中国知识产权司法保护
经典案例集

The Classical Cases of
Intellectual Property Rights on
Judicial Protection in China

中华人民共和国最高人民法院　编

The Supreme People's Court of The People's Republic of China

人 民 法 院 出 版 社

People's Court Press

图书在版编目（CIP）数据

中国知识产权司法保护经典案例集 / 中华人民共和国

最高人民法院编 . -- 北京：人民法院出版社，2018.9

ISBN 978-7-5109-2263-3

Ⅰ . ①中… Ⅱ . ①中… Ⅲ . ①知识产权保护—案例—

中国 Ⅳ . ① D923.405

中国版本图书馆 CIP 数据核字 (2018) 第 214503 号

中国知识产权司法保护经典案例集

中华人民共和国最高人民法院　编

策划编辑	韦钦平
责任编辑	李安尼　巩　雪
出版发行	人民法院出版社
地　　址	北京市东城区东交民巷 27 号（100745）
电　　话	（010）67550579（责任编辑）　　　67550558（发行部查询）
	65223677（读者服务部）
客服 QQ	2092078039
网　　址	http：//www.courtbook.com.cn
E - m a i l	courtpress@sohu.com
印　　刷	北京雅昌艺术印刷有限公司
经　　销	新华书店

开　　本	787×1092 毫米　1/16
字　　数	360 千字
印　　张	30.75
版　　次	2018 年 9 月第 1 版　2018 年 9 月第 1 次印刷
书　　号	ISBN 978-7-5109-2263-3
定　　价	98.00 元

ISBN 978-7-5109-2263-3

人民法院出版社

懂法，更懂法律人

中国审判杂志

加强国际司法交流与合作
共创知识产权保护事业的美好未来

中华人民共和国二级大法官、最高人民法院副院长　陶凯元

　　保护知识产权，就是保护智慧和创造，保护市场的创新和竞争活力，保护国家创新和发展的动力源泉。当前，全球迎来了新一轮科技革命与产业变革，在给人类经济社会发展带来深远影响的同时，也给知识产权保护事业带来新的挑战和机遇。加强知识产权保护不仅是中国履行国际义务的庄严承诺，更是中国加快创新型国家建设、实现现代化建设"两个一百年"奋斗目标的必然要求。中国始终高度重视知识产权保护工作，最高人民法院在改革完善知识产权保护体系、健全知识产权司法保护制度、明晰保护标准、加大司法保护力度等方面付出了持续不懈的努力。三十多年以来，中国的知识产权司法保护事业取得了举世公认的巨大成就。知识产权案件数量持续大幅增长，案件审判质效不断提高，审判体制机制不断健全，司法保护体系不断完善。中国法院充分发挥司法保护主导作用，通过典型案件审理、制定司法解释和司法政策、发布指导性案例等多种方式，不断提高知识产权司法保护水平，为推动科技创新、经济发展和文化繁荣作出了重要贡献。

　　案例指导制度是最高人民法院为总结审判经验、加强监督指导、统一法律适用、提高审判质量、维护司法公正而建立的一项具有中国特色的司法制度。自 2008 年起，最高人民法院即开始积极探索构

建多样化的知识产权案例指导方式，倡导在裁判文书中援引典型案例的裁判规则作为说理依据。通过在每年"世界知识产权日"期间对外公布《最高人民法院知识产权案件年度报告》、中国法院知识产权司法保护十大案件及五十个典型案例等方式，及时总结中国知识产权司法保护的新成果、新经验。本次入选《中国知识产权司法保护经典案例集》中的全部案例，均精选自最高人民法院于近年来通过各种方式公布的典型案例，涉及著作权、商标权、专利权、禁令及救济、损害赔偿的确定等多个领域，它们是鲜活的中国知识产权司法保护实践的缩影，充分体现了中国法院为知识产权司法保护做出的巨大努力和取得的显著进步。

中国法院始终坚持开放思维和世界眼光，不断加强与世界知识产权组织等国际组织以及有关国家的交流与合作，在知识产权司法保护、人员培训与交流、学术研究等方面都取得了卓有成效的合作成果。今年 8 月，世界知识产权组织首届"知识产权司法审判高级研究班"（Master Class on Intellectual Property Adjudication）在中国举办，来自 14 个国家的法官参加。这既是世界知识产权组织对中国知识产权司法保护所作努力的认可，也是进一步推进国际交流和合作的重要体现。值此之际，最高人民法院将本书以中英文双语方式出版，希望籍此继续为世界知识产权事业的发展积极贡献"中国经验"和"中国智慧"，并通过加强与世界知识产权组织等国际组织及相关国家的交流与合作，共创知识产权保护事业的美好未来！

是为序。

2018 年 8 月 6 日

Fostering International Judicial Exchanges and Cooperation for a Brighter Future of Intellectual Property Protection

Hon. Ms. TAO Kaiyuan, Justice, Vice-President of the Supreme People's Court of the People's Republic of China

To protect intellectual property rights is to protect individual intelligence and originality, market dynamics and the source of power of innovation and development for a country. Today, the globe has ushered in a new round of technological revolution and industrial transformation, which has exerted far-reaching impacts on human economic and social development, and introduced new challenges and opportunities for intellectual property protection. Strengthening intellectual property right (IPR) protection is not only a solemn commitment that China has made to perform its international obligations, but a necessary requirement for constructing an innovative country and achieving the 'Two Centenary Goals' of modernization. As China always values IPR protection very highly, the Supreme People's Court of China has been making efforts to improve the IPR system, perfect the IPR judicial protection system, clarify the protection standards and strengthen IPR protection. In the last three decades, China has made well-recognized achievements in IPR protection: the number of IP cases has grown dramatically, the quality and efficiency of trials have been improved, the trial system and mechanisms are becoming complete and sound, and the judicial protection system is witnessing continued optimization. Chinese courts have given full play to the leading role of judicial protection and continuously improved the judicial protection of intellectual property rights through such methods as hearing typical cases, formulating judicial interpretations and policies, and issuing guiding cases, thereby contributing to the promotion of scientific and technological innovation, economic prosperity and cultural development.

The case guidance system is a judicial system with Chinese characteristics established by the Supreme People's Court for summarizing trial experience, strengthening supervision and guidance, unifying the application of the law, improving trial quality and safeguarding justice. Since 2008, the Supreme People's Court has been actively exploring diversified guidance methods for IP cases and advocating the citation of typical cases in written judgments as the reasoning basis. To summarize the new achievements and experience related to China's IPR judicial protection in a timely manner, the *Annual Report on IPR Cases of the Supreme People's Court*, and *10 Cases and 50 Typical Cases Concerning the Judicial Protection of Intellectual Property Rights in Chinese Courts* are published every 'World Intellectual Property Day'. This 'Collection of Classic Chinese IPR Cases' consists of a selection of typical cases published by the Supreme People's Court in recent years, involving copyright, trademark rights, patent rights, injunctions, remedies and damages. They epitomize the actual situation of Chinese intellectual property protection and fully reflect the tremendous efforts and significant progress made by Chinese courts.

Thinking openly from a global perspective, Chinese courts have continued to strengthen their communication and cooperation with relevant countries and such international organizations as WIPO in the areas of IPR judicial protection, staff training and exchange, academic research etc., and have delivered remarkable outcomes. In this August, the first 'Master Class on Intellectual Property Adjudication' will be held in China and attended by judges from 14 countries, marking WIPO's recognition of the progress of Chinese IPR judicial protection, as well as representing further international exchanges and cooperation. It is in such a context that the Supreme People's Court has published the book in Chinese and English versions. In taking this opportunity, the Supreme People's Court wishes to provide Chinese 'experience' and 'insight' in this regard, and calls for further in-depth exchanges and cooperation with WIPO and other international organizations and countries so as to forge a brighter future of intellectual property protection.

6 August, 2018

目录

序　言

第一章　商标案件

第二章　专利案件

第三章 著作权案件

第四章　垄断、竞争案件

第五章　　植物新品种案件

第六章　　集成电路布图设计案件

第七章　　知识产权刑事案件

CONTENTS

Preface

Chapter 1
Trademark Cases

Chapter 2
Patent Cases

Chapter 3
Copyright Cases

The Copyright Law Does Not Protect Necessary Scenes and Limited Expression Forms in Original Works Created on Basis of the Same

Chapter 4
Monopoly and Competition Cases

Chapter 5
New Plant Varieties Cases

Chapter 6
Integrated Circuit Layout Design Cases

Chapter 7
Criminal Cases of Intellectual Property Right

第一章　商标案件

Chapter 1 Trademark Cases

姓名权可以构成商标法保护的"在先权利"

——迈克尔·杰弗里·乔丹与商标评审委员会、乔丹体育股份有限公司商标争议行政系列纠纷案

【裁判要旨】

姓名权是自然人对其姓名享有的重要人身权,姓名权可以构成2001年修正的《中华人民共和国商标法》第三十一条规定的"在先权利"。

"使用"是姓名权人享有的权利内容之一,并非其承担的义务,更不是姓名权人主张保护其姓名权的法定前提条件。在符合有关姓名权保护条件的情况下,自然人有权根据2001年修正的《中华人民共和国商标法》第三十一条的规定,就其并未主动使用的特定名称获得姓名权的保护。

自然人就特定名称主张姓名权保护的,该特定名称应当符合三项条件:其一,该特定名称在我国具有一定的知名度、为相关公众所知悉;其二,相关公众使用该特定名称指代该自然人;其三,该特定名称已经与该自然人之间建立了稳定的对应关系。外国人外文姓名的中文译名如符合前述三项条件,可以依法主张姓名权的保护。

商标权人主张的市场秩序或者商业成功并不完全是诚信经营的合法成果,而是一定程度上建立于相关公众误认的基础之上。维护此种市场秩序或者商业成功,不仅不利于保护姓名权人的合法权益,

3

而且不利于保障消费者的利益,更不利于净化商标注册和使用环境。

【案　　　号】　最高人民法院(2016)最高法行再27号

【案　　　由】　商标争议行政纠纷

【合议庭成员】　陶凯元　王　闯　夏君丽　王艳芳　杜微科

【关 键 词】　商标　争议程序　在先权利　姓名权　特定名称　使用恶意　诚实信用　市场秩序

【相关法条】　《中华人民共和国民法通则》第四条、第九十九条,《中华人民共和国侵权责任法》第二条、第二十条,《中华人民共和国商标法》(2001年修正)第三十一条

【基本案情】

在再审申请人迈克尔·杰弗里·乔丹(以下简称乔丹)与被申请人国家工商行政管理总局商标评审委员会(以下简称商标评审委员会)、一审第三人乔丹体育股份有限公司(以下简称乔丹公司)商标争议行政纠纷案(以下简称"乔丹"商标争议案)中,第6020569号"乔丹"商标(以下简称争议商标)由乔丹公司于2007年4月26日提出注册申请,核定使用在国际分类第28类的"体育活动器械、游泳池(娱乐用)、旱冰鞋、圣诞树装饰品(灯饰和糖果除外)"商品上,专用权期限自2012年3月28日至2022年3月27日。2012年10月31日,乔丹以争议商标的注册损害了其在先权利等为由,提出撤销申请。2014年4月14日,商标评审委员会作出商评字〔2014〕第052058号《关于第6020569号"乔丹"商标争议裁定》(以下简称第052058号裁定),对争议商标的注册予以维持。乔丹不服,提起行政诉讼。

北京市第一中级人民法院一审认为,本案证据尚不足以证明单独的"乔丹"明确指向乔丹。此外,争议商标指定使用的商品

与乔丹具有影响力的篮球运动领域差别较大，相关公众不易将争议商标与乔丹相联系，现有证据不足以证明争议商标的注册与使用不当利用了乔丹的知名度，或可能对乔丹的姓名权造成其他影响。争议商标的注册未损害乔丹的姓名权。一审法院遂判决维持第 052058 号裁定。乔丹不服，提起上诉。北京市高级人民法院二审判决驳回上诉、维持原判。乔丹仍不服，向最高人民法院申请再审，最高人民法院裁定提审本案。

 裁判结果

最高人民法院提审后，于 2016 年 12 月 8 日作出（2016）最高法行再 27 号行政判决：撤销商标评审委员会第 052058 号裁定和一审、二审判决，判令商标评审委员会对争议商标重新作出裁定。

【裁判理由】

最高人民法院提审判决认为：本案争议焦点为争议商标的注册是否损害了再审申请人就"乔丹"主张的姓名权，违反《中华人民共和国商标法》第三十一条关于"申请商标注册不得损害他人现有的在先权利"的规定。该争议焦点分为以下八个具体问题：第一，再审申请人主张保护姓名权的法律依据是什么？第二，再审申请人主张的姓名权所保护的具体内容是什么？第三，再审申请人在我国具有何种程度和范围的知名度？第四，再审申请人及其授权的耐克公司是否主动使用"乔丹"，其是否主动使用的事实对于再审申请人在本案中主张的姓名权有何影响？第五，争议商标的具体情形是否会使相关公众误认为与再审申请人具有关联？第六，乔丹公司对于争议商标的注册是否存在明显的主观恶意？第七，乔丹公司的经营状况，以及乔丹公司对其企业名称、有关商标的宣传、使用、获奖、被保护等情况，对本案具有何种影响？第八，再审申请人是否具有怠于保护其主张的姓名权的情形，该情形对本案有何影响？

对于上述八个具体问题，最高人民法院分别认定如下：

一、关于再审申请人主张保护姓名权的法律依据

《中华人民共和国商标法》（2001年修正）第三十一条规定："申请商标注册不得损害他人现有的在先权利"。对于商标法已有特别规定的在先权利，应当根据商标法的特别规定予以保护。对于商标法虽无特别规定，但根据民法通则、侵权责任法和其他法律的规定应予保护，并且在争议商标申请日之前已由民事主体依法享有的民事权利或者民事权益，应当根据该概括性规定给予保护。《中华人民共和国民法通则》第九十九条第一款、《中华人民共和国侵权责任法》第二条第二款均明确规定，自然人依法享有姓名权。故姓名权可以构成《中华人民共和国商标法》第三十一条规定的"在先权利"。争议商标的注册损害他人在先姓名权的，应当认定该争议商标的注册违反《中华人民共和国商标法》第三十一条的规定。

姓名被用于指代、称呼、区分特定的自然人，姓名权是自然人对其姓名享有的重要人身权。随着我国社会主义市场经济不断发展，具有一定知名度的自然人将其姓名进行商业化利用，通过合同等方式为特定商品、服务代言并获得经济利益的现象已经日益普遍。在适用《中华人民共和国商标法》第三十一条的规定对他人的在先姓名权予以保护时，不仅涉及对自然人人格尊严的保护，而且涉及对自然人姓名，尤其是知名人物姓名所蕴含的经济利益的保护。未经许可擅自将他人享有在先姓名权的姓名注册为商标，容易导致相关公众误认为标记有该商标的商品或者服务与

该自然人存在代言、许可等特定联系的，应当认定该商标的注册损害他人的在先姓名权，违反《中华人民共和国商标法》第三十一条的规定。

二、关于再审申请人主张的姓名权所保护的具体内容

自然人依据《中华人民共和国商标法》第三十一条的规定，就特定名称主张姓名权保护时，应当满足必要的条件。

其一，该特定名称应具有一定知名度、为相关公众所知悉，并用于指代该自然人。《最高人民法院关于审理不正当竞争民事案件应用法律若干问题的解释》第六条第二款是针对"擅自使用他人的姓名，引人误认为是他人的商品"的不正当竞争行为的认定作出的司法解释，该不正当竞争行为本质上也是损害他人姓名权的侵权行为。认定该行为时所涉及的"引人误认为是他人的商品"，与本案中认定争议商标的注册是否容易导致相关公众误认为存在代言、许可等特定联系是密切相关的。因此，在本案中可参照适用上述司法解释的规定，确定自然人姓名权保护的条件。

其二，该特定名称应与该自然人之间已建立稳定的对应关系。在解决本案涉及的在先姓名权与注册商标权的权利冲突时，应合理确定在先姓名权的保护标准，平衡在先姓名权人与商标权人的利益。既不能由于争议商标标志中使用或包含有仅为部分人所知悉或临时性使用的自然人"姓名"，即认定争议商标的注册损害该自然人的姓名权；也不能如商标评审委员会所主张的那样，以自然人主张的"姓名"与该自然人形成"唯一"对应为前提，对自然人主张姓名权的保护提出过苛的标准。自然人所主张的特定名称与该自然人已经建立稳定的对应关系时，即使该对应关系达不到"唯一"的程度，也可以依法获得姓名权的保护。综上，在适用《中华人民共和国商标法》第三十一条关于"不得损害他人现

有的在先权利"的规定时，自然人就特定名称主张姓名权保护的，该特定名称应当符合以下三项条件：其一，该特定名称在我国具有一定的知名度、为相关公众所知悉；其二，相关公众使用该特定名称指代该自然人；其三，该特定名称已经与该自然人之间建立了稳定的对应关系。

在判断外国人能否就其外文姓名的部分中文译名主张姓名权保护时，需要考虑我国相关公众对外国人的称谓习惯。中文译名符合前述三项条件的，可以依法主张姓名权的保护。本案现有证据足以证明"乔丹"在我国具有较高的知名度、为相关公众所知悉，我国相关公众通常以"乔丹"指代再审申请人，并且"乔丹"已经与再审申请人之间形成了稳定的对应关系，故再审申请人就"乔丹"享有姓名权。

三、关于再审申请人在我国具有何种程度和范围的知名度

正确认定再审申请人在我国具有何种程度和范围的知名度，对于认定再审申请人能否就"乔丹"享有姓名权，乔丹公司对于争议商标的注册是否存在明显的主观恶意，以及相关公众是否会误认为标记有争议商标的商品与再审申请人具有关联等具体问题均具有重要影响。

本案证据可以证明在争议商标的申请日之前，直至2015年，再审申请人在我国一直具有较高的知名度，其知名范围已不仅仅局限于篮球运动领域，而是已成为具有较高知名度的公众人物。

四、关于再审申请人及其授权的耐克公司是否主动使用"乔丹"，其是否主动使用的事实对于再审申请人在本案中主张的姓名权有何影响

首先，根据《中华人民共和国民法通则》第九十九条第一款的规定，"使用"是姓名权人享有的权利内容之一，并非其承担的义务，

更不是姓名权人"禁止他人干涉、盗用、假冒",主张保护其姓名权的法定前提条件。

其次,在适用《中华人民共和国商标法》第三十一条的规定保护他人在先姓名权时,相关公众是否容易误认为标记有争议商标的商品或者服务与该自然人存在代言、许可等特定联系,是认定争议商标的注册是否损害该自然人姓名权的重要因素。因此,在符合前述有关姓名权保护的三项条件的情况下,自然人有权根据《中华人民共和国商标法》第三十一条的规定,就其并未主动使用的特定名称获得姓名权的保护。

最后,对于在我国具有一定知名度的外国人,其本人或者利害关系人可能并未在我国境内主动使用其姓名;或者由于便于称呼、语言习惯、文化差异等原因,我国相关公众、新闻媒体所熟悉和使用的"姓名"与其主动使用的姓名并不完全相同。例如在本案中,我国相关公众、新闻媒体普遍以"乔丹"指代再审申请人,而再审申请人、耐克公司则主要使用"迈克尔·乔丹"。但不论是"迈克尔·乔丹"还是"乔丹",在相关公众中均具有较高的知名度,均被相关公众普遍用于指代再审申请人,且再审申请人并未提出异议或者反对。故商标评审委员会、乔丹公司关于再审申请人、耐克公司未主动使用"乔丹",再审申请人对"乔丹"不享有姓名权的主张,不予支持。

五、关于争议商标的具体情形是否会使相关公众误认为与再审申请人具有关联

本案争议商标为第6020569号"乔丹"商标,指定使用的商品类别为第28类"体育活动器械、游泳池(娱乐用)、旱冰鞋、圣诞树装饰品(灯饰和糖果除外)"。其中,"体育活动器械、游泳池(娱乐用)、旱冰鞋"均属于体育运动中常见的商品,"圣诞

树装饰品（灯饰和糖果除外）"则属于日常生活中常见的商品。上述商品的相关公众容易误认为标记有争议商标的商品与再审申请人存在代言、许可等特定联系。具体理由如下：首先，本案证据足以证明再审申请人及其姓名"乔丹"在我国具有长期、广泛的知名度，相关公众熟悉并普遍使用"乔丹"指代再审申请人。"乔丹"与再审申请人之间已经建立了稳定的对应关系。因争议商标标志仅为"乔丹"文字，故相关公众看到争议商标后，容易由此联想到再审申请人本人，进而容易误认为标记有争议商标的商品与再审申请人存在代言、许可等特定联系。其次，乔丹公司在《招股说明书》之"品牌风险"中特别注明："特别提醒投资者'可能会有部分消费者将发行人及其产品与迈克尔·乔丹联系起来从而产生误解或混淆，在此特提请投资者注意。'"这表明其已经认识到相关公众容易将"乔丹"与再审申请人相互联系，可能导致相关公众误认。乔丹公司在一审庭审笔录中，亦认可"确实会有没有购买过我方商品的公众会产生联系的可能"。最后，两份调查报告可以与其他证据结合，进一步证明相关公众容易误认为"乔丹"与再审申请人存在特定联系。

六、关于乔丹公司对于争议商标的注册是否存在明显的主观恶意

本案中，乔丹公司申请注册争议商标时是否存在主观恶意，是认定争议商标的注册是否损害再审申请人姓名权的重要考量因素。本案证据足以证明乔丹公司是在明知再审申请人及其姓名"乔丹"具有较高知名度的情况下，并未与再审申请人协商、谈判以获得其许可或授权，而是擅自注册了包括争议商标在内的大量与再审申请人密切相关的商标，放任相关公众误认为标记有争议商标的商品与再审申请人存在特定联系的损害结果，使得乔丹公司

无需付出过多成本，即可实现由再审申请人为其"代言"等效果。乔丹公司的行为有违《中华人民共和国民法通则》第四条规定的诚实信用原则，其对于争议商标的注册具有明显的主观恶意。

七、关于乔丹公司的经营状况，以及乔丹公司对其企业名称、有关商标的宣传、使用、获奖、被保护等情况，对本案具有何种影响

乔丹公司的经营状况，以及乔丹公司对其企业名称、有关商标的宣传、使用、获奖、被保护等情况，均不足以使争议商标的注册具有合法性。

其一，从权利的性质以及损害在先姓名权的构成要件来看，姓名被用于指代、称呼、区分特定的自然人，姓名权是自然人对其姓名享有的人身权。而商标的主要作用在于区分商品或者服务来源，属于财产权，与姓名权是性质不同的权利。在认定争议商标的注册是否损害他人在先姓名权时，关键在于是否容易导致相关公众误认为标记有争议商标的商品或者服务与姓名权人之间存在代言、许可等特定联系，其构成要件与侵害商标权的认定不同。因此，即使乔丹公司经过多年的经营、宣传和使用，使得乔丹公司及其"乔丹"商标在特定商品类别上具有较高知名度，相关公众能够认识到标记有"乔丹"商标的商品来源于乔丹公司，也不足以据此认定相关公众不容易误认为标记有"乔丹"商标的商品与乔丹之间存在代言、许可等特定联系。

其二，乔丹公司恶意申请注册争议商标，损害乔丹的在先姓名权，明显有悖于诚实信用原则。商标评审委员会、乔丹公司主张的市场秩序或者商业成功并不完全是乔丹公司诚信经营的合法成果，而是一定程度上建立于相关公众误认的基础之上。维护此种市场秩序或者商业成功，不仅不利于保护姓名权人的合法权

益，而且不利于保障消费者的利益，更不利于净化商标注册和使用环境。

八、关于再审申请人是否具有怠于保护其主张的姓名权的情形，该情形对本案有何影响

《中华人民共和国商标法》第四十一条第二款规定："已经注册的商标，违反本法……第三十一条规定的，自商标注册之日起五年内，……可以请求商标评审委员会裁定撤销该注册商标。"上述规定中的"自商标注册之日起五年内"是向商标评审委员会申请撤销争议商标的法定期限，立法者在规定该期限时已经充分考虑了在先权利人与商标权人之间的利益平衡。该期限可以督促权利人或者利害关系人及时主张权利，避免争议商标的法律效力在核准注册后的长时期内仍处于可争议状态，从而影响商标权人对争议商标的宣传和使用，损害商标权人的合法权益。本案中，再审申请人在争议商标注册之日起五年内向商标评审委员会提出撤销申请，符合上述法律规定。因此，商标评审委员会、乔丹公司关于再审申请人怠于保护其姓名权的主张缺乏事实和法律依据，不予支持。

【本案裁判文书】

扫描二维码，可见裁判文书

Name Right Can Constitute "pre-existing right" Protected by Trademark Law

——Michael Jeffrey Jordan v. Trademark Review and Adjudication Board and QIAODAN Sports Co., Ltd.

[Syllabus]

The name right is an important personal right of a natural person to his or her name, and the name right may constitute "pre-existing rights" under Article 31 of the Trademark Law of the People's Republic of China as amended in 2001.

"Use" is one of the bundle of rights of the name right holder, whereas not an obligation he or she undertakes, nor a legal precondition for the name right holder to claim protection over his or her name. Subject to the conditions for the protection of the name right, the natural person has the right to obtain the protection of the name right on specific names not actively used under the provisions of Article 31 of the Trademark Law of the People's Republic of China as amended in 2001.

If a natural person claims the protection of name right for a specific name, the specific name shall meet three conditions. First, the specific name has certain popularity in China and is known to the relevant public; second, the relevant public uses the specific name to refer to the natural person; third, the specific name has established a stable correspondence with the natural person. If the

Chinese translation of a foreigner's name in a foreign language meets the above three conditions, the translation may be protected as a name under the law.

The market order or commercial success advocated by the trademark owner is not an entirely legitimate outcome of good faith business but is, to some extent, based on confusion of the relevant public. Maintaining such a market order or commercial success is not only unconducive to the protection of legitimate rights and interests of the name right holder, but is also not helpful for protecting the interests of consumers or for improving the trademark registration and use environment.

[Case No.] Supreme People's Court (2016) ZGFXZ No. 27

[Cause of Action] Administrative dispute over trademark

[Collegial Panel Members] Tao Kaiyuan　Wang Chuang Xia Junli　Wang Yanfang　Du Weike

[Keywords] Trademark, dispute procedure, pre-existing right, name right, specific name, use, malice, good faith, market order

[Relevant Legal Provisions] Articles 4 and 99 of *the General Principles of the Civil Law of the People's Republic of China*, Articles 2 and 20 of *the Tort Law of the People's Republic of China*, Article 31 of *the Trademark Law of the People's Republic of China* (2001 amended version)

[Basic Facts]

In the reopen case of the administrative dispute over trademark between the appellant Michael Jeffrey Jordan (hereinafter referred to as "Michael Jordan") and the respondent the Trademark Review and Adjudication Board State Administration for Industry & Commerce of the People's Republic of China (hereinafter referred to as "TRAB") and the third party from the case of first instance QIAODAN Sports Co., Ltd. (hereinafter referred to as "QIAODAN Company"), the '乔丹（ pronounced as Qiao Dan ）' trademark No. 6020569 (hereinafter referred to as "disputed trademark") was filed by QIAODAN Company on April 26th, 2007 and was approved for use under Category No: 28 for sports equipment, swimming pools (for entertainment), roller skates and Christmas tree decorations (except lighting and candies) in the international classification, and the validity period was from March 28th, 2012 to March 27th, 2022. On October 31st, 2012, Michael Jordan filed a cancellation request on the grounds that the registration of the disputed trademark infringd his pre-existing right. On April 14th, 2014, the TRAB issued the SP ZI [2014] No. 052058 *Decision on No. 6020569* '乔丹' *Trademark Dispute* (hereinafter referred to as "Decision No. 052058") and maintained the registration of the disputed trademark. Thereafter Michael Jordan filed an administrative lawsuit.

The Beijing No. 1 Intermediate People's Court (court of first instance) held that the evidence in this case was insufficient to prove that the name '乔丹' clearly pointed to Michael Jordan. In addition, the products designated by the disputed trademark were quite different from the field of basketball where Michael Jordan bore influence. It was not easy for the relevant public to link the disputed trademark to Michael Jordan. The existing evidence was insufficient to prove that the registration and use of the disputed trademark improperly uses Michael Jordan's popularity or may have other effects on Michael Jordan's name right. The registration of the disputed trademark did not infringed Michael Jordan's name right. The court of first instance upheld the Decision No. 052058. Michael Jordan then filed an appeal to the Beijing High People's Court, which dismissed the appeal and upheld the original judgment. Michael Jordan applied to the Supreme People's Court for a reopen case, and the Supreme People's Court ruled that the case should be reviewed.

Holding

On December 8ᵗʰ, 2016, The Supreme People's Court issued the (2016) ZGFXZ No. 27 Administrative Judgment, where it stipulated that Decision no. 052058 of the TRAB and the judgments of lower court were revoked, and the TRAB is ordered to make a new decision.

[Reasoning]

The Supreme People's Court held that the issue in this case is whether the registration of the disputed trademark infringed the name right of the appellant therefore violated Article 31 of the Trademark Law of the People's Republic of China-"application for trademark registration shall not infringe the pre-existing rights of others". The issue of this case is divided into the following eight specific questions. First, what is the legal grounds for the appellant's claim to protect his name right? Second, what is the specific content protected by the name right claimed by the appellant? Third, what degree and scope of popularity does the appellant have in China? Fourth, did the appellant and Nike Company authorized by him actively use the name '乔丹' and what effect did the fact of active use have on the name right claimed by the appellant in the case? Fifth, does the specific situation of the disputed trademark cause the relevant public to mistakenly associate the disputed trademark with the appellant? Sixth, did QIAODAN Company acted in bad faith in registering the disputed trademark? Seventh, what is the impact of QIAODAN Company's business status and its efforts on promoting, marketing and protecting its own enterprise name, trademark? Eighth, whether there is a laches on the part of the appellant in protecting his name right?

For the eight specific questions, the Supreme People's Court respectively held as follows:

I. Legal grounds for the appellant to claim name right

Article 31 of *the Trademark Law of the People's Republic of China (amended in 2001)* provided that 'an application for trademark registration shall not infringe the pre-existing rights of others'. Therefore Pre-existing rights specifically enumerated by the Trademark Law should be protected in accordance with the special provisions of the Trademark Law, and Civil rights or civil interests not specifically enumerated should be protected in accordance with the provisions of the General Principles of the Civil Law, Tort Law and other laws .

Clause 1, Article 99 of the *General Principles of Civil Law of the People's Republic of China* and Clause 2, Article 2 of the *Tort Law of the People's Republic of China* stipulate that natural persons enjoy name right in accordance with the law. Therefore, the name right may constitute "pre-existing right" as stipulated in Article 31 of the *Trademark Law of the People's Republic of China*. If the registration of a disputed trademark infringes the pre-existing name right of others, it should be determined that the registration of the disputed trademark violates the provisions of Article 31 of the *Trademark Law of the People's Republic of China.*

17

Names are used to refer to, address and distinguish between specific natural persons. Name rights are important personal rights enjoyed by natural persons for their names. With the continuous development of China's socialist market economy, it has become increasingly common for natural persons with certain popularity to commercialize their names and endorse specific goods and services through contracts and other means to obtain economic benefits. When the pre-existing name right of another person is protected by the provisions of Article 31 of the *Trademark Law of the People's Republic of China*, it not only protects the personal dignity of the natural person, but also the economic interests contained in the name of the natural person, especially the name of a famous person. If the name of a person who has a pre-existing name right is registered as a trademark without permission, misleading relevant public believe that the goods or services marked with the trademark have specific connections with the natural person ,such as endorsement or permission of said natural person, The registration of the trademark should be deemed to have infringed the pre-existing name right of another person and violated the provisions of Article 31 of the *Trademark Law of the People's Republic of China*.

II. The specific content protected by the name right claimed by the appellant

When a natural person claims name right over a particular name, three requirements should be satisfied under Article 31 of the *Trademark Law of the People's Republic of China*.

First, the specific name should have certain popularity, be known to the relevant public and be used to refer to the natural person. Article 6 (2) of the *Interpretation of the Supreme People's Court on Several Issues Concerning the Application of Law in the Trial of Civil Cases of Unfair Competition* is a judicial interpretation with respect to unfair competition acts "use the name of another person without permission and mislead relevant public", which is closely related to the registration of disputed trademark which is likely to mislead relevant public. Therefore, in this case, the conditions for the protection of the natural person's name right can be determined by referring to the provisions of the above-mentioned judicial interpretation.

Second, the specific name should have established a stable correspondence with the natural person. In resolving the conflict between the pre-existing name right and the registered trademark right involved in this case, the standard of protection should be reasonably determined, and the interests of the pre-existing name right holder and the trademark owner should be balanced. When a specific name claimed by a natural person has established a stable correspondence with the natural person, even if the correspondence relationship is not "unique", the name right can be protected according to law. In summary, if a natural person claims name right for a specific name according to Article 31 of the *Trademark Law of the People's Republic of China*, the specific name should meet the following three conditions. First, the specific name has certain popularity in China and is known to the relevant public; second, the relevant public uses the specific name to refer to the natural person; third, the specific name has established a stable correspondence with the natural person.

When judging whether a foreigner can claim name right with respect to the Chinese translation of his or her name in a foreign language, it is necessary to consider the relevant public's common use of the name of the foreigner in China. If the Chinese translation meets the above three conditions, it may be claimed in accordance with the law. The existing evidence in this case is sufficient to prove that the name '乔丹' has high reputation in China and is known to the relevant public. The relevant public in China usually refers to the appellant as '乔丹', and the name '乔丹' has formed a stable correspondence with the appellant, therefore the appellant can claim name right for '乔丹'.

III. Degree and scope of popularity of the appellant in China

Correctly ascertaining the popularity degree and scope of the appellant in China has a significant impact on ascertaining specific issues, such as whether the appellant enjoys the name right for '乔丹', whether the disputed trademark is registered in bad faith , and whether the relevant public is misleaded that the products marked with the disputed trademark are related to the appellant.

The evidence in this case can prove that before the filing date of the disputed trademark until 2015, the appellant had always had a high reputation in China, and the scope of his popularity was not only limited to the field of basketball, as he had become a highly popular public figure.

IV. Whether the appellant and Nike Company authorized by the appellant actively used the name '乔丹', and what is its impact on the name right protection

First of all, according to the provisions of Article 99 (1) of the *General Principles of the Civil Law of the People's Republic of China*, the right to use is one of the bundle of rights enjoyed by name holders, rather than obligation, or precondition of protection.

Secondly, whether the relevant public mistakenly believe that the goods or services marked with the disputed trademark have specific connection with the natural person, such as being endorsed or approved by the name right holder, is an important factor for ascertaining whether or not the natural person's name right is infringed. Therefore, where the above three conditions concerning the protection of the name right are satisfied, the natural person has the right to obtain the protection of the name right for a specific name, even it is not actively used.

Finally, for foreigners who have a certain popularity in China, it is possible that he or she or interested parties did not actively use his or her name in China; or under certain circumstances, the "name" familiar to the relevant public and news media in China is not exactly the same as the name actively used. For example, in this case, the relevant public and news media in China generally refer to the appellant as '乔丹', whereas Michael Jordan and Nike Company mainly use '迈克尔·乔丹'. However, both '迈克尔·乔丹' and '乔丹' have high popularity among the relevant public and are generally used by the relevant public to refer to the appellant, and the appellant has no objection to either. Therefore, the claim of TRAB and QIAODAN Company that the appellant and Nike Company do not actively use '乔丹' and the appellant is not entitled to enjoy the name right for '乔丹'

is not persuasive.

V. Whether the specific circumstances of the disputed trademark will mislead the relevant public to associate the disputed trademark with the appellant.

The relevant public is likely to mistakenly believe that the products marked with the disputed trademark have specific connection with the appellant, such as being endorsed or approved by the appellant. The specific reasons are as follows. First of all, the evidence in this case is sufficient to prove that the appellant and his name '乔丹' have long-term and extensive popularity in China and the relevant public is familiar with and generally uses the name '乔丹' to refer to the appellant. A stable correspondence has been established between '乔丹' and the appellant. Since the disputed trademark is only the Chinese characters as '乔丹', it is easy for the relevant public to associate it with the appellant on seeing the disputed trademark and even to mistakenly believe that products marked with the disputed trademark have specific connections with the appellant. Secondly, QIAODAN Company specifically states under "Brand Risk" in its *Prospectus*: "Specially remind investors that some consumers may associate the issuer and its products with Michael Jordan, which may create a misunderstanding or confusion. Please note." This indicates that QIAODAN Company has recognized that the relevant public is likely to mistakenly associate 'QIAODAN' with the appellant. In the trial record of the court of first instance, QIAODAN Company also recognized that "there is a possibility that the public who has not purchased our products may be misleaded." Finally, the two market research reports completed by the Horizon Research Consultancy Group can further prove that the relevant public is likely to be misled.

VI. Whether the disputed trademark was registered in obvious bad faith by QIAODAN Company

In this case, whether the disputed trademark is registered in obvious bad faith by QIAODAN Company was an important factor to consider. The evidence in this case is sufficient to prove that QIAODAN Company was fully aware of the high popularity of the appellant and his name '乔 丹'. Instead of negotiating with the appellant to obtain his permission or authorization, QIAODAN Company willfully registered a large number of trademarks closely related to the appellant, including the disputed trademark, and mislead the relevant public to believe that the products marked with the disputed trademark have a specific connection with the appellant. In this way, QIAODAN Company achieved the effect of "endorsement" by the appellant without incurring relevant costs. The act of QIAODAN Company violates the principle of good faith stipulated in Article 4 of *the General Principles of Civil Law of the People's Republic of China*, shows obvious subjective malice during the registration of the disputed trademark and related trademarks.

VII. What is the impact of QIAODAN Company's business status and its efforts on promoting, marketing and protecting its own enterprise name, trademark?

QIAODAN Company's business status and enterprise name and trademark promotion, use, awards and protection situations are not sufficient to make the registration of the disputed trademark legal.

First, the name is used to refer to, call and distinguish a specific natural person, therefore the name right is an important personal right of the natural person to his or her name, whereas trademark is used for distinguishing source of goods or services, constituting a kind of property right which is substantially different from the name right. When ascertaining whether the registration of a disputed trademark infringes the prior name of another person, the key factor is whether relevant public is misled that the goods or services marked with the disputed trademark have specific connections with the name right holder such as endorsement or authorization. Therefore, even QIAODAN Company and its '乔丹' trademark have gained a high popularity in specific product categories after years of operation, marketing and use, and the relevant public can recognize that the products marked with '乔丹' are from QIAODAN Company, it is still not sufficient to prove that the relevant public will not be easily misled that there is a specific connection between the products marked with '乔丹' and Michael Jordan.

Second, since the disputed trademark was registered by QIAODAN Company in bad faith, infringing Michael Jordan's pre-existing name right, therefore the market order or commercial success argued by the TRAB and QIAODAN Company is not a legitimate outcome of QIAODAN Company's business, whereas, to some extent, is derived from confusion of relevant public. Maintaining such a market order or commercial success is in contrary to the rule of protecting legitimate rights, and is in contrary to the rule of protecting the interests of consumers and improving the trademark registration and use system.

VIII. Whether there is laches on the part of the appellant in protecting his name right?

Clause 2, Article 41 of the *Trademark Law of the People's Republic of China stipulates*: "If a registered trademark violates the provisions of Article 31 of this Law......, within five years from the date of trademark registration, ... may request the TRAB to invalidate the registered trademark." In the above-mentioned provisions, "within five years from the date of trademark registration" is the statute limitation for applying to the TRAB to invalidate a disputed trademark. The legislator has fully considered the balance of interests between pre-existing right holder and trademark owner when stipulating the 5 years statute limitation. The statute limitation may urge the right holder or the interested party to claim right protection according to law. In this case, the appellant filed an application for invalidation with the TRAB within five years from the date of registration of the disputed trademark, in compliance with the above-mentioned provisions. Therefore, the claim of the TRAB and QIAODAN Company that the appellant is negligent in protecting his name right lacks factual and legal grounds, and is not supported.

[Opinion of the Case (Chinese Version)]

Scan the QR code to see the Chinese version of the opinion

商标国际注册申请人应当获得合理的补正机会

——克里斯蒂昂迪奥尔香料公司与商标评审委员会商标申请驳回复审行政纠纷案

【裁判要旨】

商标国际注册申请人已经根据《商标国际注册马德里协定》《商标国际注册马德里协定有关议定书》的规定，完成了申请商标的国际注册程序，以及《中华人民共和国商标法实施条例》第十三条规定的声明与说明义务，应当属于申请手续基本齐备的情形。在申请材料仅欠缺商标法实施条例规定的部分视图等形式要件的情况下，商标行政机关应当秉承积极履行国际公约义务的精神，给予申请人合理的补正机会。

25

【案　　　号】	最高人民法院（2018）最高法行再26号
【案　　　由】	商标申请驳回复审行政纠纷
【合议庭成员】	陶凯元　王　闯　佟　姝
【关　键　词】	商标　行政诉讼　国际注册　领土延伸保护
【相关法条】	《中华人民共和国商标法实施条例》第十三条、第五十二条

【基本案情】

涉案申请商标为国际注册第1221382号商标（见下图），申请人为克里斯蒂昂迪奥尔香料公司（以下简称迪奥尔公司）。申请商标的原属国为法国，核准注册时间为2014年4月16日，国际注册日期为2014年8月8日，国际注册所有人为迪奥尔公司，指定使用商品为香水、浓香水等。

申请商标

申请商标经国际注册后，根据《商标国际注册马德里协定》《商标国际注册马德里协定有关议定书》的相关规定，迪奥尔公司通过世界知识产权组织国际局（以下简称国际局），向澳大利亚、丹麦、芬兰、英国、中国等提出领土延伸保护申请。2015年7月13日，国家工商行政管理总局商标局（以下简称商标局）向国际局发出申请商标的驳回通知书，以申请商标缺乏显著性为由，驳回全部指定商品在中国的领土延伸保护申请。在法定期限内，迪奥尔公司向国家工商行政管理总局商标评审委员会（以下简称商标评审委员会）提出复审申请。商标评审委员会认为，申请商标难以起到区别商品来源的作用，缺乏商标应有的显著性，遂以第13584号决定，驳回申请商标在中国的领土延伸保护申请。迪奥尔公司不服，提起行政诉讼。迪奥尔公司认为，首先，申请商标为指定颜色的三维立体商标，迪奥尔公司已经向商标评审委员会提交了申请商标的三面视图，但商标评审委员会却将申请商标作为普通商标进行审查，决定作出的事实基础有误。其次，申请商标设计独特，并通过迪奥尔公司长期的宣传推广，具有了较强的显著性，其领土延伸保护申请应当获得支持。

 裁判结果

北京知识产权法院及北京市高级人民法院均未支持迪奥尔公司的诉讼主张。其主要理由为：迪奥尔公司并未在国际局国际注册簿登记之日起 3 个月内向商标局声明申请商标为三维标志并提交至少包含三面视图的商标图样，而是直至驳回复审阶段在第一次补充理由书中才明确提出申请商标为三维标志并提交三面视图。在迪奥尔公司未声明申请商标为三维标志并提交相关文件的情况下，商标局将申请商标作为普通图形商标进行审查，并无不当。商标局在商标档案中对申请商标指定颜色、商标形式等信息是否存在登记错误，并非本案的审理范围，迪奥尔公司可通过其他途径寻求救济。迪奥尔公司不服二审判决，向最高人民法院提出再审申请。最高人民法院于 2017 年 12 月 29 日作出（2017）最高法行申 7969 号行政裁定，提审本案，并于 2018 年 4 月 26 日作出（2018）最高法行再 26 号判决，撤销一审、二审判决及被诉决定，并判令商标评审委员会重新作出复审决定。

【裁判理由】

法院生效裁判认为，申请商标国际注册信息中明确记载，申请商标指定的商标类型为"三维立体商标"，且对三维形式进行了具体描述。在无相反证据的情况下，申请商标国际注册信息中关于商标具体类型的记载，应当视为迪奥尔公司关于申请商标为三维标志的声明形式。也可合理推定，在申请商标指定中国进行领土延伸保护的过程中，国际局向商标局转送的申请信息与之相符，商标局应知晓上述信息。因国际注册商标的申请人无需在指定国家再次提出注册申请，故由国际局向商标局转送的申请商标信息，应当是商标局据以审查、决定申请商标指定中国的领土延伸保护申请能否获得支持的事实依据。根据现有证据，申请商标请求在中国获得注册的商标类型为"三维立体商标"，而非记载于商标局档案并作为商标局、商标评审委员会审查基础的"普通商标"。迪奥尔公司已经在评审程序中明确了申请商标的具体类型为三维立体商标，并通过补充三面视图的方式提出了补正要求。对此，商标评审委员会既未在第13584号决定中予以如实记载，也未针对迪奥尔公司提出的上述主张，对商标局驳回决定依据的相关事实是否有误予以核实，而仍将申请商标作为"图形商标"进行审查并迳行驳回迪奥尔公司复审申请的做法，违反法定程序，并可能损及行政相对人的合法利益，应当予以纠正。商标局、商标评审委员会应当根据复审程序的规定，以三维立体商标为基础，重新对申请商标是否具备显著特征等问题予以审查。

《商标国际注册马德里协定》及其议定书制定的主要目的是通过建立国际合作机制，确立和完善商标国际注册程序，减少和简化注册手续，便利申请人以最低成本在所需国家获得商标保护。结合本案事实，申请商标作为指定中国的马德里商标国际注册申请，有关申请材料应当以国际局向商标局转送的内容为准。现有证据可以合理推定，迪奥尔公司已经在商标国际注册程序中对申请商标为三维立体商标这一事实作出声明，说明了申请商标的具体使用方式并提供了申请商标的一面视图。在申请材料仅欠缺商标法实施条例规定的部分视图等形式要件的情况下，商标行政机关应当秉承积极履行国际公约义务的精神，给予申请人合理的补正机会。本案中，商标局并未如实记载迪奥尔公司在国际注册程序中对商标类型作出的声明，且在未给予迪奥尔公司合理补正机会，并欠缺当事人请求与事实依据的情况下，迳行将申请商标类型变更为普通商标并作出不利于迪奥尔公司的审查结论，商标评审委员会对此未予纠正的做法，均缺乏事实与法律依据，且可能损害行政相对人合理的期待利益，对此应予纠正。

综上，商标评审委员会应当基于迪奥尔公司在复审程序中提出的与商标类型有关的复审理由，纠正商标局的不当认定，并根据三维标志是否具备显著特征的评判标准，对申请商标指定中国的领土延伸保护申请是否应予准许的问题重新进行审查。商标局、商标评审委员会在重新审查认定时应重点考量如下因素：一是申请商标的显著性与经过使用取得的显著性，特别是申请商标进入中国市场的时间，在案证据能够证明的实际使用与宣传推广的情况，以及申请商标因此而产生识别商品来源功能的可能性；二是审查标准一致性的原则。商标评审及司法审查程序虽然要考虑个案情况，但审查的基本依据均为商标法及其相关行政法规规定，不能以个案审查为由忽视执法标准的统一性问题。

【本案裁判文书】

扫描二维码，可见裁判文书

An Applicant for International Trademark Registration Should Have a Reasonable Chance to Make Supplements and Corrections

——Christian Dior Perfumes LLC v. Trademark Review and Adjudication Board

[Syllabus]

Where an applicant for an international registration of trademarks has completed international registration procedures for pursuant to Madrid Agreement Concerning the International Registration of Marks and the Protocol Relating to the Madrid Agreement Concerning the International Registration of Marks and performed the representation and statement obligations set out in Article 13 of the Implementing Regulations of the Trademark Law of the People's Republic of China, the application procedures should be deemed as fundamentally complete. Where the application documents only lack procedural elements within the meaning of the Implementing Regulations of the Trademark Law, such as partial views, the competent trademark authority should adhere to the principle of performing the obligations under international agreements and give the applicant a reasonable chance to supplement and correct.

[Case No.] Supreme People's Court (2018) ZGFXZ No. 26

[Cause of Action] Administrative dispute of reviewing the rejection of trademark application

[Collegial Panel Members] Tao Kaiyuan　Wang Chuang Tong Shu

[Keywords] Trademark, administrative lawsuit, international registration and extension of territorial protection

[Relevant Legal Provisions] Articles 13 and 52 of the *Implementing Regulations of the Trademark Law of the People's Republic of China*

[Basic Facts]

The trademark at issue international registration number 1221382 (as shown in the picture below), for which the applicant is Christian Dior Perfumes LLC ("Dior"). The country of origin for the trademark at issue is France, with approved registration date: April 16, 2014 and international registration date: August 8, 2014. The international registration owner is Dior, and the designated products include perfumes and heavy perfumes.

Trademark at issue

After the trademark at issue had been registered internationally, according to relevant provisions in the *Madrid Agreement Concerning the International Registration of Marks and the Protocol Relating to the Madrid Agreement Concerning the International Registration of Marks*, Dior applied to the International Bureau of World Intellectual

Property Organization (hereinafter referred to as International Bureau) for an extension of territorial protection to Australia, Denmark, Finland, England, China, etc. On July 13, 2015, the Trademark Office of the State Administration for Industry and Commerce (hereinafter referred to as "CTMO") issued to the International Bureau a notice of rejection and rejected the application for the extension of territorial protection over all the designated products in China on the grounds that the trademark at issue lacks distinctive features. Within the statutory time limit, Dior appealed to the Trademark Review and Adjudication Board of the State Administration for Industry and Commerce ("TRAB"). TRAB concluded that the trademark at issue is not capable of distinguishing the source of goods and lacks distinctive features. Therefore, TRAB issued No. 13584 Decision, rejecting the application for the extension of territorial protection over the trademark at issue in China. Dior was dissatisfied with the decision and thus filed an administrative lawsuit. Dior argued: 1) the trademark at issue is a three-dimensional mark in a specific color, for which Dior had submitted to TRAB the three-view drawing of the trademark at issue, but TRAB made the decision on incorrect factual basis by taking the trademark at issue as an ordinary trademark. 2) the trademark at issue has a unique design which becomes very significant after long-term efforts of Dior to promote and market it, so the application for the extension of territorial protection should be approved.

 Holding

Neither Beijing Intellectual Property Court nor Being High People's Court upheld the claims of Dior on account of the following: Dior did not state to the Trademark Office that the trademark at issue is a three-dimensional mark or submit trademark designs including three-view drawing at the minimum, within 3 months after the date when it had been registered with the International Bureau, but until the phase of the review of the refused trademark when the first supplementary reasons were submitted. In the case where Dior did not state that the trademark at issue is a three-dimensional mark or submit relevant documents, the Trademark Office did not err in taking the trademark at issue as an ordinary graphic trademark. Whether the Trademark Office had errors in recording the designated color, mark form and other information the trademark at issue in the register of trademarks is out of the issues of this case, and Dior may seek relieves in any other form. Dior refused to accept the second-instance judgment and filed a retrial application with the Supreme People' Court. The Supreme People' Court issued (2017) ZGFXS No. 7969 Administrative Ruling on December 29, 2017 to hear the case, and issued (2018) ZGFXZ No. 26 Judgment on April 26, 2018, overruling the first-instance and second-instance judgments and the decision appealed against, and ordering TRAB to render a new review decision.

[Reasoning]

The effective ruling of the court indicates, as made clear in the international registration information of the trademark at issue, the designated trademark type of the trademark at issue is "a three-dimensional mark" with specific description of the three-dimensional form. Without contrary evidence, the record concerning specific trademark type in the international registration information of the trademark at issue should be deemed as a statement of Dior that the trademark at issue is a three-dimensional mark. It can also be reasonably presumed that when the application is filed for an extension of territorial protection over the trademark at issue in China, the application information transmitted by the International Bureau to the Trademark Office is as the same as above, so the Trademark Office should have known the information above. The applicant for the international registration is not required to file a registration application to a designated country, so the International Bureau is responsible for transmitting the information of the trademark at issue to the Trademark Office. The CTMO is the one to hear and decide the factual basis for the application for the extension of territorial protection over the trademark at issue in China. According to existing evidence, the trademark type of the trademark at issue over which the territorial protection is applied in China is "a three-dimensional mark", other than "an ordinary trademark" acting as the basis to be reviewed by the CTMO and TRAB as recorded in the register of the CTMO. In the review procedure, Dior made it clear that the specific type of the trademark at issue is a three-dimensional mark, and proposed the request to supplement and correct by additionally submitting the three-view drawing. However, TRAB did not keep true records in No. 13584 Decision, and did not verify whether the facts on which the CTMO had made the decision of rejection were problematic with respect to the abovementioned claim proposed by Dior. TRAB still took the trademark at issue as "a graphic trademark" and simply rejected the review application from Dior, which violates the legal procedure and may impair the legal benefits of the administrative counterpart and should be corrected. In accordance with the review procedures, the CTMO and TRAB should, on the basis of a three-dimensional mark, re-check whether the trademark at issue lacks distinctive features.

The *Madrid Agreement Concerning the International Registration of Marks* and its Protocol are designed to establish international cooperation mechanism, establish and improve procedures for international registration of trademarks, reduce and streamline registration procedures and provide applicants with convenience to obtain trademark protection at the lowest cost in any country. On the facts of the case, as the trademark at issue is under application for the Madrid International Registration with

China designated for territorial extension, relevant application documents should be transmitted by the International Bureau to the CTMO. It can be reasonably presumed from existing evidence that, in the international trademark registration procedures, Dior has made a statement that the trademark at issue is a three-dimensional mark, made clear the specific use of the trademark at issue, and submitted the one-view drawing of the trademark at issue. Where the application documents only lack procedural elements within the meaning of the Implementing Regulations of the Trademark Law, such as partial views, the competent trademark authority should adhere to the principle of performing the obligations under international agreements and give the applicant a reasonable chance to make supplements and corrections. In this case, the CTMO did not keep true records of the statement made by Dior as to trademark type in the international registration procedure, did not give Dior a reasonable chance to make supplements and corrections. Without the parties' requests or factual facts, it flatly changed the trademark at issue to an ordinary trademark, and carried out an examination decision to the disadvantage of Dior, and TRAB's failure to make corrections lacks either factual and legal basis. These acts may impair reasonably expected benefits of the administrative counterpart and should be corrected.

Therefore, TRAB should, based on the reasons for retrial as proposed by Dior in respect of the trademark type, correct the improper affirmation of the CTMO, and re-check whether the application for an extension of territorial protection over the trademark at issue in China shall be approved, according to the standards to assess whether the three-dimensional trademark has distinguishing features. In the retrial process, the CTMO and TRAB shall focus on: 1) the distinctiveness of the trademark at issue and the distinctiveness derived from use of the trademark at issue, particularly the time when the trademark at issue enters in the Chinese market, actual use, promotion and marketing that can be proved by existing evidence, and the possibility that the trademark at issue identifies the source and function of the product; and 2) the principle of unified assessing standards. In the review and judicial procedures, despite the necessity to consider the circumstances of an individual case, the basic standards for review should be the Trademark Law and other relevant administrative regulations, and the principle of unified standards should not be abandoned for any individual case.

[Opinion of the Case (Chinese Version)]

Scan the QR code to see the Chinese version of the opinion

恶意取得并行使商标权的行为不受法律保护

——王碎永与深圳歌力思服装实业有限公司等侵害商标权纠纷案

【裁判要旨】

当事人违反诚实信用原则，损害他人合法权益，扰乱市场正当竞争秩序，恶意取得、行使商标权并主张他人侵权的，人民法院应当以构成权利滥用为由，判决对其诉讼请求不予支持。

【案　　　号】最高人民法院（2014）民提字第 24 号

【案　　　由】侵害商标权纠纷

【合议庭成员】王艳芳　朱　理　佟　姝

【关　键　词】知识产权侵权　商标　诚实信用　权利滥用

【相 关 法 条】《中华人民共和国民事诉讼法》第十三条，《中华人民共和国商标法》第五十二条

【基本案情】

深圳歌力思服装实业有限公司成立于 1999 年 6 月 8 日。2008 年 12 月 18 日，该公司通过受让方式取得第 1348583 号"歌力思"商标，该商标核定使用于第 25 类的服装等商品之上，核准注册于 1999 年 12 月。2009 年 11 月 19 日，该商标经核准续展注册，有效期自 2009 年 12 月 28 日至 2019 年 12 月 27 日。深圳歌力思服

装实业有限公司还是第 4225104 号"ELLASSAY"的商标注册人。该商标核定使用商品为第 18 类的（动物）皮；钱包；旅行包；文件夹（皮革制）；皮制带子；裘皮；伞；手杖；手提包；购物袋。注册有效期限自 2008 年 4 月 14 日至 2018 年 4 月 13 日。2011 年 11 月 4 日，深圳歌力思服装实业有限公司更名为深圳歌力思服饰股份有限公司（以下简称歌力思公司，即本案一审被告人）。2012 年 3 月 1 日，上述"歌力思"商标的注册人相应变更为歌力思公司。

一审原告人王碎永于 2011 年 6 月申请注册了第 7925873 号"歌力思"商标，该商标核定使用商品为第 18 类的钱包、手提包等。王碎永还曾于 2004 年 7 月 7 日申请注册第 4157840 号"歌力思及图"商标。后因北京市高级人民法院于 2014 年 4 月 2 日作出的二审判决认定，该商标损害了歌力思公司的关联企业歌力思投资管理有限公司的在先字号权，因此不应予以核准注册。

自 2011 年 9 月起，王碎永先后在杭州、南京、上海、福州等地的"ELLASSAY"专柜，通过公证程序购买了带有"品牌中文名：歌力思，品牌英文名：ELLASSAY"字样吊牌的皮包。2012 年 3 月 7 日，王碎永以歌力思公司及杭州银泰世纪百货有限公司（以下简称杭州银泰公司）生产、销售上述皮包的行为构成对王碎永拥有的"歌力思"商标、"歌力思及图"商标权的侵害为由，提起诉讼。

 裁判结果

杭州市中级人民法院于 2013 年 2 月 1 日作出（2012）浙杭知初字第 362 号民事判决，认为歌力思公司及杭州银泰公司生产、销售被诉侵权商品的行为侵害了王碎永的注册商标专用权，判决歌力思公司、杭州银泰公司承担停止侵权行为、赔偿王碎永经济损失及合理费用共计 10 万元及消除影响。歌力思公司不服，提起上诉。浙江省高级人民法院于 2013 年 6 月 7 日作出（2013）浙知终字第 222 号民事判决，驳回上诉、维持原判。歌力思公司及王碎永均不服，向最高人民法院申请再审。最高人民法院裁定提审本案，并于 2014 年 8 月 14 日作出（2014）民提字第 24 号判决，撤销一审、二审判决，驳回王碎永的全部诉讼请求。

【裁判理由】

最高人民法院提审认为：诚实信用原则是一切市场活动参与者所应遵循的基本准则。一方面，它鼓励和支持人们通过诚实劳动积累社会财富和创造社会价值，并保护在此基础上形成的财产性权益，以及基于合法、正当的目的支配该财产性权益的自由和权利；另一方面，它又要求人们在市场活动中讲究信用、诚实不欺，在不损害他人合法利益、社会公共利益和市场秩序的前提下追求自己的利益。民事诉讼活动同样应当遵循诚实信用原则。一方面，它保障当事人有权在法律规定的范围内行使和处分自己的民事权利和诉讼权利；另一方面，它又要求当事人在不损害他人和社会公共利益的前提下，善意、审慎地行使自己的权利。任何违背法律目的和精神，以损害他人正当权益为目的，恶意取得并行使权利、扰乱市场正当竞争秩序的行为均属于权利滥用，其相关权利主张不应得到法律的保护和支持。

第 4157840 号"歌力思及图"商标迄今为止尚未被核准注册，王碎永无权据此对他人提起侵害商标权之诉。对于歌力思公司、杭州银泰公司的行为是否侵害王碎永的第 7925873 号"歌力思"商标权的问题，首先，歌力思公司拥有合法的在先权利基础。歌力思公司及其关联企业最早将"歌力思"作为企业字号使用的时间为1996年，最早在服装等商品上取得"歌力思"注册商标专用权的时间为1999年。经长期使用和广泛宣传，作为企业字号和注册商标的"歌力思"已经具有了较高的市场知名度，歌力思公司对前述商业标识享有合法的在先权利。其次，歌力思公司在本案中的使用行为系基于合法的权利基础，使用方式和行为性质均具有正当性。从销售场所来看，歌力思公司对被诉侵权商品的展示和销售行为均完成于杭州银泰公司的歌力思专柜，专柜通过标注歌力思公司的"ELLASSAY"商标等方式，明确表明了被诉侵权商品的提供者。在歌力思公司的字号、商标等商业标识已经具有较高的市场知名度，而王碎永未能举证证明其"歌力思"商标同样具有知名度的情况下，歌力思公司在其专柜中销售被诉侵权商品的行为，不会使普通消费者误认该商品来自于王碎永。从歌力思公司的具体使用方式来看，被诉侵权商品的外包装、商品内的显著部位均明确标注了"ELLASSAY"商标，而仅在商品吊牌之上使用了"品牌中文名：歌力思"的字样。由于"歌力思"本身就是歌力思公司的企业字号，且与其"ELLASSAY"商标具有互为指代关系，故歌力思公司在被诉侵权商品的吊牌上使用"歌力思"文字来指代商品生产者的做法并无明显不妥，不具有攀附王碎永"歌力思"商标知名度的主观意图，亦不会为普通消费者正确识别被诉侵权商品的来源制造障碍。在此基础上，杭州银泰公司销售被诉侵权商品的行为亦不为法律所禁止。最后，王碎永取得和行使"歌力思"商标权的行为难谓正当。"歌力思"商标由中文文字"歌力思"构成，与歌力思公司在先使用的企业字号及在先注册的"歌力思"商标的文字构成完全相同。"歌力思"本身为无固有含义的臆造词，具有较强的固有显著性，依常理判断，在完全没有接触或知悉的情况下，因巧合而出现雷同注册的可能性较低。作为地域接近、经营范围关联程度较高的商品经营者，王碎永对"歌力思"字号及商标完全不了解的可能性较低。在上述情形之下，王碎永仍在手提包、钱包等商品上申请注册"歌力思"商标，其行为难谓正当。王碎永以非善意取得的商标权对歌力思公司的正当使用行为提起的侵权之诉，构成权利滥用。

【本案裁判文书】

扫描二维码，可见裁判文书

41

Malicious Acquisition and Exercise of Trademark Rights is not Protected by Law

——Wang Suiyong v. Ellassay

[Syllabus]

Where any party violates the principle of good faith, damages legitimate interests of others, disrupts fair market competition order, maliciously obtains and exercises trademark rights and claims infringement against others, the People's court shall reject the claims on the ground of abuse of rights.

[Case No.] The Supreme People's Court (2014) MTZ No.24

[Cause of Action] Dispute over trademark infringement

[Collegial Panel Members] Wang Yanfang   Zhu Li   TongShu

[Keywords] Intellectual Property Infringement, Trademark, Good Faith, Abuse of Rights

[Relevant Legal Provisions] Article 13, *Civil Procedure Law of the People's Republic of China*; Article 52, *Trademark Law of the People's Republic of China*

[Basic Facts]

Shenzhen Ellassay Garment Industrial Co., Ltd. was founded on June 8th, 1999. On December 18th, 2008, the company acquired the trademark No.1348583 "歌力思" by way of transfer, which was approved for use on Class 25 clothing products, and was approved for registration in December 1999. On November 19th, 2009, the trademark registration was renewed with its validity from December 28th, 2009 to December 27th, 2019. At the same time, Shenzhen Ellassay Garment Industrial Co., Ltd. was also the registrant of trademark No. 4225104 "ELLASSAY", which was approved for use on Class 18 commodities such as (animal) leather, wallets, travelling bags and folders (leather products); leather belts, fur, umbrellas, canes and shopping bags, with validity from April 14th, 2008 to April 13th, 2018. On November 4th, 2011, Shenzhen Ellassay Garment Industrial Co., Ltd. changed its name to Shenzhen Ellassay Fashion Co., Ltd. (hereinafter "Ellassay", the defendant in first-instance case). On March 1st, 2012, the registrant of the above-mentioned trademark "歌力思" was accordingly changed to Ellassay.

The plaintiff in the first-instance case Wang Suiyong registered trademark No. 7925873 "歌力思", which was approved for use on Class 18 commodities such as wallets and handbags, in June 2011. Wang Suiyong also applied to register trademark No. 4157840 "歌力思 /graphic" on July 7th, 2004. Later, the Beijing High People's Court affirmed in the second-instance case on April 2nd, 2014 that the trademark infringed upon the prior trade name of Ellassay's affiliate Ellassay Investment Management Co., Ltd. and thus, didn't approve the registration.

Since September 2011, Wang Suiyong had been buying leather bags with tags bearing "Chinese Brand Name: 歌力思, English Brand Name: ELLASSAY" at Ellassay counters in Hangzhou, Nanjing, Shanghai and Fuzhou, through notarial procedures. On March 7th, 2012, Wang Suiyong filed an action claiming that Ellassay and Intime Department

Store (Group) Company Limited (hereinafter "Intime Department Store") infringed upon the trademarks "歌力思" and "歌力思 /graphic" by producing and selling the above leather bags.

 Holding

On February 1st, 2013, the Hangzhou Intermediate People's Court rendered the civil judgment (2012) Zhe-Hang-Zhi-Chu-Zi No. 362, holding that Ellassay's and Intime Department Store's production and sales of the allegedly infringing commodities infringed upon Wang Suiyong's right to the registered trademark, and ruled that Ellassay and Intime Department Store should stop the infringement, compensate Wang Suiyong RMB100,000 for economic losses and reasonable expenses, and eliminate the impact of such infringement. Not satisfied with the decision, Ellassay filed an appeal. On June 7th, 2013, the Zhejiang High People's Court passed the civil judgement (2013) Zhe-Zhi-Zhong-Zi No. 222, rejecting the appeal and upheld the original judgement. Still unsatisfied, Ellassay applied for retrial with the Supreme People's Court. The Supreme People's Court accepted the application and passed the judgment (2014) Min-Ti-Zi No. 24 on August 14th, 2014, reversing the first-instance and second-instance judgments and dismissing all Wang Suiyong's claims.

[Reasoning]

The Supreme People's Court's opinions: Good faith is a basic principle that all market players should comply with. It encourages and supports people to accumulate social wealth and create social value through honest work, and protects property interests formed on this basis as well as the freedom and rights to dispose these interests for proper and legitimate purposes. However, it also requires people to be honest and faithful in market activities, and seek interests without prejudicing others' legitimate interests, public benefits and market order. Principle of good faith should also be followed in civil proceedings. While it safeguards the parties' right to exercise and dispose their civil and procedural rights to the extent permitted by law, it requires the parties to exercise their rights in good faith and with due care without harming others' and public interests. Any malicious acquisition or exercise of rights or disruption of fair market competition order against the objective and spirit of law or for the purpose of damaging others' legitimate rights is an abuse of rights, and relevant claims shall not be protected or supported by law.

Registration of trademark No. 4157840 " 歌力思 /graphic" had not as yet been approved, hence Wang Suiyong had no right to sue others for infringement of trademark. Did Ellassay and Intime Department Store infringe upon Wang Suiyong's trademark No. 792587 " 歌力思 "? First, Ellassay owns the legitimate prior rights. Ellassay and its affiliates used "ELLASSAY" as trade name as early as 1996 and obtained the registered trademark "ELLASSAY" on commodities such as garments in 1999. Through long-term use and extensive publicity, "ELLASSAY" now enjoys high visibility in the market as its trade name and registered trademark. Therefore, Ellassay owns prior rights of the aforementioned trademark. Second, Ellassay's use in this case is based on legitimate rights, and both its methods of use and nature are legitimate. In terms of place of sales, Ellassay's allegedly infringing products were displayed and sold in Ellassay's counters in Intime Department Store, and the counters clearly indicated the provider of the allegedly infringing products by marking Ellassay's trademark "ELLASSAY". Given that Ellassay's business marks such as trade name and trademark are highly visible in the market and Wang Suiyong failed to prove that " 歌力思 " enjoys the same visibility, Ellassay's sales of allegedly infringing products at its counters will not make ordinary consumers falsely believe that these products are from Wang Suiyong. In terms of Ellassay's specific methods of use, the trademark "ELLASSAY" was marked on conspicuous areas on the packaging and inside the allegedly infringing products, and only Chinese characters " 品牌中文名 (Chinese Brand Name)：歌力思 " were printed on the product tags. As " 歌力思 " is Ellassay's trade name and is used as the substitute for the trademark "ELLASSAY", there is nothing obviously wrong with Ellassay using the Chinese characters " 歌力思 " on the tags of the allegedly infringing products to indicate the product manufacturer. It didn't intend to attach itself to Wang Suiyong's trademark " 歌力思 " and wouldn't prevent ordinary consumers from differentiating the correct source of the allegedly infringing products. On this basis, Intime Department Store's sales of the allegedly infringing products is also not prohibited by law. Finally, Wang Suiyong obtaining the trademark " 歌力思 " and exercising the trademark right wasn't justifiable or appropriate. The trademark " 歌力思 " comprises of Chinese characters " 歌力思 ", which are exactly the same as the Chinese characters of the trade name first used by Ellassay and the earlier registered trademark "ELLASSAY". " 歌力思 " is an invented phrase without any intrinsic meaning. According to common sense, it is less likely to register the exact same trademark by coincidence without seeing or knowing the prior one. As a similar region business operator with similar business scope, it is unlikely that Wang Suiyong did not know about the trade name and trademark "ELLASSAY". In such circumstances, it is difficult to say if it is appropriate for Wang Suiyong to apply for registering the trademark " 歌力思 " on handbags, wallets, etc. Accordingly, Wang Suiyong's action against Ellassay's fair use of a trademark, which

Wang Suiyang had acquired maliciously, constitutes an abuse of rights.

[Opinion of the Case (Chinese Version)]

Scan the QR code to see the Chinese version of the opinion

楼盘名称与注册商标权的保护 及擅自使用他人企业名称的判断

——广州星河湾实业发展有限公司、广州宏富房地产有限公司与
江苏炜赋集团建设开发有限公司侵害商标权及不正当竞争纠纷案

【裁判要旨】

将申请人享有注册商标专用权的商标作为楼盘名称使用构成侵犯注册商标专用权

他人善意使用诉争名称的时间早于权利人对其企业名称的使用，该使用行为不构成擅自使用他人企业名称的行为。

【案　　　号】	最高人民法院（2013）民提字第 102 号
【案　　　由】	侵害商标权及不正当竞争纠纷
【合议庭成员】	王　闯　王艳芳　朱　理
【关 键 词】	商标侵权　不正当竞争　楼盘名称　企业名称在先使用
【相 关 法 条】	《中华人民共和国商标法》（2001 年修正）第五十二条，《最高人民法院关于审理商标民事纠纷案件适用法律若干问题的解释》第九条、第十条、第二十一条

【基本案情】

在再审申请人广州星河湾实业发展有限公司（以下简称星河湾公司）、广州宏富房地产有限公司（以下简称宏富公司）与被申请人江苏炜赋集团建设开发有限公司（以下简称炜赋公司）侵害商标权及不正当竞争纠纷案（以下简称"星河湾"商标侵权及不正当竞争案）中，核定使用在第 36 类"公寓出租、公寓管理"等服务上的第 1946396 号和第 1948763 号 组合商标由宏富公司提出注册申请，后先后转让给案外人宏宇企业集团（香港）有限公司（以下简称宏宇公司）及星河湾公司。宏富公司经许可使用上述两注册商标，并有权以自身的名义提起侵权诉讼。宏富公司及其关联企业先后在广州、北京、上海等地开发以"星河湾"命名的地产项目，"星河湾"地产项目及宏宇集团、星河湾公司先后获得多项荣誉。自 2000 年起，炜赋公司在江苏省南通市先后推出"星河湾花园""星辰花园""星景花园"等多个地产项目，小区名称均报经南通市民政局批准。星河湾公司、宏富公司以炜赋公司在开发的不动产项目中使用"星河湾"字样，侵害其注册商标权并构成不正当竞争为由，提起诉讼。江苏省南通市中级人民法院一审认为，炜赋公司使用"星河湾花园"作为其开发的楼盘名称，未导致消费者对该楼盘来源产生混淆，不构成商标侵权。宏富公司开发的"星河湾"楼盘在广州地区具有较高知名度，但炜赋公司长期正当、合理使用"星河湾花园"这一名称，主观上并无搭便车之故意，客观上也未造成消费者误认，故炜赋公司使用该名称不构成不正当竞争。遂判决驳回星河湾公司、宏富公司的诉讼请求。星河湾公司、宏富公司不服，向江苏省高级人民法院提起上诉。江苏省高级人民法院二审判决驳回上诉、维持原判。星河湾公司、宏富公司仍不服，向最高人民法院申请再审。最高人民法院裁定提审本案。

> **裁判结果**
>
> 　　最高人民法院于 2015 年 2 月 26 日作出（2013）民提字第 102 号民事判决：判决撤销一审、二审判决，判令炜赋公司在其尚未出售的楼盘和将来拟开发的楼盘上不得使用相关"星河湾"名称作为其楼盘名称，并赔偿星河湾公司、宏富公司经济损失 5 万元。

【裁判理由】

　　最高人民法院提审认为：关于被申请人将申请人享有注册商标专用权的商标作为楼盘名称使用是否构成侵犯注册商标专用权的问题。根据《中华人民共和国商标法》实施条例第五十条第（一）项规定，"同一种或者类似商品上，将与他人注册商标相同或者近似的标志作为商品名称或者商品装潢使用，误导公众的"属于《中华人民共和国商标法》第五十二条第（五）项所称的侵犯注册商标专用权行为。本案中，星河湾公司享有第 1946396 号、第 1948763 号注册商标的专用权，两商标分别核定使用于第 36 类的不动产出租、不动产代理等服务和第 37 类的建筑、室内装潢修理等服务，炜赋公司在商品房上使用该商品名称。关于商品房与不动产建造是否构成商品与服务类似的问题，根据《最高人民法院关于审理商标民事纠纷案件适用法律若干问题的解释》第十一条第三款之规定，商品与服务类似，是指商品和服务之间存在特定联系，容易使相关公众混淆。本案两注册商标核定的服务类别分别是不动产管理、建筑等，与商品房销售相比，两者功能用途、消费对象、销售渠道基本相同，开发者均系相关房地产开发商，不动产管理、建筑等服务与商品房销售存在特定的联系，应当认定为商品与服务之间的类似。

关于使用"星河湾花园"商品名称是否会误导公众的问题。根据原审法院查明的事实,从 2001 年起,宏富公司等单位就开始在南方日报、羊城晚报等相关媒体上对星河湾楼盘进行宣传,"星河湾"命名的楼盘先后获得了相关荣誉,具有较高的知名度,因此"星河湾"文字系该注册商标中最具有显著性和知名度的部分。炜赋公司将其开发的楼盘命名为"星河湾花园",由于该名称事实上起到了识别该楼盘的作用,其实质也属于一种商业标识,该标识中"花园"为楼盘名称的一般用语,其最显著的部分为"星河湾"文字,与星河湾公司、宏富公司上述两个注册商标中的显著部分"星河湾"完全相同,呼叫方式一致,加之现代社会信息流通丰富快捷,相关房地产开发商在全国各地陆续开发系列房地产楼盘亦非罕见,炜赋公司此种使用方式会使相关公众误认该楼盘与星河湾公司、宏富公司开发的"星河湾"系列楼盘有一定的联系,容易误导公众。因此,炜赋公司将与星河湾公司享有商标专用权的"星河湾"商标相近似的"星河湾花园"标识作为楼盘名称使用,容易使相关公众造成混淆误认,构成对星河湾公司、宏富公司相关商标权的侵犯,应当承担相应的民事责任。原审法院认为其仅作为楼盘名称使用,不可能使相关公众对楼盘及其服务的来源产生混淆,该认定错误,最高人民法院予以纠正。

关于是否构成擅自使用他人企业名称的问题。最高人民法院认为,根据原审法院查明的事实,星河湾公司原名为广州明宇木业有限公司,2007 年 8 月更名为星河湾公司。以"星"字开头命名楼盘名称,是炜赋公司自 2000 年以来形成的习惯和传统,且早在 2006 年 5 月 15 日,炜赋公司已向南通市民政局申请命名该小区为"炜赋·星河湾",理由为:继星辰花园、星景花园后仍以"星"字开头,因保留该地原有两条河流穿过小区,故以"炜赋·星河湾"

51

命名。同年 5 月 25 日，南通市民政局批复同意炜赋公司将该住宅区命名为"星河湾花园"，因此诉争楼盘名称的使用先于星河湾公司企业名称的使用，该种使用并不属于擅自使用他人企业名称的行为。

【本案裁判文书】

扫描二维码，可见裁判文书

Protection for Name of Real Estate Property and Right to Registered Trademark, and Judgment on Unauthorized Use of Another Enterprise's Name

——Guangzhou Star River Industry Development Co., Ltd. and Guangzhou Hongfu Real Estate Co., Ltd. v. Jiangsu Weifu Group Construction & Development Co., Ltd.

[Syllabus]

If a trademark for which the petitioner enjoys the exclusive right to use as registered trademark is used as the name of a real estate property, such an act constitute an infringement of the exclusive right to use the registered trademark.

If the use of the disputed name as the enterprise name by the alleged infringing party was prior to its use by the right holder, then such an act does not constitute an unauthorized use of another enterprise's name.

[Case No.] The Supreme People's Court (2013) MTZ No. 102

[Cause of Action] Dispute over infringement of trademark right and unfair competition

[Collegial Panel Members] Wang Chuang   Wang Yanfang Zhu Li

[Keywords] Trademark infringement, unfair competition, name of real estate project, enterprise name, prior use

[Relevant Legal Provisions] Article 51 of the *Trademark Law of the People's Republic of China* (2001 revised edition), Articles 9, 10 and 21 of *Interpretation of the Supreme People's Court Concerning the Application of Laws in the Trial of Cases of Civil Disputes Arising from Trademarks.*

[Basic Facts]

In the dispute over trademark infringement and unfair competition between the retrial appellant Guangzhou Star River Industry Development Co., Ltd. (hereinafter referred to as Star River Company), Guangzhou Hongfu Real Estate Co., Ltd. (hereinafter referred to as Hongfu Company) and the retrial respondent Jiangsu Weifu Group Construction & Development Co., Ltd. (hereinafter referred to as Weifu Company) (the dispute is hereinafter referred to as the dispute over trademark infringement and unfair competition of "Star River"), the combined mark ▓▓▓▓▓ , i.e., No.1946396 and No. 1948763 authorized to be applied for Category No. 36 services – "apartment rental and apartment management" and other services, was registered based on the application by Hongfu Company, and later successively transferred to Hongyu Group (Hong Kong) Co., Ltd. (hereinafter referred to as Hongyu Company), a party not involved in the case, and Star River Company. Hongfu Company was licensed to use the abovementioned two registered trademarks and was entitled to file a suit over infringement in its own name. Hongfu Company and its affiliates developed property projects with the name "Star River" in Guangzhou, Beijing, Shanghai and other places successively. The "Star River" property projects as well as Hongyu Group and Star River Company won many honors. Since 2000, Weifu Company successively launched several real estate projects including "Star River Garden", "Star Garden" and "Star View Garden" in Nantong, Jiangsu, and all such names were submitted to the Nantong Municipal Bureau of Civil Affairs for approval. Star River Company and Hongfu Company initiated legal proceedings on the grounds that the use of the wording "Star River" in Weifu Company's real estate projects infringed its registered trademark right and constituted unfair competition. The court of first instance, the Intermediate People's Court of Nantong, Jiangsu held that the use of "Star River Garden" by Weifu Company as the name of a real estate property it had developed did not cause confusion among consumers towards the source of such property and therefore did not constitute a trademark infringement of. The "Star River" property developed by Hongfu Company enjoyed a high profile in Guangzhou, however, Weifu Company neither showed any subjective intention of freely utilizing the value of the name "Star River", nor was there objectively speaking, any possibility of consumer confusion over the name. Hence, Weifu Company's action of using such a name did not constitute unfair competition. Therefore, the Court rejected the claims filed by Star River Company and Hongfu Company. Following this, Star River Company and Hongfu Company appealed to the High People's Court of Jiangsu. In the court of second instance, the Higher People's Court of Jiangsu, upheld the original judgment. Dissatisfied with the ruling, Star River Company and Hongfu Company further appealed and filed an application for retrial with the Supreme People's Court. The Supreme People's Court directly reviewed the case and entered a judgment.

Holding

On February 26ᵗʰ, 2015, the Supreme People's Court entered a civil judgment ([2013] MTZ No. 102), in which the judgment of the court of first instance and court of second instance were revoked, and Weifu Company was ordered not to use "Star River" as the name for its real estate property not yet sold or which is to be developed in the future, and to pay Star River Company and Hongfu Company damages in the amount of RMB 50,000 for economic losses.

[Reasoning]

The Supreme People's Court held that: with respect to the question on whether the respondent's use of the trademark in which the petitioner enjoyed the exclusive right, as the name of a real estate property constituted an infringement of the exclusive right to use the registered trademark, Article 50 (1) of the *Implementing Rules of the Trademark Law of the People's Republic of China* prescribe that, "the use of words or designs that are identical with or similar to another person's registered trademark for the same kind of goods or similar goods as the name or decoration of the goods to an extent that is sufficient to cause misidentification", shall constitute an infringement of the exclusive right to use of a registered trademark referred to in Paragraph (5), Article 52 of the *Trademark Law of the People's Republic of China*. In this case, Star River Company owned the exclusive right to use the registered trademarks No. 1946396 and No. 1948763 星河湾 , which were approved to be applied for Category No. 36 services including real estate rental and real estate agency and Category No. 37 services including building, interior decoration & maintenance, separately; Weifu Company had applied such a name in its housing product. With respect to the question whether housing product and real estate building constituted similar goods and services, pursuant to provisions in Clause 3, Article 11 of the *Interpretation of the Supreme People's Court Concerning the Application of Laws in the Trial of Cases of Civil Disputes Arising from Trademarks*, similar goods and services shall mean that there is a specific link between the goods and the services, wherein the relevant public may be easily confused. Service categories approved for the two registered trademarks involved herein were real estate management and construction. When compared to the sale of housing product, both were the same in terms of functions, purposes, targeted consumers, sales channels, etc., and both developers were real estate developers. As there was a specific link between real estate management and construction, and the sale of housing product, they should be considered to be similar goods and services.

With respect to the question whether the use of "Star River Garden" as the product name will mislead the public, based on the facts established by the court of first instance, Hongfu Company and its related business units promoted Star River real estate on *Nanfang Daily, Yangcheng Evening News* and related media since 2001, and such properties with the name "Star River" won relevant honors, gaining a high profile, therefore, the term "Star River" was the most prominent and renowned component of such a registered trademark. Whereas, Weifu Company named its real estate properties as "Star River Garden", which in fact played a role in identifying such property, and essentially belonged to a type of business marks. The word "Garden" in such a mark was a general term for the name of the property, however its most prominent parts were the words "Star River", which were identical in both wording and recall to the significant part "Star River" in the above two registered trademarks of Star River Company and Hongfu Company. Furthermore, as modern society features rich and convenient information flow, it is not uncommon to see real estate developers develop a series of real estate properties nationwide, and such kind of use by Weifu Company would cause confusion in the minds of the public that such property has a certain link with the "Star River" series properties developed by Star River Company and Hongfu Company, thus misleading the public. Therefore, Weifu Company applying the mark "Star River Garden" as the name of its property, which was similar to the trademark "Star River" in which Star River Company enjoyed an exclusive right to use, constituted an infringement on the related trademark of Star River Company and Hongfu Company, as the relevant public may be easily confused. Hence, Weifu Company should bear corresponding civil liability. While the court of first instance and court of second instance held that it was impossible to cause confusion among relevant public over the property and its service as it was only used as the property name, the Supreme People's Court stipulated that such a judgment was incorrect and hence corrected the same.

With respect to the question whether it constituted an unauthorized use of another enterprise's name. In the view of the Supreme People's Court, based on facts established by the court of first instance, Star River Company, formerly Guangzhou Minyu Wood Co., Ltd. changed its current name in August 2007. It was a custom and tradition developed since 2000 for Weifu Company to name its properties with the word "Star", and early on May 15th, 2006, Weifu Company applied to Nantong Municipal Bureau of Civil Affairs for naming a residential community as "Weifu Star River" on the grounds that "Star" was taken as the first word based on its existing "Star Garden" and "Star View Garden" properties, and the word river was indicative of the two rivers running through the community.

On May 25th, 2006, Nantong Municipal Bureau of Civil Affairs replied and approved that Weifu Company could name such a residential community as "Star River Garden". The use of the disputed property name was earlier than its use by Star River Company as its enterprise's name, and as such it was not an act of unauthorized use of another enterprise's name.

[Opinion of the Case (Chinese Version)]

Scan the QR code to see the Chinese version of the opinion

判断中外文商标是否构成近似
应当考虑二者是否已经形成了稳定的对应关系

——拉菲罗斯柴尔德酒庄与商标评审委员会、南京金色希望酒业有限公司商标争议行政纠纷案

【裁判要旨】

判断中文商标与外文商标是否构成近似，不仅要考虑商标构成要素及其整体的近似程度、相关商标的显著性和知名度、所使用商品的关联程度等因素，还应考虑二者是否已经在相关公众之间形成了稳定的对应关系。

【案　　　　号】　最高人民法院（2016）最高法行再34号

【案　　　　由】　商标争议行政纠纷

【合议庭成员】　王艳芳　钱小红　杜微科

【关　键　词】　商标　争议程序　商标近似　对应关系

【相关法条】　《中华人民共和国商标法》第二十八条

【基本案情】

在再审申请人拉菲罗斯柴尔德酒庄（以下简称拉菲酒庄）与被申请人国家工商行政管理总局商标评审委员会（以下简称商标评审委员会）、南京金色希望酒业有限公司（以下简称金色希望公

司）商标争议行政纠纷案（以下简称"拉菲庄园"商标争议案）中，第 4578349 号"拉菲庄园"商标（即争议商标）的申请日为 2005年 4 月 1 日，核定使用在第 33 类葡萄酒、酒（饮料）、果酒（含酒精）、蒸馏酒精饮料、苹果酒、含酒精液体、含水果的酒精饮料、米酒、青稞酒、料酒商品上，注册商标专用权人为金色希望公司。"LAFITE"商标（即引证商标）申请日为 1996 年 10 月 10 日，核定使用在第 33 类的含酒精饮料（啤酒除外）商品上，注册商标专用权人为拉菲酒庄。在法定期限内，拉菲酒庄以争议商标违反《中华人民共和国商标法》（2001 年修正）第二十八条等规定为由，向商标评审委员会提出争议申请。商标评审委员会于 2013 年 9 月2 日作出商评字 ［2013］ 第 55856 号《关于第 4578349 号"拉菲庄园"商标争议裁定书》（以下简称第 55856 号裁定），以争议商标违反《中华人民共和国商标法》第二十八条规定为由，对争议商标予以撤销。金色希望公司不服，提起行政诉讼。北京市第一中级人民法院一审判决维持第 55856 号裁定。金色希望公司不服，提起上诉。北京市高级人民法院二审认为，难以认定引证商标在争议商标申请日之前，已经在中国大陆地区具有市场知名度，相关公众已经能够将引证商标与"拉菲"进行对应性识别。争议商标的注册和使用长达十年之久，其已经形成稳定的市场秩序，从维护已经形成和稳定的市场秩序考虑，本案争议商标的注册应予维持。遂判决撤销一审判决及第 55856 号裁定。拉菲酒庄不服，向最高人民法院申请再审。经查明，中国经济网 2014 年 2 月 12日《质检总局公布六款进口"拉菲"葡萄酒质量不合格》报道记载，"'拉菲'葡萄酒一直让中国消费者对其趋之若鹜，……然而近日，国家质检总局公布六款洋拉菲酒质量不合格，让'拉菲迷'们大跌眼镜。中国经济网了解到，六款不合格产品为：拉菲庄园 2012

干红葡萄酒……。"2016 年 8 月 1 日搜狐财经刊登图文消息"'拉菲庄园'隆重登陆糖酒会消费者不知其为山寨"。最高人民法院裁定提审本案。

 裁判结果

最高人民法院于 2016 年 12 月 23 日作出（2016）最高法行再 34 号行政判决：撤销二审判决，维持一审判决及第 55856 号裁定。

【裁判理由】

最高人民法院提审认为：认定商标是否近似，既要考虑商标构成要素及其整体的近似程度，也要考虑相关商标的显著性和知名度、所使用商品的关联程度等因素，以是否容易导致混淆作为判断标准。争议商标由中文文字"拉菲庄园"构成，"庄园"用在葡萄酒类别上显著性较弱，"拉菲"系争议商标的主要部分，判断争议商标与引证商标是否构成近似，关键在于判断"拉菲"与"LAFITE"是否构成近似或者形成了较为稳定的对应关系。在争议商标申请日前，根据法院查明的事实，各类宣传报道中即有将引证商标"LAFITE"音译为"拉菲"的情况，且《新快报》《扬子晚报》《北京日报》等刊物属于消费者容易接触到的，受众面较大的宣传媒介。相关媒体所载文章均对"LAFITE"葡萄酒给予了极高评价，引证商标具有较高的知名度。此外，拉菲酒庄通过多年的商业经营活动，客观上在"拉菲"与"LAFITE"之间建立了稳固的联系，我国相关公众通常以"拉菲"指代"LAFITE"商标，争议商标与引证商标构成近似商标。此外，对于已经注册使用一段时间的商标，是否已经通过使用建立较高市场声誉和形成自身的相关公众群体，并非由使用时间决定，而是要看相关公众能否通过其使用行为，在客观上实现了与其他商标的区分。根据法院查明的事实，有关新闻报道所涉不合格产品，均系使用了争议商标的相关产品。从相关新闻报道也可以看出，相关公众对争议商标与引证商标已经混淆误认。因此，金色希望公司提交的证据未能证明其通过对争议商标的使用已经形成了相关公众群体，二审法院所作争议商标已经形成了稳定的市场秩序的结论并无事实依据，最高人民法院予以纠正。

【本案裁判文书】

扫描二维码，可见裁判文书

Judging Whether Two Trademarks in Chinese and Foreign Languages are Similar Requires Considering Whether the Two Constitute a Stable Correspondence

——Chateau Lafite Rothschild v. Trademark Review and Adjudication Board and Nanjing Gold Hope Wine Industry

[Syllabus]

To judge whether the trademarks in Chinese and foreign language are similar, we should not only consider the components of the trademarks, their overall similarity, significance and reputation of relevant trademarks and the correlation between the products used, but should also whether the two have formed a stable correspondence among relevant public.

[Case No.] Supreme People's Court (2016) ZGFXZ No. 34

[Cause of Action] Administrative case regarding trademark dispute

[Collegial Panel Members] Wang Yanfang　Qian Xiaohong Du Weike

[Keywords] Trademark, dispute procedure, trademark similarity, correspondence

[Relevant Legal Provisions] Article 28 of *Trademark Law of the People's Republic of China*

[Basic Facts]

In the retrial of the administrative case on trademark dispute (hereinafter referred to as "Chateau Lafite" trademark dispute case") between the Applicant–Chateau Lafite Rothschild (hereinafter referred to as "Chateau Lafite") and the Respondents – Trademark Review and Adjudication Board of the State Administration for Industry and Commerce (hereinafter referred to as "TRAB") and Nanjing Gold Hope Wine Industry (hereinafter referred to as "Gold Hope Company"), the date of the application f the trademark No. 4578349 "Chateau Lafei" (i.e. the disputed trademark) was April 1st, 2005. The disputed trademark was approved for use in Category No. 33 products, including wine, liquor (beverage), fruit wine (including alcohol), distilling spirit beverage, apple wine, alcohol-containing liquid, fruit-containing spirit beverage, rice wine, highland barley wine and cooking wine, and the registered trademark's exclusive owner was stipulated as Gold Hope Company. The application date for the "LAFITE" trademark (i.e. the reference trademark) was October 10th, 1996, and the trademark was approved for use in Category No. 33 product – alcohol-containing beverage (except for beer), and the registered trademark's exclusive owner was stipulated as Chateau Lafite. Within the statutory time limit, Chateau Lafite filed an opposition application regarding the disputed trademark with the TRAB on the grounds that it violated Article 28 of the *Trademark Law of the People's Republic of China* (2001 revised edition). The Trademark Review Committee rendered the Decision No. 55856 for *Application No. 4578349 "Chateau Lafei" Trademark Opposition* S.P.Z. [2013] (hereinafter referred to as Decision No. 55856) on September 2nd, 2013, and cancelled the disputed trademark on the grounds that the disputed trademark violated Article 28 of the Trademark Law of the People's Republic of China. Gold Hope Company refused to accept the ruling and instituted administrative proceedings. Beijing No.1 Intermediate People's Court maintained Decision no. 55856. Gold Hope Company refused to accept the ruling and instituted an appeal. In the court of second instance, the Beijing High People's Court held that it was difficult to affirm that the reference trademark had a market reputation in China's mainland before the application date of the disputed trademark and that relevant public had been able to identify the reference trademark and "Lafei". The disputed trademark had been registered and used for up to 10 years and had established a stable market order. Thus, from the perspective of maintaining the established and stable market order, the registration of the disputed trademark in this case shall be maintained. Therefore, the court overruled the judgment of the court of first instance and Decision No. 55856. Chateau Lafite refused to accept the ruling and applied to the Supreme People's Court for retrial. Upon investigation, China Economic Net reported in an article titled *AQSIQ Announces six kinds of imported "Lafite" wine that do not conform to quality standard*, "Chinese consumers have always been enticed by 'Lafite' Wine, however, recently, the Administration of Quality Supervision, Inspection and Quarantine announced six kinds of imported Lafite wine that did not conform with the quality standard, which left admirers of Lafite shocked. According to China Economic Net, the six kinds of products that did not conform with the quality standard are: Chateau Lafei 2012 dry red wine..." On August 1st, 2016, Sohu Finance published an article with text and photos "'Chateau Lafite' showcased at China Food and Drinks Fair, consumers don't know it is a knockoff." The Supreme People's Court ruled that the case should be reviewed.

Holding

The Supreme People's Court made an administrative judgment (2016) ZGFXZ No. 34 on December 23rd, 2016, to overrule the judgment of the court of second instance and maintain the judgment of the court of first instance and Decision No. 55856.

[Reasoning]

The Supreme People's Court held that the decision on whether the trademarks are similar requires considering the components of trademarks and their overall similarity, and also the significance and reputation of relevant trademarks and the correlation between the trademarks, and whether it is easy to cause confusion, which shall be used as the judgment standard. The disputed trademark consists of the words "Chateau Lafei" in Chinese, "Chateau" has weak significance with respect to the wine category and "Lafei" is the main component of the disputed trademark. The key to judge whether the disputed trademark is similar to the reference trademark is to judge whether "Lafei" is similar with "LAFITE" or whether the two have a stable correspondence. Before the application date of the disputed trademark, according to the facts ascertained by the court, there have been situations where all kinds of publicity reports transliterated "LAFITE" into "Lafei", in *New Express*, *Yangtze Evening Post* and *Beijing Daily*, which are publication that are easily accessible and have a large audience. The articles stated in relevant media highly commended "LAFITE" wine, and the reference trademark has a high reputation. In addition, through many years' commercial operation activities, Chateau Lafei has established a stable connection between "Lafei" and "LAFITE" objectively, and relevant public in China often refer to "Lafei" as "Lafite", and the disputed trademark is similar to the reference trademark. In addition, for a trademark that has been registered and used for a period of time, whether the relevant public groups have been formed by establishing a high market reputation is not decide based on time, but by whether the relevant public can distinguish from other trademarks through their use. As per the facts ascertained by the court, the substandard products involved in relevant news reports are all relevant products of the disputed trademark. Also, according to news reports, relevant public have confused the disputed trademark with the reference trademark. Therefore, the evidence submitted by Gold Hope Company failed to prove that relevant public groups have been formed by the use of the disputed trademark. The conclusion made by the court of second instance that the disputed trademark has formed a stable market order has no factual basis, and the Supreme People's Court corrected the same.

[Opinion of the Case (Chinese Version)]

Scan the QR code to see the Chinese version of the opinion

商标法关于"其他不正当手段取得注册"的认定

——李隆丰与商标评审委员会、三亚市海棠湾管理委员会
商标争议行政纠纷案

【裁判要旨】

2001 年《中华人民共和国商标法》第四十一条第一款规定的"以其他不正当手段取得注册",是指以欺骗手段以外,扰乱商标注册秩序、损害公共利益、不正当占用公共资源或者以其他方式谋取不正当利益的手段取得注册;民事主体申请注册商标,应该有使用的真实意图,其申请注册商标行为应具有合理性或正当性。

69

【案　　　号】	最高人民法院（2013）知行字第 41、（2013）知行字第 42 号
【案　　　由】	商标争议行政纠纷
【合议庭成员】	夏君丽　殷少平　董晓敏
【关　键　词】	商标注册　其他不正当手段
【相　关　法条】	《中华人民共和国商标法》（2001 年修正）第四条、第四十一条

【基本案情】

再审申请人李隆丰与国家工商行政管理总局商标评审委员会（以下简称商标评审委员会）、一审第三人三亚市海棠湾管理委员会（以下简称海棠湾管委会）商标争议行政纠纷案中，李隆丰于2005年6月8日在第36类的不动产出租、不动产管理、住所(公寓)等服务上注册了第4706493号"海棠湾"商标，在第43类住所（旅馆、供膳寄宿处）、旅游房屋出租、饭店、餐馆等服务上注册了第4706970号"海棠湾"商标（即两争议商标）。海棠湾管委会依据《中华人民共和国商标法》第三十一条、第四十一条第一款、第十条规定向商标评审委员会申请撤销上述两争议商标。商标评审委员会分别作出商评字〔2011〕第13255号《关于第4706493号"海棠湾"商标争议裁定书》（以下简称第13255号裁定）和〔2011〕第12545号《关于第4706970号"海棠湾"商标争议裁定书》（以下简称第12545号裁定），裁定撤销上述两个"海棠湾"商标。李隆丰不服，分别提起行政诉讼。北京市第一中级人民法院一审分别判决撤销第13255号裁定和第12545号裁定。商标评审委员会和海棠湾管委会不服，提出上诉。北京市高级人民法院二审分别判决撤销一审判决，维持第13255号裁定和第12545号裁定。李隆丰不服，向最高人民法院申请再审。最高人民法院于2013年8月12日分别裁定驳回李隆丰的再审申请。

 裁判结果

商标评审委员会分别作出商评字〔2011〕第13255号《关于第4706493号"海棠湾"商标争议裁定书》和〔2011〕第12545号《关于第4706970号"海棠湾"商标争议裁定书》，裁定撤销上述两个"海棠湾"商标。李隆丰不服，分别提起行政诉讼。北京市第一中级人民法院一审分别判决撤销第 13255 号裁定和第 12545 号裁定。商标评审委员会和海棠湾管委会不服，提出上诉。北京市高级人民法院二审分别判决撤销一审判决，维持第 13255 号裁定和第 12545 号裁定。李隆丰不服，向最高人民法院申请再审。最高人民法院于 2013 年 8 月 12 日分别裁定驳回李隆丰的再审申请。

【裁判理由】

最高人民法院认为：根据 2001 年《中华人民共和国商标法》第四十一条第一款的规定，已经注册的商标是以欺骗手段或者其他不正当手段取得注册的，其他单位或者个人可以请求商标评审委员会裁定撤销。审查判断诉争商标是否属于该条款规定的"以其他不正当手段取得注册"的情形，要考虑其是否属于欺骗手段以外的扰乱商标注册秩序、损害公共利益、不正当占用公共资源或者以其他方式谋取不正当利益的手段。依据《中华人民共和国商标法》第四条的规定，自然人、法人或者其他组织对其生产、制造、加工、拣选或者经销的商品或者提供的服务，需要取得商标专用权的，应当向商标局申请商标注册。从该条规定的精神来看，民事主体申请注册商标，应该有使用的真实意图，以满足自己的商标使用需求为目的，其申请注册商标行为应具有合理性或正当性。根据商标评审委员会及原审法院查明的事实，在李隆丰申请注册争议商标之前，"海棠湾"标志经过海南省相关政府机构的宣传推广，已经成为公众知晓的三亚市旅游度假区的地名和政府规划的大型综合开发项目的名称，其含义和指向明确。李隆丰自己在接受媒体采访时也承认是在看到报纸报道香港著名企业家将参与开发海棠湾的消息后，认为该标志会非常知名，作为商标会具有较高的价值，因而才将其申请注册为商标。李隆丰作为个人，不仅在第 36 类的不动产出租、不动产管理、住所（公寓）等服务上和第 43 类的住所（旅馆、供膳寄宿处）、旅游房屋出租、饭店、餐馆等服务上注册了本案争议商标，还在其他商品或服务类别上申请注册了"海棠湾"商标。此外，李隆丰在多个类别的商品或服务上还注册了"香水湾""椰林湾"等 30 余件商标，其中不少与公众知晓的海南岛的地名、景点名称有关。李隆丰利用政府部门宣传推广海棠湾休闲度假区及其开发项目所产生的巨大影响力，抢先申请注册多个"海棠湾"商标的行为，以及没有合理理由大量注册囤积其他商标的行为，并无真实使用意图，不具备注册商标应有的正当性，属于不正当占用公共资源、扰乱商标注册秩序的情形。

【本案裁判文书】

扫描二维码，可见裁判文书

Recognition of "Registration Obtained by Other Improper Means" Under the Trademark Law

——Li Longfeng v. Trademark Review and Adjudication Board and Sanya Haitangwan Management Committee

[Syllabus]

Under Article 41 (1) of the Trademark Law of the People's Republic of China (as amended in 2001), "registration obtained in any other improper means" refers to the acquisition of a registered trademark, not by fraud, but in any means that disturbs the trademark registration order, impairs public interests, improperly occupies public resources or otherwise seeks unjust profits; to apply for a registered trademark, a civil subject should have the real intent to use.

[Case No.] Supreme People's Court (2013) ZXZ No. 41 & (2013) ZXZ No. 42
[Cause of Action] Trademark administrative dispute
[Collegial Panel Members] Xia Junli   Yin Shaoping Dong Xiaomin
[Keywords] Trademark registration, other improper means
[Relevant Legal Provisions] Articles 4 and 41 of the Trademark Law of the People's Republic of China (as amended in 2001)

[Basic Facts]

In the retrial case of Li Longfeng v. the Trademark Review and Adjudication Board of the State Administration for Industry & Commerce (hereinafter referred to as TRAB) and Sanya Haitangwan Management Committee (hereinafter referred to as Haitangwan Management Committee) as the third party in the first instance in respect of a trademark administrative dispute 1, on June 8, 2005, Li Longfeng registered Trademark No. 4706493 "Haitangwan" in Type 36: Real Estate Lease, Real Estate Management, Residence (Apartment) and other Services, and also registered Trademark No. 4706970 "Haitangwan" in Type 43: Residence (Inns and Boarding House), Tourist Homes, Hotels, Restaurants and Other Services (i.e. the two trademarks at issue). Under the provisions of Articles 31, 41(1) and 10 of the Trademark Law of the People's Republic of China, Haitangwan Management Committee applied to TRAB a request for cancellation of the registration of the Disputed Trademarks. TRAB, through SPZ (2011) No. 13255 Decision on Trademark Dispute over Trademark No. 4706493 "Haitangwan" ("No. 13255 Decision") and SPZ (2011) No. 12545 Decision on Trademark Dispute over Trademark No. 4706970 "Haitangwan" ("No. 12545 Decision"), ruled to respectively cancel the two "Haitangwan" trademarks. Li Longfeng found it dissatisfactory and brought administrative lawsuits against the aforementioned decisions respectively. On first instance, Beijing No. 1 Intermediate People's Court ordered to overrule No. 13255 Award and No. 12545 Award. TRAB and Haitangwan Management Committee appealed. On second instance, the Beijing High People's Court ordered to overrule the first instance judgment and uphold No. 13255 Award and No. 12545 Award. Li Longfeng applied to the Supreme People's Court for retrial. On August 12, 2013, the Supreme People's Court denied the application for retrial from Li Longfeng.

Holding

TRAB, through SPZ (2011) No. 13255 Decision on Trademark Dispute over Trademark No. 4706493 "Haitangwan" and SPZ (2011) No. 12545 Decision on Trademark Dispute over Trademark No. 4706970 "Haitangwan", ruled to cancel the two "Haitangwan" trademarks respectively. Li Longfeng found it dissatisfactory and brought administrative lawsuits against the aforementioned decisions respectively. On first instance, Beijing No. 1 Intermediate People's Court ordered to overrule No. 13255 Award and No. 12545 Award. TRAB and Haitangwan Management Committee appealed. On second instance, the Beijing High People's Court ordered to overrule the first instance judgment and uphold No. 13255 Award and No. 12545 Award. Li Longfeng applied to the Supreme People's Court for retrial. On August 12, 2013, the Supreme People's Court denied the application for retrial from Li Longfeng.

[Reasoning]

The Supreme People's Court holds that: under Article 41 (1) of the Trademark Law of the People's Republic of China (as amendment in 2001), if the registration of a registered trademark is obtained by fraud or any other improper means, any organization or individual may petition to TRAB for an order to cancel such registration. To review and determine whether the Disputed Trademarks are "registered in any other improper means", it is necessary to consider whether the registration is acquired, not by fraud, but in any means that disturbs the trademark registration order, impairs public interests, improperly occupies public resources or otherwise seeks unjust profits. Article 4 of the Trademark Law of the People's Republic of China says that any natural person, legal person, or other organization that needs to obtain the proprietary rights to use a trademark for the goods or services he produces, manufactures, processes, selects, or markets shall file an application for registration of the trademark of the goods with the Trademark Office. It can be seen from the forgoing article that to apply for a registered trademark, the civil subject should have the real intent for its own use, and it should be reasonable or legitimate to apply for the registered trademark. According to the facts collected and ascertained by TRAB and the original court, prior to Li Longfeng's application for registering the Dispute Trademarks, "Haitangwan" has been used and promoted by relevant governmental authorities of Hainan Province and become a publicly-known name of resort area in Sanya City and the name of a major comprehensive development project with clear meaning and designation. In the media interview, Li Longfeng also made it clear that he registered the trademark because he believed that the mark would be very famous when he learnt on a Hong Kong newspaper that renowned entrepreneurs from Hong Kong would participate in the development of the Haitangwan Project and that the trademark would have high value. As an individual, Li Longfeng registered the trademarks at issue not only in Type 36: Real Estate Lease, Real Estate Management, Residence (Apartment) and other Services and Type 43: Residence (Inns and Boarding House), Tourist Homes, Hotels, Restaurants and Other Services, but also in other types of goods and services. In addition, Li Longfeng registered more than 30 trademarks, such as "Xiangshuiwan" and "Yelinwan", in various types of goods and services, and some of them are related to place names and scenic spot names in Hainan Island that are known to the public. Li Longfeng exploited the huge influence from governmental authorities' efforts to promote and market Haitangwan Resort Area and its development project, squatted several trademarks related to "Haitangwan", and registered a large number of other trademarks without justifiable reasons. His conducts show that he lacks the intent to use the mark and does not have the justification required to register a trademark, and constitutes improperly occupying public resources and disturbing trademark registration order.

[Opinion of the Case (Chinese Version)]

Scan the QR code to see the Chinese version of the opinion

77

电视节目名称在商标法意义上的使用与侵权判断

——金阿欢与江苏省广播电视总台、深圳市珍爱网信息技术有限公司侵害商标权纠纷案

【裁判要旨】

相关标识具有节目名称的属性并不能当然排斥该标识作为商标的可能性。判断被诉标识是否属于商标性使用，关键在于相关标识的使用是否能指示相关商品／服务的来源，起到使相关公众区分不同商品／服务的提供者的作用。

电视节目大多以现实生活为题材，这些现实生活题材只是电视节目的组成要素。在判断此类电视节目是否与某一服务类别相同或类似时，应当综合考察节目的整体和主要特征，把握其行为本质，作出全面、合理、正确的审查认定。

【案　　　号】　广东省高级人民法院（2016）粤民再447号
【案　　　由】　侵害商标权纠纷
【合议庭成员】　徐春建　邱永清　肖海棠
【关　键　词】　电视节目名称　商标　类别　混淆
【相关法条】　《中华人民共和国商标法》第五十七条第（一）项、第（二）项，《最高人民法院关于审理商标民事纠纷

案件适用法律若干问题的解释》第九条、第十条、第
十一条、第十二条

【基本案情】

在再审申请人江苏省广播电视总台（以下简称江苏电视台）、深圳市珍爱网信息技术有限公司（以下简称珍爱网公司）与被申请人金阿欢侵害商标权纠纷案中，金阿欢系第7199523号"非诚勿扰"商标权利人，该商标于2009年2月16日申请注册，2010年9月7日获得核准注册，核定服务项目包括第45类的"交友服务、婚姻介绍所"。

江苏电视台旗下的江苏卫视于2010年开办了以婚恋交友为主题、名称为《非诚勿扰》的电视节目。江苏卫视在节目简介中称："《非诚勿扰》是一档适应现代生活节奏的大型婚恋交友节目，我们将为您提供公开的婚恋交友平台，高质量的婚恋交友嘉宾，全新的婚恋交友模式。"报名方法包括"在珍爱网登记报名资料"。珍爱网曾在深圳南山区招募嘉宾，为该节目推选相亲对象。该案中，被诉"非诚勿扰"标识主要体现为两种形态：一是"非诚勿扰"纯文字标识；二是，即"非诚勿扰"文字与女性剪影组合的图文标识。

金阿欢以江苏电视台和珍爱网侵害其注册商标专用权为由，向广东省深圳市南山区法院提起诉讼，请求法院判令：1.江苏电视台所属的江苏卫视频道立即停止使用"非诚勿扰"栏目名称；2.珍爱网公司立即停止使用"非诚勿扰"名称进行广告推销、报名筛选、后续服务等共同侵权行为；3.两被告共同承担本案全部诉讼费用。

广东省深圳市南山区人民法院认为：金阿欢的文字商标"非诚勿扰"与江苏台电视节目的名称"非诚勿扰"相同，被诉"非诚勿扰"电视节目虽然与婚恋交友有关，但终究是电视节目，相关公众

一般认为两者不存在特定联系，不容易造成公众混淆，两者属于不同类别服务，不构成侵权。一审遂判决：驳回金阿欢的诉讼请求。金阿欢不服，提起上诉。广东省深圳市中级人民法院认为，从《非诚勿扰》节目简介、开场白、结束语，参加报名条件、节目中男女嘉宾互动内容，以及广电总局的发文、媒体评论，可认定江苏电视台的《非诚勿扰》为相亲、交友节目。故江苏电视台的《非诚勿扰》节目与金阿欢涉案注册商标所核定的"交友、婚姻介绍"服务相同。本案金阿欢涉案注册商标已投入商业使用，被诉行为影响了该商标正常使用，相关公众容易对权利人的注册商标使用与江苏电视台产生错误认识及联系，构成商标侵权。珍爱网公司参与了节目嘉宾招募、宣传，还与江苏电视台签订有《合作协议书》，构成共同侵权。遂判决江苏电视台与珍爱网公司停止侵权行为。江苏电视台与珍爱网公司不服二审判决，以被诉标识不属于商标性使用、类别与金阿欢注册商标核定使用类别不同、不构成混淆为由，向广东省高级人民法院申请再审。

 裁判结果

广东省深圳市南山区人民法院于 2014 年 9 月 29 日作出一审判决：驳回金阿欢诉讼。金阿欢不服，提起上诉。广东省深圳市中级人民法院于 2015 年 12 月 11 日作出二审判决：1. 撤销（2013）深南法知民初字第 208 号民事判决；2. 江苏电视台所属的江苏卫视频道于判决生效后立即停止使用"非诚勿扰"栏目名称；3. 珍爱网公司于判决生效后立即停止使用"非诚勿扰"名称进行广告推销、报名筛选、后续服务等行为。江苏电视台与珍爱网公司不服二审判决，向广东省高级人民法院申请再审。广东省高级人民法院裁定提审本案，并于 2016 年 12 月 30 日判决撤销二审判决，维持一审判决。

【裁判理由】

广东省高级人民法院提审认为：

一、关于被诉标识是否属于商标性使用的问题

判断被诉"非诚勿扰"标识是否属于商标性使用，关键在于相关标识的使用是否为了指示相关商品／服务的来源，起到使相关公众区分不同商品／服务的提供者的作用。本案中，"非诚勿扰"原是江苏电视台为了区分其台下多个电视栏目而命名的节目名称，但从本案的情况来看，江苏电视台对被诉"非诚勿扰"标识的使用，并非仅仅为概括具体电视节目内容而进行的描述性使用，而是反复多次、大量地在其电视、官网、招商广告、现场宣传等商业活动中单独使用或突出使用，使用方式上具有持续性与连贯性，其中 标识更在整体呈现方式上具有一定独特性，这显然超出对节目或者作品内容进行描述性使用所必需的范围和通常认知，具备了区分商品／服务的功能。江苏电视台在播出被诉节目同时标注"江苏卫视"台标的行为，客观上并未改变"非诚勿扰"标识指示来源的作用和功能，反而促使相关公众更加紧密地将"非诚勿扰"标识与江苏电视台下属频道"江苏卫视"相联系。随着该节目持续热播及广告宣传，被诉"非诚勿扰"标识已具有较强显著性，相关公众看到被诉标识，将联想到该电视节目及其提供者江苏电视台下属江苏卫视，客观上起到了指示商品／服务来源的作用。而且，江苏电视台在不少广告中，将被诉"非诚勿扰"标识与"江苏卫视"台标、"途牛""韩束"等品牌标识并列进行宣传，在再审审查程序中提交的证据表明江苏电视台曾就该标识的使用向华谊公司谋求商标授权，以上均直接反映江苏电视台主观上亦存在将被诉标识作为识别来源的商标使用、作为品牌而进行维护的意愿。因此，江苏电视台仅以"非诚勿扰"属于节目名称、

同时标注台标明晰来源为由，否认相关行为属于商标性使用，不能成立。

二、关于江苏电视台是否侵害金阿欢涉案注册商标权的问题

在商标侵权裁判中，必须对被诉标识与注册商标是否相同或近似、两者服务是否相同或类似，以及是否容易引起相关公众的混淆误认作出判断。

（一）关于被诉标识与涉案商标是否相同或近似的问题

本案中，将被诉"非诚勿扰"文字标识及 图文标识分别与金阿欢涉案第 7199523 号注册商标 相比对，文字形态上均存在繁体字与简体字的区别，在字体及文字排列上亦有差异。被诉图文组合标识与金阿欢注册商标相比，还多了颜色及图案差异。故该两被诉标识与金阿欢涉案第 7199523 号注册商标相比，均不属于相同标识。该两被诉标识与金阿欢涉案注册商标的显著部分与核心部分均为"非诚勿扰"，文字相同，整体结构相似，在自然组成要素上相近似。但客观要素的相近似并不等同于商标法意义上的近似。商标法所要保护的，并非仅以注册行为所固化的商标标识本身，而是商标所具有的识别和区分商品／服务来源的功能。如果被诉行为并非使用在相同或类似商品／服务上，或者并未损害涉案注册商标的识别和区分功能，亦未因此导致市场混淆后果的，不应认定构成商标侵权。

（二）关于两者服务类别是否相同或类似的问题

对于电视节目是否与某一服务类别相同或类似进行司法判断时，不能简单、孤立地将某种表现形式或某一题材内容从整体节目中割裂开来，应当综合考察节目的整体和主要特征，把握其行为本质，作出全面、合理、正确的审查认定。以此考察被诉《非诚勿扰》电视节目，从相关服务的目的、内容、方式、对象等方

面情况来看，正是典型的使用在电视文娱节目上。具体言之，被诉《非诚勿扰》节目系一档以相亲、交友为题材的电视文娱节目，其借助相亲、交友场景中现代未婚男女的言行举止，结合现场点评嘉宾及主持人的评论及引导，通过剪辑编排成电视节目予以播放，使社会公众在娱乐、放松、休闲的同时，了解当今社会交友现象及相关价值观念，引导树立健康向上的婚恋观与人生观。其服务目的在于向社会公众提供旨在娱乐、消遣的文化娱乐节目，凭节目的收视率与关注度获取广告赞助等经济收入；服务的内容和方式为通过电视广播这一特定渠道和大众传媒方式向社会提供和传播文娱节目；服务对象是不特定的广大电视观众等。而第45类中的"交友服务、婚姻介绍"系为满足特定个人的婚配需求而提供的中介服务，服务目的系通过提供促成婚恋配对的服务来获取经济收入；服务内容和方式通常包括管理相关需求人员信息、提供咨询建议、传递意向信息等中介服务；服务对象为特定的有婚恋需求的未婚男女。故两者无论是在服务目的、内容、方式和对象上均区别明显。以相关公众的一般认知，能够清晰区分电视文娱节目的内容与现实中的婚介服务活动，不会误以为两者具有某种特定联系，两者不构成相同服务或类似服务。

退一步而言，即使认定其为类似服务，也必须紧扣商标法宗旨，考虑涉案注册商标的显著性与知名度，在确定其保护范围与保护强度的基础上考虑相关公众混淆、误认的可能性，从而判断是否构成商标侵权。本案中，金阿欢涉案注册商标中的"非诚勿扰"文字本系商贸活动中的常见词汇，用于婚姻介绍服务领域显著性较低，其亦未经过金阿欢长期、大量的使用而获得后天的显著性。故本案对该注册商标的保护范围和保护强度，应与金阿欢对该商标的显著性和知名度所作出的贡献相符。反观被诉《非诚勿扰》节目，其将"非诚勿扰"作为相亲、交友题材的节目名称具有一定合理性，经过长期热播，作为娱乐、消遣的综艺性文娱电视节目为公众所熟知。即使被诉节目涉及交友方面的内容，相关公众也能够对该服务来源作出清晰区分，不会产生两者误认和混淆，不构成商标侵权。

【本案裁判文书】

扫描二维码，可见裁判文书

Judgment on Use and Infringement of TV Program Names from the Perspective of Trademark Law

——Jin Ahuan v. Jiangsu Broadcasting Corporation and Shenzhen Zhenai.com Information Technology Co., Ltd.

[Syllabus]

A relevant logo with an attribute of program's name does not exclude the possibility of the logo being a trademark. The key to judging whether the alleged logo is used as trademark lies in whether the relevant logo is used to indicate the source of relevant goods/services to enable the relevant public to distinguish the providers of different goods/services.

Most TV programs are based on real life. These real-life themes are only the elements of TV programs. In judging whether such TV programs are the same as or similar to a certain service category, we shall comprehensively examined the entirety and main features of the programs, grasp its nature, and thus make a comprehensive, reasonable and correct determination.

[Case No.] Guangdong High People's Court (2016) YMZ No. 447
[Cause of Action] Dispute over infringement on trademark rights
[Collegial Panel Members] Xu Chunjian   Qiu Yongqing
Xiao Haitang

[Keywords] TV program name, trademark, category, confusion
[Relevant Legal Provisions] Items 1 and 2, Article 57 of the
Trademark Law of the People's Republic of China, Articles 9, 10, 11
and 12 of the *Interpretation of the Supreme People's Court on Several
Issues Concerning the Application of Law in the Trial of Civil Dispute
Cases over Trademarks*

[Basic Facts]

In the retrial of the dispute case over infringement of trademark rights by
the appellant Jiangsu Broadcasting Corporation (hereinafter referred
to as "Jiangsu TV Station") and Shenzhen Zhenai.com Information
Technology Co., Ltd. (hereinafter referred to as "Zhenai.com"), and
the respondent Jin Ahuan, wherein Jin Ahuan is the holder of the
trademark " 非誠勿擾 " No. 7199523. The trademark was applied for
registration on February 16th, 2009 and was approved for registration
on September 7th, 2010, and the approved service items include items
under Category No.45 "Dating Service and Marriage Agency".

In 2010, JSTV under Jiangsu TV Station launched a TV program titled
"If You Are the One" based on the theme of marriage and dating. JSTV
informs in the program introduction that "If You Are the One" is a large-
scale dating program that adapts to the rhythm of modern life, and
provides an open platform for marriage and dating, high-quality dating
friends and a brand-new marriage and dating model. The registration
method includes "registering the materials at Zhenai.com". Zhenai.com
recruited guests from Nanshan District in Shenzhen City and selected the
blind date guests for the program. In this case, the alleged "If You Are
the One" logo is mainly reflected in two forms: one is the "If You Are the
One" text logo, and the other is 非誠勿擾 graphic logo, which combines the
text "If You Are the One" and a female silhouette.

Jin Ahuan filed a lawsuit in the People's Court of Nanshan District of Shenzhen, Guangdong Province, on the grounds that Jiangsu TV Station and Zhenai.com infringed on the exclusive right to use their registered trademarks, and requested the court to order that: 1. JSTV under Jiangsu TV Station immediately stop using the "If You Are the One" name; 2. Zhenai.com immediately stopped using the "If You Are the One" name for advertising, registration, follow-up services and other joint infringement acts; 3. the two defendants jointly bear all the litigation costs of the case.

The People's Court of Nanshan District of Shenzhen, Guangdong Province affirmed that Jin Ahuan's text-based trademark "If You Are the One" is the same as the name "If You Are the One" of Jiangsu TV program, however, the alleged "If You Are the One" TV program is related to marriage and dating and is only a TV program; the relevant public generally believes that there is no specific connection between the two, and it is not easy to cause public confusion. The two belong to different types of services and it does not constitute infringement. The court of first instance rejected Jin Ahuan's claim. Jin Ahuan refused to accept the judgement and filed an appeal. The Shenzhen Intermediate People's Court of Guangdong Province affirmed that Jiangsu TV Station's "If You Are the One" can be identified as a marriage and dating program based on the program introduction, opening remarks, concluding remarks, participation, registration conditions, interactive content of the male and female guests in the program, and the publication of the State Administration of Radio, Film and Television and media comments. Therefore, the "If You Are the One" program of Jiangsu TV Station is the same as the approved "Dating and Marriage Introduction" service for Jin Ahuan's registered trademark. In this case, the registered trademark of Jin Ahuan has been put into commercial use. The use of the alleged logo affects the normal use of the trademark. The relevant public can easily misunderstand and connect the use of the registered trademark of the right holder with the program of

87

Jiangsu TV station, which constitutes trademark infringement. Zhenai. com participated in the recruitment of the guests and promotion, and also signed a *Cooperation Agreement* with Jiangsu TV Station, constituting joint infringement. Hence, the court ruled that Jiangsu TV Station and Zhenai.com should cease infringement. Jiangsu TV Station and Zhenai. com refused to accept the judgement of the appellate court and applied for retrial with the Guangdong High People's Court on the grounds that the use of the alleged logo does not belong to the use of a trademark as the category is different from the approved use category of the registered trademark of Jin Ahuan, and it does not cause confusion.

 Holding

On first instance, the People's Court of Nanshan District of Shenzhen, Guangdong Province made a judgment on September 29th, 2014, and rejected Jin Ahuan's claims. Jin Ahuan refused to accept the judgment and filed an appeal. on appeal, the Shenzhen Intermediate People's Court of Guangdong Province made a judgment on December 11th, 2015 stipulating that: 1. The civil judgment (2013) SNFZMC ZI No. 208 be revoked; 2. JSTV under Jiangsu TV Station immediately cease using the "If You Are the One" name after the judgment takes effect; 3. Zhenai.com immediately stop using the "If You Are the One" name for advertising, registration and follow-up services after the judgment takes effect. Jiangsu TV Station and Zhenai.com refused to accept the judgment of the court of second instance, and applied for retrial in the Guangdong High People's Court. The Guangdong High People's Court ruled that the case was to be reviewed, and on December 30th, 2016, the judgment of the court of second instance was revoked and the judgment of the court of first instance was upheld.

[Reasoning]

The Guangdong High People's Court reviewed the case and held that:

I. Issue on whether the alleged logo is used as a trademark

The key to judging whether the alleged "If You Are the One" logo is a trademark, lies in whether the relevant logo aims to indicate the source of the relevant goods/services to enable the relevant public to distinguish the providers of different goods/services. In this case, "If You Are the One" is originally the name of the program named by Jiangsu TV Station, to distinguish it from its multiple TV programs. However, judging from the circumstances of this case, Jiangsu TV Station's use of the alleged "If You Are the One" logo is not merely a descriptive use for summarizing the content of the TV program, but rather, involves repeated and extensive independent or prominent use in commercial activities such as television, official website, investment attracting advertisement and onsite publicity, and the manner of use is continuous and coherent. The logo is somewhat unique in its overall presentation, which clearly goes beyond the scope and general awareness necessary for the descriptive use of the program or work content and has the function of distinguishing goods/services. Jiangsu TV Station broadcasted the alleged program with the "JSTV" logo, which objectively does not change the role and function of the "If You Are the One" logo indication source, but instead prompts the relevant public to more closely associate the "If You Are the One" logo with JSTV under Jiangsu TV Station. As the program continued to be broadcasted and advertised, the alleged "If You Are the One" logo became more distinctive. The relevant public sees the alleged logo and will associate it with the TV program and its provider JSTV under Jiangsu TV Station, which objectively plays a role in indicating the source of goods/services. Moreover, in many advertisements, Jiangsu TV Station combined the alleged "If You Are the One" logo with the "JSTV" logo, "Tuniu.com" "KanS" and other brand logos for joint publicity, and the evidence submitted in the retrial review process indicates that Jiangsu TV station had sought trademark authorization from Huayi Company for the use of the logo. All of the above directly reflect that Jiangsu TV

Station subjectively was willing to use the alleged logo as the trademark to identify the source and maintain it as a brand. Therefore, it could not be established that Jiangsu TV Station denied that the relevant behavior was trademark use on the grounds that "If You Are the One" was a program name and the TV Station logo was clearly marked to distinguish its source.

II. Issue on whether Jiangsu TV station infringes on the registered trademark rights of Jin Ahuan

In the trademark infringement judgment, it must be evaluated whether the alleged logo is the same as or similar to the registered trademark, whether the two services are the same or similar, and whether it is easy to cause confusion and misunderstanding in the minds of the relevant public.

(I) Issue on whether the alleged logo is the same as or similar to the registered trademark

In this case, the alleged "If You Are the One" text logo and graphic logo were compared with the registered trademark No. 7199523 of Jin Ahuan. There are differences in the form of characters between the traditional Chinese characters used in Jin Ahuan's mark and simplified Chinese characters used in the respondent's logo, and there are also differences in fonts and text sequence. Compared with Jin Ahuan's registered trademark, the alleged combined graphic and text logo has differences in color and pattern. Therefore, the alleged logos are not the same as Jin Ahuan's registered trademark no. 7199523. The prominent part and the core part of the alleged logos and Jin Ahuan's registered trademark are "If You Are the One", wherein the text is the same, the overall structure is similar, and the natural components are similar. However, the similarity of objective factors is not equivalent to similarity with respect to the Trademark Law. What the Trademark Law wants to protect is not the trademark logo itself which is fixed by the act of registration, but the trademark's function of identifying and distinguishing goods/services. If the alleged logo is not used for the same or similar goods/services or does not damage the identification and distinguishing factor of the registered trademark involved and does not result in market confusion, it should not be deemed to constitute a trademark infringement.

(II) Issue on whether the two service categories are the same or similar

When a TV program is judged to be the same or similar to a service category, it is not reasonable to simply and independently isolate the manifestation or a theme content from the overall program to make a one-sided and inflexible identification. The entirety and main features of the program should be comprehensively examined. It is necessary to grasp the essence of its behavior, and make a comprehensive, reasonable and correct review and determination. In this respect, when the TV program of the alleged "If You Are the One" logo was investigated from the perspectives of purpose, content, method and object of related services, its use was typical in TV entertainment programs. Specifically, "If You Are the One" TV program is a TV entertainment program featuring blind dates and dating. It uses the words and actions of modern unmarried men and women in a scenario of a blind date and dating, combines the same with comments and guidance from onsite commenters and the host, and is broadcast as a TV program after editing, so that the public can understand the phenomenon of current social dating and related values, while enjoying and relaxing, and are guided to establish a healthy and active view of marriage and love and view of life. The purpose of its service is to provide the public with a cultural and entertainment program and to obtain economic benefits such as sponsorship and advertisements, based on audience rating and interest in the program; the service content and method is provided through specific channels of television broadcasting and mass media, to disseminate cultural entertainment programs to the public; and the service objects are unspecified TV viewers. The "dating service and marriage introduction" as per Category No. 45 is an intermediary service provided to meet the needs of pairing a specific individual. The purpose of the service is to obtain economic benefit by providing services that promote marriage and love matchmaking; the service content and method usually include managing related personal information of participants, providing consulting and advice, and transmitting information on intention and other intermediary services; the service objects are specific unmarried men and women who are interested in marriage. Therefore, the differences between the two are obvious in terms of service purpose, content, method and object. Based on the general knowledge of the relevant public, it is possible to clearly distinguish the content of the TV entertainment program from the real matchmaking service activities, and it is not possible for the relevant public to mistakenly believe that the two have a certain relationship; furthermore, the two do not constitute the same services or similar services.

Taking a step back, even if they are identified to be similar services, it must closely follow the purpose of the Trademark Law, and consider the significance and popularity of the registered trademark involved as well as the possibility of confusion and misunderstanding in the minds of the relevant public, based on determining the scope of protection and the intensity of protection, to decide whether it constitutes a trademark infringement. In this case, the "If You Are the One" text in Jin Ahuan's registered trademark is a common phrase in business activities, which is used in the field of marriage introduction services, and is not significantly used on a long-term and large-scale basis by Jin Ahuan. Therefore, the scope of protection and intensity of protection of the registered trademark in this case should be consistent with Jin Ahuan's contribution to the significance and popularity of the trademark. In contrast, the alleged "If You Are the One" program uses "If You Are the One" as the name of a blind date and dating program based on certain rational use of the phrase. After long-term broadcast, the entertainment TV program can be well-known to the public. Even if the alleged program involves content related to dating, the relevant public can make a clear distinction on the source of the service without having any misunderstanding or confusion with respect to the two, and thus, it does not constitute trademark infringement.

[Opinion of the Case (Chinese Version)]

Scan the QR code to see the Chinese version of the opinion

商品名称作为未注册驰名商标保护的司法标准

——"新华字典"侵害商标权及不正当竞争纠纷案

【裁判要旨】

显著性是商标的基本特征，是一个标志可以作为商标的基本属性。只有具有显著特征的标识才能发挥区别商品来源的作用，进而可以作为商标注册或保护。商品名称只有在具备显著性的情况下，才能够发挥识别商品来源的作用，同时，在达到驰名商标的程度时，可以获得未注册驰名商标的保护。"新华字典"具有特定的历史起源、发展过程和长期唯一的提供主体以及客观的市场格局，保持着产品和品牌混合属性的商品名称，已经在相关消费者中形成了稳定的认知联系，具有指示商品来源的意义和作用，具备商标的显著特征。从商务印书馆对"新华字典"进行宣传所持续的时间、程度和地理范围来看，"新华字典"已经获得较大的影响力和较高的知名度。综合以上因素，可以认定"新华字典"构成未注册驰名商标。

【案　　　号】　北京知识产权法院（2016）京73民初277号

【案　　　由】　侵害商标权及不正当竞争纠纷

【合议庭成员】　张玲玲　冯　刚　杨　洁

【关　键　词】　商标　未注册驰名商标　不正当竞争　知识传播

【相关法条】　《中华人民共和国侵权责任法》第十五条，《中华人民

共和国商标法》第十三条、第十四条,《中华人民共
和国反不正当竞争法》第五条第(二)项、第二十
条第一款

【基本案情】

原告商务印书馆有限公司(以下简称务印书馆)与被告华语教学
出版社有限责任公司(以下简称华语出版社)同为出版机构。原告商
务印书馆自 1957 年至今,连续出版《新华字典》通行版本至第 11 版,
2010 ~ 2015 年,原告商务印书馆出版的《新华字典》在字典类图书
市场的平均占有率超过 50%,截至 2016 年,原告商务印书馆出版的《新
华字典》全球发行量超过 5.67 亿册,获得"最受欢迎的字典"吉尼斯
世界纪录及"最畅销的书(定期修订)"吉尼斯世界纪录等多项荣誉。

原告商务印书馆诉称被告华语出版社生产、销售"新华字典"
辞书的行为侵害了原告商务印书馆"新华字典"未注册驰名商标,
且被告华语出版社使用原告商务印书馆《新华字典》(第 11 版)
知名商品的特有包装装潢的行为已构成不正当竞争。请求法院判
令被告立即停止侵害商标权及不正当竞争行为;在《中国新闻出
版广电报》等相关媒体上刊登声明,消除影响;赔偿原告经济损
失 300 万元及合理支出 40 万元。

被告华语出版社辩称,"新华字典"由国家项目名称发展为公共
领域的辞书通用名称,原告无权就"新华字典"主张商标权益,无
权禁止他人正当使用。涉案《新华字典》(第 11 版)的装潢不属于《中
华人民共和国反不正当竞争法》第五条第(二)项规定的"特有装潢",
不会使购买者产生混淆或误认。原告提起诉讼旨在通过司法判决的
方式独占"新华字典"这一辞书通用名称,具有排除竞争、实现垄
断辞书类市场的不正当目的。

北京知识产权法院认为，"新华字典"具备商标的显著特征，且经过原告商务印书馆的使用已经达到驰名商标的程度，构成未注册驰名商标，被告华语出版社复制、摹仿原告商务印书馆的未注册驰名商标"新华字典"的行为，容易导致混淆，构成商标侵权。原告商务印书馆出版的《新华字典》（第11版）构成知名商品的特有包装装潢，被告华语出版社擅自使用《新华字典》（第11版）知名商品的特有装潢的行为构成不正当竞争。一审法院判决：被告华语出版社立即停止涉案侵害商标权及不正当竞争行为；在《中国新闻出版广电报》等相关媒体上刊登声明，消除影响；赔偿原告商务印书馆经济损失300万元及合理支出27万余元。

本案一审宣判后，双方当事人达成执行和解，一审生效。

 裁判结果

北京知识产权法院于2017年12月28日作出（2016）京73民初277号判决：判令被告华语出版社立即停止使用原告商务印书馆的"新华字典"未注册驰名商标的行为及立即停止使用与原告商务印书馆《新华字典》（第11版）知名商品的特有装潢相同或近似装潢的不正当竞争行为；在相关媒体上发布声明并承担赔偿经济损失3,000,000元及合理费用277,989.2元的赔偿责任。

【裁判理由】

北京知识产权法院判决认为：本案的焦点问题为：1.涉案"新华字典"是否构成未注册驰名商标，如果"新华字典"构成未注册驰名商标，华语出版社实施的被诉行为是否构成侵权；2.商务印书馆出版的《新华字典》（第11版）是否构成知名商品的特有包装装潢，如果构成知名商品的特有包装装潢，华语出版社的被诉行为是否构成不正当竞争；3. 如果前述侵权行为成立，华语出版社应当如何承担法律责任。

一、涉案"新华字典"是否构成未注册驰名商标？如果"新华字典"构成未注册驰名商标，华语出版社实施的被诉行为是否构成侵权？

1. 法院认为，涉案"新华字典"构成未注册驰名商标。

首先，"新华字典"具备商标的显著特征。显著识别性是商标的基本特征，是一个标志可以作为商标的基本属性。只有具有显著特征的标识才能发挥区别商品来源的作用，进而可以作为商标注册或保护。本案中，"新华字典"具有特定的历史起源、发展过程和长期唯一的提供主体以及客观的市场格局，保持着产品和品牌混合属性的商品名称，已经在相关消费者中形成了稳定的认知联系，具有指示商品来源的意义和作用，具备商标的显著特征。本案遵循在先案例（2011）民提字第 55 号民事判决及（2013）民申字第 371 号民事裁定中确立的裁判标准，认定"新华字典"具有商标的显著特征，能够发挥商品来源的识别作用。

其次，"新华字典"构成未注册驰名商标。从相关公众对涉案"新华字典"的知晓程度来看，"新华字典"已经在全国范围内被相关公众广为知晓。从商务印书馆使用"新华字典"持续的时间和销售数量来看，"新华字典"近 60 年间已经在全国范围内销售数亿册，销售量巨大，销售范围非常广泛。从商务印书馆对"新华字典"进行宣传所持续的时间、程度和地理范围来看，"新华字典"已经获得较大的影响力和较高的知名度。综合以上因素，可以认定"新华字典"构成未注册驰名商标。

最后，商务印书馆可以就"新华字典"主张未注册驰名商标。

至被诉行为发生之时，"新华字典"标识尚未获准商标注册，但"新华字典"经过商务印书馆的使用已经达到驰名商标的程度，应该得到《中华人民共和国商标法》的保护。将"新华字典"作为商务印书馆的未注册驰名商标给予保护，不仅是对于之前商务印书馆在经营"新华字典"辞书商品中所产生的识别来源作用和凝结的商誉给予保护，更是通过商标保护的方式使其承担商品质量保障的法定义务和社会责任。这不仅不会损害知识的传播，相反，为了维护"新华字典"良好的品牌商誉，商务印书馆对其出版、发行的标有"新华字典"标识的辞书更会注重提升品质，促进正确知识的广泛传播。

2. 法院认为，华语出版社复制、摹仿商务印书馆的未注册驰名商标"新华字典"的行为，容易导致混淆，构成商标侵权。

商务印书馆和华语出版社使用"新华字典"的商品均为第16类辞书，属于相同商品，且华语出版社在其出版的字典上使用了与商务印书馆未注册驰名商标"新华字典"完全相同的商标，该行为属于以复制的方式使用商务印书馆的未注册驰名商标。根据在案证据显示，华语出版社在其出版的第16类字典商品上使用"新华字典"标识，已经使消费者在购买和使用字典的过程中将其出版的《新华字典》误认成商务印书馆出版的《新华字典》。华语出版社的上述行为已经导致相关公众发生混淆和误认。因此，华语出版社在第16类辞书上使用"新华字典"标识的行为已经构成在相同商品上复制他人未在中国注册的驰名商标，容易导致混淆，违反了《中华人民共和国商标法》第十三条第二款的规定。

二、商务印书馆出版的《新华字典》（第11版）是否构成知名商品的特有包装装潢？如果构成知名商品的特有包装装潢，华语出版社的被诉行为是否构成不正当竞争？

1.法院认为，商务印书馆出版的《新华字典》(第11版)构成知名商品的特有包装装潢。

首先，商务印书馆出版的《新华字典》(第11版)属于知名商品。《新华字典》第11版自2011年6月出版发行，至被诉行为发生时已经在全国范围大量出版发行，并取得较高的知名度。结合商务印书馆在全国范围内宣传和经营《新华字典》的情况，以及《新华字典》辞书获得的系列荣誉和重要奖项，可以认定商务印书馆的《新华字典》(第11版)属于知名商品。

其次，《新华字典》(第11版)的装潢属于特有装潢。《新华字典》(第11版)使用的装潢是对与其功能性无关的构成要素进行了独特的排列组合，形成了能够与其他经营者的同类商品相区别的整体形象。经过商务印书馆长期的宣传和使用，使得相关公众能够将上述装潢的整体形象与《新华字典》(第11版)的商品来源联系起来，该装潢所体现的文字、图案、色彩及其排列组合具有识别和区分商品来源的作用，具备特有性。因此，《新华字典》(第11版)的装潢属于《中华人民共和国反不正当竞争法》第五条第(二)项所保护的知名商品的特有装潢。

2.法院认为，华语出版社擅自使用《新华字典》(第11版)知名商品的特有装潢的行为构成不正当竞争。

商务印书馆提交了原、被告的产品对比图如下：

第11版 单色本　　　　第11版 双色本　　　　第11版 平装本　　　　第11版 大字本

(2011年6月出版)　　　(2011年6月出版)　　　(2011年6月出版)　　　(2012年1月出版)

| 被诉1 | 被诉2 | 被诉3 | 被诉4 | 被诉5 | 被诉8 | 被诉10 |

（——————————2012年7月首印至今——————————）　（--2014年2月首印至今--）

从以上产品对比图可见，被诉侵权产品在《新华字典》（第11版）之后出版，且在字典封面的整体设计、封面中上部的文字设计、封面中部的版次设计、封面下部的图形设计、字典书脊的颜色及文字设计方面构成近似。由此，华语出版社的被诉侵权产品的装潢与商务印书馆《新华字典》（第11版）的装潢在文字结构、图案设计、色彩搭配、排列位置等整体视觉效果上相近似，普通消费者施以一般注意力，容易对原、被告商品的来源发生混淆和误认。且根据在案证据，被诉侵权产品已经在市场上引起了相关消费者的混淆和误认。因此，华语出版社因擅自使用《新华字典》（第11版）知名商品的特有装潢而构成《中华人民共和国反不正当竞争法》第五条第（二）项规定的不正当竞争行为。

三、华语出版社应当如何承担法律责任？

法院判决华语出版社立即停止侵权并刊登声明、消除影响，对商务印书馆300万元赔偿数额的诉讼请求予以全额支持，另判决赔偿合理支出277,989.2元。

首先，鉴于华语出版社实施了上述被诉侵权行为，其应当立即停止使用商务印书馆的"新华字典"未注册驰名商标，并禁止在第16类辞书商品上使用与"新华字典"相同或近似的商标。同时，其还应当立即停止使用与商务印书馆《新华字典》（第11版）知名商品的特有装潢相同或近似的装潢的行为，并刊登声明，消除其侵权行为给商务印书馆带来的负面影响。

其次，本院参考北京市新闻出版广电局备案的部分被控侵权字典印刷委托书的信息统计数量、2014 年内地上市的出版企业年度平均净资产收益情况、华语出版社在全国的销售情况，综合考虑华语出版社被诉侵权行为的性质及主观故意，参照《中华人民共和国商标法》第六十三条第一款规定，按照上述方法确定数额的 1.5 倍确定本案的赔偿数额。具体计算如下：2012 年 9 月 30 日至 2016 年 9 月 30 日期间，华语出版社因出版印刷被控侵权字典而获利为 $20,310,160 \times 11.29\% = 2,293,017.64$ 元。该数额的 1.5 倍已经超出了商务印书馆 300 万元赔偿数额的诉讼请求，故，本院对商务印书馆 300 万元赔偿数额的诉讼请求予以全额支持。

最后，商务印书馆主张合理支出 40 万元，并提交了部分维权合理支出的证据。考虑到商务印书馆提交的合理支出凭证与本案的关联性、必要性，本院对于具有凭证的合理支出 277,989.2 元予以支持，超出部分不予支持。

【相关裁判文书】

扫描二维码，可见裁判文书

Judicial Protection Standard for Product Name Constitute of Unregistered Well-Known Trademark

——Commercial Press Co.,Ltd v. Sinolingua Co., Ltd.

[Syllabus]

In the network environment, if the alleged infringement act is not prohibited in time, it will cause the respondent to improperly use the rights of others to gain further market share ,which may cause economic losses to the petitioner, and such damage will be difficult to make up. Therefore, the respondent's alleged infringement act should be prohibited, and under such a circumstance,an pre-litigation injunction should be granted.

[Case No.] Beijing Intellectual Property Court (2016) J 73 MC No. 277
[Cause of Action] Disputes over infringement on trademarks and unfair competition
[Collegial Panel Members] Zhang Lingling　Feng Gang　Yang Jie
[Keywords] Trademark, unregistered well-known trademark, unfair competition, knowledge spreading
[Relevant Legal Provisions] Article 15 of the *Tort Law of the People's Republic of China*, Articles 13 and 14 of the *Trademark Law of the People's Republic of China*, Article 5 (2) and Article 20 (1) of the *Law of the People's Republic of China on Anti-Unfair Competition*

[Basic Facts]

Both the Plaintiff the Commercial Press Co., Ltd. (hereinafter referred to as Commercial Press) and the Defendant Sinolingua Co., Ltd. (hereinafter referred to as Sinolingua) are the publishing agency. The Plaintiff the Commercial Press has continuously published the popular version of Xinhua Dictionary to 11th edition since 1957, and in 2010-2015, the average market share of Xinhua Dictionary published by Commercial Press in the dictionary market exceeded 50%, and as of 2016, the global distribution volume for Xinhua Dictionary published by the Commercial Press exceeded 567 million, for which it has been listed in the Guinness World Records "the Most Popular Dictionary" and the Guinness World Records "the Bestselling Book (as revised on a regular basis)" and many other honors.

The Plaintiff the Commercial Press alleged that the acts of the Defendant Sinolingua, i.e. producing and selling the "Xinhua Dictionary", infringed the unregistered well-known trademark "Xinhua Dictionary" of the Plaintiff, and the Defendant Sinolingua applying the special package of the famous product *Xinhua Dictionary* (11th Edition) of Commercial Press constituted unfair competition. The Court is requested to render the following judgements: the Defendant should immediately stop the infringement of trademark rights and the acts of unfair competition; the Defendant should post statements in the relevant media including *China Press and Publication TV Broadcast Newspaper* to eliminate the effects arising from the infringement; the Defendant should pay the Plaintiff damages for economic losses in the amount of RMB 3 million and for reasonable costs and expenses in RMB 400,000.

The Defendant Sinolingua argued that "Xinhua Dictionary" was developed from the national project name to the common name of dictionary in the public domain and the Plaintiff had no right to assert the interests of trademark in relation to "Xinhua Dictionary" and to prohibit others from properly using it. The decoration of involved Xinhua Dictionary (11th Edition) did not belong to the "special package" as specified in Article 5 (2) of the Anti-unfair Competition Law of the People's Republic of China and would not cause confusion or misunderstanding of the buyers. The Plaintiff filing a lawsuit aimed to monopolize the common name of dictionary (i.e. "Xinhua Dictionary") by way of judicial judgment, which had the improper purpose of eliminating competition and achieving monopoly on the dictionary market.

Beijing Intellectual Property Court believes that "Xinhua Dictionary" has the distinctive features of a trademark and upon the use of the Plaintiff the Commercial Press, it has become a well-known trademark and constitutes an unregistered well-known trademark. The Defendant Sinolingua's replication and imitation of the Plaintiff's unregistered well-known trademark "Xinhua Dictionary" has infringed on the trademark. Xinhua Dictionary (11th Edition) published by the Plaintiff the Commercial Press falls into the special package and decoration of famous products, and the Defendant Sinolingua's use of the special decoration of famous product Xinhua Dictionary (11th Edition) without consent constitutes unfair competition. The Court of first instance ruled as follows: the Defendant Sinolingua should immediately cease the infringement of the trademark at issue and the unfair competition conduct; the Defendant should post statements in the relevant media including *China Press and Publication TV Broadcast Newspaper* to eliminate the effects arising from the infringement; it shall compensate the Plaintiff the Commercial Press for economic losses of RMB 3 million and for reasonable costs and expenses of more than RMB 270,000.

After the judgment of the trial court was rendered, the Parties involved reached a settlement on the execution of the judgement and the judgment in the first instance went into effect.

Holding

Beijing Intellectual Property Court made the following judgment ((2016) J73 MC No.277) on December 28, 2017: the Defendant Sinolingua was ordered to immediately cease to use the unregistered well-known trademark "Xinhua Dictionary" of the Plaintiff the Commercial Press and immediately cease the unfair competition of using the same or similar decoration as or to the special decoration of famous product Xinhua Dictionary (11th Edition) of the Plaintiff the Commercial Press; the Defendant shall post statements in the relevant media and assume the liability for compensating the economic loss of RMB 3 million (RMB THREE MILLION ONLY) and reasonable costs and expenses of RMB 277,989.2 (RMB TWO HUNDRED SEVENTY SEVEN THOUSAND NINE HUNDRED EIGHTY NINE POINT TWO ONLY).

[Reasoning]

The judgment of Beijing Intellectual Property Court believes that the issue of the Case focuses on the following two points: first, whether the involved "Xinhua Dictionary" constitutes an unregistered well-known trademark, and if so, whether the alleged conduct of Sinolingua constitutes an infringement; second, whether Xinhua Dictionary (11th Edition) published by the Commercial Press constitutes special package and decoration of a famous product, and if so, whether the alleged behavior of Sinolingua constitutes unfair competition; third, if the aforementioned infringements are confirmed, what legal liabilities should be borne by Sinolingua.

I. whether the involved "Xinhua Dictionary" constitutes the unregistered well-known trademark? If so, whether the alleged conduct of Sinolingua constitutes an infringement?

(I) The Court holds that the involved "Xinhua Dictionary" constitutes a registered well-known trademark.

Firstly, "Xinhua Dictionary" has the distinctive features of trademark. The distinctiveness is a basic feature of the trademark, and is a basic attribute that a mark can be considered as a trademark. The mark with distinctive features only can play a role that distinguishes the source of goods and then can be registered or protected as a trademark. In the Case, "Xinhua Dictionary" has formed stable cognitive connections in the relevant consumers, with specific historical origin, development process and long-term sole provider and objective market pattern, maintaining the mixed attributes of product and brand as the product name, and it has the meaning and role indicating the source of goods and the distinctive features of trademark. In this Case, pursuant to the trial standard as established in the prior cases ((2011) MTZ No.55 Civil Judgment and (2013) MSZ No.371 Civil Ruling), it is confirmed that "Xinhua Dictionary" has the distinctive features of trademark and can play a role in identifying the source of goods.

Secondly, "Xinhua Dictionary" constitutes the unregistered well-known trademark. Judging from the extent of knowledge the relevant public has on the "Xinhua Dictionary" at issue, "Xinhua Dictionary" has been widely known to the relevant public across the whole country. Based on the duration that the Commercial Press uses the name "Xinhua Dictionary" and the sales volume of the dictionary, hundreds of millions of "Xinhua Dictionary" copies have been sold across the whole country in the past 60 years, with very huge sales volume and extremely extensive sales range. Based on the duration, extent and geographical range that the Commercial Press publicizes "Xinhua Dictionary", it has obtained great influence and high popularity. Taking the above facts into consideration, "Xinhua Dictionary" can be confirmed as constituting an unregistered well-known trademark.

Lastly, the Commercial Press can assert the unregistered well-known trademark with respect to the name of "Xinhua Dictionary". As of the time when the alleged acts took place, the mark "Xinhua Dictionary" has not been granted for trademark registration, but "Xinhua Dictionary" has reached the extent of well-known trademark upon use of the Commercial Press, which should be protected by the *Trademark Law of the People's Republic of China*. The protection should be made to "Xinhua Dictionary" as the unregistered well-known trademark of the Commercial Press, which not only protects the role of identifying the source and the goodwill as a result of Commercial Press's operation of the "Xinhua Dictionary" but also makes it assume the legal obligation and social liability for product quality assurance by way of trademark protection. This will not jeopardize the spreading of knowledge. Instead, in order to maintain the good brand reputation of "Xinhua Dictionary", the Commercial Press will pay much more attention to promoting the quality for the dictionary published and issued by it with the mark of "Xinhua Dictionary" and facilitate the extensive spreading of correct knowledge.

(II) The Court holds that Sinolingua's to replication and imitatation of the unregistered well-known trademark "Xinhua Dictionary" of the Commercial Press are prone to cause confusion, which constitutes trademark infringement.

The products on which the Commercial Press and Sinolingua use the name "Xinhua Dictionary" are dictionaries under Category 16, which are identical products. Sinolingua uses completely identical trademark as the unregistered well-known trademark "Xinhua Dictionary" of the Commercial Press in its published dictionary, which constitutes using the unregistered well-known trademark of the Commercial Press by way of replication. According to documented evidence, Sinolingua used the mark "Xinhua Dictionary" in its published dictionary products under Class 16, which has caused the consumers to confuse its published *Xinhua Dictionary* as the one published by the Commercial Press when they buy and use the dictionary. The abovementioned behavior of Sinolingua has caused relevant public confusion and misunderstanding. Therefore, the conduct that Sinolingua uses the mark of "Xinhua Dictionary" in the dictionary for Class 16 has constituted replicating others' well-known trademark not registered in the same products in China, and would easily cause confusion. It is a breach ofs the provisions of Article 13 (2) of the *Trademark Law of the People's Republic of China*.

II. Whether Xinhua Dictionary (11th Edition) published by the Commercial Press constitutes the special package and decoration for famous product? If does so, whether the alleged behavior of Sinolingua constitutes the unfair competition?

(I) The Court holds that Xinhua Dictionary (11th Edition) published by the Commercial Press constitutes the special package and decoration for famous product.

Firstly, Xinhua Dictionary (11th Edition) published by the Commercial Press is a famous product. Xinhua Dictionary (11th Edition) has been largely published and issued across the whole country since it has been firstly published and issued in June 2011, up to the time that the alleged behaviors occur, which has obtained greater popularity Based on the situation that the Commercial Press promotes and operates Xinhua Dictionary across the whole country, and the a series of honors and important awards obtained by Xinhua Dictionary, the Xinhua Dictionary (11th

Edition) published by the Commercial Press can be confirmed to be a famous product.

Secondly, the decoration of Xinhua Dictionary (11th Edition) belongs to the special decoration. The decoration used in the Xinhua Dictionary (11th Edition) is a unique arrangement and combination made to the elements unrelated to its functionalities, forming the overall image that can distinguish from other operators' similar products. After long-term promotion and use by the Commercial Press, the abovementioned decoration can be associated with the source of goods of "Xinhua Dictionary" (11th Edition) by the relevant; the words, image, color and their arrangement and combination reflected in such decoration can play a role in identifying and distinguishing the source of goods, with the nature of specificity. Therefore, the decoration of "Xinhua Dictionary" (11th Edition) falls into the special decoration of famous products as protected in Article 5 (2) of the Anti-unfair Competition Law of the People's Republic of China.

(II) The Court believes the conduct that Sinolingua uses the special decoration of "Xinhua Dictionary" (11th Edition) without consent constitutes unfair competition.

The Commercial Press has provided the comparison pictures of the Plaintiff's and the Defendant's products as follows:

11th Edition Single Color 11th Edition Double Color 11th Edition Paperback 11th Edition Large-Character

(Published in June 2011) (Published in June 2011) (Published in June 2011)(Published in January 2012)

| Alleged Version 1 | Alleged Version2 | Alleged Version3 | Alleged Version4 | Alleged Version5 | Alleged Version8 | Alleged Version10 |

(------------------Firstly published in July 2012 up to now--------------------) (--Firstly published in February 2014 up to now--)

As shown in the comparison pictures above, the alleged infringing products are published upon the issuance of *Xinhua Dictionary* (11th Edition) and they are similar to *Xinhua Dictionary* (11th Edition) in the aspects of their overall design in the dictionary cover, word design in the top part of cover, edition design of the middle part of the cover, graphic design of the bottom part of the cover, color and word design of the dictionary's backbone. Thus, the decoration of the alleged infringing products of Sinolingua is similar to the one of *Xinhua Dictionary* (11th Edition) of the Commercial Press in the word structure, graphic design, color matching, arrangement position and other overall visual effects, and common consumers with general attention can easily be confused and mistaken about the source of the Plaintiff's and the Defendant's products. And according to documented evidence, the alleged infringing products have caused the relevant consumers to be confused and mistaken in the market. Therefore, Sinolingua violates the unfair competition as specified in Article 5 (2) of the Anti-unfair Competition Law of the People's Republic of China by using the special decoration of famous product *Xinhua Dictionary* (11th Edition) without consent.

III. what legal liabilities shall be borne by Sinolingua?

The Court renders the following ruling: Sinolingua should immediately cease infringement and post statements to eliminate the effects; full support should be given to the claims of the Commercial Press for damages of RMB 3 million and it shall also be ordered to compensate RMB 277,989.2 for reasonable costs and expenses.

Firstly, in consideration of the above alleged infringements implemented by Sinolingua, it should immediately cease to use the unregistered well-known trademark "Xinhua Dictionary" of the Commercial Press, and it should be prohibited from using the same or similar trademark as or to "Xinhua Dictionary" in the dictionary products for Class 16. Meanwhile, it should also immediately cease to use the same or similar decoration as or to the special decoration of famous product *Xinhua Dictionary* (11th Edition) of the Commercial Press, and post statements to eliminate the negative effects of its infringement on the Commercial Press.

Secondly, by reference to the information statistical quantity of the dictionary printing power of attorney for partly alleged infringement as recorded by Beijing Municipal Bureau of Press, Publication, Radio, Film and Television, annual average return on net assets for publishing enterprises listed in the mainland in 2014, the sales status of Sinolingua across the whole country, taking the nature of alleged infringements of Sinolingua and subjective intention into the overall consideration, the Court determines the amount of damages of the Case as 1.5 times the amount that is determined according to the aforesaid methods, subject to Article 63 (1) of the *Trademark Law of the People's Republic of China*. The specific calculation is as follows: during the period from September 30, 2012 to September 30, 2016, Sinolingua made a profit by publishing the alleged infringing dictionary, i.e.: 20 ,310,160* 11.29% = RMB 2,293,017.064. That amount by multiplying 1.5 times has exceeded the claims of the Commercial Press for compensation of RMB 3 million; thus, the Court makes fully support to the claims of the Commercial Press for compensation of RMB 3 million.

Lastly, the Commercial Press asserts the compensation of RMB

400,000 for reasonable costs and expenses, and provides the evidence proving the reasonable expenses for the purpose of partly protecting legal rights. Taking into consideration the relevance and necessity between the evidences of reasonable expense provided by the Commercial Press and the Case, the Court affirms the reasonable expenses of RMB 277,989.2 with evidences and the exceeded part is not be affirmed.

[Opinion of the Case (Chinese Version)]

Scan the QR code to see the Chinese version of the opinion

第二章　专利案件

Chapter 2 Patent Cases

药品制备方法专利侵权纠纷中
被诉侵权药品制备工艺的查明

——礼来公司与常州华生制药有限公司侵害发明专利权纠纷案

【裁判要旨】

药品制备方法专利侵权纠纷中，在无其他相反证据的情形下，应当推定被诉侵权药品在药监部门的备案工艺为其实际的制备工艺；有证据证明被诉侵权药品备案工艺不真实的，应当充分审查被诉侵权药品的技术来源、生产规程、批生产记录、备案文件等证据，依法确定被诉侵权药品的实际制备工艺。

对于被诉侵权药品制备工艺等复杂的技术事实，可以综合运用技术调查官、专家辅助人、司法鉴定以及科技专家咨询等多种途径进行查明。

【案　　　号】最高人民法院（2015）民三终字第 1 号

【案　　　由】侵害发明专利权纠纷

【合议庭成员】周　翔　吴　蓉　宋淑华

【关　键　词】侵害发明专利权　药品制备方法发明专利　保护范围
　　　　　　　技术调查官　被诉侵权药品制备工艺查明

【相关法条】《中华人民共和国专利法》（2000 年修正）第五十六条
　　　　　　第一款、第五十七条第二款、第六十二条第一款，《中

华人民共和国民事诉讼法》第七十八条、第七十九条

【基本案情】

2013 年 7 月 25 日，礼来公司（又称伊莱利利公司）向江苏省高级人民法院（以下简称江苏高院）诉称，礼来公司拥有涉案 91103346.7 号方法发明专利权，涉案专利方法制备的药物奥氮平为新产品。常州华生制药有限公司（以下简称华生公司）使用落入涉案专利权保护范围的制备方法生产药物奥氮平并面向市场销售，侵害了礼来公司的涉案方法发明专利权。为此，礼来公司提起本案诉讼，请求法院判令：1. 华生公司赔偿礼来公司经济损失人民币 151,060,000 元、礼来公司为制止侵权所支付的调查取证费和其他合理开支人民币 28,800 元；2. 华生公司在其网站及《医药经济报》刊登声明，消除因其侵权行为给礼来公司造成的不良影响；3. 华生公司承担礼来公司因本案发生的律师费人民币 1,500,000 元；4. 华生公司承担本案的全部诉讼费用。

江苏高院一审查明：涉案专利为英国利利工业公司 1991 年 4 月 24 日申请的名称为"制备一种噻吩并苯二氮杂䓬化合物的方法"的第 91103346.7 号中国发明专利申请，授权公告日为 1995 年 2 月 19 日。2011 年 4 月 24 日涉案专利权期满终止。1998 年 3 月 17 日，涉案专利的专利权人变更为英国伊莱利利有限公司；2002 年 2 月 28 日专利权人变更为礼来公司。

涉案专利授权公告的权利要求为：1. 一种制备 2- 甲基 -10-（4- 甲基 -1- 哌嗪基 ）-4H- 噻吩并［2,3,-b］［1,5］苯并二氮杂䓬，或其酸加成盐的方法。

所述方法包括：

（a）使 N- 甲基哌嗪与下式化合物反应，

式中 Q 是一个可以脱落的基团，或

（b）使下式的化合物进行闭环反应

2001 年 7 月，中国医学科学院药物研究所（简称医科院药物所）和华生公司向国家药品监督管理局（简称国家药监局）申请奥氮平及其片剂的新药证书。2003 年 5 月 9 日，医科院药物所和华生公司获得国家药监局颁发的奥氮平原料药和奥氮平片《新药证书》，华生公司获得奥氮平和奥氮平片《药品注册批件》。新药申请资料中《原料药生产工艺的研究资料及文献资料》记载了制备工艺，即加入 4- 氨基 -2- 甲基 -10- 苄基 - 噻吩并苯并二氮杂䓬，盐酸盐，甲基哌嗪及二甲基甲酰胺搅拌，得粗品，收率94.5%；加入 2- 甲基 -10- 苄基 -（4- 甲基 -1- 哌嗪基）-4H-噻吩并苯并二氮杂䓬、冰醋酸、盐酸搅拌，然后用氢氧化钠中和后得粗品，收率 73.2%；再经过两次精制，总收率为 39.1%。从反应式分析，该过程就是以式四化合物与甲基哌嗪反应生成式五化合物，再对式五化合物脱苄基，得式一化合物。2003 年 8 月，华生公司向青岛市第七人民医院推销其生产的"华生－奥氮平"5mg-新型抗精神病药，其产品宣传资料记载，奥氮平片主要成份为奥氮平，其化学名称为 2- 甲基 -10-（4- 甲基 -1- 哌嗪）-4H-噻吩并苯并二氮杂䓬。

在另案审理中，根据江苏高院的委托，2011 年 8 月 25 日，上海市科技咨询服务中心出具（2010）鉴字第 19 号《技术鉴定报告书》。该鉴定报告称，按华生公司备案的"原料药生产工艺的研究资料及文献资料"中记载的工艺进行实验操作，不能获得原料药奥氮平。鉴定结论为：华生公司备案资料中记载的生产原料药奥氮平的关键反应步骤缺乏真实性，该备案的生产工艺不可行。

经质证，礼来公司认可该鉴定报告，华生公司对该鉴定报告亦不持异议，但是其坚持认为采取两步法是可以生产出奥氮平的，只是因为有些内容涉及商业秘密没有写入备案资料中，故专家依据备案资料生产不出来。

华生公司认为其未侵害涉案专利权，理由是：2003 年至今，华生公司一直使用 2008 年补充报批的奥氮平备案生产工艺，该备案文件已于 2010 年 9 月 8 日获国家药监局批准，具备可行性。在礼来公司未提供任何证据证明华生公司生产工艺的情况下，应以华生公司 2008 年奥氮平备案工艺作为认定侵权与否的比对工艺。

华生公司提交的 2010 年 9 月 8 日国家药监局《药品补充申请批件》中"申请内容"栏为："（1）改变影响药品质量的生产工艺;（2）修改药品注册标准。""审批结论"栏为："经审查，同意本品变更生产工艺并修订质量标准。变更后的生产工艺在不改变原合成路线的基础上，仅对其制备工艺中所用溶剂和试剂进行调整。质量标准所附执行，有效期 24 个月。"

上述 2010 年《药品补充申请批件》所附《奥氮平药品补充申请注册资料》中 5.1 原料药生产工艺的研究资料及文献资料章节中 5.1.1 说明内容为："根据我公司奥氮平原料药的实际生产情况，在不改变原来申报生产工艺路线的基础上，对奥氮平的制备工艺过程做了部分调整变更，对工艺进行优化，使奥氮平各中间体的质量得到进一步的提高和保证，其制备过程中的相关杂质得到有效控制……由于工艺路线没有变更，并且最后一步的结晶溶剂亦没有变更，故化合物的结构及晶型不会改变。"

最高人民法院二审审理过程中，为准确查明本案所涉技术事实，根据《中华人民共和国民事诉讼法》第七十九条、《最高人民法院关于适用〈中华人民共和国民事诉讼法〉的解释》（以下简称《民事诉讼法解释》）第一百二十二条之规定，对礼来公司的专家辅助人出庭申请予以准许；根据《民事诉讼法解释》第一百一十七条之规定，对华生公司的证人出庭申请予以准许；根据《中华人民共和国民事诉讼法》第七十八条、《民事诉讼法解释》第二百二十七条之规定，通知出具（2014）司鉴定第 02 号《技术鉴定报告》的江苏省科技咨询中心工作人员出庭；根据《最高人民法院关于知识产权法院技术调查官参与诉讼活动若干问题的暂行规定》第二条、第十条之规定，首次指派技术调查官出庭，就相关技术问题与各方当事人分别询问了专家辅助人、证人及鉴定人。

最高人民法院二审另查明：1999 年 10 月 28 日，华生公司与医科院药物所签订《技术合同书》，约定医科院药物所将其研制开发的抗精神分裂药奥氮平及其制剂转让给华生公司，医科院药物所负责完成临床前报批资料并在北京申报临床；验收标准和方法按照新药审批标准，采用领取临床批件和新药证书方式验收；在其他条款中双方对新药证书和生产的报批作出了约定。

医科院药物所 1999 年 10 月填报的（京 99）药申临字第 82 号《新药临床研究申请表》中，"制备工艺"栏绘制的反应路线如下：

1999 年 11 月 9 日，北京市卫生局针对医科院药物所的新药临床研究申请作出《新药研制现场考核报告表》，"现场考核结论"栏记载："该所具备研制此原料的条件，原始记录、实验资料基本完整，内容真实。"

2001 年 6 月，医科院药物所和华生公司共同向国家药监局提交《新药证书、生产申请表》[（2001）京申产字第 019 号]。针对该申请，江苏省药监局 2001 年 10 月 22 日作出《新药研制现场考核报告表》，"现场考核结论"栏记载："经现场考核，样品制备及检验原始记录基本完整，检验仪器条件基本具备，研制单位暂无原料药生产车间，现申请本品的新药证书。"

根据华生公司申请，江苏药监局 2009 年 5 月 21 日发函委托江苏省常州市食品药品监督管理局药品安全监管处对华生公司奥氮平生产现场进行检查和产品抽样，江苏药监局针对该检查和抽样出具了《药品注册生产现场检查报告》（受理号 CXHB0800159），其中"检查结果"栏记载："按照药品注册现场检查的有关要求，2009 年 7 月 7 日对该品种的生产现场进行了第一次检查，该公司的机构和人员、生产和检验设施能满足该品种的生产要求，原辅材料等可溯源，主要原料均按规定量投料，生产过程按申报的工艺进行。2009 年 8 月 25 日，按药品注册现场核查的有关要求，检查了 70309001、70309002、70309003 三批产品的批生产记录、检验记录、原料领用使用、库存情况记录等，已按抽样要求进行了抽样。""综合评定结论"栏记载："根据综合评定，现场检查结论为：通过"。

国家药监局 2010 年 9 月 8 日颁发给华生公司的《药品补充申请批件》所附《奥氮平药品补充申请注册资料》中，5.1 "原料药生产工艺的研究资料及文献资料"之 5.1.2 "工艺路线"中绘制的反应路线如下：

5.1.2 工艺路线

2015 年 3 月 5 日，江苏省科技咨询中心受上海市方达（北京）律师事务所委托出具（2014）司鉴字第 02 号《技术鉴定报告》，其"鉴定结论"部分记载："1. 华生公司 2008 年向国家药监局备案的奥氮平制备工艺是可行的。2. 对比华生公司 2008 年向国家药监局备案的奥氮平制备工艺与礼来公司第 91103346.7 号方法专利，两者起始原料均为仲胺化物，但制备工艺路径不同，具体表现在：（1）反应中产生的关键中间体不同；（2）反应步骤不同：华生公司的是四步法，礼来公司是二步法；（3）反应条件不同：取代反应中，华生公司采用二甲基甲酰胺为溶媒，礼来公司采用二甲基亚砜和甲苯的混合溶剂为溶媒。"

二审庭审中，礼来公司明确其在本案中要求保护涉案专利权利要求 1 中的方法（a）。

 裁判结果

江苏省高级人民法院于 2014 年 10 月 14 日作出（2013）苏民初字第 0002 号民事判决：1. 常州华生制药有限公司赔偿礼来公司经济损失及为制止侵权支出的合理费用人民币计 350 万元；2. 驳回礼来公司的其他诉讼请求。案件受理费人民币 809,744 元，由礼来公司负担 161,950 元，常州华生制药有限公司负担 647,794 元。礼来公司、常州华生制药有限公司均不服，提起上诉。最高人民法院 2016 年 5 月 31 日作出（2015）民三终字第 1 号民事判决：1. 撤销江苏省高级人民法院（2013）苏民初字第 0002 号民事判决；2. 驳回礼来公司的诉讼请求。一、二审案件受理费各人民币 809,744 元，由礼来公司负担 323,897 元，常州华生制药有限公司负担 1,295,591 元。

【裁判理由】

最高人民法院二审认为：《最高人民法院关于审理侵犯专利权纠纷案件应用法律若干问题的解释》第七条规定："人民法院判定

被诉侵权技术方案是否落入专利权的保护范围，应当审查权利人主张的权利要求所记载的全部技术特征。被诉侵权技术方案包含与权利要求记载的全部技术特征相同或者等同的技术特征的，人民法院应当认定其落入专利权的保护范围；被诉侵权技术方案的技术特征与权利要求记载的全部技术特征相比，缺少权利要求记载的一个以上的技术特征，或者有一个以上技术特征不相同也不等同的，人民法院应当认定其没有落入专利权的保护范围。"本案中，华生公司被诉生产销售的药品与涉案专利方法制备的产品相同，均为奥氮平，判定华生公司奥氮平制备工艺是否落入涉案专利权保护范围，涉及以下三个问题：

一、关于涉案专利权的保护范围

《中华人民共和国专利法》第五十六条第一款规定："发明或者实用新型专利权的保护范围以其权利要求的内容为准，说明书及附图可以用于解释权利要求。"本案中，礼来公司要求保护涉案专利权利要求1中的方法(a)，该权利要求采取开放式的撰写方式，其中仅限定了参加取代反应的三环还原物及N-甲基哌嗪以及发生取代的基团，其保护范围涵盖了所有采用所述三环还原物与N-甲基哌嗪在Q基团处发生取代反应而生成奥氮平的制备方法，无论采用何种反应起始物、溶剂、反应条件，均在其保护范围之内。基于此，判定华生公司奥氮平制备工艺是否落入涉案专利权保护范围，关键在于两个技术方案反应路线的比对，而具体的反应起始物、溶剂、反应条件等均不纳入侵权比对范围，否则会不当限缩涉案专利权的保护范围，损害礼来公司的合法权益。

二、关于华生公司实际使用的奥氮平制备工艺

《中华人民共和国专利法》第五十七条第二款规定："专利侵权纠纷涉及新产品制造方法的发明专利的，制造同样产品的单位

或者个人应当提供其产品制造方法不同于专利方法的证明。"本案中，双方当事人对奥氮平为专利法中所称的新产品不持异议，华生公司应就其奥氮平制备工艺不同于涉案专利方法承担举证责任。具体而言，华生公司应当提供证据证明其实际使用的奥氮平制备工艺反应路线未落入涉案专利权保护范围，否则，将因其举证不能而承担推定礼来公司侵权指控成立的法律后果。

本案中，华生公司主张其自 2003 年至今一直使用 2008 年向国家药监局补充备案工艺生产奥氮平，并提交了其 2003 年和 2008 年奥氮平批生产记录（一审补充证据 6）、2003 年、2007 年和 2013 年生产规程（一审补充证据 7）、《药品补充申请批件》（一审补充证据 12）等证据证明其实际使用的奥氮平制备工艺。如前所述，本案的侵权判定关键在于两个技术方案反应路线的比对，华生公司 2008 年补充备案工艺的反应路线可见于其向国家药监局提交的《奥氮平药品补充申请注册资料》，其中 5.1 "原料药生产工艺的研究资料及文献资料"之 5.1.2 "工艺路线"图显示该反应路线为：先将"仲胺化物"中的仲氨基用苄基保护起来，制得"苄基化物"（苄基化），再进行闭环反应，生成"苄基取代的噻吩并苯并二氮杂䓬"三环化合物（还原化物）。"还原化物"中的氨基被 N- 甲基哌嗪取代，生成"缩合物"，然后脱去苄基，制得奥氮平。本院认为，现有在案证据能够形成完整证据链，证明华生公司 2003 年至涉案专利权到期日期间一直使用其 2008 年补充备案工艺的反应路线生产奥氮平，主要理由如下：

首先，华生公司 2008 年向国家药监局提出奥氮平药品补充申请注册，在其提交的《奥氮平药品补充申请注册资料》中，明确记载了其奥氮平制备工艺的反应路线。针对该补充申请，江苏省药监部门于 2009 年 7 月 7 日和 8 月 25 日对华生公司进行了生产现场检查和产品抽样，并出具了《药品注册生产现场检查报告》（受理号 CXHB0800159），该报告显示华生公司的"生产过程按申报的工艺进行"，三批样品"已按抽样要求进行了抽样"，现场检查结论为"通过"。也就是说，华生公司 2008 年补充备案工艺经过药监部门的现场检查，具备可行性。基于此，2010 年 9 月 8 日，国家药监局向华生公司颁发了《药品补充申请批件》，同意华生公司奥氮平"变更生产工艺并修订质量标准"。对于华生公司 2008 年补充备案工艺的可行性，礼来公司专家辅助人在二审庭审中予以认可，江苏省科技咨询中心出具的（2014）司鉴字第 02 号《技术鉴定报告》在其鉴定结论部分也认为"华生公司 2008 年向国家药监局备案的奥氮平制备工艺是可行的"。因此，在无其他相反证据的情形下，应当推定华生公司 2008 年补充备案工艺即为其取得《药品补充申请批件》后实际使用的奥氮平制备工艺。

其次，一般而言，适用于大规模工业化生产的药品制备工艺步骤繁琐，操作复杂，其形成不可能是一蹴而就的。从研发阶段到实际生产阶段，其长期的技术积累过程通常是在保持基本反应路线稳定的情况下，针对实际生产中发现的缺陷不断优化调整反应条件和操作细节。华生公司的奥氮平制备工艺受让于医科院药物所，双方于 1999 年 10 月 28 日签订了《技术转让合同》。按照合同约定，医科院药物所负责完成临床前报批资料并在北京申报临床。在医科院药物所 1999 年 10 月填报的（京 99）药申临字第 82 号《新药临床研究申请表》中，"制备工艺"栏绘制的反应路线显示，其采用了与华生公司 2008 年补充备案工艺相同的反应路线。针对该新药临床研究申请，北京市卫生局 1999 年 11 月 9 日作出《新药研制现场考核报告表》，确认"原始记录、实验资料基本完整，内容真实。"在此基础上，医科院药物所和华生公司按照《技术转让合同》的约定，共同向国家药监局提交新药证书、生产申请表〔（2001）京申产字第019号〕。针对该申请，江苏省药监局2001年10月22日作出《新药研制现场考核报告表》，确认"样品制备及检验原始记录基本完整"。通过包括前述考核在内的一系列审查后，2003年5月9日，医科院药物所和华生公司获得国家药监局颁发的奥氮平原料药和奥氮平片《新药证书》。由此可见，华生公司自1999年即拥有了与其2008年补充备案工艺反应路线相同的奥氮平制备工艺，并以此申报新药注册，取得新药证书。因此，华生公司在2008补充备案工艺之前使用反应路线完全不同的其他制备工艺生产奥氮平的可能性不大。

最后，国家药监局2010年9月8日向华生公司颁发的《药品补充申请批件》"审批结论"栏记载："变更后的生产工艺在不改变原合成路线的基础上，仅对其制备工艺中所用溶剂和试剂进行调整"，即国家药监局确认华生公司2008年补充备案工艺与其之前的制备工艺反应路线相同。华生公司在一审中提交了其2003年、2007年和2013年的生产规程，2003年、2008年的奥氮平批生产记录，华生公司主张上述证据涉及其商业秘密，一审法院组织双方当事人进行了不公开质证，确认其真实性和关联性。本院经审查，华生公司2003年、2008年的奥氮平批生产记录是分别依据2003年、2007年的生产规程进行实际生产所做的记录，上述生产规程和批生产记录均表明华生公司奥氮平制备工艺的基本反应路线与其2008年补充备案工艺的反应路线相同，只是在保持该基本反应路线不变的基础上对反应条件、溶剂等生产细节进行调整，不断优化，这样的技术积累过程是符合实际生产规律的。

综上，本院认为，华生公司2008年补充备案工艺真实可行，2003年至涉案专利权到期日期间华生公司一直使用2008年补充备案工艺的反应路线生产奥氮平。

三、关于礼来公司的侵权指控是否成立

对比华生公司奥氮平制备工艺的反应路线和涉案方法专利，二者的区别在于反应步骤不同，关键中间体不同。具体而言，华生公司奥氮平制备工艺使用的三环还原物的胺基是被苄基保护的，由此在取代反应之前必然存在苄基化反应步骤以生成苄基化的三环还原物，相应的在取代反应后也必然存在脱苄基反应步骤以获得奥氮平。而涉案专利的反应路线中并未对三环还原物中的胺基进行苄基保护，从而不存在相应的苄基化反应步骤和脱除苄基的反应步骤。

《最高人民法院关于审理专利纠纷案件适用法律问题的若干规定》第十七条第二款规定："等同特征，是指与所记载的技术特征以基本相同的手段，实现基本相同的功能，达到基本相同的效果，并且本领域普通技术人员在被诉侵权行为发生时无需经过创造性劳动就能够联想到的特征。"本案中，就华生公司奥氮平制备工艺的反应路线和涉案方法专利的区别而言，首先，苄基保护的三环还原物中间体与未加苄基保护的三环还原物中间体为不同的化合物，两者在化学反应特性上存在差异，即在未加苄基保护的三环还原物中间体上，可脱落的 Q 基团和胺基均可与 N- 甲基哌嗪发生反应，而苄基保护的三环还原物中间体由于其中的胺基被苄基保护，无法与 N- 甲基哌嗪发生不期望的取代反应，取代反应只能发生在 Q 基团处；相应地，涉案专利的方法中不存在取代反应前后的加苄基和脱苄基反应步骤。因此，两个技术方案在反应中间物和反应步骤上的差异较大。其次，由于增加了加苄基和脱苄基步骤，华生公司的奥氮平制备工艺在终产物收率方面会有所减损，而涉案专利由于不存在加苄基保护步骤和脱苄基步骤，收率不会因此而下降。故两个技术方案的技术效果如收率高低等方面存在较大差异。最后，尽管对所述三环还原物中的胺基进行苄基保护以减少副反应是化学合成领域的公知常识，但是这种改变是实质性的，加苄基保护的三环还原物中间体的反应特性发生了改变，增加反应步骤也使收率下降。而且加苄基保护为公知常识仅说明华生公司的奥氮平制备工艺相对于涉案专利方法改进有限，但并不意味着两者所采用的技术手段是基本相同的。

综上，华生公司的奥氮平制备工艺在三环还原物中间体是否为苄基化中间体以及由此增加的苄基化反应步骤和脱苄基步骤方面，与涉案专利方法是不同的，相应的技术特征也不属于基本相同的技术手段，达到的技术效果存在较大差异，未构成等同特征。因此，华生公司奥氮平制备工艺未落入涉案专利权保护范围。

综上所述，华生公司奥氮平制备工艺未落入礼来公司所有的涉案专利权的保护范围，一审判决认定事实和适用法律存在错误，依法予以纠正。

【本案裁判文书】

扫描二维码，可见裁判文书

Identification of the Preparation Nethod of the Alleged Infringing Drug in Patent Infringement Dispute

——Eli Lilly & Co. v. Watson Pharmaceuticals (Changzhou) Co., Ltd.

[Syllabus]

In the patent infringement dispute over drug preparation method, in the absence of other evidence to the contrary, the preparatory method of the alleged infringing drug filed with the pharmaceutical supervisory department should be presumed as its actual preparation method. In case there is evidence proving that the preparatory method of the alleged infringing drug that has been filed is not true, then evidence including the technical sources, production procedures, batch manufacturing records and filing documents of the alleged infringing drug should be fully reviewed in order to determine the actual preparation method of the alleged infringing drug in accordance with the law.

With respect to complicated technical facts such as the preparation method of the alleged infringing drugs, they can be verified by comprehensive application of various approaches, such as the use of technical investigators, expert advisors, judicial appraisal and technology expert consultation.

[Case No.] Supreme People's Court (2015) MSZZ No.1

[Cause of Action] Dispute over invention patent right infringement

[Collegial Panel Members] Zhou Xiang　Wu Rong　Song Shuhua

[Keywords] Invention patent right infringement, invention patent of drug preparation method, scope of protection, technical investigator, ascertainment of preparation methodology of alleged infringing drug

[Relevant Legal Provisions] Paragraph 1, Article 56, Paragraph 2, Article 57 and Paragraph 1, Article 62 of *Patent Law of the People's Republic of China* (2000 amendment), Articles 78 and 79 of *Civil Procedure Law of the People's Republic of China*

[Basic Facts]

On July 25th, 2013, Lilly (also known as Eli Lilly and Company) filed a lawsuit to the Jiangsu High People's Court (hereinafter referred to as Jiangsu High Court), claiming that Lilly has the invention patent right No. 91103346.7 for the preparation method of the case involved, and that the drug olanzapine prepared with the patent method involved, is a new product. Watson Pharmaceuticals (Changzhou) Co., Ltd (hereinafter referred to as Watson) produced olanzapine using the preparation method within the scope of patent right protection and sold it in the market, which has infringed upon the invention patent right for the involved method of Lilly. To this end, Lilly filed this lawsuit and requested the court order that: 1. Watson shall compensate Lilly for its economic losses of RMB151,060,000 and pay another RMB28,800 for the investigation fee and other reasonable expenses incurred by Lilly to deter the infringement. 2. Watson shall post a statement on its website and *Medical Economics* to eliminate the adverse effects of its infringement on Lilly. 3. Watson shall bear the attorney fee of RMB1,500,000 incurred by Lilly in this case. 4. Watson shall bear for all litigation costs incurred in this case.

The Jiangsu High Court, the court of first instance found that: the patent involved is the Chinese invention patent application No. 91103346.7, titled "Method to prepare a thieno- benzodiazepines compound", which was applied by Lilly Industrial Company of the UK on April 24th, 1991. The patent right involved was authorized and proclaimed on February 19th, 1995 and expired on April 24th, 2011. The patentee of the patent involved was changed to Eli Lilly Ltd of the UK on March 17th, 1998 and then changed to Eli Lilly and Company on February 28th, 2002.

The claim of the authorized patent involved is: 1. A method to prepare 2-methyl-10-(4-methyl-1- piperazine)-4H-thieno-[2,3,-b][1,5] benzodiazepine, or add its acid into salt.

The described method includes:

(a) having N-methyl piperazine react with following compound,

In the equation, Q is a group that may exfoliate, or

(b) having following compound set off a ring-closure reaction

In July 2001, The Institute of Materia Medica (IMM) of the Chinese Academy of Medical Sciences (CAMS) (hereinafter referred to as Institute of Medicine), along with Watson, applied for a new drug certificate for olanzapine and its tablets, to the State Food and Drug Administration (Hereinafter referred to as SFDA). On May 9th, 2003, the Institute of Medicine and Watson obtained the New Drug Certificate for olanzapine and its tablets issued by SFDA, and Watson obtained the *Drug Registration Approval* for olanzapine and olanzapine tablets. The preparation method was recorded in the new drug application document "*Research Materials and Literature on the Producing Methodology of API*", that is: "add 4-amino -2-methyl -10-benzyl-thieno-benzodiazepines, hydrochloride, methyl piperazine and dimethyl formamide, stir to get the crude product, with a yield coefficient of 94.5%; then add 2-methyl -10-benzyl-(4- methyl -1- piperazine)-4H- thieno- benzodiazepines, glacial acetic acid and hydrochloric acid, stir to get the crude product, with a yield coefficient of 73.2%; then with two more refinements, the total yield coefficient becomes 39.1%". Based on the analysis of the equation, the process is to have compound in Equation 4 react with methyl piperazine to create the compound in Equation 5, and then debenzylate the compound in Equation 5 to create the compound in Equation 1. In August 2003, Watson marketed its self-produced novel antipsychotic drug "Watson-Olanzapine" to Qingdao Seventh People's Hospital. As recorded in the product publicity materials, the main component of olanzapine tablet is olanzapine whose chemical name is 2-methyl-10-(4-methyl-1-piperazine)-4H-thieno-benzodiazepines.

In another trial, Shanghai Science and Technology Consulting Service Center issued (2010) JZ No.19 *Technical Expert Report* on August 25th, 2011 upon the entrustment of Jiangsu High Court. According to the said report, the active pharmaceutical ingredient (API) olanzapine could not be obtained according to the process described in the *Research Materials and Literature on the Producing Methodology of API* filed by Watson. The expert conclusion is that the key reaction step as recorded in the document filed by Watson to produce the API olanzapine lacks authenticity, and the filed production methodology is not feasible.

After cross-examination, Lilly accepted the expert report and Watson did not raise any objection, either. However, Watson insisted that the Two-Step Method could produce olanzapine. The failure of the experts to replicate the production method based on the filing documents is only because some contents that involved trade secrets were not included in the filing document.

Watson did not think that it had infringed upon the patent right involved for the following reasons: Watson had been using the filed olanzapine producing technology since 2003 after it submitted the supplementary application, which was approved in 2008. The filing document had been approved by SFDA on September 8th, 2010 after its feasibility was evaluated. In the absence of any evidence provided by Lilly proving Watson's production methodology, the production methodology for olanzapine filed by Watson in 2008 should be the methodology used to ascertain infringement.

It is stated in the Application Content column of the *Approval Letter on Supplementary Application for Drugs* submitted to SFDA by Watson on September 8th, 2010 that: "1. change the production methodology that may affect the quality of drug; 2. revise the drug registration standard"; the Approval Conclusion column states: "After review, agree to change the production methodology and revise the quality standard. There is no other change in the production methodology other than with respect to the solvents and reagents used in the preparation method on the basis of without changing the original route of synthesis. The quality standard is attached and is valid for 24 months."

It is stated in the Descriptions of Subsection 5.1.1 "Technology Route" of Section 5.1 "Research Materials and Literature on the Production Methodology of API" in the *Supplementary and Registration Information for Olanzapine attached in the Approval Letter on Supplementary Application for Drugs* (2010) that: "Based on the actual production condition of the API olanzapine, we have made partial adjustment and optimization of the olanzapine preparation methodology on the basis of without changing the original reported producing route, to further guarantee and improve the quality of olanzapine intermediates and to effectively control relevant impurities during preparation process ....As neither the technology route nor the crystal-solvent used in the last step has been changed, the structure and morphology of the compound will not change."

At the Supreme People's Court, the court of second instance, to ascertain the technical facts involved in this case, the expert advisor of Lilly was allowed to appear in the court in accordance with the provisions of Article 79 of *Civil Procedure Law of the People's Republic of China and Article 122 of Interpretation of the Supreme People's Court Concerning the Application of Civil Procedure Law of the People's Republic of China* (hereinafter referred to as *Interpretation of Civil Procedure Law*). The witness of Watson was allowed to appear in the court in accordance with the provision of Article 117 of *Interpretation of Civil Procedure Law*. The staff from Jiangsu Science and Technology Consulting Service Center which has issued the (2014) SJD No. 02 of *Technical Expert Report* were notified to appear in the court in accordance with the provisions of Article 78 of *Civil Procedure Law of the People's Republic of China* and Article 227 of *Interpretation of Civil Procedure Law*. Technical investigators were appointed to appear in court for the first time in accordance with the provisions of Article 2 and Article 10 of *Temporary Provisions of the Supreme People's Court on Several Issues Concerning the Litigation Participation by Technical Investigator of Intellectual Property Court*. The Supreme People's Court asked the relevant expert advisor, witnesses and appraiser to communicate with all parties on relevant technical issues.

The Supreme People's Court, the court of second instance, found that: Watson had signed the *Technology Transfer Contract* with Institute of Medicine on October 28th, 1999, pursuant to which, Institute of Medicine transfers its independently-developed anti-schizophrenia drug olanzapine and its formulation to Watson. The Institute of Medicine was responsible for completing the pre-clinical application for approval and the clinical approval in Beijing. The acceptance criteria and methods were subject to the approval standards for new drug and the acceptance was conducted by obtaining clinical approval documents and new drug certificates. In other words, both parties agreed on the new drug certificate and approval for production.

In the (J99) YSLZ No. 82 *Application Form for Clinical Research of New Drugs* filled and submitted by the Institute of Medicine in October 1999, the reaction route in the "Preparation Methodology" column is described as below:

On November 9th, 1999, Beijing Municipal Health Bureau issued the *New Drug Development Site Assessment Report* after receiving the clinical research application for new drugs from the Institute of Medicine and recorded in the "Site Assessment Conclusion" column that: "The Institute has the conditions for development of this raw material. The original records and experimental data are basically complete, and the contents are true."

In June 2001, the Institute of Medicine and Watson jointly submitted the *Application Form for New Drug Certificate and Production* [(2001) JSCZ No. 019]. After receiving the application, Jiangsu SFDA issued the *New Drug Development Site Assessment Report* on October 22nd, 2001 and recorded in the "Site Assessment Conclusion" conclusion that: "After site assessment, the original records of sample preparation and inspection are basically complete, the inspection equipment conditions are basically in place, the research and development unit has no API production workshop at the moment, and is now applying for the new drug certificate for this product."

According to Watson's application, Jiangsu Food and Drug Administration issued a letter to entrust the Pharmaceutical Safety Supervision Department of Changzhou Food and Drug Administration of Jiangsu Province to conduct an inspection and sample the products at Watson's olanzapine production site. After inspection and sampling, Jiangsu Pharmaceutical Safety Supervision Department issued the *Inspection Report on Drug Registration and Production Site* (reference no. CXHB0800159) and recorded in the "Inspection Result" column that: "In accordance with the requirements of the drug registration site inspection, we have inspected the production site for the first time on July 7, 2009, and found that: The company's facilities and personnel, production and inspection facilities meet the production requirements for this variety, its raw and auxiliary materials can be traced back to the source, main raw materials are supplied according to the specified quantity, and the production process is carried out according to the reported process. On August 25th, 2009, we inspected the batch manufacturing records, inspection records, raw materials requisition and use, and inventory records for the products of batch Nos. 70309001, 70309002 and 70309003, and took samples in accordance with the sampling requirement." It is recorded in the "Comprehensive

Evaluation Conclusion" column that: "According to the comprehensive evaluation, the site inspection conclusion is: Passed".

In Subsection 5.1.2 "Technology Route" of Section 5.1 "Research Materials and Literature Materials on the Production Technology of API" in *Supplementary and Registration Information for Olanzapine* attached in *Approval Letter on Supplementary Application for Drugs* issued to Watson by the Institute of Medicine, the reaction route is described as below:

5.1.2 工艺路线

On March 5th, 2015, Jiangsu Science and Technology Consulting Center upon entrustment by Shanghai Fangda Law Firm (Beijing), issued the (2014) SJZ No. 02 *Technical Expert Report*, and recorded in the "Expert Conclusion" column that: "1. The olanzapine preparation methodology filed by Watson with the SFDA is feasible. 2. By comparing the olanzapine preparation methodology filed by Watson in 2008 with the SFDA, with Lilly's methodology patent no. 91103346.7, it is found that the initial materials of both are secondary amine compounds, however, their preparation methodology differs in: 1) the key intermediates produced in the reaction are different; 2) the reaction steps are different: it is a Four-Step Method for Watson and Two-Step Method for Lilly, respectively; 3) the reaction conditions are different: the solvent used by Watson in the substitution reaction is dimethylformamide and that used by Lilly is a mixed solvent composed of dimethyl sulfoxide and methylbenzene."

In the Court of Second Instance, Lilly clarified that it requested to protect the method (a) in Claim 1 of the patent involved in the case.

 Holding

Jiangsu High People's Court made a civil ruling (2013) SMCZ No.0002 on October 14th, 2014 requesting: 1. Watson Pharmaceuticals (Changzhou) Co., Ltd. compensate Lilly RMB3,500,000 for its economic loss and other reasonable fees involved to deter the infringement; 2. to dismiss other claims of Lilly. With respect to the court fee of RMB809,744, Lilly should pay RMB161,950 and Watson should pay RMB647,794. Both Lilly and Watson refused to accept the ruling and appealed. The Supreme People's Court made a civil ruling (2015) MSZZ No.1: 1. to reverse the Civil Ruling (2013) SMCZ No.0002 of Jiangsu High People's Court; 2. to dismiss the claim of Lilly. The court fees in the First and Second Instances are RMB809,744 respectively, of which Lilly should pay RMB323,897 and Watson should pay RMB1,295,591.

[Reasoning]

In the Second Instance, the Supreme People's Court held that: it is stipulated in Article 7 of the *Interpretation of the Supreme People's Court on Several Issues Concerning the Application of Law in the Trial of Cases of Infringement upon Intellectual Property Rights* that: "When the People's Court determines whether the alleged infringing technical solution falls within the scope of patent right protection, all technical features recorded in the claim by the patentee should be reviewed. In case the alleged infringing technical solution contains the same or equivalent technical features as those of the claim, the People's Court shall determine that it falls within the scope of patent right protection; in case the alleged infringing technical solution lacks one or more technical features compared to all of those recorded by the claim, or contains one or more technical features that is (are) not the same or not equivalent with those of the claim, the People's Court shall determine that it doesn't fall within the scope of patent right protection." In this case, the alleged drug produced and sold by Watson is the same as the product prepared by using the patent method involved in this case, both are olanzapine; therefore, the following three questions would be involved in order to determine whether the olanzapine preparation methodology falls within the scope of protection for the patent right involved in this case:

I. Scope of protection for patent right involved

It is stipulated in Paragraph 1, Article 56 of the *Patent Law of People's Republic of China* that: "The scope of protection for the patent right to invention or utility model shall be subject to the content of its claim, both instructions and drawings can be used to interpret the claim." In this case, Lilly required protection of the method (a) of Claim 1 of the patent right involved. The claim adopts an open composition method, in which only the tricyclic reduction, N-methyl piperazine and group participating in the substitution reaction are defined. The scope of protection covers all preparation methods to produce olanzapine by using the aforesaid tricyclic reduction and N-methyl piperazine having substitution reaction with Q group, regardless of the reaction starting materials, solvent and reaction conditions used. Otherwise, the scope of protection for the patent right involved will be reduced improperly, and the legitimate rights and interests of Lilly will be damaged.

II. Olanzapine preparation methodology actually used by Watson

It is stipulated in Paragraph 2, Article 57 of the *Patent Law of People's Republic of China* that: "In case the invention patent of a new product's manufacturing method is involved in the patent infringement dispute, the unit or individual who manufactures the same product shall provide evidence proving their manufacturing methods differ from the patented method." In this case, neither party has any objection to the fact that the new product claimed in the patent method is olanzapine; Watson should bear the burden of proof evidencing its olanzapine preparation methodology is different from the patent method involved. Specifically, Watson should provide evidence to prove the reaction route of the olanzapine preparation methodology actually used by it does not fall within the scope of protection of the patent right involved, or else it will be liable for the legal consequences of the establishment of Lilly's allegation for its infringement due to its inability to provide evidence.

In this case, Watson claimed that it has been using a methodology that it had placed in a supplementary filing with the FSDA in 2008 since 2003, and submitted the olanzapine batch manufacturing records of 2003 and 2008 (supplementary evidence 6 in the First Instance), the production regulations of 2003, 2007 and 2013 (supplementary evidence 7 in the First Instance) and *Approval Letter on Supplementary Application for Drugs* (supplementary evidence 12 in the First Instance) to prove the olanzapine preparation methodology actually used by it. As mentioned above, the key to the infringement judgement of this case lies in the comparison of the reaction routes of the two technical solutions. The reaction route of the process in Watson's 2008 supplementary filed technology can be seen in the *Registration Information on the Supplementary Application for Olanzapine* submitted to the SFDA, wherein Subsection 5.1.2 "Technology Route" of Section 5.1 *"Research Materials and Literature Materials on the Manufacturing Technique of API"* shows the reaction route as follows: First, to protect the secondary amino group of "secondary amine compound" with benzyl to produce a "benzyl compound" (benzylation) and then to have ring-closure reaction to produce "benzyl substituted thienobenzodiazepines" tricyclic compound (reduction compound). The amine group of the "reduction compound" is substituted by N-methyl piperazine to produce "condensation compound", and lastly, the olanzapine is produced through a debenzylation reaction. The court held that there is documented evidence which can form a complete chain of evidence, proving that Watson has been using the reaction route described in 2008 supplementary filed technology since 2003 till the expiry date of the patent right involved, to produce olanzapine. The main reasons are as follows:

First, Watson submitted the supplementary application for registration of olanzapine to SFDA in the *Registration Information on Supplementary Application for Olanzapine*, which clearly records the reaction route of the olanzapine preparation methodology. After receiving the supplementary application, the Pharmaceutical Administration of Jiangsu Province conducted onsite inspection on the production site of Watson and made product sampling on July 7th and August 25th, 2009, respectively, and issued the *Report on Production Site Inspection for Drug Registration* (reference No. CXHB0800159), which shows that Watson's "production process is conducted in accordance with the declared methodology", three batches of products "were sampled in accordance with the sampling requirements", and the onsite inspection conclusion is "Passed". That means that Watson's 2008 supplementary filed methodology is feasible, based on the onsite inspection by the Pharmaceutical Administration. Based on this, SFDA issued the *Approval Letter on Supplementary Application for Drugs* dated

September 8, 2010 to Watson, agreeing that Watson may "change the production process and revise the quality standard" of olanzapine. The expert advisor from Lilly recognized the feasibility of Watson's 2008 supplementary filed methodology in the Court of Second Instance. The (2014) SJZ No.02 *Technical Expert Report* issued by Jiangsu Science and Technology Consulting Service Center also held in the conclusion that "Watson's 2008 supplementary filed methodology for olanzapine is feasible". In conclusion, in absence of other evidence to the contrary, it should be presumed that Watson's 2008 supplementary filed methodology is the olanzapine preparation methodology actually used by it after the *Approval Letter on Supplementary Application for Drugs* was obtained.

Secondly, Drug preparation methodology applied in large-scale industrial production is often cumbersome and complicated, due to which, its formation cannot be achieved overnight. The long-term technology accumulation process from research & development to actual production would usually involve optimization of reaction conditions and operation details based on the defects found during actual production, under the condition of maintaining basic reaction route stability. Watson's olanzapine preparation methodology was transferred by the Institute of Medicine according to the *Technology Transfer Contract* dated October 28th, 1999 between the Parties, pursuant to which, the Institute of Medicine was responsible for completing the pre-clinical application for approval and the clinical approval in Beijing. In the (J99) YSLZ No.82 *Application Form for Clinical Research of New Drugs* filed and submitted by the Institute of Medicine in October 1999, the reaction route described in the "Preparation Methodology" column shows that the same reaction route has been used with that of Watson's 2008 supplementary filed technology. On November 9th, 1999, the Beijing Municipal Health Bureau issued the *New Drug Development Site Assessment*

Report based on the said clinical research application for new drug, confirming that: "The original records and experimental data are basically complete and the contents thereof are true." Based on this, the Institute of Medicine and Watson jointly submitted the *Application Form for New Drug Certificate and Production* [(2001) JSCZ No.019] pursuant to the Technology Transfer Contract. After the application, Jiangsu Food and Drug Administration issued the *New Drug Development Site Assessment Report* on October 22nd, 2001, confirming that: "The original records of sample preparation and inspection are basically complete". After passing all reviews including the above said assessment, the Institute of Medicine and Watson obtained the *New Drug Certificate* for olanzapine and olanzapine tablets, issued by the SFDA. Thus, it can be seen that Watson has used the same olanzapine preparation methodology with the reaction route stipulated in the 2008 supplementary filed methodology and had already obtained the *New Drug Certificate* by registering for new drug application. Therefore, it is unlikely for Watson to produce olanzapine with a very different preparation methodology before the 2008 supplementary filed technology.

Finally, it is recorded in the "Approval Conclusion" column of *Approval Letter on Supplementary Application for Drugs* that: "The revised production methodology has no other adjustment except with respect to the solvents and reagents used in the preparation methodology on the basis of not changing the original synthetic route". That is to say, SFDA confirmed that the reaction route of Watson's 2008 supplementary filed methodology is the same as that of former preparation methodology. Watson submitted the production regulations of year 2003, 2007 and 2013 as well as the olanzapine batch manufacturing records of year 2003 and 2008 in the First Instance. Since Watson claimed that the above evidence involved its trade secrets, the Court of First Instance organized both parties to make closed cross-examination in order to determine the authenticity and relevance. After the review, the court found that the olanzapine batch manufacturing records of year 2003 and 2008 are the records of actual production conducted according to the production regulations of year 2003 and 2007. Both the above production regulation and batch manufacturing records show that the basic reaction route of Watson's olanzapine preparation methodology is the same as that it had filed in its 2008 supplementary filing. There are just some adjustments and optimization with respect to details such as reaction conditions and solvents on the basis without changing the basic reaction route. Such technology accumulation process is in line with the actual production approach.

To sum up, the court held that, Watson's 2008 supplementary filed methodology is true and feasible, and it has been using the reaction route of supplementary methodology filed by the Institute of Medicine in 2008, since 2003 to the expiry date of the patent right involved to produce olanzapine.

III. Whether the alleged infringement claim by Lilly could be established

By comparing the reaction route of Watson's olanzapine preparation methodology with the patent method involved, the differences between them were with respect to the reaction steps and key intermediates. To be more specific, the amine group of the tricyclic reduction used by Watson's olanzapine preparation methodology is protected by benzyl, thereby the benzylation reaction certainly existed before the substitution reaction in order to produce the benzylated tricyclic reduction, and the debenzylation reaction step also certainly existed after the substitution reaction in order to produce olanzapine. On the other hand, there is no benzyl protection for the amine group of tricyclic reduction used by the patent involved, and there are no corresponding steps for benzylation and debenzylation.

It is stipulated in Paragraph 2, Article 17 of *Several Provisions of the Supreme People's Court Concerning the Application of Law in the Trial of Cases Involving Patent Disputes* that: "The equivalent feature means to basically realize the same function and achieve the same effect by using the same means as the recorded technical features, and the features that can be associated by a person having ordinary skill in this field without creative labor, upon the occurrence of alleged infringing acts." In this case, the differences in reaction routes between Watson's olanzapine preparation methodology and the patent method involved lie on: firstly, the intermediate of tricyclic reduction protected by benzyl differs from that of tricyclic reduction without benzyl protection. There are differences in chemical reaction characteristics between them, namely, both the Q group and amine group on the tricyclic reduction intermediate without benzyl protection can react with N-methyl piperazine, while that on the tricyclic reduction intermediate protected by benzyl does not have undesired substitution reactions with N-methyl piperazine. The substitution reaction happens only at Q group. Correspondingly, there are no steps of benzylation and debenzylation. Therefore, there is a big difference between the two technical solutions in reaction intermediates and reaction steps. Secondly, the final product yield coefficient of Watson's olanzapine preparation methodology is reduced due to the steps of benzylation and debenzylation compared to that of the patent method involved. Therefore, there is a big difference between the two technical solutions in technical effects such as yield coefficient. Lastly, although it is a common knowledge in the field of chemical synthesis to impose benzyl protection for the amine group of tricyclic reduction in order to reduce adverse reaction, such change is substantial. It will change the reaction characteristics of tricyclic reduction intermediate, and the added reaction step will reduce the yield coefficient. Moreover, the common knowledge of imposing benzyl protection only indicates that Watson's olanzapine preparation methodology is relatively limited compared with the patent method involved and doesn't mean that the technical means used by the two are basically the same.

In summary, Watson's olanzapine preparation methodology differs with the patent method involved in whether the intermediates of tricyclic reduction are benzylated intermediates and with respect to the added steps of benzylation and debenzylation. The corresponding technical features do not belong to the same technical means. There is a big difference in the technical effects achieved and no equivalent feature has been constituted. For this reason, Watson's olanzapine preparation methodology does not fall within the scope of protection of the patent method involved.

In conclusion, Watson's olanzapine preparation methodology does not fall within the scope of protection of the patent method involved. The Court of First Instance erred in its ascertainment of facts and application of law in its judgment, which should be corrected in accordance with the law.

[Opinion of the Case (Chinese Version)]

Scan the QR code to see the Chinese version of the opinion

设计特征的认定
及对外观设计近似性判断的影响

——浙江健龙卫浴有限公司与高仪股份公司
侵害外观设计专利权纠纷案

【裁判要旨】

设计特征体现了授权外观设计不同于现有设计的创新内容，也体现了设计人对现有设计的创造性贡献。如果被诉侵权产品未包含授权外观设计区别于现有设计的全部设计特征，一般可以推定二者不构成近似外观设计。设计特征的存在应由专利权人进行举证，允许第三人提供反证予以推翻，并由人民法院依法予以确定。

【案　　　　号】最高人民法院（2015）民提字第 23 号
【案　　　　由】侵害外观设计专利权纠纷
【合议庭成员】周　翔　吴　蓉　宋淑华
【关　键　词】外观设计专利　近似判断　设计特征
【相关法条】《中华人民共和国专利法》第五十九条第二款

【基本案情】

高仪股份公司（以下简称高仪公司）为"手持淋浴喷头（No. A4284410X2）"外观设计专利的权利人，该外观设计专利现合法有效。2012 年 11 月，高仪公司以浙江健龙卫浴有限公司（以下简称健龙公司）生产、销售和许诺销售的丽雅系列等卫浴产品侵害其"手持淋浴喷头"外观设计专利权为由提起诉讼，请求法院判令健龙公司立即停止被诉侵权行为，销毁库存的侵权产品及专用于生产侵权产品的模具，并赔偿高仪公司经济损失 20 万元。经一审庭审比对，健龙公司被诉侵权产品与高仪公司涉案外观设计专利的相同之处为：二者属于同类产品，从整体上看，二者均是由喷头头部和手柄两个部分组成，被诉侵权产品头部出水面的形状与涉案专利相同，均表现为出水孔呈放射状分布在两端圆、中间长方形的区域内，边缘呈圆弧状。两者的不同之处为：1. 被诉侵权产品的喷头头部四周为斜面，从背面向出水口倾斜，而涉案专利主视图及左视图中显示其喷头头部四周为圆弧面；2. 被诉侵权产品头部的出水面与面板间仅由一根线条分隔，涉案专利头部的出水面与面板间由两条线条构成的带状分隔；3. 被诉侵权产品头部出水面的出水孔分布方式与涉案专利略有不同；4. 涉案专利的手柄上有长椭圆形的开关设计，被诉侵权产品没有；5. 涉案专利中头部与手柄的连接虽然有一定的斜角，但角度很小，几乎为直线形连接，被诉侵权产品头部与手柄的连接产生的斜角角度较大；6. 从涉案专利的仰视图看，手柄底部为圆形，被诉侵权产品仰视的底部为曲面扇形，涉案专利手柄下端为圆柱体，向与头部连接处方向逐步收缩压扁呈扁椭圆体，被诉侵权产品的手柄下端为扇面柱体，且向与喷头连接处过渡均为扇面柱体，过渡中的手柄中段有弧度的突起；7. 被诉侵权产品的手柄底端有一条弧形的装饰线，将手柄底端与产品的背面连成一体，涉案专利的手柄底端没有这样的设计；8. 涉案专利头部和手柄的长度比例与被诉侵权产品有所差别，两者的头部与手柄的连接处弧面亦有差别。

> ### 裁判结果
>
> 　　浙江省台州市中级人民法院于 2013 年 3 月 5 日作出（2012）
> 浙台知民初字第 573 号民事判决，驳回高仪公司诉讼请求。高仪公
> 司不服，提起上诉。浙江省高级人民法院于 2013 年 9 月 27 日作出
> （2013）浙知终字第 255 号民事判决：1. 撤销浙江省台州市中级人
> 民法院（2012）浙台知民初字第 573 号民事判决；2. 浙江健龙公司
> 立即停止制造、许诺销售、销售侵害高仪公司"手持淋浴喷头"外观
> 设计专利权的产品的行为，销毁库存的侵权产品；3. 浙江健龙公司赔
> 偿高仪股份公司经济损失（含高仪公司为制止侵权行为所支出的合理
> 费用）人民币 10 万元；4. 驳回高仪公司的其他诉讼请求。浙江健龙
> 公司不服，提起再审申请。最高人民法院于 2015 年 8 月 11 日作出
> （2015）民提字第 23 号民事判决：1. 撤销二审判决；2. 维持一审判决。

【裁判理由】

　　最高人民法院提审认为：外观设计专利制度的立法目的在于
保护具有美感的创新性工业设计方案，一项外观设计应当具有区
别于现有设计的可识别性创新设计才能获得专利授权，该创新设
计即是授权外观设计的设计特征。由于设计特征的存在，一般消
费者容易将授权外观设计区别于现有设计，因此，其对外观设计
产品的整体视觉效果具有显著影响，如果被诉侵权产品未包含授
权外观设计区别于现有设计的全部设计特征，一般可以推定被诉
侵权产品与授权外观设计不近似。专利权人可能将设计特征记载
在简要说明中，也可能会在专利授权确权或者侵权程序中对设计
特征作出相应陈述。无论是专利权人举证证明的设计特征，还是
通过授权确权有关审查文档记载确定的设计特征，如果第三人提

出异议，都应当允许其提供反证予以推翻。人民法院在听取各方当事人质证意见的基础上，对证据进行充分审查，依法确定授权外观设计的设计特征。本案专利的设计特征有三点：一是喷头及其各面过渡的形状，二是喷头出水面形状，三是喷头宽度与手柄直径的比例。虽然被诉侵权产品采用了与本案专利高度近似的跑道状出水面，但在喷头及其各面过渡的形状这一设计特征上，二者在设计风格上呈现明显差异。二审判决仅重点考虑了本案专利跑道状出水面的设计特征，而对于其他设计特征，以及产品正常使用时容易被直接观察到的其他区别设计特征未予考虑，从而认定二者构成近似外观设计的结论是错误的。

【本案裁判文书】

扫描二维码，可见裁判文书

Judgment on Determination
of Design Features and Their Influence
on Design Similarity

—— Jianlong v. Grohe

[Syllabus]

Design features comprise innovative content that distinguishes an authorized design from a prior design and the designer's creative contribution to the prior design. If a product allegedly infringes but does not contain all design features that differentiate the authorized design from the prior design, it is generally presumed that they are not similar designs. Existence of design features shall be proved by the patentee who shall bear the burden of proof, a third party shall be allowed to rebut the same, and it shall be determined by a People's court according to law.

151

[Case No.] The Supreme People's Court (2015) Min-Ti-Zi No.23
[Cause of Action] Dispute over design patent infringement
[Collegial Panel Members] Zhou Xiang   Wu Rong   Song Shuhua
[Keywords] Design Patent Infringement, Similarity Judgment, Design Features
[Relevant Legal Provisions] Paragraph 2, Article 59, *Patent Law of the People's Republic of China*

[Basic Facts]

Grohe Ag ("Grohe") is the patentee of the design patent "handheld shower head No.A4284410X2", and this patent is now legal and valid. In November 2012, Grohe brought an action against Zhejiang Jianlong Sanitary Ware Co., Ltd. ("Jianlong") which produces, sells and offers to sell sanitary products on the ground that it infringes its "handheld shower head" design patent, and requested the court to rule that Jianlong immediately stop the infringement, destroy infringing products in stock and the molds that are specially used for producing infringing products, and compensate Grohe RMB200,000 for its economic loss. Based on the comparison conducted in the court of first instance, similarities between Jianlong's allegedly infringing product and Grohe's design patent are that they are both the same product type. Both designs have a shower head and a handle. Spray from the shower head of the allegedly infringing product is the same as that of the involved patent, that is, holes are distributed in a radial pattern in a region that is round on both ends and rectangular in the middle with arc-shaped edges. The differences are: 1. Peripheries of the shower head of the allegedly infringing product are inclined planes, while the front and left view of the patent involved shows that the peripheries of the shower head have arc-shaped surfaces.2. Spray from the shower head of the allegedly infringing product is separated from the panel only by a single line, while spray from the shower head of the patent involved is separated from the panel by a band made up of two lines.3. Distribution of holes on the shower head of the allegedly infringing product is slightly different from the patented product.4. There is an oblong switch on the handle of the patent involved, while there is no such switch on the allegedly infringing product. 5. There is an oblique angle where the head of the patented product and the handle connect, but the angle is so small that it almost appears as a straight line, while the connecting angle between the head and the handle of the allegedly infringing product is wide.6. The bottom view of the patent involved shows the handle has a round bottom, while the bottom of the allegedly infringing product's handle is a fan-shaped curved surface. The lower end of the handle of the patent involved is a cylinder, which gradually turns into an ellipsoid at the point of its connection with the head, while the lower end of the handle of the allegedly infringing product is a fan-shaped cylinder, and also presents a fan-shaped cylinder at the point of its connection with the shower head, and there is an arc-like protuberance in the middle of the handle. 7. There is a decorative arc on the bottom of the allegedly infringing product's handle that integrates the bottom of the handle and the back of the product into a whole, while there is no such design on the bottom of the handle of the patent involved.8. The proportion of the length between the head and handle of the patent involved differs from the allegedly infringing product, and the arc-shaped surface at the connection between the head and handle of the two is also different.

 Holding

On March 5th, 2013, Zhejiang Taizhou Intermediate People's Court rendered the civil judgment (2012) Zhe-Tai-Zhi-Min-Chu-Zi No.573 and dismissed Grohe's claims. Not accepting the result, Grohe appealed to the higher court. On September 27th, 2013, Zhejiang High People's Court passed the civil judgment (2013) Zhe-Zhi-Min-Zhong-Zi No. 255: (1) It reversed the civil judgment (2012) Zhe-Tai-Zhi-Min-Chu-Zi No.573 made by Zhejiang Taizhou Intermediate People's Court; (2) It asked Jianlong to immediately stop producing, offering for sale and selling products that infringe Grohe's "handheld shower head" design patent and to destroy the infringing products in stock; (3) It asked Jianlong to compensate Grohe RMB100,000 for its economic loss (including reasonable expenses of Grohe for stopping the infringement); (4) It rejected Grohe's other claims. Jianlong was unsatisfied with the decision, and appealed the case in the higher court. On August 11th, 2015, the Supreme People's

Court made the civil judgment (2015) Min-Ti-Zi No.23: (1) It reversed the second-instance judgment; (2) It maintained the first-instance judgement.

[Reasoning]

The Supreme People's Court's opinions: Laws for design patent system are formulated to protect aesthetic and innovative industrial designs; a patented design should feature identifiable innovative characteristics distinctive from prior designs, and such innovative characteristics should represent the design features of authorized designs. Due to existence of these features, ordinary consumers should find it easier to differentiate authorized designs from prior designs. Therefore, they have significant impact on the product's overall visual effect from the perspective of the design. If an allegedly infringing product does not contain all the design features that differentiate the authorized design from the prior design, it is generally presumed that the allegedly infringing product does not resemble the authorized design. The patentee may specify design features in a brief description or state the design features in the patent authorization or infringement procedures in a pertinent manner. Whether proved by the patentee bearing the burden of proof or recorded in relevant review documents of the authorization, these specific design features can be overturned by counter-evidence if any third party raises an objection. Based on cross-examination of the parties, the People's court shall fully examine the evidence and determine design features of the authorized design according to law. The patent in this case has three design features: first, shape of the shower head and plane transitions; second, shape of the shower head spray; third, proportion between the width of the shower head and the handle diameter. Though the allegedly infringing product adopts a similar spray as the patent involved in this case, the two have large differences in design style in terms of design feature – the shape of shower head and plane transition. The second-instance judgment only considered design features of the runway-shaped spray while neglecting other design features as well as other distinctive design features that are easily noticeable in normal use of the product. Therefore, reaching a conclusion that the two are similar designs based on this is wrong.

[Opinion of the Case (Chinese Version)]

Scan the QR code to see the Chinese version of the opinion

马库什权利要求的性质、在无效程序中的修改方式和创造性判断方法

——专利复审委员会与北京万生药业有限责任公司、第一三共株式会社发明专利权无效行政纠纷案

【裁判要旨】

以马库什方式撰写的化合物权利要求应当被理解为一种概括性的技术方案，而不是众多化合物的集合。

允许对马库什权利要求进行修改的原则，应当是不能因为修改而产生具有新性能和作用的一类或单个化合物，但是同时也要充分考量个案因素。

对于以马库什方式撰写的化合物权利要求的创造性的判断，应当遵循创造性判断的基本方法，即专利审查指南所规定的"三步法"。意料不到的技术效果是创造性判断的辅助因素，通常不宜跨过"三步法"，直接适用具有意料不到的技术效果来判断专利申请是否具有创造性。

【案　　　号】最高人民法院（2016）最高法行再 41 号

【案　　　由】发明专利权无效行政纠纷

【合议庭成员】秦元明　李　嵘　马秀荣

【关　键　词】无效程序　马库什权利要求　修改方式　创造性

【相关法条】《中华人民共和国专利法》第三十一条第一款,《中华人民共和国专利法实施细则》第三十四条

【基本案情】

在再审申请人国家知识产权局专利复审委员会(以下简称专利复审委员会)与被申请人北京万生药业有限责任公司(以下简称万生公司)、一审第三人第一三共株式会社发明专利权无效行政纠纷案(简称"马库什权利要求"专利无效行政纠纷案)中,第一三共株式会社系名称为"用于治疗或预防高血压症的药物组合物的制备方法"、专利号为97126347.7的发明专利(即涉案专利)的权利人。涉案专利权利要求以马库什方式撰写。万生公司以涉案专利不具备创造性等为由向专利复审委员会提出无效宣告请求。2010年8月30日,第一三共株式会社对权利要求进行了修改,其中包括:删除了权利要求1中"或其可作药用的盐或酯"中的"或酯"两字;删除权利要求1中R4定义下的"具有1至6个碳原子的烷基";删除了权利要求1中R5定义下除羧基和式COOR5a外的其他技术方案。专利复审委员会在口头审理过程中告知第一三共株式会社,对于删除权利要求1中"或酯"的修改予以认可,但其余修改不符合《中华人民共和国专利法实施细则》第六十八条的相关规定,该修改文本不予接受。第一三共株式会社和万生公司对此无异议。2011年1月14日,第一三共株式会社提交了修改后的权利要求书替换页,其中删除权利要求1中的"或酯"。专利复审委员会作出第16266号无效宣告请求审查决定(简称第16266号决定),认为涉案专利权利要求1相比于证据1是非显而易见的,具有创造性,符合《中华人民共和国专利法》第二十二条第三款的规定。遂在第一三共株式会社于2011年1月14日提交的修改文本的基础上,维持涉案专利权有效。万生公

司不服，提起行政诉讼。北京市第一中级人民法院认为，专利复审委员会以不符合《中华人民共和国专利法实施细则》第六十八条的规定对第一三共株式会社于 2010 年 8 月 30 日提交的修改文本不予接受，不存在法律适用错误。涉案专利权利要求 1 相对于证据 1 是非显而易见的，具备创造性。遂判决维持第 16266 号决定。万生公司不服，提起上诉。北京市高级人民法院二审认为，马库什权利要求属于并列技术方案的特殊类型，第一三共株式会社于 2010 年 8 月 30 日提交的修改文本缩小了涉案专利权的保护范围，符合《中华人民共和国专利法实施细则》第六十八条第一款规定。涉案专利权利要求所涵盖的一个具体实施例的效果与现有技术的证据 1 中实施例 329 的技术效果相当，因此，涉案专利权利要求 1 未取得预料不到的技术效果，不具备创造性。

 裁判结果

专利复审委员会于 2011 年 4 月 1 日作出第 16266 号无效宣告请求审查决定，维持本专利权全部有效。万生公司不服第 16266 号决定，向北京市第一中级人民法院提起行政诉讼。北京市第一中级人民法院于 2011 年 12 月 20 日一审判决维持专利复审委员会作出的第 16266 号决定。万生公司不服一审判决，向北京市高级人民法院提起上诉，请求撤销一审判决及第 16266 号决定，责令专利复审委员会重新作出审查决定。北京市高级人民法院于 2013 年 9 月 24 日二审判决撤销一审判决、撤销专利复审委员会第 16266 号决定、专利复审委员会重新作出无效宣告请求审查决定。专利复审委员会不服，向最高人民法院申请再审。最高人民法院裁定提审本案，并于 2017 年 12 月 20 日判决撤销二审判决，维持一审判决。

【裁判理由】

最高人民法院提审认为：

一、关于马库什权利要求的性质

马库什权利要求是化学发明专利申请中一种特殊的权利要求撰写方式，即一项申请在一个权利要求中限定多个并列的可选要素概括的权利要求。马库什权利要求撰写方式的产生是为了解决化学领域中多个取代基基团没有共同上位概念可概括的问题，其本身一直被视为结构式的表达方式，而非功能性的表达方式。马库什权利要求限定的是并列的可选要素而非权利要求，其所有可选择化合物具有共同性能和作用，并且具有共同的结构或者所有可选择要素属于该发明所属领域公认的同一化合物。虽然马库什权利要求的撰写方式特殊，但是也应当符合专利法和专利法实施细则关于单一性的规定。马库什权利要求具有极强的概括能力，一旦获得授权，专利权保护范围将涵盖所有具有相同结构、性能或作用的化合物，专利权人权益将得到最大化实现。而从本质而言，专利权是对某项权利的垄断，专利权人所享有的权利范围越大，社会公众所受的限制也就越多，因此，从公平角度出发，对马库什权利要求的解释应当从严。马库什权利要求不管包含多少变量和组合，都应该视为一种概括性的组合方案。选择一个变量应该生成一种具有相同效果药物，即选择不同的分子式生成不同的药物，但是这些药物的药效不应该有太大差异，相互应当可以替代，而且可以预期所要达到的效果是相同的，这才符合当初创设马库什权利要求的目的。因此，马库什权利要求应当被视为马库什要素的集合，而不是众多化合物的集合，马库什要素只有在特定情况下才会表现为单个化合物，但通常而言，马库什要素应当理解为具有共同性能和作用的一类化合物。如果认定马库什权利要求所表述的化合物是众多化合物的集合，就明显与单一性要求不符，因此二审判决认为马库什权利要求属于并列技术方案不妥，应当予以纠正。

二、关于马库什权利要求在无效程序中的修改方式

2010 年《专利审查指南》规定无效宣告请求审查阶段，发明和实用新型专利文件的修改应仅限于权利要求书，其遵循的基本原则是：1. 不得改变原权利要求的主题名称；2. 与授权的权利要求相比，不得扩大原专利的保护范围；3. 不得超出原说明书和权利要求书中技术特征；4. 一般不得增加未包含在授权权利要求书中的技术特征。但是，目前修改方式已经改为在满足上述修改原则的前提下，修改权利要求书的具体方式一般限于权利要求的删除、技术方案的删除、权利要求的进一步限定、明显错误的修正。权利要求进一步限定是指在权利要求中补入其他权利要求中记载的一个或者多个技术特征，以缩小保护范围。可见，在无效程序中，专利文件修改方式更加多样化。但是，化学领域发明专利申请审查存在诸多特殊问题，如化学发明是否能够实施需要借助于实验结果才能确认，有的化学产品需要借助于参数或者制备方法定义，已知化学产品新的性能和用途并不意味着结构或者组分的改变等。鉴于化学发明创造的特殊性，同时考虑到在马库什权利要求撰写之初，专利申请人为了获得最大的权利保护范围就有机会将所有结构方式尽可能写入一项权利要求，因此在无效阶段对马库什权利要求进行修改必须给予严格限制，允许对马库什权利要求进行修改的原则应当是不能因为修改而产生新性能和作用的一类或单个化合物，但是同时也要充分考量个案因素。如果允许专利申请人或专利权人删除任一变量的任一选项，即使该删除使得权利要求保护范围缩小，不会损伤社会公众的权益，但是由于是否因此会产生新的权利保护范围存在不确定性，不但无法给予社会公众稳定的预期，也不利于维护专利确权制度稳定，因此二

审法院相关认定明显不妥，应当予以纠正。

三、关于马库什权利要求的创造性判断方法

马库什权利要求创造性判断应当遵循创造性判断的基本方法，即专利审查指南所规定的"三步法"。意料不到的技术效果是创造性判断的辅助因素，而且作为一种倒推的判断方法，具有特殊性，不具有普遍适用性。因此，只有在经过"三步法"审查和判断得不出是否是非显而易见时，才能根据具有意料不到的技术效果认定专利申请是否具有创造性，通常不宜跨过"三步法"直接适用具有意料不到的技术效果来判断专利申请是否具有创造性。关于技术效果比对结果的问题，本案中，专利复审委员会在无效程序中并未将比文件1实施例10、17、50和69和涉案专利的实施例进行比对且就此作出认定，而二审直接进行比对并作出认定，明显超出了无效审查决定的审查范围，不符合行政诉讼法和相关司法解释的规定，应当予以纠正。无效宣告请求人万生公司认为涉案专利权利要求1不具备创造性，并将证据1作为最接近的对比文件。专利复审委员会和一审法院在对涉案专利权利要求1的创造性进行判断时，严格遵循了"三步法"，认定权利要求1的式I化合物和证据1的式I化合物相比较具有两项区别技术特征，然后对两项区别技术特征的非显而易见性进行了分析，从而认定涉案专利权利要求1具有创造性并无不当。

【本案裁判文书】

扫描二维码，可见裁判文书

The Nature of the Markush Claim, the Amendment to It in the Invalidation Proceeding and the Method for the Inventive Step Judgment

——Patent Reexamination Board v. Beijing Winsunny Harmony Science & Technology Co., Ltd., Daiichi Sankyo Co.,Ltd.

[Syllabus]

The compound claim written as a Markush Claim should be understood as a general technical solution rather than a collection of many compounds.

Amendment to the Markush Claim shall be allowed when a class of compounds or a single compound with new properties and effects is not produced due to the modification, however, individual cases that are an exception should also be considered.

*The inventive step judgment of the compound claim written as a Markush Claim should follow the basic method for the inventive step judgment, that is, the "three-step method" stipulated in the **Guidelines for Patent Examination**. The unexpected technical effect is a contributing factor in the inventive step judgment. Normally it will be inappropriate to skip the "three-step method" and directly apply the unexpected technical effect to determine whether a patent application involves an inventive step or not.*

[Case No.] Supreme People's Court 41 [2016], Administrative Retrial, SPC

[Cause of Action] Administrative dispute over invalidation of an invention patent

[Collegial Panel Members] Qin Yuanming   Li Rong   Ma Xiurong

[Keywords] Invalidation proceeding, Markush Claim, Amendment, Inventive Step (Non-obviousness)

[Relevant Legal Provisions] Paragraph 1, Article 31 of the *Patent Law of the People's Republic of China*, Article 34 of the *Detailed Rules for the Implementation of the Patent Law of the People's Republic of China*

[Basic Facts]

In the retrial of the administrative dispute over the invalidation of the invention patent (the administrative dispute over the invalidation of the patent under the "Markush Claim") between the Patent Reexamination Board of the State Intellectual Property Office (hereinafter referred to as the Patent Reexamination Board) (the applicant), Beijing Winsunny Harmony Science & Technology Co., Ltd. (hereinafter referred to as Winsunny) (the respondent), and Daiichi Sankyo Company Limited (the third-party in the first instance); the last party is the holder of the patent titled "The preparation method of the pharmaceutical composition for the treatment or prevention of hypertension," numbered 97126347.7 (i.e., the patent involved in the case). The patent claims are written in the form of a Markush Claim. Winsunny requested the Patent Reexamination Board for invalidation of the said patent on the ground that it involved no inventive step. On August 30, 2010, Daiichi Sankyo Company Limited made the following amendments to the claim: deleted "or ester" in the phrase "or its salt or ester which can be used for medicinal purposes" in Claim 1; deleted "alkyl with 1 to 6 carbon atoms" under the definition of R4 in Claim 1; and deleted the other technical schemes except carboxyl and Formula COOR5a under the definition of R5 in Claim 1. During the oral proceedings, the Patent Reexamination Board informed Daiichi Sankyo Company Limited that the deletion of "or ester" in Claim 1 was approved, but other deletions were unacceptable since they did not conform to the relevant provisions of Article 68 in the *Detailed Rules for the Implementation of the Patent Law of the People's Republic of China*. Daiichi Sankyo Company Limited and Winsunny did not object to this. On January 14, 2011, Daiichi Sankyo Company Limited submitted a revised claim for replacement, in which the "or ester" in Claim 1 was deleted. The Patent Reexamination Board made Decision No. 16266 on the examination request for invalidation, in which it decided that Claim 1 of the patent involved in the case is non-obvious as compared to that in Evidence 1, has an inventive step and conforms to Paragraph 3, Article 22 of the Patent Law of the People's Republic of China. Thus, on the basis of the revised version submitted by Daiichi Sankyo Company Limited on January 14, 2011, the patent right involved was upheld as valid. Opposing the decision, Winsunny initiated an administrative litigation. Beijing No.1 Intermediate People's Court ruled that the Patent Reexamination Board had no error in the application of law for rejecting the revised text submitted by Daiichi Sankyo Company Limited on August 30, 2010, on the ground that it did not comply with Article 68 of the *Detailed Rules for the Implementation of the Patent Law of the People's Republic of China*. Claim 1 of the concerned patent is non-obvious as compared to that in Evidence 1 and involves an inventive step. Therefore, the Court decided to affirm the Decision No.16266. Winsunny was not satisfied with the ruling and made an appeal. In the second instance, Beijing Higher People's Court held that the Markush Claim is a special type of parallel technical solution, and that the revised text submitted by Daiichi Sankyo Company Limited on August 30, 2010 narrowed the scope of protection for the patent involved, which complies with Paragraph 1, Article 68 of the *Detailed*

Rules for the Implementation of the Patent Law of the People's Republic of China. The effect of a specific embodiment covered by the claim of the patent involved is similar to the technical effect of Embodiment 329 of the existing technology in Evidence 1. Claim 1 of the patent involved did not achieve the unexpected technical effect and therefore does not have inventive step.

 Holding

On April 1, 2011, the Patent Reexamination Board made Decision No. 16266 on the examination request for invalidation, in which it affirmed that the patent right involved is valid. Opposing the Decision, Winsunny filed an administrative lawsuit with Beijing No.1 Intermediate People's Court, which decided on December 20, 2011 to uphold Decision No. 16266 made by the Patent Reexamination Board. Winsunny refused to accept the first-instance judgment and appealed to Beijing Higher People's Court for revocation of the first-instance judgment and Decision No. 16266, and ordering the Patent Reexamination Board to make a new decision. On September 24, 2013, Beijing Higher People's Court decided that the decision of the first instance and Decision No. 16266 made by the Patent Reexamination Board shall be revoked, and that a new decision shall be made by the Patent Reexamination Board on the examination request for invalidation. Opposing the decision, the Patent Reexamination Board applied for retrial to the Supreme People's Court, which tried the case and ruled on December 20, 2017 that the decision of the second instance shall be revoked and that of the first instance shall be upheld.

[Reasoning]

The Supreme People's Court held that:

I . Nature of the Markush Claim

The Markush Claim is a special way of writing a claim to apply for chemical invention patents, i.e., a claim which applies for the identification of multiple parallel optional elements in one claim. The way a Markush Claim is written, is designed to solve the problem in the field of chemistry wherein many substituent groups cannot be summarized by a common upper-level concept. It has been considered as a structural expression rather than a functional expression. The Markush Claim requires the definition of parallel optional elements instead of additional claims, and all of its optional compounds have common properties and functions and a common structure, or that all the optional elements belong to the same compound recognized in the domain of the invention. Although the Markush Claim is written in a special way, it shall also comply with the provisions of the *Patent Law and the Detailed Rules for the Implementation of the Patent Law*. The Markush Claim has a very strong ability to generalize. Once authorized, the scope of patent protection will cover all compounds with the same structure, property or function, and the patentee's rights and interests will be maximized. In essence, a patent right is the monopoly on a certain right, which means that the greater the scope of the rights enjoyed by the patentee, the more restrictions the public will be subject to. Therefore, from the point of view of fairness, the Markush Claim interpretation should be strict. No matter how many variables and combinations it includes, the Claim should be regarded as a general combination solution. The choice of a variable should generate a drug with the same effect – the choice of different molecular formulas should produce different drugs, but there should not be too much difference in the drug's efficacy and the drugs should be mutually replaceable, and the expected effect should remain the same. That is the reason why the Markush Claim was created in the first place. Therefore, the Markush Claim should be regarded as a collection of the Markush elements rather than of many compounds. Normally the Markush elements should be understood as a class of compounds with common properties and functions, and would present themselves as a single compound only under certain circumstances. If it is determined that the compounds expressed under the Markush Claim are a collection of many compounds, it is inconsistent with the requirement of singularity. Therefore, it is incorrect for the court of second instance to decide that the Markush Claim is a parallel technical solution, and the decision should be corrected.

II. Amendment to the Markush Claim in the Invalidation Proceeding

The 2010 *Guidelines for Patent Examination* stipulates that during the invalidation request review stage, the amendment to the new invention and utility patent documents shall be limited to the claim and shall follow the basic principles: 1. The title of the original claim shall not be changed; 2. The scope of protection of the original patent shall not be extended as compared to the authorized claim; 3. The technical features shall not go beyond the original specification and claim; 4. Generally, technical features that are not included in the authorized claim shall not be added. However, the current method of amendment employed, aside from meeting the above principles, was specifically limited to the deletion of the claim, the deletion of the technical solution, the further limitation of the claim and the correction of an obvious error. Further limitation of the claim refers to the addition of one or more technical features recorded in other claims, so as to narrow the scope of protection. It can be seen that in the invalidation proceeding, the amendment to the patent documents can be conducted in multiple ways. However, there are many special issues in the examination of patent application for chemical inventions. For example, whether a chemical invention can be implemented needs to be confirmed by the result of the experiment; some chemical products need to be defined by means of parameters or preparation methods; and new properties and use of a chemical product do not mean changes in its structure or components. In view of the particularity of chemical inventions and given the fact that in writing the Markush Claim, the patent applicant has had the opportunity to put as many structures and formulas as possible into one claim in order to obtain the maximum scope of protection, the amendment to the Markush Claim should be strictly restricted in the invalidation stage. The amendment to the Markush Claim shall be allowed when a class of compounds or a single compound with new properties and functions will not be generated because of the amendment; however, individual cases that are an exception should also be considered. If a patent applicant or a patentee is allowed to delete any option of any variable, even if such deletion will narrow the scope of protection and will not impair the rights and interests of the public, there will be uncertainty in the possible new scope of rights protection, which will neither offer a stable expectation to the public nor maintain a stable patent right confirmation system. Therefore, the decisions made by the court of second instance are obviously improper and should be corrected.

III. Method for Judgment of the Inventive Step of Markush Claim

The judgment of the inventive step of Markush claim should follow the basic method for such judgment, that is, the "three-step method" stipulated in the *Guidelines for Patent Examination*. The unexpected technical effect is a contributing factor in judging the inventive step – it is a kind of backward judgment method, and it is special and does not have universal applicability. Therefore, only when a judgment on non-obviousness can be made based on the "three-step method" can a patent application be decided as involving an inventive step based on the unexpected technical effect. Generally, it would be inappropriate to skip the "three-step method" and directly apply the unexpected technical effect to determine whether a patent application involves an inventive step or not. As for the comparison of technical effects, in this case, the Patent Reexamination Board did not, in the invalidation proceedings, compare Embodiments 10, 17, 50 and 69 of Document 1 with those of the concerned patent and decide upon that comparison, whereas in the court of second instance, a direct comparison and decision was made, which obviously went beyond the scope of invalidation review. Such a practice does not conform to the provisions of the *Administrative Procedure Law* and relevant judicial interpretations and should be corrected. Winsunny, the requester for the invalidation, held that Patent Claim 1 involved in the case lacked the inventive step, and used Evidence 1 as the closest comparative document. When deciding whether Patent Claim 1 involves an inventive step or not, the Patent Reexamination Board and the court of first instance strictly followed the "three-step method," and found that there are two distinguishing technical features between the compounds of Formula I in Claim 1 and the compounds of Formula I in Evidence 1. After analyzing the non-obviousness of the two distinguishing technical features, they believed that it was justified to declare the Patent Claim 1 involves an inventive step.

[Opinion of the Case (Chinese Version)]

Scan the QR code to see the Chinese version of the opinion

产品说明书是否属于专利法意义上的公开出版物

——蒂森克虏伯机场系统（中山）有限公司与中国国际海运集装箱（集团）股份有限公司、深圳中集天达空港设备有限公司、广州市白云国际机场股份有限公司侵害发明专利权纠纷案

【裁判要旨】

产品操作和维护说明书随产品销售而交付使用者，使用者及接触者均没有保密义务，且其能够为不特定公众所获取，属于专利法意义上的公开出版物。其中记载的技术方案，以交付给使用者的时间作为公开时间。

【案　　　号】	最高人民法院（2016）最高法民再179号
【案　　　由】	侵害发明专利权纠纷
【合议庭成员】	李　剑　宋淑华　吴　蓉
【关　键　词】	发明专利　侵权　产品说明书　出版物公开
【相关法条】	《中华人民共和国专利法》（2000年修正）第二十二条，《中华人民共和国专利法》（2008年修正）第六十二条

【基本案情】

在再审申请人蒂森克虏伯机场系统（中山）有限公司（以下简称蒂森中山公司）与被申请人中国国际海运集装箱（集团）股份有限公司（以下简称中集公司）、深圳中集天达空港设备有限公司（以下简称天达公司）、一审被告广州市白云国际机场股份有限公司（以下简称白云机场）侵害发明专利权纠纷案中，中集公司系名称为"登机桥辅助支撑装置和带有该装置的登机桥及其控制方法"的第 200410004652.9 号发明专利（即本案专利）的权利人，本案专利的申请日为 2004 年 2 月 26 日，授权公告日为 2007 年 8 月 22 日。授权时的专利权人是中集公司。2009 年 5 月 8 日，本案发明专利权人变更为中集公司和天达公司。中集公司与天达公司以白云机场和蒂森中山公司未经许可擅自实施本案专利的技术方案侵害其专利权为由，提起诉讼。蒂森中山公司在一审诉讼过程中提出现有技术抗辩，并提交了蒂森克虏伯机场系统公司运营总监雷蒙德·K·斯特里特的证言及来源于该公司的佐证证言的附件作为支持其现有技术抗辩的证据。该证据记载，从 2000 年 10 月至 2001 年 3 月，蒂森克虏伯集团派往旧金山国际机场的现场小组为消除晃动幅度过大的问题研究出一种技术解决方案，其中包括在登机桥的横梁／负重轮的两侧均安装一个液压稳定器，以增强登机桥的稳定性。这种方法被称为"悬臂梁设计"或"悬臂梁装置"。用户接受使用"悬臂梁设计"或"悬臂梁装置"的建议。随后便进行了生产和安装。《手册》的附录 Y "液压稳定器"（以下简称附录 Y）经更新后发布并交付用户。蒂森中山公司主张，附录 Y 证明其使用的为现有技术。广东省广州市中级人民法院一审认为，附录 Y 是一份由蒂森中山公司关联公司自行印制的非正规出版物。在蒂森中山公司不能证明其关联公司曾使用"悬臂梁装置"技术的情况下，一审法院难以确认该附录 Y 内容的真实性及其印制及交付给旧金山国际机场的时间。因蒂森中山公司不能证明"悬臂梁装置"技术于 2000～2001 年就已通过附录 Y 公开发表，故其现有技术抗辩不能成立。一审法院遂判决蒂森中山公司、白云机场立即停止侵权行为，蒂森中山公司赔偿中集公司与天达公司经济损失 50 万元并驳回中集公司与天达公司的其他诉讼请求。蒂森中山公司不服，提起上诉。广东省高级人民法院二审判决驳回上诉、维持原判。蒂森中山公司仍不服，向最高人民法院申请再审。最高人民法院裁定提审本案，并于 2016 年 10 月 10 日判决撤销一审、二审判决，驳回中集公司与天达公司的诉讼请求。

 裁判结果

广东省广州市中级人民法院于 2012 年 9 月 24 日作出（2011）穗中法民三初字第 107 号民事判决：1. 蒂森中山公司、白云机场立即停止侵权行为；2. 蒂森中山公司赔偿中集公司与天达公司经济损失 50 万元；3. 驳回中集公司与天达公司的其他诉讼请求。蒂森中山公司不服一审判决，向广东省高级人民法院提起上诉。广东省高级人民法院于 2014 年 7 月 16 日作出（2013）粤高法民三终字第 38 号民事判决：驳回上诉，维持原判。蒂森中山公司仍不服，向最高人民法院申请再审。最高人民法院裁定提审本案，并于 2016 年 10 月 10 日作出（2016）最高法民再 179 号民事判决：1. 撤销广东省高级人民法院（2013）粤高法民三终字第 38 号民事判决；2. 撤销广东省广州市中级人民法院（2011）穗中法民三初字第 107 号民事判决；3. 驳回被申请人中国国际海运集装箱（集团）股份有限公司和深圳中集天达空港设备有限公司的诉讼请求。

【裁判理由】

　　最高人民法院提审认为：蒂森中山公司在本案中主张现有技术抗辩，即因附录 Y 构成出版物公开，故其使用的是现有技术，不侵害本案专利权。专利法意义上的出版物是指记载有技术或设计内容的独立存在的传播载体，并且应当表明或者有其他证据证明其公开发表或出版的时间。附录 Y 虽是一份产品操作和维护说明书并随产品销售而交付使用者，但其使用者以及接触者均没有保密义务，也即附录 Y 是可公开的，且其能够为不特定公众通过复印的方式获取。由此可见，附录 Y 系独立存在的传播载体，鉴于其也记载了涉案专利技术的技术特征，其交付给旧金山国际机场的时间，即公开时间亦能确定，故其属于专利法意义上的出版物公开，蒂森中山公司据此主张现有技术抗辩，有事实和法律依据，应当予以支持。

【本案裁判文书】

扫描二维码，可见裁判文书

Whether or Not Product Manuals Are Considered as Publications as Defined in the Patent Law

——ThyssenKrupp Airport Systems (Zhongshan) Co., Ltd.

v. China International Marine Containers (Group) Ltd.,

Shenzhen CIMC Tianda Airport Equipment Co., Ltd.,

and Guangzhou Baiyun International Airport Co., Ltd.

[Syllabus]

Product operation and maintenance manuals are delivered to users together with the sold products. Neither the users nor those who come in contact with the product have the duty of confidentiality. In addition, they can be accessed by the unspecified public and are considered as publications as defined in the Patent Law. The technical schemes recorded in the manuals shall be deemed as publicly accessible from the moment when the manuals are delivered to users.

[Case No.] Supreme People's Court (2016) ZGFXZ No. 179

[Cause of Action] Dispute over infringement on patent right for invention

[Collegial Panel Members] Li Jian   Song Shuhua   Wu Rong

[Keywords] Patent for invention, infringement, product manual, publication

[Relevant Legal Provisions] Article 22 of the *Patent Law of the*

People's Republic of China (revised in 2000) and Article 62 of the *Patent Law of the People's Republic of China* (revised in 2008)

[Basic Facts]

In the dispute over infringement of patent for invention between the applicant ThyssenKrupp Airport Systems (Zhongshan) Co., Ltd. (hereinafter referred to as ThyssenKrupp Zhongshan) and the respondents China International Marine Containers (Group) Ltd. (hereinafter referred to as CIMC), Shenzhen CIMC Tianda Airport Equipment Co., Ltd. (hereinafter referred to as Tianda), and Guangzhou Baiyun International Airport Co., Ltd. (hereinafter referred to as Baiyun Airport), the Defendant of first instance, CIMC is the holder of the patent for invention No. 200410004652.9 (i.e. Patent Involved hereby in this Case) named "Supporting Device for Boarding Bridge and Boarding Bridge with the Device and the Control Methodology". The Patent involved in this Case was applied on February 26, 2004 and authorized on August 22, 2007. The patent owner was CIMC at the time of authorization. On May 8, 2009, the holder of the Patent Involved in this Case was changed from CIMC to Tianda. CIMC and Tianda filed a lawsuit claiming that the implementation of the technical schemes of the Patent Involved in this Case by Baiyun Airport and ThyssenKrupp Zhongshan without permission from the patent holder had infringed upon their patent. During the first instance, ThyssenKrupp Zhongshan made its defenses based on prior technologies, and submitted testimonies of Raymond•K•Streat, chief operating director of ThyssenKrupp Zhongshan, and attached supporting documents to support its defenses about prior technologies. As recorded in the evidences, from October 2000 to March 2001, the on-site team sent by ThyssenKrupp to San Francisco International Airport developed a technical solution to eliminate the large amplitude of shaking. The solution included the installation of a hydraulic stabilizer on both sides of the

175

beam/loading wheel of the boarding bridge, for the purpose of promoting the stability of the boarding bridge. It was called "cantilever beam design" or "cantilever beam device". The user accepted and applied the suggestion of "cantilever beam design" or "cantilever beam device", and then the production and installation work was carried out. Appendix Y "Hydraulic Stabilizer" of the *Manual* (hereinafter referred to as Appendix Y) was released and delivered to the user after being updated. ThyssenKrupp Zhongshan claimed that Appendix Y proved that they were using an prior technology. In first instance, Guangzhou Municipal Intermediate People's Court of Guangdong Province held that, Appendix Y was an informal publication printed by the affiliated company of ThyssenKrupp Zhongshan. If ThyssenKrupp Zhongshan failed to prove its affiliated company had used the technology of "cantilever beam device", it was difficult for the first instance court to confirm the authenticity of Appendix Y and the time when the manual was printed to San Francisco International Airport. Because ThyssenKrupp Zhongshan failed to prove the technology of "cantilever beam device" had been publicized through Appendix Y in 2000-2001, the defense concerning prior technologies shall not be justified. The first instance court hereby made the judgment that ThyssenKrupp Zhongshan and Baiyun Airport should cease the act of infringement immediately, ThyssenKrupp Zhongshan should compensate CIMC and Tianda for their economic losses in the amount of RMB 500,000, and other claims by CIMC and Tianda were rejected. ThyssenKrupp Zhongshan refused to accept the judgment and filed an appeal. The High People's Court of Guangdong Province rejected the appeal and upheld the original judgment in the second instance. ThyssenKrupp Zhongshan still refused to accept the ruling and applied to the Supreme People's Court for a retrial. The Supreme People's Court decided to bring this Case to trial, and on October 10, 2016 revoked the judgments made in first and second instances, and rejected the claims of CIMC and Tianda.

Holding

On September 24, 2012, Guangzhou Municipal Intermediate People's Court of Guangdong Province made (2011) SZFMSCZ No. 107 Civil Judgment as follows: I. ThyssenKrupp Zhongshan and Baiyun Airport should cease the infringing act immediately; II. ThyssenKrupp Zhongshan should compensate CIMC and Tianda for their economic losses in the amount of RMB 500,000; III. Other claims by CIMC and Tianda were rejected. ThyssenKrupp Zhongshan refused to accept the judgment of the first instance, and appealed to the Higher People's Court of Guangdong Province. On July 16, 2014, High People's Court of Guangdong Province entered (2013) YGFMSZZ No. 38 Civil Judgment as follows: the appeal was rejected and the original judgment was upheld. ThyssenKrupp Zhongshan still refused to accept the ruling and applied to the Supreme People's Court for a retrial. The Supreme People's Court decided to bring this Case to trial, and made (2016) ZGFMZ No. 179 Civil Judgment on October 10, 2016: I. the (2013) YGFMSZZ No. 38 Civil Judgment made by the High People's Court of Guangdong Province was revoked; II. the (2011) SZFMSCZ No. 107 Civil Judgment made by Guangzhou Municipal Intermediate People's Court of Guangdong Province was revoked; III. Claims of ThyssenKrupp Airport Systems (Zhongshan) Co., Ltd. and China International Marine Containers (Group) Ltd. were rejected.

[Reasoning]

During the trial, the Supreme People's Court held that: in this Case, ThyssenKrupp Zhongshan made a defense of prior technologies, i.e. because Appendix Y was a publication, the technology it used was available as an prior technology and it did not constitute an infringement upon the patent involved in this Case. Publications as defined in the Patent Law refer to independent communication media containing contents of technologies or designs, with the time of release or publishing indicated in the publication or can be proved via other evidences. Appendix Y as a product manual for operation and maintenance had been delivered to the users along with the products sold, but neither the user nor those who had contact with the product had the duty of confidentiality, which meant that Appendix Y was open and was accessible to the unspecified public through photocopies. In regard of this, Appendix Y was an independent communication medium, containing the technical features of the patented technologies involved, and it was possible to ascertain the time when it was delivered to San Francisco International Airport, i.e. the time of public release. So, Appendix Y conformed to a publication as defined in the Patent Law. The defense concerning prior technologies made by ThyssenKrupp Zhongshan related to Appendix Y had factual and legal basis, and therefore should be adopted.

[Opinion of the Case (Chinese Version)]

Scan the QR code to see the Chinese version of the opinion

专利权人与侵权人的事先约定可以作为确定专利侵权损害赔偿数额的依据

——中山市隆成日用制品有限公司与湖北童霸儿童用品有限公司侵害实用新型专利权纠纷案

【裁判要旨】

权利人与侵权人就侵权损害赔偿数额作出的事先约定，不构成权利人与侵权人之间的交易合同，故侵权人应承担的民事责任仅为侵权责任，不属于《中华人民共和国合同法》第一百二十二条规定的侵权责任与违约责任竞合的情形。

权利人与侵权人就侵权损害赔偿数额作出的事先约定，是双方就未来发生侵权时权利人因被侵权所受到的损失或者侵权人因侵权所获得的利益所预先达成的一种计算方法。在无法律规定无效等情形下，人民法院可直接以权利人与侵权人的事先约定作为确定侵权损害赔偿数额的依据。

【案　　　号】　最高人民法院（2013）民提字第116号
【案　　　由】　侵害实用新型专利权纠纷
【合议庭成员】　王　闯　朱　理　何　鹏
【关　键　词】　实用新型专利侵权　损害赔偿　竞合
【相关法条】　《中华人民共和国合同法》第一百二十二条，《中华人

【基本案情】

中山市隆成日用制品有限公司（以下简称隆成公司）是名称为"前轮定位装置"实用新型专利（以下简称涉案专利）的专利权人。2008年4月,隆成公司曾以湖北童霸儿童用品有限公司（以下简称童霸公司）侵犯涉案专利为由向武汉市中级人民法院提起诉讼，法院判决童霸公司停止侵权并赔偿损失。童霸公司不服，提起上诉。二审期间，双方达成调解协议并由湖北省高级人民法院制作了（2009）鄂民三终字第42号民事调解书,其主要内容为：童霸公司保证不再侵犯隆成公司的专利权，如发现一起侵犯隆成公司实用新型专利权的行为，自愿赔偿隆成公司100万元。后隆成公司发现童霸公司仍在从事侵害涉案专利权的经营行为，遂于2011年5月再次向武汉市中级人民法院提起诉讼，请求法院判令童霸公司赔偿隆成公司100万元并承担诉讼费用。一审庭审中，经法院释明，隆成公司明确本案依据专利侵权起诉，不选择合同违约之诉，但请求法院对侵权赔偿数额按双方约定的标准计算。一审法院认为：根据《中华人民共和国合同法》第一百二十二条的规定，侵权责任与违约责任竞合时，受损害方有选择权。隆成公司明确选择提起侵权之诉，应根据侵权责任法确定赔偿数额。若赔偿标准以前案民事调解书的约定为准，则与合同法的上述规定相冲突。因隆成公司主张侵权之诉，违约之诉无法纳入法庭调查和辩论的范围，法院无须对违约行为及违约责任作出判断，故不宜适用当事人约定的违约赔偿金。一审法院遂适用法定赔偿判决童霸公司赔偿隆成公司14万元。隆成公司不服，提起上诉。湖北省高级人民法院二审认为，侵权行为成立与否是本案双方当事人权利义务关系的基础，前案中被诉侵权童车产品的型号与本案中被诉侵权童车产品的型号不同，故调解协议约定的赔偿数额不能适用于本案，遂判决驳回上诉，维持一审判决。隆成公司仍不服，向最高人民法院申请再审。最高人民法院裁定提审本案，并于 2013 年 12 月 7 日判决撤销原一、二审判决，判令童霸公司赔偿隆成公司 100 万元。

 裁判结果

> 武汉市中级人民法院于 2011 年 10 月 24 日作出（2011）武知初字第 467 号民事判决，判令童霸公司赔偿隆成公司 14 万元，驳回隆成公司其他诉讼请求。隆成公司不服一审判决，向湖北省高级人民法院提起上诉，请求撤销一审判决，并依法改判。湖北省高级人民法院于 2012 年 5 月 11 日作出二审判决，驳回上诉，维持一审判决。隆成公司不服二审判决，向最高人民法院申请再审。最高人民法院裁定提审本案，并于 2013 年 12 月 7 日判决撤销原一、二审判决，判令童霸公司赔偿隆成公司 100 万元。

【裁判理由】

最高人民法院提审认为：

一、关于双方当事人在前案中达成的调解协议的效力

由于调解协议系双方当事人自愿达成，其内容仅涉及私权处分，不涉及社会公共利益、第三人利益，也不存在法律规定的其他无效情形，且湖北省高级人民法院对调解协议进行审查确认后制作了民事调解书，故双方在前案中达成的调解协议合法有效。

二、关于本案能否适用双方在调解协议中约定的赔偿数额确定方法

首先，本案中童霸公司应承担的民事责任，不属于侵权责任与违约责任竞合之情形。《中华人民共和国合同法》第一百二十二条所规定的侵权与违约责任的竞合，其法律要件是"因当事人一方的违约行为，侵害对方人身、财产权益"。就该规定来看，违约责任与侵权责任发生竞合的前提是当事人双方之间存在一种基础的交易合同关系。基于该交易合同关系，一方当事人违反合同约定的义务，该违约行为侵害了对方权益而产生侵权责任。因此，该规定中的违约行为应当是指对基础交易合同约定义务的违反，且该违约行为同时侵害了对方权益，而不是指对侵权行为发生之后当事人就如何承担赔偿责任所作约定的违反。就调解协议的内容来看，该协议并非隆成公司与童霸公司之间的基础交易合同，而是对侵权行为发生后如何承担侵权赔偿责任（包括计算方法和数额）的约定。因此，本案中童霸公司应承担的民事责任，不属于《中华人民共和国合同法》第一百二十二条规定的侵权责任与违约责任竞合的情形。其次，本案中童霸公司应承担的民事责任系侵权责任。一方面，前已述及，隆成公司与童霸公司之间并不存在基础合同关系；另一方面，调解协议的法律意义与效果，不在于对童霸公司的合同交易义务作出约定，而在于对侵权责任如何承担作出约定。即使没有调解协议，童霸公司基于法律规定也同样负有不侵权的义务。当事人双方将童霸公司将来侵权行为发生后的具体赔偿方法和数额写进调解协议，只是为了便于进一步约定当童霸公司再次侵权时其侵权责任应如何承担。第三，侵权责任法、专利法等法律，并未禁止被侵权人与侵权人就侵权责任的方式、侵权赔偿数额等预先作出约定。这种约定的实质是，双方就未来发生侵权时权利人因被侵权所受到的损失或者侵权人因侵权所获得的利益，预先达成的一种简便的计算和确定方法。基于举证困难、诉讼耗时费力等因素的考虑，双方当事人在私法自治的范畴内完全可以对侵权赔偿数额作出约定，这种约定既包括侵权行为发生后的事后约定，也包括侵权行为发生前的事先约定。因此，本案适用调解协议中双方约定的赔偿数额确定方法，与《中华人民共和国专利法》第六十五条的有关规定并不冲突。综上，本案可以适用隆成公司与童霸公司在前案调解协议中约定的赔偿数额确定方法。

【本案裁判文书】

扫描二维码，可见裁判文书

Prior Agreements Between the Patentee and Infringer Can Be the Basis to Determine the Damages of Patent Infringement

——Zhongshan Longcheng Daily Use Products Co., Ltd. v. Hubei Tongba Children Ltd.

[Syllabus]

The agreement on the sum of damages between the patentee and the infringer in advance does not constitute a transactional agreement between them. Hence, the civil liability of the infringer is only confined to tort liability, which does not fall into the circumstance described in Article 122 of the Contract Law of the People's Republic of China, i.e., concurrence between tort liability and liability for breach of contract.

A prior agreement on the sum of damages between the patentee and the infringer is a calculation method agreed by both parties in advance regarding the loss of the patentee or the proceeds by the infringer due to future infringement. In absence of any laws or regulations that may render the agreement invalid, the people's court may directly determine the sum of tort damages on the basis of the prior agreement between the patentee and the infringer in advance.

[Case No.] Supreme People's Court (2013) MTZ No. 116

[Cause of Action] Utility model patent infringement dispute

[Collegial Panel Members] Wang Chuang   Zhu Li   He Peng

[Keywords] Utility model patent infringement, compensation, concurrence

[Relevant Legal Provisions] Article 122 of the *Contract Law of the People's Republic of China* and Article 65 (1) of the *Patent Law of the People's Republic of China*

[Basic Facts]

Zhongshan Longcheng Daily Use Products Co., Ltd. (hereinafter referred to as "Longcheng") is the patentee of the utility model ("Patent at Issue") named "Wheel Alignment Device". In April 2008, Longcheng filed a lawsuit to Wuhan Intermediate People's Court against Hubei Tongba Children Ltd. (hereinafter referred to as Tongba) on the grounds of patent infringement, and the court ordered Tongba to cease the infringement and compensate. Tongba refused to accept the judgment and filed an appeal. During the appeal, the Parties reached a mediation agreement and Hubei High People's Court made a civil paper of mediation ([2009] EMSZZ No. 42), main contents of which included: Tongba should promise not to infringe the patent of Longcheng any further, and in case of any further infringement on the utility model of Longcheng, Tongba should voluntarily indemnify Longcheng in the amount of RMB 1 million. After that, Longcheng found that Tongba was still engaging in business activities that infringed on the Patent at Issue, and thus lodged another lawsuit with Wuhan Intermediate People's Court in May 2011, requesting the court to rule that Tongba should compensate Longcheng in the amount of RMB 1 million, and bear the litigation costs. On first instance, after interpretation by the court, Longcheng made it clear that it was lodging this lawsuit on the grounds of patent infringement rather than breach of contract, but it requested the court to calculate the amount of compensation according to the amount agreed by both parties. The court of first instance held that, in accordance with Article 122 of the Contract Law of the People's Republic of China, the injured party should have the right of choice in the event of concurrence of tort liability and liability for breach of contract. Longcheng expressly chose to lodge the lawsuit for infringement, so the amount of compensation would be determined according to the Tort Law. If the standard for compensation were subject to the agreement in the civil mediation paper of the previous case, this would conflict with the above provisions of the Contract Law. Longcheng lodged the lawsuit for infringement, the lawsuit concerning breach of contract could not be included in the investigation and debate, and the court need not to decide on the breach and liabilities therein, thus it would have been inappropriate to apply the amount of compensation for the breach as agreed by both parties. Therefore, the court of first instance applied the statutory standard of compensation, and ruled that Tongba should compensate Longcheng RMB 140,000. Longcheng refused to accept this ruling and filed an appeal. On appeal, Hubei Provincial High People's Court held that the rights and liabilities between Parties of the case at issue should be whether the infringement in fact took place. The model of the allegedly infringing baby buggy involved in the previous case was different from the model of the allegedly infringing baby buggy involved in this case, and thus the amount of damages agreed in the mediation agreement could not be applied to this case. Therefore, the court dismissed the appeal and upheld the ruling of the trial court. Longcheng still refused to accept the ruling as final and applied to the Supreme People's Court for retrial. The Supreme People's Court determined to review this case, and on December 7, 2013, ruled that the judgments made in the first instance and second instance should be overruled, and that Tongba should compensate Longcheng RMB 1 million.

⚖ Holding »»»»»»»

On October 24, 2011, Wuhan Intermediate People's Court made (2011) WZCZ No. 467 Civil Judgment, ordering Tongba to compensate Longcheng RMB 140,000 and rejecting other claims of Longcheng. Longcheng refused to accept the ruling of first instance and instituted an appeal before Hubei High People's Court for overruling the judgment and amending the judgment according to law. Hubei High People's Court made the judgment of second instance on May 11, 2012, rejected the appeal and upheld the first instance judgment. Longcheng refused to accept the judgment of second instance and applied to the Supreme People's Court for a retrial. The Supreme People's Court determined to review this case, and on December 7, 2013, ruled that the judgments made in the first instance and second instance should be overruled, and that Tongba should compensate Longcheng in the amount of RMB 1 million.

[Reasoning]

After the retrial, the SPC held that: I. The effect of the mediation agreement made by both parties in the previous case.

The mediation agreement is made by both parties on their free will, the contents are only concerning the dispose of private rights, not involving social public interests and third party interests, there is no other circumstances under the law which would render the agreement invalid, and Hubei High People's Court made the civil paper of mediation after reviewing and confirming the mediation agreement, thus the mediation agreement made by both parties in the previous case should be legally valid.

II. With regard to whether this case could apply the way of determining damages as agreed by both parties in the mediation agreement entered into in the previous case, firstly, the civil liabilities that Tongba should have borne did not fall within the scope of concurrence between tort liability and liability for breach of contract. The premise for concurrence between tort liability and liability for breach of contract as stipulated in Article 122 of the Contract Law of the People's Republic of China should be "the personal and property rights of the other party is damaged due to breach of contract by one party". According to that provision, the premise for concurrence between tort liability and liability for breach of contract should be a basic transaction relation between the parties. Based on such a transaction relation, one party breached the contractual obligation, and such breach infringed upon the other party's interests, incurring tort liability. Therefore, the 'breach' stipulated in such provision should refer to the fact that one party violates an obligation agreed in the basic transaction contract, and that violation infringes upon the rights and interests of the other party at the same time, rather than referring to the violation of the agreement concerning the way to assume the liabilities for damages concluded by the parties after the infringement has taken place. Subject to the contents, the mediation agreement made in the previous case was not a basic transaction contract between Longcheng and Tongba, but an agreement concerning how to assume the liabilities for damages for infringement (including calculation methods and amount) after occurrence of infringing act. Therefore, in this case, the civil liabilities that Tongba should have borne did not fall within the circumstance of concurrence between tort liability and liability for breach of contract as stipulated in Article 122 of the Contract Law of the People's Republic of China. Secondly, the civil liabilities that Tongba should assume in this case should be the liability for infringement. On one hand, as afore-said, Longcheng and Tongba were not of a basic contractual relation; on the other hand, the legal significance and effect of the mediation agreement made in the previous case did not lie in the agreement on the contractual obligations of Tongba, but in the agreement on how to assume the liability for infringement. Even in absence of the mediation agreement, Tongba should bear the obligation of non-infringement according to the law. Both parties wrote the specific methods and amount of compensation for future infringement by Tongba into the mediation agreement only to specify how Tongba should assume the liability for infringement when infringing upon the Patent at Issue once again. Thirdly, the Tort Law, Patent Law and other laws do not prohibit the infringed party and infringer from making an agreement in advance on the method for assuming the liability for infringement, the amount of damages, etc. The substance of such an agreement is a simple method for calculating and determining losses of the patentee or benefits of the infringer as a result of any future infringement, as agreed by both parties in advance. Considering such factors as the difficulty in furnishing evidence, the time-consuming litigation, etc., both parties concerned can definitely make an agreement on the amount of damages for infringement to the extent of the autonomy of private law, and such an agreement includes prior agreements before occurrence of infringement. Therefore, the application of the method for determining the amount of compensation as agreed by both parties in the mediation agreement in this case did not conflict with relevant provisions of Article 65 of the Patent Law of the People's Republic of China. In conclusion, the method for determining the amount of compensation as agreed by Longcheng and Tongba in the mediation agreement of previous case could be applied in this case.

[Opinion of the Case (Chinese Version)]

Scan the QR code to see the Chinese version of the opinion

被侵权人向网络服务提供者所发出的有效通知、网络服务提供者接到通知后所应采取的必要措施的判断方法

——威海嘉易烤生活家电有限公司与永康市金仕德工贸有限公司、浙江天猫网络有限公司侵害发明专利权纠纷案

【裁判要旨】

　　网络用户利用网络服务实施侵权行为，被侵权人依据侵权责任法向网络服务提供者所发出的要求其采取必要措施的通知，包含被侵权人身份情况、权属凭证、侵权人网络地址、侵权事实初步证据等内容的，即属有效通知。网络服务提供者自行设定的投诉规则，不得影响权利人依法维护其自身合法权利。

　　《中华人民共和国侵权责任法》第三十六条第二款所规定的网络服务提供者接到通知后所应采取的必要措施包括但并不限于删除、屏蔽、断开链接。"必要措施"应遵循审慎、合理的原则，根据所侵害权利的性质、侵权的具体情形和技术条件等来加以综合确定。

【案　　　号】　浙江省高级人民法院（2015）浙知终字第 186 号
【案　　　由】　发明专利权侵权纠纷
【合议庭成员】　周　平　陈　宇　刘　静
【关　键　词】　民事　侵害发明专利权　有效通知　必要措施

网络服务提供者连带责任

【相关法条】 《中华人民共和国侵权责任法》第三十六条

【基本案情】

原告威海嘉易烤生活家电有限公司（以下简称嘉易烤公司）诉称：永康市金仕德工贸有限公司（以下简称金仕德公司）未经其许可，在天猫商城等网络平台上宣传并销售侵害其ZL200980000002.8号专利权的产品，构成专利侵权；浙江天猫网络有限公司（以下简称天猫公司）在嘉易烤公司投诉金仕德公司侵权行为的情况下，未采取有效措施，应与金仕德公司共同承担侵权责任。请求判令：1.金仕德公司立即停止销售被诉侵权产品；2.金仕德公司立即销毁库存的被诉侵权产品；3.天猫公司撤销金仕德公司在天猫平台上所有的侵权产品链接；4.金仕德公司、天猫公司连带赔偿嘉易烤公司50万元；5.本案诉讼费用由金仕德公司、天猫公司承担。

金仕德公司答辩称：其只是卖家，并不是生产厂家，嘉易烤公司索赔数额过高。

天猫公司答辩称：1.其作为交易平台，并不是生产销售侵权产品的主要经营方或者销售方；2.涉案产品是否侵权不能确定；3.涉案产品是否使用在先也不能确定；4.在不能证明其为侵权方的情况下，由其连带赔偿50万元缺乏事实和法律依据，且其公司业已删除了涉案产品的链接，嘉易烤公司关于撤销金仕德公司在天猫平台上所有侵权产品链接的诉讼请求亦不能成立。

法院经审理查明：2009年1月16日，嘉易烤公司及其法定代表人李琎熙共同向国家知识产权局申请了名称为"红外线加热烹调装置"的发明专利，并于2014年11月5日获得授权，专利

191

号为 ZL200980000002.8。该发明专利的权利要求书记载："1. 一种红外线加热烹调装置,其特征在于,该红外线加热烹调装置包括:托架,在其上部中央设有轴孔,且在其一侧设有控制电源的开关;受红外线照射就会被加热的旋转盘,作为在其上面可以盛食物的圆盘形容器,在其下部中央设有可拆装的插入到上述轴孔中的突起;支架,在上述托架的一侧纵向设置;红外线照射部,其设在上述支架的上端,被施加电源就会朝上述旋转盘照射红外线;上述托架上还设有能够从内侧拉出的接油盘;在上述旋转盘的突起上设有轴向的排油孔。"2015 年 1 月 26 日,涉案发明专利的专利权人变更为嘉易烤公司。涉案专利年费缴纳至 2016 年 1 月 15 日。

2015 年 1 月 29 日,嘉易烤公司的委托代理机构北京商专律师事务所向北京市海诚公证处申请证据保全公证,其委托代理人王永先、时寅在公证处监督下,操作计算机登入天猫网(网址为 http : //www.tmall.com),在一家名为"益心康旗舰店"的网上店铺购买了售价为 388 元的 3D 烧烤炉,并拷贝了该网店经营者的营业执照信息。同年 2 月 4 日,时寅在公证处监督下接收了寄件人名称为"益心康旗舰店"的快递包裹一个,内有韩文包装的 3D 烧烤炉及赠品、手写收据联和中文使用说明书、保修卡。公证员对整个证据保全过程进行了公证并制作了(2015)京海诚内民证字第 01494 号公证书。同年 2 月 10 日,嘉易烤公司委托案外人张一军向淘宝网知识产权保护平台上传了包含专利侵权分析报告和技术特征比对表在内的投诉材料,但淘宝网最终没有审核通过。同年 5 月 5 日,天猫公司向浙江省杭州市钱塘公证处申请证据保全公证,由其代理人刁曼丽在公证处的监督下操作电脑,在天猫网益心康旗舰店搜索"益心康 3D 烧烤炉韩式家用不粘电烤炉无烟烤肉机电烤盘铁板烧烤肉锅",显示没有搜索到符合条件的商品。

公证员对整个证据保全过程进行了公证并制作了（2015）浙杭钱证内字第 10879 号公证书。

一审庭审中，嘉易烤公司主张将涉案专利权利要求 1 作为本案要求保护的范围。经比对，嘉易烤公司认为除了开关位置的不同，被控侵权产品的技术特征完全落入了涉案专利权利要求 1 记载的保护范围，而开关位置的变化是业内普通技术人员不需要创造性劳动就可解决的，属于等同特征。两原审被告对比对结果不持异议。另查明，嘉易烤公司为本案支出公证费 4,000 元，代理服务费 81,000 元。

 裁判结果

浙江省金华市中级人民法院于 2015 年 8 月 12 日作出（2015）浙金知民初字第 148 号民事判决：1. 金仕德公司立即停止销售侵犯专利号为 ZL200980000002.8 的发明专利权的产品的行为；2. 金仕德公司于判决生效之日起十日内赔偿嘉易烤公司经济损失 150,000 元（含嘉易烤公司为制止侵权而支出的合理费用）；3. 天猫公司对上述第二项中金仕德公司赔偿金额的 50,000 元承担连带赔偿责任；4. 驳回嘉易烤公司的其他诉讼请求。一审宣判后，天猫公司不服，提起上诉。浙江省高级人民法院于 2015 年 11 月 17 日作出（2015）浙知终字第 186 号民事判决：驳回上诉，维持原判。

【裁判理由】

法院生效裁判认为：各方当事人对于金仕德公司销售的被诉侵权产品落入嘉易烤公司涉案专利权利要求 1 的保护范围，均不持异议，原审判决认定金仕德公司涉案行为构成专利侵权正确。

关于天猫公司在本案中是否构成共同侵权，《中华人民共和国侵权责任法》第三十六条第二款规定，网络用户利用网络服务实施侵权行为的，被侵权人有权通知网络服务提供者采取删除、屏蔽、断开链接等必要措施。网络服务提供者接到通知后未及时采取必要措施的，对损害的扩大部分与该网络用户承担连带责任。上述规定系针对权利人发现网络用户利用网络服务提供者的服务实施侵权行为后"通知"网络服务提供者采取必要措施，以防止侵权后果不当扩大的情形，同时还明确界定了此种情形下网络服务提供者所应承担的义务范围及责任构成。本案中，天猫公司涉案被诉侵权行为是否构成侵权应结合对天猫公司的主体性质、嘉易烤公司"通知"的有效性以及天猫公司在接到嘉易烤公司的"通知"后是否应当采取措施及所采取的措施的必要性和及时性等加以综合考量。

第一，天猫公司依法持有增值电信业务经营许可证，系信息发布平台的服务提供商，其在本案中为金仕德公司经营的"益心康旗舰店"销售涉案被诉侵权产品提供网络技术服务，符合《中华人民共和国侵权责任法》第三十六条第二款所规定网络服务提供者的主体条件。

第二，天猫公司在二审庭审中确认嘉易烤公司已于2015年2月10日委托案外人张一军向淘宝网知识产权保护平台上传了包含被投诉商品链接及专利侵权分析报告、技术特征比对表在内的投诉材料，且根据上述投诉材料可以确定被投诉主体及被投诉商品。

《中华人民共和国侵权责任法》第三十六条第二款所涉及的"通知"是认定网络服务提供者是否存在过错及应否就危害结果的不当扩大承担连带责任的条件。"通知"是指被侵权人就他人利用网络服务商的服务实施侵权行为的事实向网络服务提供者所发出的要求其采取必要技术措施,以防止侵权行为进一步扩大的行为。"通知"既可以是口头的,也可以是书面的。通常,"通知"内容应当包括权利人身份情况、权属凭证、证明侵权事实的初步证据以及指向明确的被诉侵权人网络地址等材料。符合上述条件的,即应视为有效通知。嘉易烤公司涉案投诉通知符合侵权责任法规定的"通知"的基本要件,属有效通知。

第三,经查,天猫公司对嘉易烤公司投诉材料作出审核不通过的处理,其在回复中表明审核不通过原因是:请在实用新型、发明的侵权分析对比表表二中详细填写被投诉商品落入贵方提供的专利权利要求的技术点,建议采用图文结合的方式一一指出。(需注意,对比的对象为卖家发布的商品信息上的图片、文字),并提供购买订单编号或双方会员名。

二审法院认为,发明或实用新型专利侵权的判断往往并非仅依赖表面或书面材料就可以作出,因此专利权人的投诉材料通常只需包括权利人身份、专利名称及专利号、被投诉商品及被投诉主体内容,以便投诉接受方转达被投诉主体。在本案中,嘉易烤公司的投诉材料已完全包含上述要素。至于侵权分析比对,天猫公司一方面认为其对卖家所售商品是否侵犯发明专利判断能力有限,另一方面却又要求投诉方"详细填写被投诉商品落入贵方提供的专利权利要求的技术点,建议采用图文结合的方式一一指出",该院认为,考虑到互联网领域投诉数量巨大、投诉情况复杂的因素,天猫公司的上述要求基于其自身利益考量虽也具有一定的合理性,而且也有利于天猫公司对于被投诉行为的性质作出初步判断并采取相应的措施。但就权利人而言,天猫公司的前述要求并非权利人投诉通知有效的必要条件。况且,嘉易烤公司在本案的投诉材料中提供了多达5页的以图文并茂的方式表现的技术特征对比表,天猫公司仍以教条的、格式化的回复将技术特征对比作为审核不通过的原因之一，处置失当。至于天猫公司审核不通过并提出提供购买订单编号或双方会员名的要求，该院认为，本案中投诉方是否提供购买订单编号或双方会员名并不影响投诉行为的合法有效。而且，天猫公司所确定的投诉规制并不对权利人维权产生法律约束力，权利人只需在法律规定的框架内行使维权行为即可，投诉方完全可以根据自己的利益考量决定是否接受天猫公司所确定的投诉规制。更何况投诉方可能无需购买商品而通过其他证据加以证明，也可以根据他人的购买行为发现可能的侵权行为，甚至投诉方即使存在直接购买行为，但也可以基于某种经济利益或商业秘密的考量而拒绝提供。

第四，《中华人民共和国侵权责任法》第三十六条第二款所规定的网络服务提供者接到通知后所应采取必要措施包括但并不限于删除、屏蔽、断开链接。"必要措施"应根据所侵害权利的性质、侵权的具体情形和技术条件等来加以综合确定。

本案中，在确定嘉易烤公司的投诉行为合法有效之后，需要判断天猫公司在接受投诉材料之后的处理是否审慎、合理。该院认为，本案系侵害发明专利权纠纷。天猫公司作为电子商务网络服务平台的提供者，基于其公司对于发明专利侵权判断的主观能力、侵权投诉胜诉概率以及利益平衡等因素的考量，并不必然要求天猫公司在接受投诉后对被投诉商品立即采取删除和屏蔽措施，对被诉商品采取的必要措施应当秉承审慎、合理原则，以免损害被投诉人的合法权益。但是将有效的投诉通知材料转达被投诉人并通知被投诉人申辩当属天猫公司应当采取的必要措施之一。否则权利人投诉行为将失去意义，权利人的维权行为也将难以实现。网络服务平台提供者应该保证有效投诉信息传递的顺畅，而不应成为投诉信息的黑洞。被投诉人对其生产、或销售的商品是否侵权，以及是否应主动自行停止被投诉行为，自会作出相应的判断及应对。而天猫公司未履行上述基本义务的结果导致被投诉人未收到任何警示从而造成损害后果的扩大。至于天猫公司在嘉易烤公司起诉后即对被诉商品采取删除和屏蔽措施，当属审慎、合理。综上，天猫公司在接到嘉易烤公司的通知后未及时采取必要措施，对损害的扩大部分应与金仕德公司承担连带责任。天猫公司就此提出的上诉理由不能成立。关于天猫公司所应承担责任的份额，一审法院综合考虑侵权持续的时间及天猫公司应当知道侵权事实的时间，确定天猫公司对金仕德公司赔偿数额的 50,000 元承担连带赔偿责任，并无不当。

【本案裁判文书】

扫描二维码，可见裁判文书

Judging Whether the Notice Sent by the Victim of the Tort to the Network Service Provider Is Effective and Whether the Network Service Provider Has Taken Necessary Measures Upon Receipt of Such Notice

——Weihai Jiayikao Home Appliances Co., Ltd. v. Yongkang Jinshide Industry and Trade Co., Ltd. and Zhejiang Tmall Network Co., Ltd.

[Syllabus]

Where after a network user commits an infringing act by using network services, the victim of infringement issues a notice to the network service provider in accordance with the Tort Law and requires the network service provider to take necessary measures, if the notice includes identity of the victim of infringement, the ownership certificate, the website of the infringing party, and the preliminary evidence of the infringement fact, it is a valid and effective notice. The rules of complaint set by the network service provider may not affect the obligee to legally safeguard its legiminate rights and interests.

Necessary measures that shall be taken by a network service provider upon receipt of a notice as prescribed in paragraph 2, Article 36 of the Tort Law of the People's Republic of China include but are not limited to deletion, blockage, and disconnection of the links. "Necessary measures" shall observe the principle of prudence and rationality and they shall be comprehensively determined according to the nature of the infringed right, the specific infringement circumstances, and the technical conditions.

[Case No.] Zhejiang High People's Court (2015) ZZZZ No.186

[Cause of Action] Patent Infringement Dispute

[Collegial Panel Members] Zhou Ping   Chen Yu   Liu Jing

[Keywords] Civil, infringement upon patent for invention, effective notice, necessary measures, network service provider, joint and several liability

[Relevant Legal Provisions] Article 36 of the *Tort Law of the People's Republic of China*

[Basic Facts]

The Plaintiff Weihai Jiayikao Home Appliances Co., Ltd. ("Jiayikao Company") alleged that: without its licensing, Yongkang Jinshide Industry and Trade Co., Ltd. ("Jinshide Company") publicized and sold products infringing its patent (No. ZL200980000002.8) on Tmall and other network platforms, which constituted patent infringement; under the circumstance where Jiayikao Company filed a complaint against Jinshide Company for infringement, Zhejiang Tmall Network Co., Ltd. ("Tmall Company") failed to take any effective measures and it shall jointly assume the infringement liability with Jinshide Company. Jiayikao Company requested the court to order that, 1. Jinshide Company immediately cease the sale of the alleged infringing products; 2. Jinshide Company immediately destroy the alleged infringing products in stock; 3. Tmall Company delete all links to the alleged infringing products on Tmall; 4. Jinshide Company and Tmall Company jointly and severally compensate Jiayikao Company RMB 500,000; and 5. the litigation fee of this case be assumed by Jinshide Company and Tmall Company.

Jinshide Company contended that: it was just a seller, not a producer and the amount of compensation claimed by Jiayikao Company was excessive.

Tmall Company contended that: (1) as a trading platform, it was not the key operator engaged in the production or sale of the alleged infringing products or the seller of such products; (2) whether the products involved infringed upon the patent involved was uncertain; (3) whether the products involved were first to be used was also uncertain; (4) where evidence failed to prove that it was the infringing party, it lacked factual and legal basis for it to be jointly and severally liable for compensation of RMB 500,000; further, it has deleted the links to the products involved, and the claim of Jiayikao Company that all links to the infringing products shall be deleted was untenable.

After a trial, the court found that: on January 16, 2009, Jiayikao Company and its legal representative Li Jinxi jointly applied for a patent for invention for a product titled "infrared heating and cooking appliance" to the State Intellectual Property Office; on November 5, 2014, Jiayikao Company was granted the patent (No. ZL200980000002.8). It was recorded in the claims of the patent for invention that: "1. An infrared heating and cooking appliance, which has the following features: this infrared heating and cooking appliance includes: a bracket, in the upper central part, there is an axle hole and on one side, there is a switch for controlling power supply; a rotating disk that is heated once under infrared radiation, serving as a disc-shaped round container for containing food, and there is a removable ledge in the lower central part that may be inserted into the aforesaid axle hole; a holder, which is a longitudinal appliance on one side of the aforesaid bracket; a part of infrared radiation, which is located in the upper end of the aforesaid holder and once powered, it will launch infrared radiation to the aforesaid rotating disk; an oil drip pan, which is located in the aforesaid bracket and can be pulled out from the inner side; and axial oil outlets on the ledge of the aforesaid rotating disk." On January 26, 2015, the patentee of the patent for invention involved was changed to Jiayikao Company. The annual fee of the patent involved has been paid to January 15, 2016.

On January 29, 2015, Beijing Shangzhuan Law Firm, the agency engaged by Jiayikao Company, filed an application for evidence preservation notarization with Beijing Haicheng Notarial Public Office. Under the supervision of the Notarial Public Office, the agents Wang Yongxian and Shi Yin logged onto the website of Tmall (http://www.tmall.com), bought a 3D BBQ grill at a price of RMB 388 from an online shop "Yixinkang Flagship Store," and copied the business license of the operator of this online shop. On February 4 of the same year, under the supervision of the Notarial Public Office, Shi Yin received an express package with the addresser being "Yixinkang Flagship Store," which included a 3D BBQ grill packaged in Korean, a gift, a hand-written receipt, and instructions and warranty card in Chinese. The notary notarized the whole process of evidence preservation and issued the notarial deed ((2015) JHCNMZZ No. 01494). On February 10 of the same year, Jiayikao Company entrusted Zhang Yijun, a person not involved in the case, with uploading complaint materials including the analysis report on patent infringement and the form of comparisons on technical features, to the intellectual property right protection platform of Taobao, but Taobao did not approve such materials finally. On May 5 of the same year, Tmall Company filed an application with Qiantang Notary Public Office of Hangzhou City, Zhejiang Province for evidence preservation notarization. Under the supervision of the Notary Public Office, its agent Diao Manli logged onto the website of Tmall (http://www.tmall.com) and searched "Yixinkang 3D BBQ Grill; Korean Household; Non-stick Electric Oven; Smoke-free BBQ Machine; Electric Baking Pan; Teppanyaki; Oven" in the "Yixinkang Flagship Store." No commodity satisfying the conditions was available. The notary notarized the whole process of evidence preservation and issued the notarial deed ((2015) ZHQZNZ No. 10879).

In the court trial of the first instance, Jiayikao Company claimed that Claim 1 in the patent involved shall be considered as the scope of protection in this case. After comparing the alleged infringing product with Claim 1 of the patent involved, Jiayikao Company held that, all technical features of the alleged infringing product fell within the scope of protection recorded in Claim 1 of the patent involved, except for the location of the switch, which may be changed by an ordinary technician in the field without any creative work and shall be considered as equivalent to that recorded in Claim 1. The two Defendants in the first trial raised no objection to the result of the comparison. Moreover, the court found that, Jiayikao Company paid notarization fee of RMB 4,000 and service charge of RMB 81,000 for this case.

 Holding

Jinhua Intermediate People's Court of Zhejiang Province entered a civil judgment ((2015) ZJZMCZ No. 148) on August 12, 2015 as follows: "I. Jinshide Company shall immediately cease the sale of the products infringing the patent (No. ZL200980000002.8); II. Jinshide Company shall compensate Jiayikao Company RMB 150,000 for its economic loss (including reasonable expenses paid by Jiayikao Company for stopping infringement) within ten days after the Judgment takes effects; III. Tmall Company shall bear joint liability for RMB 50,000 of the amount that Jinshide Company shall compensate as mentioned above; IV. Other claims of Jiayikao Company are rejected." Tmall Company refused to accept the judgment made in the first trial and filed an appeal. However, Zhejiang Higher People's Court entered a civil judgment ((2015) ZZZZ No. 186) on November 17, 2015, rejecting the appeal and affirming the original judgment.

[Reasoning]

According to the effective judgment of the court, since the parties to this case raised no objection to the fact that the features of the alleged infringing product fell within the scope of protection recorded in Claim 1 of the patent involved of Jiayikao Company, the original judgment that the behavior of Jinshide constituted patent infringement was correct. As for whether the behavior of Tmall Company shall constitute joint infringement, according to Clause 2, Article 36 of the Tort Law of the People's Republic of China, where after a network user commits an infringing act by using network services, the victim of infringement shall have the right to send a notice to the network service provider and requires the network service provider to take necessary measures, including but not limited to deletion, block, and disconnection of the links. If, after being notified, the network service provider fails to take necessary measures in a timely manner, it shall be jointly and severally liable for any additional harm with the network user. The above provisions regulate the circumstances where the obligee sends a "notice" to the network service provider and requires the network service provider to take necessary measures after it finds that a network user commits an infringing act by using network services so as to prevent additional damage and specifically specify the scope of obligations and the composition of liabilities that the network service provider shall assume under such circumstances. In this case, whether the behavior of Tmall Company shall constitute an infringement shall be determined based on several factors such as the nature of Tmall Company, the effectiveness of the "notice" sent by Jiayikao Company, whether Tmall Company shall take measures upon receipt of the "notice" from Jiayikao Company, and the necessity and timeliness of the measures taken.

Firstly, Tmall Company holds the Value-added Telecommunication Services License by law and is a network service provider on an information publishing platform. In this case, it provides network services for "Yixinkang Flagship Store" operated by Jinshide Company to sell the alleged infringing product involved and satisfies the requirements for a network service provider as specified in paragraph 2, Article 36 of the Tort Law of the People's Republic of China.

Secondly, Tmall confirmed in the court trial of second instance that, on February 10, 2015, Jiayikao Company entrusted Zhang Yijun, a person not involved in this case, with uploading complaint materials including the links to the product complained, the analysis report on patent infringement and the form of comparisons on technical features, to the intellectual property right protection platform of Taobao, and Tmall Company could find out which product was complained about and who the complaint was reported against based on such materials.

The determination of whether the network service provider is at fault and whether the network service provider shall be jointly and severally liable for additional damages caused by the infringement shall be based on the "notice" referred to in Clause 2, Article 36 of the Tort Law of the

People's Republic of China. "Notice" refers to a notice sent by the victim of infringement after a network user commits an infringing act by using network services to require the network service provider to take necessary measures and prevent further infringement. The "notice" may be oral or written. Generally, the "notice" shall include materials such as the identity of the obligee, the ownership certificate, the preliminary evidence of the infringement fact, and the website of the alleged infringing party. If a notice satisfies the above requirements, it shall be deemed effective and valid. The notice sent by Jiayikao Company complies with the requirements for the "notice" as specified in the Tort Law and shall be deemed valid and effective.

Thirdly, upon investigation, Tmall did not approve complaint materials of Jiayikao Company and gave the following reasons for such disapproval in the reply: please detail the technical features of the product involved that are covered by your patent in the Analysis and Comparison Sheet on the Infringement upon the Patent for Utility Model and Invention (II); a combination of pictures and text is recommended. (Note: the comparison shall be made with pictures and text in the commodity information published by the seller). You also need to provide the purchase order number or the user name of the parties involved.

It is held by the court of second instance that, it is difficult to judge the infringement upon the patent for invention or utility model based on the conditions or written documents, so the obligee generally may only provide the complaint materials such as the identity of the obligee, name and number of the patent, the product in question and the other party, so that the receiver of the complaint can inform the other party. In this case, the complaint materials provided by Jiayikao Company included all the materials above-mentioned. As for comparison and analysis report, on the one hand, Tmall Company believed that it only had limited ability to judge whether the product sold by the seller infringed the patent for invention; one the other hand, it required Jiayikao Company to "detail the technical features of the product involved that are covered by your patent; a combination of pictures and text is recommended". The court held that, considering the huge number of complaints and the complexity of complaints in the internet field, it was reasonable for Tmall to make this request for its own interests and such behavior could help Tmall make preliminary judgment on the nature of the alleged infringement and take measures accordingly. But for the obligee, the above requirements of Tmall Company was not essential for the notice sent by the obligee to be valid and effective. Moreover, Jiayikao Company provided in the complaint materials a five-page form of comparison on technical features including pictures and text but Tmall Company still replied in an inflexible manner and took the comparison on technical features as a reason for disapproval, which was improper. As for the disapproval from Tmall Company and the request of Tmall Company for providing the purchase order number or user name of the parties involved, the court held that, whether Jiayikao Company provided the purchase order number or user name of the parties involved would not affect the validity and effectiveness of the complaint. In addition, the rules of complaint set by Tmall Company shall not be legally binding upon the obligee and the obligee may safeguard its rights in accordance with law and could, for its own interests, decide whether to accept such rules or not. Moreover, the obligee may not purchase the product involved but provide other evidence to prove the alleged infringement such as others' purchase; even the obligee directly purchased the product involved, it may refuse to provide relevant information for the purposes of safeguarding its economic interests or trade secret.

Lastly, necessary measures that shall be taken by a network service provider upon receipt of a notice as prescribed in paragraph 2, Article 36 of the Tort Law of the People's Republic of China include but are not limited to deletion, blockage, and disconnection of the links. "Necessary measures" shall be comprehensively determined according to the nature of the infringed right, the specific infringement circumstances, and the technical conditions.

In this case, after determining that the complaint reported by Jiayikao Company was valid and effective, the court needed to judge whether the handling of complaint materials by Tmall Company was prudent or reasonable. The court held that, this case involved a dispute over infringement upon patent for invention. Considering its subjective judgment on infringement upon patent for invention, the possibility of the complaint being recognized and balance of interests as well as other factors, Tmall Company, as a provider of e-commerce network service platform, was not required to immediately delete or block the product involved after receipt of complaint; the taking of necessary measures against the product involved shall comply with the principle of prudence and rationality so as to prevent the lawful rights and interests of the party complained. However, one of the necessary measures that Tmall Company shall take was transferring effective complaint materials to the party against whom the complaint is filed and requiring it to defend itself. Otherwise the complaint of the obligee would be meaningless and may not be successfully handled. The network service provider shall ensure the smooth exchange of effective complaint information and shall not just leave complaints aside. The party complained will make judgment on whether the products owned, produced or sold by itself infringe upon others' rights and whether it shall voluntarily stop the alleged infringement, and take measures accordingly. However, the party against whom the complaint is filed did not receive any warning due to Tmall Company's failure to perform the above obligations and additional damages were caused. The deletion and blockage of the product involved by Tmall Company after Jiayikao Company filed a lawsuit shall be deemed to be prudent and reasonable. In conclusion, as, after being notified by Jiayikao Company, Tmall Company failed to take necessary measures in a timely manner, it shall, together with Jinshide Company, be jointly and severally liable for any further damages. The grounds of appeal of Tmall Company shall not be established. As for the liability that Tmall Company shall assume, it was not inappropriate for the court of first instance to determine that Tmall shall be jointly and severally liable for paying RMB 50,000, the amount that Jinshide Company is liable for compensation, by taking comprehensive consideration of the duration of the infringement and the time when Tmall Company shall be aware of the infringement.

[Opinion of the Case (Chinese Version)]

Scan the QR code to see the Chinese version of the opinion

第三章 著作权案件

Chapter 3 Copyright Cases

根据同一历史题材创作作品中的必要场景和
有限表达方式不受著作权法保护

—— 张晓燕与雷献和、赵琪、山东爱书人音像图书有限公司
著作权侵权纠纷案

【裁判要旨】

根据同一历史题材创作的作品中的题材主线、整体线索脉络，是社会共同财富，属于思想范畴，不能为个别人垄断，任何人都有权对此类题材加以利用并创作作品。

判断作品是否构成侵权，应当从被诉侵权作品作者是否接触过权利人作品、被诉侵权作品与权利人作品之间是否构成实质相似等方面进行。在判断是否构成实质相似时，应比较作者在作品表达中的取舍、选择、安排、设计等是否相同或相似，不应从思想、情感、创意、对象等方面进行比较。

按照《中华人民共和国著作权法》保护作品的规定，人民法院应保护作者具有独创性的表达，即思想或情感的表现形式。对创意、素材、公有领域信息、创作形式、必要场景，以及具有唯一性或有限性的表达形式，则不予保护。

211

【案　　　　号】 最高人民法院（2013）民申字第 1049 号
【案　　　　由】 著作权纠纷

【合议庭成员】 于晓白 骆 电 李 嵘

【关 键 词】 著作权侵权 影视作品 历史题材 实质相似

【相 关 法 条】《中华人民共和国著作权法》第二条,《中华人民共
和国著作权法实施条例》第二条

【基本案情】

原告张晓燕诉称:其于 1999 年 12 月开始改编创作《高原骑
兵连》剧本,2000 年 8 月根据该剧本筹拍 20 集电视连续剧《高
原骑兵连》(以下将该剧本及其电视剧简称"张剧"),2000 年 12
月该剧摄制完成,张晓燕系该剧著作权人。被告雷献和作为《高
原骑兵连》的名誉制片人参与了该剧的摄制。被告雷献和作为第
一编剧和制片人、被告赵琪作为第二编剧拍摄了电视剧《最后的
骑兵》(以下将该电视剧及其剧本简称"雷剧")。2009 年 7 月 1
日,张晓燕从被告山东爱书人音像图书有限公司购得《最后的骑兵》
DVD 光盘,发现与"张剧"有很多雷同之处,主要人物关系、故
事情节及其他方面相同或近似,"雷剧"对"张剧"剧本及电视剧
构成侵权。故请求法院判令:三被告停止侵权,雷献和在《齐鲁
晚报》上公开发表致歉声明并赔偿张晓燕剧本稿酬损失、剧本出
版发行及改编费损失共计 80 万元。

被告雷献和辩称:"张剧"剧本根据张冠林的长篇小说《雪域
河源》改编而成,"雷剧"最初由雷献和根据师永刚的长篇小说《天
苍茫》改编,后由赵琪参照其小说《骑马挎枪走天涯》重写剧本
定稿。2000 年上半年,张晓燕找到雷献和,提出合拍反映骑兵生
活的电视剧。雷献和向张晓燕介绍了改编《天苍茫》的情况,建
议合拍,张晓燕未同意。2000 年 8 月,雷献和与张晓燕签订了合
作协议,约定拍摄制作由张晓燕负责,雷献和负责军事保障,不

参与艺术创作,雷献和没有看到张晓燕的剧本。"雷剧"和"张剧"创作播出的时间不同,"雷剧"不可能影响"张剧"的发行播出。

法院经审理查明:"张剧""雷剧"、《骑马挎枪走天涯》《天苍茫》,均系以二十世纪八十年代中期精简整编中骑兵部队撤(缩)编为主线展开的军旅、历史题材作品。短篇小说《骑马挎枪走天涯》发表于《解放军文艺》1996 年第 12 期总第 512 期;长篇小说《天苍茫》于 2001 年 4 月由解放军文艺出版社出版发行;"张剧"于 2004 年 5 月 17 日至 5 月 21 日由中央电视台第八套节目在上午时段以每天四集的速度播出;"雷剧"于 2004 年 5 月 19 日至 29 日由中央电视台第一套节目在晚上黄金时段以每天两集的速度播出。

《骑马挎枪走天涯》通过对骑兵连被撤销前后连长、指导员和一匹神骏的战马的描写,叙述了骑兵在历史上的辉煌、骑兵连被撤销、骑兵连官兵特别是骑兵连长对骑兵、战马的痴迷。《骑马挎枪走天涯》存在如下描述:神马(15 号军马)出身来历中透着的神秘、连长与军马的水乳交融、指导员孔越华的人物形象、连长作诗、父亲当过骑兵团长、骑兵在未来战争中发挥的重要作用、连长为保留骑兵连所做的努力、骑兵连最后被撤销、结尾处连长与神马的悲壮。"雷剧"中天马的来历也透着神秘,除了连长常问天的父亲曾为骑兵师长外,上述情节内容与《骑马挎枪走天涯》基本相似。

《天苍茫》是讲述中国军队最后一支骑兵连充满传奇与神秘历史的书,书中展示草原与骑兵的生活,如马与人的情感、最后一匹野马的基因价值,以及研究马语的老人,神秘的预言者,最后的野马在香港赛马场胜出的传奇故事。《天苍茫》中连长成天的父亲是原骑兵师的师长,司令员是山南骑兵连的第一任连长、成天父亲的老部下,成天从小暗恋司令员女儿兰静,指导员王青衣与

213

兰静相爱，并促进成天与基因学者刘可可的爱情。最后连长为救被困沼泽的研究人员牺牲。雷剧中高波将前指导员跑得又快又稳性子好的"大喇嘛"牵来交给常问天作为临时坐骑。结尾连长为完成抓捕任务而牺牲。"雷剧"中有关指导员孔越华与连长常问天之间关系的描述与《天苍茫》中指导员王青衣与连长成天关系的情节内容有相似之处。

　　法院依法委托中国版权保护中心版权鉴定委员会对张剧与雷剧进行鉴定，结论如下：1. 主要人物设置及关系部分相似；2. 主要线索脉络即骑兵部队缩编（撤销）存在相似之处；3. 存在部分相同或者近似的情节，但除一处语言表达基本相同之外，这些情节的具体表达基本不同。语言表达基本相同的情节是指双方作品中男主人公表达"愿做牧马人"的话语情节。"张剧"电视剧第四集秦冬季说："草原为家，以马为伴，做个牧马人"；"雷剧"第十八集常问天说："以草原为家，以马为伴，你看过电影《牧马人》吗？做个自由的牧马人"。

 裁判结果

　　山东省济南市中级人民法院于 2011 年 7 月 13 日作出（2010）济民三初字第 84 号民事判决：驳回张晓燕的全部诉讼请求。张晓燕不服，提起上诉，山东省高级人民法院于 2012 年 6 月 14 日作出（2011）鲁民三终字第 194 号民事判决：驳回上诉，维持原判。张晓燕不服，向最高人民法院申请再审。最高人民法院经审查，于 2014 年 11 月 28 日作出（2013）民申字第 1049 号民事裁定：驳回张晓燕的再审申请。

【裁判理由】

最高人民法院审查认为：本案的争议焦点是"雷剧"的剧本及电视剧是否侵害"张剧"的剧本及电视剧的著作权。

判断作品是否构成侵权，应当从被诉侵权作品的作者是否"接触"过要求保护的权利人作品、被诉侵权作品与权利人的作品之间是否构成"实质相似"两个方面进行判断。本案各方当事人对雷献和接触"张剧"剧本及电视剧并无争议，本案的核心问题在于两部作品是否构成实质相似。

我国著作权法所保护的是作品中作者具有独创性的表达，即思想或情感的表现形式，不包括作品中所反映的思想或情感本身。这里指的思想，包括对物质存在、客观事实、人类情感、思维方法的认识，是被描述、被表现的对象，属于主观范畴。思想者借助物质媒介，将构思诉诸形式表现出来，将意象转化为形象、将抽象转化为具体、将主观转化为客观、将无形转化为有形，为他人感知的过程即为创作，创作形成的有独创性的表达属于受著作权法保护的作品。著作权法保护的表达不仅指文字、色彩、线条等符号的最终形式，当作品的内容被用于体现作者的思想、情感时，内容也属于受著作权法保护的表达，但创意、素材或公有领域的信息、创作形式、必要场景或表达唯一或有限则被排除在著作权法的保护范围之外。必要场景，指选择某一类主题进行创作时，不可避免而必须采取某些事件、角色、布局、场景，这种表现特定主题不可或缺的表达方式不受著作权法保护；表达唯一或有限，指一种思想只有唯一一种或有限的表达形式，这些表达视为思想，也不给予著作权保护。在判断"雷剧"与"张剧"是否构成实质相似时，应比较两部作品中对于思想和情感的表达，将两部作品表达中作者的取舍、选择、安排、设计是否相同或相似，而不是离开表达看思想、情感、创意、对象等其他方面。结合张晓燕的主张，从以下几个方面进行分析判断：

关于张晓燕提出"雷剧"与"张剧"题材主线相同的主张，因"雷剧"与《骑马挎枪走天涯》都通过紧扣"英雄末路、骑兵绝唱"这一主题和情境描述了"最后的骑兵"在撤编前后发生的故事，可以认定"雷剧"题材主线及整体线索脉络来自《骑马挎枪走天涯》。"张剧""雷剧"以及《骑马挎枪走天涯》《天苍茫》4部作品均系以二十世纪八十年代中期精简整编中骑兵部队撤（缩）编为主线展开的军旅历史题材作品，是社会的共同财富，不能为个别人所垄断，故4部作品的作者都有权以自己的方式对此类题材加以利用并创作作品。因此，即便"雷剧"与"张剧"题材主线存在一定的相似性，因题材主线不受著作权法保护，且"雷剧"的题材主线系来自最早发表的《骑马挎枪走天涯》，不能认定"雷剧"抄袭自"张剧"。

关于张晓燕提出"雷剧"与"张剧"人物设置与人物关系相同、相似的主张，鉴于前述4部作品均系以特定历史时期骑兵部队撤（缩）编为主线展开的军旅题材作品，除了《骑马挎枪走天涯》受短篇小说篇幅的限制，没有三角恋爱关系或军民关系外，其他3部作品中都包含三角恋爱关系、官兵上下关系、军民关系等人物设置和人物关系，这样的表现方式属于军旅题材作品不可避免地采取的必要场景，因表达方式有限，不受著作权法保护。

关于张晓燕提出"雷剧"与"张剧"语言表达及故事情节相同、相似的主张，从语言表达看，如"雷剧"中"做个自由的'牧马人'"与"张剧"中"做个牧马人"语言表达基本相同，但该语言表达属于特定语境下的惯常用语，非独创性表达。从故事情节看，用于体现作者的思想与情感的故事情节属于表达的范畴，具有独创性的故事情节应受著作权法保护，但是，故事情节中仅部分元素相同、相似并不能当然得出故事情节相同、相似的结论。前述4部作品相同、相似的部分多属于公有领域素材或缺乏独创性的素材，有的仅为故事情节中的部分元素相同，但情节所展开的具体内容和表达的意义并不相同。二审法院认定"雷剧"与"张剧"6处相同、相似的故事情节，其中老部下关系、临时指定马匹等在《天苍茫》中也有相似的情节内容，其他部分虽在情节设计方面存在相同、相似之处，但有的仅为情节表达中部分元素的相同、相似，情节内容相同、相似的部分少且微不足道。

整体而言，"雷剧"与"张剧"具体情节展开不同、描写的侧重点不同、主人公性格不同、结尾不同，二者相同、相似的故事情节在"雷剧"中所占比例极低，且在整个故事情节中处于次要位置，不构成"雷剧"中的主要部分，不会导致读者和观众对两部作品产生相同、相似的欣赏体验，不能得出两部作品实质相似的结论。根据《最高人民法院关于审理著作权民事纠纷案件适用法律若干问题的解释》第十五条"由不同作者就同一题材创作的作品，作品的表达系独立完成并且有创作性的，应当认定作者各自享有独立著作权"的规定，"雷剧"与"张剧"属于由不同作者就同一题材创作的作品，两剧都有独创性，各自享有独立著作权。

【本案裁判文书】

扫描二维码，可见裁判文书

The Copyright Law Does Not Protect Necessary Scenes and Limited Expression Forms in Original Works Created on Basis of the Same Historical Theme

——Zhang Xiaoyan v. Lei Xianhe, Zhao Qi and Shandong Book Lover Audio-Video and Book Co., Ltd.

[Syllabus]

The theme mainline and the overall sequence of clues in a work created on basis of the same historical theme is the common treasure of the society, which is within the scope of ideas and cannot be monopolized by any individual. Any person has the right to create a work by using such theme.

Whether a work constitutes infringement shall be judged from such aspects as whether the author of the alleged infringing work has come into contact with the work of the copyright holder and whether the alleged infringing work and the work of the copyright holder constitute substantial similarity. In judging whether substantial similarity is constituted, comparisons shall be made on whether the acceptance or rejection, choices, arrangements, and designs in the works are identical or similar rather than comparisons in ideas, emotions, originality, objects, etc.

In accordance with provisions of the Copyright Law of the People's

Republic of China on protection of works, the people's court shall protect the author's expressions with originality, namely, expression forms of ideas or emotions. Creative ideas, materials, information in public domains, creation forms, necessary scenes as well as unique or limited expression forms shall not be protected.

[Case No.] Supreme People's Court (2013) MSZ No. 1049

[Cause of Action] Copyright dispute

[Collegial Panel Members] Yu Xiaobai　Luo Dian　Li Rong

[Keywords] Copyright infringement, film and TV works, historical themes, substantial similarity

[Relevant Legal Provisions] Article 2 of *Copyright Law of the People's Republic of China*, Article 2 of *Regulations on the Implementation of the Copyright Law of the People's Republic of China*

[Basic Facts]

Plaintiff Zhang Xiaoyan alleged that: she began to produce and adapt the script of '高原骑兵连' in December 1999. In August 2000, a 20-episode TV series named '高原骑兵连' (the script and the TV play are hereinafter referred to as the 'TV Play of Miss Zhang') was prepared to shoot, and completed in December 2000. Zhang Xiaoyan was the copyright holder of such TV series. Defendant Lei Xianhe participated in the production of the TV series as the honorary producer of '高原骑兵连'. Defendant Lei Xianhe as the first scriptwriter and producer, and Defendant Zhao Qi as the second scriptwriter, shot the TV series of '最后的骑兵' (the TV play and the script thereto are hereinafter referred to as the 'TV Play of Mr. Lei'). On July 1, 2009, Zhang Xiaoyan bought the DVD of '最后的骑兵' from Defendant Shandong Book Lover Audio-Video and Book Co., Ltd., and found that '最后的骑兵' was same as or similar to the 'TV Play of Miss Zhang' in terms of relationship of main characters and story line and other aspects, therefore, the 'TV Play of Mr. Lei' infringed the script and TV play of 'TV Play of Miss Zhang'. She therefore applied to the court requesting to order: the three Defendants stop infringement, and Lei Xianhe make a public statement of apology in *Qilu Evening News,* and compensate Zhang Xiaoyan for her losses of script remunerations, publication and distribution as well as adaptation of script, i.e. RMB 800,000 in total.

Defendant Lei Xianhe argued that: the script of the 'TV Play of Miss Zhang' was adapted from the full-length novel of Zhang Guanlin ' 雪域 河源 ', but the 'TV Play of Mr. Lei' was first adapted by Lei Xianhe on basis of Shi Yonggang's full-length novel ' 天苍茫 ' and rewritten by Zhao Qi on basis of ' 骑马挎枪走天涯 '. In the first half of 2000, Zhang Xiaoyan proposed to make a TV play reflecting the life of cavalry with Lei Xianhe. Lei Xianhe introduced the adaption of ' 天苍 茫 ' to Zhang Xiaoyan, and proposed to make the film together, but Zhang Xiaoyan refused. In August 2000, Lei Xianhe and Zhang Xiaoyan signed a cooperative agreement, pursuant to which Zhang Xiaoyan is in the charge of the shooting, and Lei Xianhe is responsible for the military security, but does not participate in the artistic creation. Lei Xianhedid not see the script of Zhang Xiaoyan. As the 'TV Play of Mr. Lei' was created and broadcast in different time with the 'TV Play of Miss Zhang', the 'TV Play of Mr. Lei' was unlikely to affect the creation and broadcast of the 'TV Play of Miss Zhang'.

It was found by the court through investigation that: 'TV Play of Miss Zhang', 'TV Play of Mr. Lei', ' 骑马挎枪走天涯 ', and ' 天苍茫 ' were four works that are on military and historical subject matters and take the demobilization (or reduction) of cavalry units during the military "streamlining and reorganization" of the mid-1980s as their main line. The short story ' 骑马挎枪走天涯 ' was published in Issue 512 of *Literature and Art of the People's Liberation Army* (Issue 12, 1996);

the full-length novel ' 天苍茫 ' was published by the Liberation Army Art Press in April 2001; the 'TV Play of Miss Zhang' was broadcast on CCTV-8 in the morning from May 17, 2004 to May 21, 2004, with four episodes a day; the 'TV Play of Mr. Lei' was broadcast on CCTV-1 in the evening prime time during May 19-29, 2004, with two episodes a day.

' 骑马挎枪走天涯 ' describes the bright moment of cavalry in history, withdrawal of the cavalry and obsession of cavalry soldiers (especially the company commander) with cavalry and war horse through the description of the company commander, instructor and a strong war horse before and after withdrawal of the cavalry. ' 骑马挎枪走天涯 ' includes the following descriptions: the war horse (War Horse No. 15) has a mysterious family background and origin, the company commander and the war horse get along with each other in harmony, the personalities of the instructor Kong Yuehua, the company commander makes poems, father of the company commander was the regiment commander of cavalry, the cavalry plays an important role in the future war, the company commander makes great efforts to retain the squadron of cavalry, the squadron of cavalry is withdrawn at last and the solemnity of the company commander and war horse at the end of the novel. In the 'TV Play of Mr. Lei', the horse is also mysterious, and except that the father of Chang Wentian, the company commander, was a division commander, the 'TV Play of Mr. Lei' is basically the same as " 骑马挎枪走天涯 " in terms of the aforesaid plots and contents.

' 天苍茫 ' is a book of the legendary and mysterious history of the last squadron of cavalry of Chinese army, describing the lives in prairie and lives of cavalry, such as the emotions between horse and human, the value of the genes of the last wild horse, the elder studying horse language and the mysterious prophet, telling a story that the last wild horse won the game in the race course of Hong Kong. In '天苍茫', father of the company commander Cheng Tian was the division commander of cavalry, and the region commander was the first company commander of Shannan Squadron of Cavalry and a former subordinate of Cheng Tian's father. Cheng Tian secretly fell in love with the region commander's daughter Lan Jing when he was young, but the instructor Wang Qingyi was in love with Lan Jing, and he helped the romance between Cheng Tian and Liu Keke, a genetics researcher. At last, the company commander sacrificed for saving the researchers trapped in marsh. In the 'TV Play of Mr. Lei', Gao Bo leads the horse "Da Lama" of former instructor, which runs fast and steady and has a good temper, to Chang Wentian for his use temporarily. In the end, the company commander sacrifices for completing the arresting task. The descriptions on the relation between the instruction Kong Yuehua and the company commander Chang Wentian in the 'TV Play of Mr. Lei' are similar to those on the relation between instruction Wang Qingyi and the company commander Cheng Tian in '天苍茫'.

The court entrusted the Copyright Identification Commission of the Copyright Protection Center of China to legally identify the 'TV Play of Miss Zhang' and the 'TV Play of Mr. Lei', and concludes that: 1. the two TV Plays are similar in their setting and relations of main characters; 2. the main line, i.e. withdrawing (downsizing) the cavalry unit are similar; 3. the two TV Plays are same or similar in some plots, but they are different in specific language expressions except one is basically the same. The plot point with a basically identical verbal expression refers to the statement, made by the male lead of each work, that he is "willing to be a herdsman". In the 4th episode of the TV series of the 'TV Play of Miss Zhang', Qin Dongji says: "The green-land is my home, treat my horse as my partner, I want to be a herdsman." In the 18th episode of the 'TV Play of Mr. Lei', Chang Wentian says: "I treat the green-land as my home and my horse as my partner. Have you seen the film *The Herdsman*? I want to be a free herdsman."

Holding

On July 13, 2011, the Intermediate People's Court of Jinan Municipality, Shandong Province, rendered the Civil Judgment (2010) JMSCZ No. 84 rejecting all claims of Zhang Xiaoyan's. Unconvinced, Zhang Xiaoyan appealed. On June 14, 2012, the Higher People's Court of Shandong Province rendered the Civil Judgment (2011) LMSZZ No. 194 rejecting the appeal and affirming the original judgment. Unconvinced, Zhang Xiaoyan applied to the Supreme People's Court for a retrial. On November 28, 2014, the Supreme People's Court, after review, rendered the Civil Ruling (2013) MSZ No. 1049 rejecting Zhang Xiaoyan's application for a retrial.

[Reasoning]

After trial, the Supreme People's Court holds that: the focal point of the dispute in this Case is whether the script and television series of the 'TV Play of Mr. Lei' infringed upon the copyrights associated with the script and television series of the 'TV Play of Miss Zhang'.

A judgment as to whether a work constitutes an infringement of copyright should be made from two aspects: whether the author of the allegedly infringing work has ever been "exposed" to the work of the copyright holder who demands protection and whether there is any "substantive similarity" between the allegedly infringing work and the copyright holder's work. None of the parties in this Case disputes the fact that Lei Xianhe has been exposed to the script and television series of the 'TV Play of Miss Zhang'. The key question of this Case is whether there is any "substantive similarity" between the two works.

The Copyright Law of China protects the expressions of an author, in a work, that have originality, i.e., forms of showing the author's thoughts or emotions. The protection does not cover the thoughts or emotions themselves reflected in the work. Thoughts, as referred to here, include understandings of material existence, objective facts, human emotions, and thinking methods. Thoughts are objects that a person describes and shows and they fall within the ambit of subjectivity. Creation is a process that can be perceived by others and during which thinkers, by means of material media, show ideas by recourse to forms, convert imagery to images, and convert something abstract, subjective, or intangible to something concrete, objective, or tangible. Expressions which are formed by creation and which have originality are a type of work protected by the Copyright Law. Expressions protected by the Copyright Law do not merely refer to the text, color, lines, and symbols of the final form of a work. When the content of a work is used to manifest the author's thoughts and emotions, the content is also a type of expression protected by the Copyright Law. However, creative ideas, source material, or public domain information as well as forms of creation, necessary scenes, or expressions that are unique or limited are excluded from the scope of protection of the Copyright Law. Necessary scenes refer to certain events, roles, layouts, and scenes that are inevitable and must be used when a certain theme is selected for creation. Such indispensable ways of giving expression to a particular theme are not protected by the Copyright Law. The term "expressions that are unique or limited" refers to instances where there are unique or limited forms of expression for a certain thought. These expressions are deemed as thoughts and are also not provided with copyright protection. When judging whether there is any substantive similarity between the 'TV Play of Mr. Lei' and the 'TV Play of Miss Zhang', comparisons shall be made with respect to the expressions of thoughts and emotions in two works, whether or not the authors' choices, selections, arrangements, and designs, as expressed in the works are same or similar, rather than departing from expressions to look at other aspects, such as thoughts, emotions, creative ideas, objects, etc. The analysis and judgment are made on basis of the following aspects, in combination with Zhang Xiaoyan's claims:

Concerning the claim made by Zhang Xiaoyan that the main line of the subject matter in the 'TV Play of Mr. Lei' and that in the 'TV Play of Miss Zhang' are the same. Because both the 'TV Play of Mr. Lei' and '骑马挎枪走天涯', by closely following the theme and situation about "a hero's dead end, a cavalryman's swan song", describe stories about "the last cavalryman" before and after demobilization, it can be determined that the main line of the subject matter as well as the overall thread and sequence of ideas in the 'TV Play of Mr. Lei' are from '骑马挎枪走天涯'. The 'TV Play of Miss Zhang', the 'TV Play of Mr. Lei', '骑马挎枪走天涯' and '天苍茫' are four works that are on military and historical subject matters and take the demobilization (or reduction) of cavalry units during the military "streamlining and reorganization" of the mid-1980s as their main line. This main line is common wealth of society and cannot be monopolized by individuals. Therefore, the authors of these four works have the right to use, in their own ways, such historical subject matter and to create works based on it. Consequently, even if there are some similarities between the main line of the subject matter in the 'TV Play of Mr. Lei' and [that in] the 'TV Play of Miss Zhang', because the main line of the subject matter is not protected by the Copyright Law, and the main line of the subject matter in the 'TV Play of Mr. Lei' is from '骑马挎枪走天涯', which was the earliest of the works published, the court could not determine that the 'TV Play of Mr. Lei' was copied from the 'TV Play of Miss Zhang'.

225

Concerning the claim made by Zhang Xiaoyan that the setups of the main characters and their relationships in the 'TV Play of Mr. Lei' and 'TV Play of Miss Zhang' are the same or similar. The aforementioned four works are all on military subject matters and take the demobilization (or reduction) of cavalry units during a certain historical period as their main line. Except for '骑马挎

枪走天涯 ', which is limited by the length of short fiction and, thus, does not include any triangular love relationship or relationship between the military and civilians, the other three works all cover such setups of the main characters and their relationships as the triangular love relationships, the superior-inferior relationships between officials and soldiers, and the relationship between the military and civilians. These ways of depicting this subject matter involve necessary scenes that are inevitable and must be used in a work about the military subject matter. Because the ways of giving expression to this subject matter are limited, they are not protected by the Copyright Law.

Concerning the claim made by Zhang Xiaoyan that the verbal expressions and the plots of the stories in the 'TV Play of Mr. Lei' and the 'TV Play of Miss Zhang' are the same or similar. Looking at verbal expressions, for example, the verbal expressions "be a free herdsman" and "be a herdsman" used in the 'TV Play of Mr. Lei' and 'TV Play of Miss Zhang', respectively, are basically the same. However, these verbal expressions are a type of phrase customarily used in a specific context; they are not original expressions. From the plots of the stories, a story plot that is used to manifest an author's thoughts and emotions falls within the ambit of expressions. A story plot that has originality should be protected by the Copyright Law. However, if only some elements of the plots of the stories are the same or similar, one cannot necessarily draw the conclusion that the plots of the stories are the same or similar. The parts of the aforementioned four works that are the same or similar are mostly a type of public domain source material or source material that lacks originality. In some of these parts, only some elements in the plots of stories are the same, but the specific contents and the meanings expressed by these elements as unfolded by the plots are not the same. The second-instance court determined that six points of the plots in the 'TV Play of Mr. Lei' and 'TV Play of Miss Zhang' are the same or similar. Among these points are those about the relationship with a former subordinate, about assigning a temporary mount, etc., and similar plot content also appears in ' 天 苍 茫 '. Although the plot design in other parts of the two series is same or similar, some of these merely show that a few elements used in the expression of the plots are the same or similar. The parts of the two series with the same or similar plot content are few and insignificant.

Generally speaking, in the 'TV Play of Mr. Lei' and the 'TV Play of Miss Zhang', the specific unfolding is different, the focuses of depiction are different, the personalities of the lead characters are different, and the endings are different. The plots of the two series that are the same or similar only take an extremely low proportion in the 'TV Play of Mr. Lei' and are of secondary importance in its entire story plot. They do not constitute the main parts of the 'TV Play of Mr. Lei' and will not cause the readers and viewers to have the same or similar experiences in appreciating the two works. Therefore, one cannot draw the conclusion that the two works have any substantive similarity. Article 15 of the *Interpretation of the Supreme People's Court on Several Issues Concerning the Application of Law in the Adjudication of Copyright Civil Disputes* provides: where works on the same subject matter are created by different authors and the expression of each work is completed independently and has creativity, a people's court should determine that each author enjoys independent copyrights. The 'TV Play of Mr. Lei' and the 'TV Play of Miss Zhang' are works on the same subject matter created independently by different authors. Accordingly, the two series have originality and each author enjoyed independent copyright.

[Opinion of the Case (Chinese Version)]

Scan the QR code to see the Chinese version of the opinion

民间文学艺术衍生作品的表达系独立完成
且有创作性的部分受著作权法保护

——洪福远、邓春香与贵州五福坊食品有限公司、贵州今彩民族文化研发有限公司著作权侵权纠纷案

【裁判要旨】

　　民间文学艺术衍生作品的表达系独立完成且有创作性的部分，符合著作权法保护的作品特征的，应当认定作者对其独创性部分享有著作权。

【案　　　号】	贵州省贵阳市中级人民法院（2015）筑知民初字第17号
【案　　　由】	著作权侵权纠纷
【合议庭成员】	唐有临　刘永菊　袁波文
【关　键　词】	著作权侵权　民间文化艺术衍生作品　独创性
【相 关 法 条】	《中华人民共和国著作权法》第三条，《中华人民共和国著作权法实施条例》第二条

【基本案情】

　　原告洪福远、邓春香诉称：原告洪福远创作完成的《和谐共生十二》作品，发表在 2009 年 8 月贵州人民出版社出版的《福远

蜡染艺术》一书中。洪福远曾将该涉案作品的使用权（蜡染上使用除外）转让给原告邓春香，由邓春香维护著作财产权。被告贵州五福坊食品有限公司（以下简称五福坊公司）以促销为目的，擅自在其销售的商品上裁切性地使用了洪福远的上述画作。原告认为被告侵犯了洪福远的署名权和邓春香的著作财产权，请求法院判令：被告就侵犯著作财产权赔偿邓春香经济损失 20 万元；被告停止使用涉案图案，销毁涉案包装盒及产品册页；被告就侵犯洪福远著作人身权刊登声明赔礼道歉。

被告五福坊公司辩称：第一，原告起诉其拥有著作权的作品与贵州今彩民族文化研发有限公司（以下简称今彩公司）为五福坊公司设计的产品外包装上的部分图案，均借鉴了贵州黄平革家传统蜡染图案，被告使用今彩公司设计的产品外包装不构成侵权；第二，五福坊公司的产品外包装是委托本案第三人今彩公司设计的，五福坊公司在使用产品外包装时已尽到合理注意义务；第三，本案所涉作品在产品包装中位于右下角，整个作品面积只占产品外包装面积的二十分之一左右，对于产品销售的促进作用影响较小，原告起诉的赔偿数额 20 万元显然过高。原告的诉请没有事实和法律依据，故请求驳回原告的诉讼请求。

第三人今彩公司述称：其为五福坊公司进行广告设计、策划，2006 年 12 月创作完成"四季如意"的手绘原稿，直到 2011 年 10 月五福坊公司开发针对旅游市场的礼品，才重新截取该图案的一部分使用，图中的鸟纹、如意纹、铜鼓纹均源于贵州黄平革家蜡染的"原形"，原告作品中的鸟纹图案也源于贵州传统蜡染，原告方主张的作品不具有独创性，本案不存在侵权的事实基础，故原告的诉请不应支持。

法院经审理查明：原告洪福远从事蜡染艺术设计创作多年，

先后被文化部授予"中国十大民间艺术家""非物质文化遗产保护工作先进个人"等荣誉称号。2009 年 8 月其创作完成的《和谐共生十二》作品发表在贵州人民出版社出版的《福远蜡染艺术》一书中，该作品借鉴了传统蜡染艺术的自然纹样和几何纹样的特征，色彩以靛蓝为主，描绘了一幅花、鸟共生的和谐图景。但该作品对鸟的外形进行了补充，对鸟的眼睛、嘴巴丰富了线条，使得鸟图形更加传神，对鸟的脖子、羽毛融入了作者个人的独创，使得鸟图形更为生动，对中间的铜鼓纹花也融合了作者自己的构思而有别于传统的蜡染艺术图案。2010 年 8 月 1 日，原告洪福远与原告邓春香签订《作品使用权转让合同》，合同约定洪福远将涉案作品的使用权（蜡染上使用除外）转让给邓春香，由邓春香维护受让权利范围内的著作财产权。

被告五福坊公司委托第三人今彩公司进行产品的品牌市场形象策划设计服务，包括进行产品包装及配套设计、产品手册以及促销宣传品的设计等。根据第三人今彩公司的设计服务，五福坊公司在其生产销售的产品贵州辣子鸡、贵州小米渣、贵州猪肉干的外包装礼盒的左上角、右下角使用了蜡染花鸟图案和如意图案边框。洪福远认为五福坊公司使用了其创作的《和谐共生十二》作品，一方面侵犯了洪福远的署名权，割裂了作者与作品的联系，另一方面侵犯了邓春香的著作财产权。经比对查明，五福坊公司生产销售的上述三种产品外包装礼盒和产品手册上使用的蜡染花鸟图案与洪福远创作的《和谐共生十二》作品，在鸟与花图形的结构造型、线条的取舍与排列上一致，只是图案的底色和线条的颜色存在差别。

　　贵州省贵阳市中级人民法院于 2015 年 9 月 18 日作出（2015）
筑知民初字第 17 号民事判决：1. 被告贵州五福坊食品有限公司于
本判决生效之日起 10 日赔偿原告邓春香经济损失 10 万元；2. 被告
贵州五福坊食品有限公司在本判决生效后，立即停止使用涉案《和谐
共生十二》作品；3. 被告贵州五福坊食品有限公司于本判决生效之
日起 5 日内销毁涉案产品贵州辣子鸡、贵州小米渣、贵州猪肉干的包
装盒及产品宣传册页；4. 驳回原告洪福远和邓春香的其余诉讼请求。
一审宣判后，各方当事人均未上诉，判决已发生法律效力。

【裁判理由】

　　法院生效裁判认为：本案的争议焦点一是本案所涉《和谐共
生十二》作品是否受《中华人民共和国著作权法》保护；二是案
涉产品的包装图案是否侵犯原告的著作权；三是如何确定本案的
责任主体；四是本案的侵权责任方式如何判定；五是本案的赔偿
数额如何确定。

　　关于第一个争议焦点。本案所涉原告洪福远的《和谐共生
十二》画作中两只鸟尾部重合，中间采用铜鼓纹花连接而展示对
称的美感，而这些正是传统蜡染艺术的自然纹样和几何纹样的主
题特征，根据本案现有证据，可以认定涉案作品显然借鉴了传统
蜡染艺术的表达方式，创作灵感直接来源于黄平革家蜡染背扇图
案。但涉案作品对鸟的外形进行了补充，对鸟的眼睛、嘴巴丰富
了线条，对鸟的脖子、羽毛融入了作者个人的独创，使得鸟图形
更为传神生动，对中间的铜鼓纹花也融合了作者的构思而有别于
传统的蜡染艺术图案。根据《中华人民共和国著作权法实施条例》

第二条"著作权法所称作品，是指文学、艺术和科学领域内具有独创性并能以某种有形形式复制的智力成果"的规定，本案所涉原告洪福远创作的《和谐共生十二》画作属于传统蜡染艺术作品的衍生作品，是对传统蜡染艺术作品的传承与创新，符合《中华人民共和国著作权法》保护的作品特征，在洪福远具有独创性的范围内受著作权法的保护。

关于第二个争议焦点。根据《中华人民共和国著作权法实施条例》第四条第（九）项"美术作品，是指绘画、书法、雕塑等以线条、色彩或者其他方式构成的有审美意义的平面或者立体的造型艺术作品"的规定，绘画作品主要是以线条、色彩等方式构成的有审美意义的平面造型艺术作品。经过庭审比对，本案所涉产品贵州辣子鸡等包装礼盒和产品手册中使用的花鸟图案与涉案《和谐共生十二》画作，在鸟与花图形的结构造型、线条的取舍与排列上一致，只是图案的底色和线条的颜色存在差别，就比对的效果来看图案的底色和线条的颜色差别已然成为侵权的掩饰手段而已，并非独创性的智力劳动；第三人今彩公司主张其设计、使用在五福坊公司产品包装礼盒和产品手册中的作品创作于 2006 年，但其没有提交任何证据可以佐证，而洪福远的涉案作品于 2009 年发表在《福远蜡染艺术》一书中，且书中画作直接注明了作品创作日期为 2003 年，由此可以认定洪福远的涉案作品创作并发表在先。在五福坊公司生产、销售涉案产品之前，洪福远即发表了涉案《和谐共生十二》作品，五福坊公司有机会接触到原告的作品。据此，可以认定第三人今彩公司有抄袭洪福远涉案作品的故意，五福坊公司在生产、销售涉案产品包装礼盒和产品手册中部分使用原告的作品，侵犯了原告对涉案绘画美术作品的复制权。

关于第三个争议焦点。庭前准备过程中，经法院向洪福远释明是否追加今彩公司为被告参加诉讼，是否需要变更诉讼请求，原告以书面形式表示不同意追加今彩公司为被告，并认为五福坊公司与今彩公司属于另一法律关系，不宜与本案合并审理。事实上，五福坊公司与今彩公司签订了合同书，合同约定被告生产的所有产品的外包装、广告文案、宣传品等皆由今彩公司设计，合同也约定今彩公司提交的设计内容有侵权行为，造成的后果由今彩公司全部承担。但五福坊公司作为产品包装的委托方，并未举证证明其已尽到了合理的注意义务，且也是侵权作品的最终使用者和实际受益者，根据《中华人民共和国著作权法》第四十八条第二款第（一）项"有下列侵权行为的，应当根据情况，承担停止侵害、消除影响、赔礼道歉、赔偿损失等民事责任……（一）未经著作权人许可，复制、发行、表演、放映、广播、汇编、通过信息网络向公众传播其作品的，本法另有规定的除外"，以及《最高人民法院关于审理著作权民事纠纷案件适用法律若干问题的解释》（以下简称《著作权纠纷案件解释》）第十九条、第二十条第二款的规定，五福坊公司依法应承担本案侵权的民事责任。五福坊公司与第三人今彩公司之间属另一法律关系，不属于本案的审理范围，当事人可另行主张解决。

关于第四个争议焦点，根据《中华人民共和国著作权法》第四十七条、第四十八条规定，侵犯著作权或与著作权有关的权利的，应当根据案件的实际情况，承担停止侵害、消除影响、赔礼道歉、赔偿损失等民事责任。本案中，第一，原告方的部分著作人身权和财产权受到侵害，客观上产生相应的经济损失，对于原告方的第一项赔偿损失的请求，依法应当获得相应的支持；第二，无论侵权人有无过错，为防止损失的扩大，责令侵权人立即停止正在实施的侵犯他人著作权的行为，以保护权利人的合法权益，也是法律实施的目的，对于原告方第二项要求被告停止使用涉案图案，销毁涉案包装盒及产品册页的诉请，依法应予支持；第三,五福坊公司事实上并无主观故意，也没有重大过失，只是没有尽到合理的审查义务而基于法律的规定承担侵权责任，洪福远也未举证证明被告侵权行为造成其声誉的损害,故对于洪福远要求五福坊公司在《贵州都市报》综合版面刊登声明赔礼道歉的第三项诉请，不予支持。

关于第五个争议焦点，本案中，原告方并未主张为制止侵权行为所支出的合理费用，也没有举证证明为制止侵权行为所支出的任何费用。庭审中，原告方没有提交任何证据以证明其实际损失的多少，也没有提交任何证据以证明五福坊公司因侵权行为的违法所得。事实上，原告方的实际损失本身难以确定，被告方因侵权行为的违法所得也难以查清。根据《著作权纠纷案件解释》第二十五条第一款、第二款"权利人的实际损失或者侵权人的违法所得无法确定的，人民法院根据当事人的请求或者依职权适用著作权法第四十八条第二款（现为第四十九条第二款）的规定确定赔偿数额。人民法院在确定赔偿数额时，应当考虑作品类型、合理使用费、侵权行为性质、后果等情节综合确定"的规定，结合本案的客观实际，主要考量以下5个方面对侵犯著作权赔偿数额的影响:第一,洪福远的涉案《和谐共生十二》作品属于贵州传统蜡染艺术作品的衍生作品，著作权作品的创作是在传统蜡染艺术作品基础上的传承与创新，涉案作品中鸟图形的轮廓与对称的美感来源于传统艺术作品，作者构思的创新有一定的限度和相对局限的空间；第二，贵州蜡染有一定的区域特征和地理标志意义，以花、鸟、虫、鱼等为创作缘起的蜡染艺术作品在某种意义上属于贵州元素或贵州符号，五福坊公司作为贵州的本土企业，其使用贵州蜡染艺术作品符合民间文学艺术作品作为非物质文化遗产固有的民族性、区域性的基本特征要求；第三，根据洪福远与邓春香签订的《作品使用权转让合同》，洪福远已经将

其创作的涉案《和谐共生十二》作品的使用权（蜡染上使用除外）
转让给邓春香，即涉案作品的大部分著作财产权转让给了传统民间
艺术传承区域外的邓春香，由邓春香维护涉案作品著作财产权，基
于本案著作人身权与财产权的权利主体在传统民间艺术传承区域范
围内外客观分离的状况，传承区域范围内的企业侵权行为产生的后
果与影响并不显著；第四，洪福远几十年来执着于民族蜡染艺术的
探索与追求，在创作中将传统的民族蜡染与中国古典文化有机地揉
和，从而使蜡染艺术升华到一定高度，对区域文化的发展起到一定
的推动作用。尽管涉案作品的大部分著作财产权已经转让给了传统
民间艺术传承区域外的邓春香，但洪福远的创作价值以及其在蜡染
艺术业内的声誉应得到尊重；第五，五福坊公司涉案产品贵州辣子
鸡、贵州小米渣、贵州猪肉干的生产经营规模、销售渠道等应予以
参考，根据五福坊公司提交的五福坊公司与广州卓凡彩色印刷有限
公司的采购合同，尽管上述证据不一定完全客观反映五福坊公司涉
案产品的生产经营状况，但在原告方无任何相反证据的情形下，被
告的证明主张在合理范围内应为法律所允许。综合考量上述因素，
参照贵州省当前的经济发展水平和人们的生活水平，酌情确定由五
福坊公司赔偿邓春香经济损失 10 万元。

【本案裁判文书】

扫描二维码，可见裁判文书

Expressions Independently Created and with Originality in a Derivative Folk Literary and Artistic Work Shall Be Protected by the Copyright Law

——Hong Fuyuan and Deng Chunxiang v. Guizhou Wufufang Food Co., Ltd. and Guizhou Jincai Natural Culture Research & Development Co., Ltd.

[Syllabus]

Where part of a derivative folk literary and artistic work is independently created and has originality, it conforms to the characteristics of a work protected by the Copyright Law, it shall be determined that the author enjoys copyright to such part with originality.

236

[Case No.] Guiyang Intermediate People's Court of Guizhou Province (2015) ZZMCZ No. 17

[Cause of Action] Copyright infringement dispute

[Collegial Panel Members] Tang Youlin   Liu Yongju
Yuan Bowen

[Keywords] Copyright infringement, derivative folk literary and artistic work, originality

[Relevant Legal Provisions] Article 3 of the *Copyright Law of the People's Republic of China* and Article 2 of the *Regulation on*

the Implementation of the Copyright Law of the People's Republic of China

---

[Basic Facts]

Plaintiffs Hong Fuyuan and Deng Chunxiang claimed that: the work created by Hong Fuyuan, *Harmonious Coexistence XII*, was published in the book, *Fuyuan's Batik Arts* published by Guizhou People's Publishing House in August 2009. Hong Fuyuan once transferred the right to use the work involved (excluding the right to use on batik) to the Plaintiff Deng Chunxiang, who was responsible for maintaining the copyright-related property rights. Without permission of Plaintiffs, for the purpose of sales promotion, Defendant Guizhou Wufufang Food Co., Ltd. (hereinafter referred to as "Wufufang Company") used a selective part of the aforesaid painting of Hong Fuyuan on commodities it sold. Plaintiffs believed that Defendant infringed upon the right of signature of Hong Fuyuan and the copyright-related property right of Deng Chunxiang and requested the court to order that: the Defendant pay Deng Chunxiang RMB200,000 as compensation for Deng Chunxiang's economic loss caused by its infringement upon her copyright-related property right; and cease the use of the pattern involved and destroy packaging boxes and product brochures involved; and the Defendant publish a formal apology for its infringement upon Hong Fuyuan's copyright-related personal right.

Defendant Wufufang Company contended that: first, both the work whose copyright was owned by Plaintiffs in the action they filed and some patterns on the exterior packages of products designed by Guizhou Jincai National Cultural Research & Development Co., Ltd. (hereinafter referred to as "Jincai Company") for Wufufang Company used the traditional batik patterns of Gejia People in Huangping County of Guizhou Province and its use of product exterior packages designed by Jincai Company did not constitute an infringement. Second, the exterior packages of Wufufang Company's products were designed by the third party Jincai Company and Wufufang Company has exercised due care when using the exterior packages of such products. Third, the work involved was placed in the right lower corner of the product packages and the area of the work involved accounted for only about 1/20 of the total area of the package, which had little effect of promoting the product sales, and the amount of compensation of RMB200,000 claimed by Plaintiffs was excessively high. Therefore, the claims by Plaintiffs lacked factual and legal basis and Wufufang Company requested the court to dismiss the claims of Plaintiffs.

The third party Jincai Company stated that: it engaged in advertisement design and planning for Wufufang Company, and completed the sketching of "Best Wishes for Four Seasons" in December 2006. The pattern was not used until October 2011 when a part of the pattern was intercepted and used by Wufufang Company in its development of gifts for the tourism market. The bird pattern, Ru-Yi pattern, and copper drum pattern in the design were all originated from the "primary form" of the batik of Gejia People in Huangping County of Guizhou Province, and the design of bird pattern in the work of Hong Fuyuan was also originated from the traditional batik of Guizhou Province. The work of Hong Fuyuan was not original and there was no factual basis for infringement in this case. Therefore, the claims of Plaintiffs should not be upheld.

Upon trial, the court found that: Plaintiff Hong Fuyuan has been engaged in the artistic design and creation of batik for many years and was awarded such honorary titles as "China Top Ten Folk Artists" and "Advanced Individual of Intangible Cultural Heritage Protection" by the Ministry of Culture. The work, *Harmonious Coexistence XII*, he created in August 2009 was published in the book *Fuyuan's Batik Arts* published by Guizhou People's Publishing House. This work used characteristics of natural patterns and geometrical patterns of the traditional batik arts as the reference and indigo as the main color, and described a harmonious picture where flowers and birds coexisted. However, the outlines of birds were supplemented in this work. The lines of the birds' eyes and mouths were enriched, which made the patterns of birds more vivid. The original creation of Hong Fuyuan was integrated into the necks and feathers of birds, which made the patterns of birds livelier. The conception of Hong Fuyuan was also integrated into the copper drum patterns in the middle, which were different from patterns in traditional batik arts. On August 1, 2010, Plaintiff Hong Fuyuan and Plaintiff Deng Chunxiang entered into a *Contract on Transfer of the Right to Use Work*, pursuant to which, Hong Fuyuan transferred the right to use the work involved (excluding the use on batik) to Deng Chunxiang and Deng Chunxiang was responsible for maintaining the property right of the work involved within the scope of rights transferred.

Defendant Wufufang Company authorized the third party Jincai Company to provide planning and design services for the brand market image of products, including the product packaging and packaged design, product brochures, and design of marketing materials. According to the design services provided by the third party Jincai Company, Wufufang Company used the pattern of flowers and birds in batik and the frame of Ru-Yi pattern on the left upper corner and right lower corner of the exterior packages of Guizhou Peppery Chicken, Guizhou Milet Dreg, and Guizhou Dried Pork produced and sold by it. Hong Fuyuan believed that: the use of his work *Harmonious Coexistence XII* by Wufufang Company infringed upon his right of signature, which split the connection between the author and the work, and infringed upon the property right of the work enjoyed by

Deng Chunxiang. It was found upon comparison that the design of flowers and birds in batik used on the exterior packages and product brochures of the aforesaid three products sold by Wufufang Company were consistent with the work *Harmonious Coexistence XII* created by Hong Fuyuan in aspects of the pattern structure of birds and flowers as well as the choice and arrangement of lines, and they were different only in the bottom color of the pattern and the color of lines.

 Holding

On September 18, 2015, the Intermediate People's Court of Guiyang City, Guizhou Province rendered a Civil Judgment (2015) ZZMCZ No. 17 that: I. Defendant Wufufang Company should, within 10 days after the Judgment came into force, pay Plaintiff Deng Chunxiang RMB 100,000 as compensation for her economic loss; II. after the Judgment came into force, Defendant Wufufang Company should immediately cease the use of the work *Harmonious Coexistence XII* involved; III. the Defendant Wufufang Company should, within 5 days after the Judgment came into force, destroy the packages and product brochures of the products involved, including Guizhou Peppery Chicken, Guizhou Milet Dreg, and Guizhou Dried Pork; IV. other claims of Plaintiffs Hong Fuyuan and Deng Chunxiang should be dismissed. After the Judgment of first instance was pronounced, none of the parties appealed and the Judgment has come into force.

[Reasoning]

In the effective judgment, the court held that: the dispute focuses of this Case were (1) whether the work *Harmonious Coexistence XII* involved was protected by the Copyright Law; (2) whether the package patterns of the products involved infringed upon Plaintiffs' copyright; (3) how to determine the responsible parties in this Case; (4) how to determine the infringement liability methods in this Case; and (5) how to determine the amount of compensation in this Case.

For the first dispute focus, the tails of the two birds in the work involved *Harmonious Coexistence XII* created by Hong Fuyuan overlapped each other, and in the middle, copper drum patterns were used as connection to show the beauty of symmetry, reflecting the characteristics of natural patterns and geometrical patterns of the traditional batik arts. Based on existing evidence of this Case, it could be determined that, although the work involved used the expression forms of the traditional batik arts, the creative inspiration directly originated from batik patterns of Gejia People in Huangping County. However, the outlines of birds were supplemented in the work involved. The lines of the birds' eyes and mouths were enriched, and the author integrated his original creation into the necks and feathers of birds, making the patterns of birds more vivid and lively. The conception of Hong Fuyuan was also integrated into the copper drum patterns in the middle, which were different from patterns in traditional batik arts. According to Article 2 of the *Regulation on the Implementation of the Copyright Law*, "The works defined in the Copyright Law refer to original intellectual creations in the domain of literature art and science that are capable of being reproduced in a fixed tangible form." The work involved *Harmonious Coexistence XII* created by Defendant Hong Fuyuan is a derivative work of traditional batik art. It is the inheritance and innovation of traditional batik art, conforms to the characteristics of works protected by the Copyright Law, and therefore is protected by the Copyright Law within the scope of originality by Hong Fuyuan.

241

As to the second dispute focus, according to Article 4(9) of the *Regulations on the Implementation of the Copyright Law*: "Works of fine art are two or three dimensional works created in lines, colors or other medium which, when being viewed, impart esthetic effects, such as paintings, works of calligraphy, sculptures, etc." Painting works are two-dimensional works created in lines, colors, etc. which impart esthetic effects. It was found upon comparison in the trial that the pattern of flowers and birds used on the exterior packages and product brochures of such products as Guizhou Peppery Chicken were consistent with the work *Harmonious Coexistence XII* involved in the pattern structure of birds and flowers as well as the choice and arrangement of lines, and they were different only in the bottom color of the pattern and the color of lines. Based on the results of comparison, the difference in the bottom color of the pattern and the color of lines was only a way to conceal the infringement, not intellectual work with originality. The third party Jincai Company alleged that the works it designed and used on the exterior packages and product brochures sold by Wufufang Company were created in 2006, but it failed to provide any evidence to prove the same. While the works involved were published by Hong Fuyuan in the book *Fuyuan's Batik Arts* in 2009, and it was indicated in the book that the painting was created in 2003. Therefore, it can be determined that Hong Fuyuan's works involved in this case were previously created and published. Before Wufufang Company produced and sold the products involved, Hong Fuyuan had published the work *Harmonious Coexistence XII*, so Wufufang Company was likely to be exposed to the works of the Plaintiff. Accordingly, it can be determined that the third party Jincai Company was intentionally infringing upon Hong Fuyuan's works involved. Partial use by Wufufang Company of the Plaintiff's works on the exterior packages and product brochures when producing and selling the products involved infringed upon the right of reproduction enjoyed by the Plaintiff to the painting works involved.

With reference to the third dispute focus, during the pre-trial preparation, the court asked Hong Fuyuan whether he wanted to add Jincai Company as a Defendant of the litigation, and whether he wanted to change the claims. The Plaintiff refused to add Jincai Company as a Defendant in writing, and believed that Wufufang Company and Jincai Company were of another legal relation, which was improper to be trialed together with this Case. As a matter of fact, Wufufang Company and Jincai Company had signed a contract, pursuant to which the exterior packages, advertising copies and materials of all products produced by the Defendant were designed by Jincai Company, the design contents submitted by Jincai Company were infringing, and the consequences caused thereby should be fully borne by Jincai Company. However, as the client for product packaging, Wufufang Company failed to provide evidence proving that it has exercised due care. Wufufang Company was also the final user and actual beneficiary of the infringing works. Subject to item (1), paragraph 2 of Article 48 of the Copyright Law: "In case of any of the following acts of infringement, the infringer shall, depending on its circumstances, be demanded for such civil liabilities as ceasation of the infringement, elimination of influences, public apology and compensation for loss......(1) Without the license of the copyright owner, to reproduce, distribute, perform, show, broadcast, compile or disseminate to the public through information networks his work, unless this Law provided otherwise". Article 19 and paragraph 2 of Article 20 of the *Interpretation of the Supreme People's Court Concerning the Application of Laws in the Trial of Civil Disputes over Copyright* (hereinafter referred to as the *Interpretation Concerning Civil Disputes over Copyright*), Wufufang Company should legally bear the civil liability for infringement of this Case. Wufufang Company and Jincai Company were of another legal relation, which

243

was not covered by this Case. The parties may make a separate settlement.

As to the fourth dispute focus, according to provisions of Articles 47 and 48 of the Copyright Law, if a copyright or copyright-related right is infringed, depending on facts of the case, the infringer shall be demanded for civil responsibility such as ceasation of the infringement, elimination of effects, public apology and compensation for loss. In this Case, first, the copyright-related personal rights and property rights of the Plaintiffs were infringed, and objectively, economic loss was caused thereby, thus, the first claim of the Plaintiffs for compensation of loss should be upheld by law; second, whether the infringer had fault or not, in order to avoid further loss, the infringer was ordered to immediately cease the behavior of infringing the copyright of others for the purposes of protecting the right holder's legitimate rights and interests and law enforcement, and the court adopted the second claim by the Plaintiffs to require the Defendant to cease the use of the patterns involved and destroy the packing boxes and product brochures involved; third, because there was no subjective intention and gross negligence in Wufufang Company, which is only liable for infringement according to law due to its failure in duly performing the examination duty, and Hong Fuyuan failed to submit evidence proving his reputational damages caused by the Defendants' infringing act, the court rejected the third claim by Hong Fuyuan to require Wufufang Company publish a formal apology in the comprehensive layout of *Guizhou City News*.

For the fifth dispute focus, in this Case, the Plaintiffs did not claim or submit evidence for the reasonable expenses incurred from deterrence of the infringing act. During the trial, the Plaintiffs did not submit evidence proving the amount of actual losses suffered by them and the illegal gains received by Wufufang Company from the infringing act. In fact, it was difficult to determine the actual losses of the Plaintiffs, and the illegal gains received by Wufufang Company from the infringing act. According to paragraphs 1 and 2 of Article 25 of the *Interpretation Concerning Civil Disputes over Copyright*: "In case the actual losses of the copyright owners or the illegal gains of the infringing party cannot be determined, the people's court shall determine the amount of compensations as per request of the parties concerned or provisions in paragaph 2 of Article 48 of the Copyright Law (i.e. the current paragraph 2 of Article 49) at its discretion within its powers. When determining the amount of compensations, the people's court shall comprehensively consider the work type, reasonable use fee, nature of infringing acts, consequences, and other relevant circumstances.", taking consideration of objective facts of this Case, there were 5 main factors to be considered which had an impact on the amount of compensations for infringing copyright: first, the work involved *Harmonious Coexistence XII* created by Hong Fuyuan is a derivative work of traditional batik art in Guizhou Province. The creation of the copyrighted work was the inheritance and innovation of traditional batik art, and the outline of bird patterns and the beauty of symmetry showed in the work involved originated from traditional artistic works. The innovation in the author's work was limited and the room for innovation was also limited; second, batik art in Guizhou Province featured with certain regional characteristics and geographic significance. In a sense, the artistic works in batik created on flowers, birds, insects, fishes, etc. belonged to elements and symbols of Guizhou Province. As a local company in Guizhou Province, Wufufang Company used the artistic works in batik of Guizhou Province in a manner conforming to the basic national and regional characteristics inherent in folk literary art works as intangible cultural heritage; third, according to the *Contract on Transfer of the*

Right to Use the Work signed by and between Hong Fuyuan and Deng Chunxiang, Hong Fuyuan had transferred the right to use the work involved *Harmonious Coexistence XII* created by him (excluding the use on batik) to Deng Chunxiang, i.e. a large part of the copyright-related property rights of the work involved was transferred to Deng Chunxiang, who was not the inheritor of traditional folk art. Deng Chunxiang was responsible for maintaining the copyright-related property rights of the work involved. Because not all the subjects of the copyright-related personal rights and property rights in this Case were inheritors of traditional folk art, the results and consequences of corporate infringements within the scope of inheritance were insignificant; fourth, Hong Fuyuan devoted himself to the exploration and pursuit of national batik art for several decades, and integrated traditional batik art and Chinese ancient culture in his creation, uplifting the batik art to a certain degree and pushing forward the development of regional culture. Although a large part of the copyright-related property rights of the work involved was transferred to Deng Chunxiang, who was not the inheritor of traditional folk art, the creative value of Hong Fuyuan and his reputation in the field of batik art should be respected; fifth, production scale and selling channels of the involved products of Wufufang Company, Guizhou Peppery Chicken, Guizhou Milet Dreg, and Guizhou Dried Pork, should also be considered. Pursuant to the purchase contract between Wufufang Company and Guangzhou Zhuofan Color Printing Co., Ltd. submitted by Wufufang Company, although the afore-said evidence might not fully and objectively reflect the production and operation concerning the products involved of Wufufang Company, the claims of Plaintiffs should be admitted by law to the reasonable extent in absence of any contrary evidence made available by Plaintiffs. Upon comprehensive consideration of the factors above, and based on the current economic development level and living standard of Guizhou Province, a discretional decision was made that Wufufang Company should compensate RMB 100,000 to Deng Chunxiang for her economic loss.

[Opinion of the Case (Chinese Version)]

Scan the QR code to see the Chinese version of the opinion

书信手稿的性质，手稿拍卖
与著作权侵权纠纷案件中的诉前行为保全

——杨季康与中贸圣佳国际拍卖有限公司
书信手稿拍卖诉前行为保全案

【裁判要旨】

私人书信作为人类沟通感情交流思想的载体，通常是写信人独立构思并创作而成的文字作品，在无相反证据的情况下，应认定为写信人创作的作品，应受我国著作权法保护。

收信人可以取得书信手稿的物权，但行使物权时不得侵害写信人的著作权。违背著作权人及其继承人意志公开发表书信手稿构成对作品发表权的侵害。

由于侵害著作人格权的后果将导致作者人格利益与精神受到伤害，其受害状态具有不可逆转性，一般难以通过金钱赔偿等方式完全消弭。此外，发表权是著作权人行使和保护其他权利的基础，一旦作品被非法发表，极易导致权利人对复制、发行等行为难以控制。在作者反对的情况下，明确表示即将公开展览作品系对发表权的即发侵害行为,符合"如不及时制止将会给权利人造成难以弥补的损害"的行为保全条件。

【案　　　　号】　北京市第二中级人民法院（2013）二中保字第 09727 号
【案　　　　由】　著作权诉前行为保全纠纷

【合议庭成员】 张 剑 杨 静 刘 娟

【关 键 词】 钱钟书 杨绛 诉前行为保全

【相关法条】 《中华人民共和国著作权法》第十条第一款第（一）项、第十九条第一款、第二十一条第一款、第五十条，《中华人民共和国著作权法实施条例》第十七条，《中华人民共和国继承法》第十条、第十一条，《中华人民共和国民事诉讼法》第一百条、第一百零一条、第一百零八条，《最高人民法院关于审理著作权民事纠纷案件适用法律若干问题的解释》第三十条第二款

【基本案情】

申请人杨季康（笔名杨绛，我国著名作家、翻译家）系钱钟书（已故著名作家、文学研究家）的配偶，二人育有一女钱瑗（已故）。被申请人李国强曾任《广角镜》月刊总编辑。钱钟书与李国强于1979年相识后，钱氏一家与李国强往来密切，通信频繁，钱氏家人的书信手稿一直由李国强收存。

2013年5月，被申请人中贸圣佳国际拍卖有限公司在其官方网站发布公告称，其将于6月21日拍卖"也是集——钱钟书书信手稿"，其中包括钱钟书、杨季康、钱瑗写给李国强的若干封信札、手稿作品百余件，此前还将举行预展和研讨会。随即新华网、人民网等多家媒体对此事进行了报道，宣称这将是"首次大规模曝光钱钟书手稿"，其中还刊登了中贸圣佳国际拍卖有限公司公布的少量手稿照片。经查，上述书信手稿多自李国强处取得，内容涉及私人交流、家庭琐事、个人情感以及文学历史时事评论等，均未曾公开发表。

杨季康强烈反对公开拍卖和展出手稿，经交涉未果，向北京市第二中级人民法院提出诉前停止侵害著作权行为的保全申请。经查，钱瑗、钱钟书相继于1997年、1998年病故，杨季康为二人继承人，

钱瑗的另一继承人其配偶杨伟成同意杨季康的维权主张。

法院审理过程中，案外人紫光集团有限公司向法院出具了合法有效的财产担保申请和相关材料，承诺承担如因杨季康申请错误给被申请人造成的全部财产损失。

 裁判结果

北京市第二中级人民法院经审理后，裁定如下：中贸圣佳国际拍卖有限公司在拍卖、预展及宣传等活动中不得以公开发表、展览、复制、发行、信息网络传播等方式实施侵害钱钟书、杨季康、钱瑗写给李国强的涉案书信手稿著作权的行为。

本裁定送达后立即执行。如不服本裁定，可在裁定书送达之日起十日内向本院申请复议一次。复议期间不停止裁定的执行。

【裁判理由】

北京市第二中级人民法院经审理认为：

诉前行为保全又称为诉前禁令，是指人民法院为及时制止正在实施或即将实施的侵害权利人知识产权或有侵害之虞的行为，在起诉前根据当事人申请发布的一种禁止或限制行为人从事某种行为的强制命令，其目的在于保护权利人知识产权免遭继续侵害，预防难以弥补损害的发生。

诉前行为保全需符合以下要件：（1）申请人享有知识产权，被申请人正在实施或即将实施侵犯知识产权行为；（2）不采取有关措施会给申请人的合法权益造成难以弥补的损害；（3）申请人提供了有效担保；（4）行为保全的作出不会损害公共利益。

一、书信手稿是受著作权法保护的作品

我国著作权法所称的作品，是指文学、艺术和科学领域内具有独创性并能以某种有形形式复制的智力创造成果。书信作为人类沟通感情、交流思想、洽谈事项的工具，通常是写信人独立构思并创作而成的文字作品，其内容或表现形式通常不是或不完全是对他人已发表的作品的引用、抄录，即不是单纯摹仿、抄袭、篡改他人的作品。因此，在无相反证据的情况下，书信通常具有独创性和可复制性，符合著作权法关于作品的构成要件，可以成为著作权法保护的作品，其著作权应当由作者即发信人享有。根据我国著作权法的相关规定，钱钟书、杨季康、钱瑗分别对各自创作的书信作品享有著作权。

二、申请人依据继承法享有行为保全请求权

钱钟书去世后，杨季康作为其唯一继承人，有权依法继承其著作权中的财产权，依法保护其著作权中的署名权、修改权和保护作品完整权，依法行使其著作权中的发表权。钱瑗去世后，杨季康、杨伟成作为其继承人，享有同上权利。鉴于杨伟成明确表示在本案中不主张权利，故杨季康依法有权主张相关权利。任何人包括收信人及其他合法取得书信手稿物权的人，对于书信手稿进行处分时均不得侵害作者及其继承人的著作权。

三、被申请人正在实施或即将实施侵权行为

判断作品是否已经发表的标准在于确定作品是否被公之于众，即将作品置于为不特定人所知的状态。本案中，中贸圣佳国际拍卖有限公司即将公开预展、公开拍卖涉案书信手稿，其为拍卖而正在或即将通过报刊、光盘、宣传册、计算机网络等方式复制发行涉案书信手稿的行为，将客观上使得作品被公开发表，不仅构成对发表权的侵犯，而且还构成对权利人复制权、发行权的侵犯。

四、被申请人的行为将造成"难以弥补的损害"

发表权属于著作人身权之一，是指决定作品是否公之于众以及何时、何地、以何种方式公之于众的权利。作品的发表是一次性行为,作品一旦被非法发表,将导致权利人的意志被违背。就本案而言,它意味着私人书信进入公众视野,该行为存在不可逆转性,这种为公众所知悉的状态将不可逆转的、无法回复到为权利人所控制的私密状态。因此,一旦以公开拍卖等方式非法发表他人私人书信手稿作品,将造成对权利人发表权难以弥补的损害。

更为重要的是,发表权不仅作为著作权中一项独立的人身权,更是著作权人行使和保护其他权利的基础。虽然不论作品是否发表,著作权人都依法享有著作权,但是作品是否已经发表对于著作权人对自身权利的保护和控制能力以及他人获取作品、使用作品的难易程度、合法性均有重大影响。一旦作品被非法发表,就如同打开了私人与公共状态之间的"开关",只有打开这个"开关",社会公众才有可能接触、传播、复制到涉案作品。涉案钱氏一家的书信手稿均为写给李国强的私人书信,从私人书信本身的功能和涉案书信的具体内容可以看出,写信人的本意在于向友人传递信息、沟通感情、探讨观点,而非将所写内容公之于众、为世人所品评。在杨季康强烈反对公开的情况下,擅自公开涉案书信手稿极易导致权利人对其他人实施后续的复制、发行、信息网络传播等行为难以控制,极易导致连锁侵权行为,此乃给权利人造成难以弥补的损害。

此外,法院充分评估了行为保全可能带来的影响后认为,在申请人提供了有效担保的情况下,做出行为保全不会损害社会公共利益。保护作品著作权与鼓励作品传播均为法律保护的价值,然而私人书信作品与普通文字作品相比具有一定的特殊性,其承载的价值更多的是私人思想感情的表达,而非面向公众的文化传播,权利人对私人书信的控制权属于典型的私权,应得到充分尊重。禁止违背意愿的发表不仅不会对公共利益造成不良影响，反而将有助于明确书信著作权及隐私权保护规则，收信人和拍卖公司在行使物权时不得侵害作品著作权。

综上，做出诉前行为保全裁定。

【本案裁判文书】

扫描二维码，可见裁判文书

Nature of Letters and Manuscripts, Manuscript Auction and Preliminary Injunction for Copyright

——Yang Jikang v. Sungari International Auction Co., Ltd.

[Syllabus]

Private letters, as a carrier to communicate human feelings and exchange ideas, usually are written works independently conceived and created by the sender, which shall be deemed as the works created by the sender. In absence of contrary evidence, private letters shall be protected by the Copyright Law of China.

Although a receiver has obtained the real right to the letters and manuscripts, it shall be exercised in a manner that does not infringe upon the copyright of the sender. The publication of the letters and manuscripts against the will of the copyright holder or any of his successors constitutes an infringement upon his copyright.

In general, infringement relating to the personality rights of copyright would result in personality and spiritual harm. As such kind of aggrieved state is irreversible, it is difficult to completely recover the damages resulting from infringement upon the personality rights of copyright through monetary compensation or non-monetary compensation. Besides, the publication right of the writer is the basis and guarantee for the exercise and protection of other related rights.. Once the work is published against the writer's will, it might make copying and issuing of the work fall out of the writer's control as well. Therefore, despite of the objection of the writer, explicitly declaring the exhibition of the work in public constitutes an infringement upon the publication right, which fulfill the requirement-- "failure in timely deterrence of such infringement will cause irreparable harm to the right holder"--for granting a preliminary injunction. The court shall, upon request by the right holder, grant the preliminary injunction.

[Case No.] Beijing No. 2 Intermediate People's Court (2013) EZMCZ No. 09727

[Cause of Action] Dispute over preliminary behavior preservation of infringement upon copyrights

[Collegial Panel Members] Zhang Jian Yang Jing Liu Juan

[Keywords] Letters, real right, copyright,privacy right,auction, pre-action injunction

[Relevant Legal Provisions] Item (1), paragraph one of Article 10, paragraph one of Article 19, paragraph one of Article 21, and Article 50 of the Copyright Law of the People's Republic of China, Article 17 of the Regulation on the Implementation of the Copyright Law of the People's Republic of China, Articles 10 and 11 of the Law of Succession of the People's Republic of China, Articles 100, 101 and 108 of the Civil Procedure Law of the People's Republic of China, and paragraph two of Article 30 of the Interpretation of the Supreme People's Court Concerning the Application of Laws in the Trial of Civil Disputes over Copyright.

[Basic Facts]

The applicant Yang Jikang (pen name: Yang Jiang, a famous writer and translator) is the wife of Qian Zhongshu (deceased, a famous writer and researcher in literature), and they had a daughter named Qian Yuan (deceased). The respondent Li Guoqiang is the former editor in chief of a monthly publication titled Wide Angle. After Li Guoqiang was acquainted with Qian Zhongshu in 1979, he become close friends with Qian Zhongshu, Yang Jikang, and their daughter Qian Yuan and they wrote to each other frequently. The Qians' letters have been kept by Li Guoqiang.

In the May of 2013, the respondent Sungari, a comprehensive auction company, announced on its official website that it would held a public auction for a Collection, Letters and Manuscripts of Qian Zhongshu on June 21, including more than 100 letters and manuscripts sent by Qian Zhongshu, Yang Jikang and Qian Yuan to Li Guoqiang. Before the auction, pre-auction exhibitions and seminars would also be hold. Later, several media like Xinhua Net and People.cn reported that they would "reveal a large scale of manuscripts of Qian Zhongshu for the first time". Through investigation, it was found that the letters and manuscripts of Qian Zhongshu involved were mainly obtained from Li Guoqiang, their content covering private communications, household affairs, personal emotions, literary reviews, historic reviews, running comments and others that have never been known to the public.

Yang Jikang strongly opposed the public auction of the private letters and manuscripts from the Qians', and applied to Beijing No. 2 Intermediate People's Court for a preliminary injunction to stop the behavior of infringement upon copyrights. Qian Yuan and Qian Zhongshu died of illness in 1997 and 1998 successively. Yang Jikang is the successor of Qian Yuan and Qian Zhongshu. Another successor of Qian Yuan, who is her husband named Yang Weicheng, agreed that Yang Jikang shall claim the rights concerned as the only successor.

During the process, A third party, Tsinghua Unigroup, issued a letter of guarantee to the court, together with the photocopy of its business license and latest financial statements, stating it is willing to act as a guarantor to provide guarantee for the applicant Yang Jikang. And it also agrees in writing that it will bear joint liability for all the economic losses of the respondent that might be incurred from any applicant's fault.

 Holding

Beijing No. 2 Intermediate People's Court ruled that Sungari should stop any conduct that infringes the copyright of the letters and manuscripts involved sent from Qian Zhongshu, Yang Jikang and Qian Yuan to Li Guoqiang in the auction, exhibitions and publicity activities by means of publication, exhibition, reproduction, distribution or network dissemination.

The ruling shall be immediately executed after service. In case any party is dissatisfied with the ruling, it may apply to the court for reconsideration within ten days after receipt of the judgment. The execution of the ruling shall not be suspended during the reconsideration.

257

[Reasoning]

Through the trial, Beijing No. 2 Intermediate People's Court holds that:

Preliminary behavior preservation is also called preliminary injunction, which refers to a kind of compulsory order granted by the people's court before trial upon the request of one party as to prohibit or limit a certain conduct of another party where a infringement upon the copyright of the party is happening or is about to happen. It aims to protect the party's intellectual property rights and prevent irreparable damages from happening.

The requirements for granting a preliminary injunction are mainly the four listed below. 1.the applicant is the subject of the intellectual property right, and the respondent is conducting and is about to conduct an infringement to the intellectual property right. 2.Failure in timely deterrence of such infringement will cause irreparable harm to the right holder. 3.The applicant has provided valid guarantee. 4.The granting of the preliminary injunction is not detrimental to social interests.

I.Letters and manuscripts are the works protected by the Copyright Law

Works defined in the Copyright Law of China refer to intellectual results that are unique in the fields of literature, arts and science and can be reproduced in a tangible way. Letters, as a human tool to communicate feelings, exchange ideas and discuss issues, usually are written works independently conceived and created by the sender, and the content or form of expression is usually not or not fully a citation or transcription of published works by others, namely, not a simple imitation, reproduction, tampering of others' works. Therefore, letters usually feature originality and replicability in line with requirements of works set forth in the Copyright Law and may become works protected by the Copyright Law. Therefore, the author (i.e., the sender) should be entitled to the copyright. According to relevant provisions of the Copyright Law, Qian Zhongshu, Yang Jikang and Qian Yuan each is entitled to the copyright of the letters created by her/himself.

II. The applicant is entitled to request for an injunction under the Law of Succession.

After the death of Qian Zhongshu, Yang Jikang, his only successor, has the right to legally inherit the property rights of his copyright, protect his rights of authorship, alteration and integrity, and exercise his right of publication. After the death of Qian Yuan, Yang Jikang and Yang Weicheng become her successors and have the right to own the property rights of her copyright, protect her rights of authorship, alteration and integrity, and exercise her right of publication. Given that Yang Weicheng has expressly given up the aforesaid rights, Yang Jikang has been entitled to the aforesaid rights. Anyone, including the receiver of the letters and other recipients legally obtaining the letters, shall not impair the legal rights and interests of the copyright holder when they dispose of the legally obtained letters and manuscripts.

III.The conduct of the respondent has been preliminarily identified as infringing act.

The criterion to determine whether a work is published or not is to identify whether the work is released to the public, namely the work is at a state where it could be known by an uncertain number of people. In this case, Sungari is about to exhibit and auction the letters and manuscripts involved. The reproduction and issuing of the aforesaid letters and manuscripts through newspapers, light disks, brochures and online means by Sungari in process or to be done for the purpose of auction objectively exposes the works at issue to the public. It is not only an infringement upon the publication right, but also an infringement upon the reproduction right and the issuing right of the copyright holder.

IV.The respondent's conduct will cause "irreparable harm".

The publication right is one important personality right of copyright. It is the right determining whether the work to be exposed to the public and when, where and by what means the work to be exposed to the public. The publication of the work is a one-off conduct. Once the work is illegally published, it would cause an objection to the will of the copyright holder. It terms of this case, it means that the private letters and manuscripts enter the public area, which is irreversible. The state of being known to the public cannot goes back to the state of being in private control of the copyright holder. Therefore, the illegal publication of the private letters and manuscripts through the means of public auction could cause irreparable harm to the copyright holder.

More importantly, the right to publication is not only an independent and important personality right of copyright, but also the basis for the copyright holder to exercise and protect other related rights. Published or not, copyright over the work is protected by law. However, the publication of the work has a great influence on the copyright holder's ability to control and protect his/her own rights, and it would also affect whether other people could obtain and utilize the work easily or legally. If there were a switch between private and public, publish the work illegally is just like turning the switch on. The public could only have access to the work and distribute and reproduce the work when the switch is on. The Qians' letters and manuscripts involved are private letters written to Li Guoqiang. From the function of private letters and the specific content of the letters involved, it could be seen that the intent of the sender is to transmit information, communicate feelings and discuss issues, instead of exposing what have been written to the public for their appreciation and comment. Where Yang Jikang made clear her intent not to make the works involved to the public, the unauthorized publication of the works would make the copyright holder loss control over other reproduction and distribution behaviors, which is likely to cause chain copyright infringement actions. This is to cause irreparable harm to the copyright holder.

Additionally, the court has sufficiently evaluated the afterwards influence what the preliminary injunction might bring. On the condition that applicant has provided valid guarantee, granting the preliminary injunction would not be detrimental to social interests. Both protecting the copyright of the work and encouraging the distribution of the work are values guarded by law. Compared to ordinary literary works, private letters are somewhat peculiar as it functions more like a carrier of private emotions and a means of expressing private feelings. It serves no way as public cultural distribution. The copyright holder's control over the private letters is a typical private right, which should be highly respected. Prohibiting the publication of private letters against the copyright holder's will is not detrimental to social interests, instead, it will help make clear the rules as to the copyright of private letters and the protection of privacy. The receiver and the auction company shall not infringe upon the copyright of the works involved even though they are entitled to exercise their property rights.

Bases on analysis above, the court ruled the preliminary injunction to be granted.

[Opinion of the Case (Chinese Version)]

261

Scan the QR code to see the Chinese version of the opinion

"云音乐"平台侵害信息网络传播权
诉前行为保全的审查判断

——深圳市腾讯计算机系统有限公司与广州网易计算机系统有限公司、网易（杭州）网络有限公司、杭州网易雷火科技有限公司、中国联合网络通信有限公司湖北省分公司、广东欧珀移动通信有限公司侵害音乐作品信息网络传播权纠纷行为保全申请案

【裁判要旨】

在网络环境下，被诉侵权行为如及时予以禁止，将会使被申请人不当利用他人权利获得的市场份额进一步快速增长，损害申请人的利益，且这种损害将难以弥补。故对被申请人的被诉侵权行为应予禁止，应依法准许申请人对本案提起的诉前行为保全申请。

【案　　　　号】	湖北省武汉市中级人民法院（2014）鄂武汉中知禁字第00005号、（2014）鄂武汉中知禁字第00005-2号
【案　　　　由】	侵害音乐作品信息网络传播权纠纷
【合议庭成员】	何　震　许继学　陈　峰
【关 键 词】	云音乐平台　信息网络传播权　诉前行为保全
【相 关 法 条】	《中华人民共和国著作权法》第五十条，《中华人民共和国民事诉讼法》第一百条

【基本案情】

申请人深圳市腾讯计算机系统有限公司（以下简称腾讯公司）与被申请人广州网易计算机系统有限公司（以下简称广州网易）、网易（杭州）网络有限公司（以下简称杭州网易）、杭州网易雷火科技有限公司（下称网易雷火）、中国联合网络通信有限公司湖北省分公司（以下简称湖北联通）、广东欧珀移动通信有限公司（以下简称广东欧珀）发生著作权争议，于2014年11月10日向湖北省武汉市中级人民法院申请诉前行为保全，腾讯公司请求：1. 责令被申请人广州网易、被申请人杭州网易、被申请人网易雷火停止通过"网易云音乐"平台（music.163.com 及其 PC 端、移动客户端）向公众传播申请人享有专有著作权的歌曲，这些歌曲包括《时间都去哪了》《爱的供养》《画心》等 623 首歌曲（见附件清单）；2. 责令被申请人湖北联通停止提供网易云音乐畅听流量包服务；3. 责令被申请人广东欧珀停止在其 OPPO 品牌手机中内置网易云音乐行为。申请人腾讯公司为前述诉前行为保全申请，向法院提交了湖北省武汉市琴台公证处（2014）鄂琴台内证字第 13911、14057、15782、15783、15784、15785、15786 号公证书、音乐专辑、相关网页打印件及工信部 IP/ICP 备案信息查询结果等证据，以证明申请人享有的涉案音乐作品（词曲作品、制品，以下通称音乐作品）著作权遭受侵权损害的事实。同时，担保人腾讯科技（深圳）有限公司广州分公司为申请人腾讯公司此次诉前行为保全申请提供了人民币 300 万元的银行存款进行担保。

263

 裁判结果

对申请人腾讯公司诉前行为保全申请及提交的证据，湖北省武汉市中级人民法院依法组成合议庭进行了审查。经审查，法院依法准许申请人腾讯公司对本案提起的诉前行为保全申请，发布如下行为保全措施：1. 被申请人广州网易计算机系统有限公司、被申请人网易（杭州）网络有限公司、被申请人杭州网易雷火科技有限公司于本裁定生效之日起立即停止通过网易云音乐平台向公众提供本裁定书附件所列623 首音乐作品的行为；2. 被申请人中国联合网络通信有限公司湖北省分公司于本裁定生效之日起立即停止向其移动手机客户提供网易云音乐畅听流量包中的涉案 623 首音乐作品的移动网络服务行为；3. 被申请人广东欧珀移动通信有限公司于本裁定书生效次日起十日内停止通过其品牌为 OPPO R830S 型号（合约机）移动手机中内置的网易云音乐客户端向移动手机客户传播涉案 623 首音乐作品的行为；4. 冻结担保人腾讯科技（深圳）有限公司广州分公司在招商银行广州分行环市东路支行（广州）开立的银行账号为 2005xxxxxxx0001 账户内的银行存款人民币 300 万元；5. 驳回申请人广州网易计算机系统有限公司提出的其他行为保全申请；6. 申请人腾讯公司应当在本裁定书生效后三十日内起诉，逾期不起诉的，将解除本裁定指定的行为保全措施。

禁止令发布后，被申请人湖北联通及被申请人广东欧珀立即停止了被诉行为，表示积极履行法院禁令义务。被申请人广州网易、杭州网易、网易雷火不服该行为保全，向湖北省武汉市中级人民法院提出复议申请。湖北省武汉市中级人民法院于 2014 年 12 月 3 日以开庭听证方式审查了三复议申请人的复议申请，认为复议申请人提出的复议理由均不能成立，裁定驳回复议申请人广州网易计算机系统有限公司、网易（杭州）网络有限公司、杭州网易雷火科技有限公司的复议申请。

复议中，申请人腾讯公司发现被诉行为仍在继续，向湖北省武汉市中级人民法院提交了违反行为保全应予处罚的书面申请。法院在听证中对申请人提出的触犯申请也进行了听证，并作出相应的处罚措施。至复议决定书发出后，被诉行为已经按照行为保全要求全面停止。

【裁判理由】

湖北省武汉市中级人民法院经审查认为：

1. 根据申请人腾讯公司提交的音乐版权授权合同、涉案音乐专辑等版权文件，申请人腾讯公司依法享有本裁定书附件所列包括《绿色玫瑰》在内 623 首音乐作品的信息网络传播权。

2. 根据湖北省武汉市琴台公证处向申请人腾讯公司提交的编号为（2014）鄂琴台内证字第 14057 号公证书显示内容，被申请人广州网易、杭州网易、网易雷火共同运营由广州网易主办的涉案网易云音乐平台（网址：music.163.com），并通过网易云音乐平台向公众提供本裁定书附件所列 623 首音乐作品。三被申请人的行为涉嫌侵犯申请人腾讯公司依法享有的附件所列 623 首音乐作品的信息网络传播权。

3. 根据申请人腾讯公司提交的湖北省武汉市琴台公证处（2014）鄂琴台内证字第 13911 号公证书载明内容，可以确认被申请人湖北联通与涉案网易云音乐平台合作，并以网易云音乐畅听流量包的模式，向其移动手机客户传播申请人腾讯公司附件所列 623 首音乐作品。被申请人湖北联通的上述行为涉嫌侵犯申请人涉案音乐作品信息网络传播权。

4. 根据申请人腾讯公司提交的湖北省武汉市琴台公证处（2014）鄂琴台内证字第 13911 号公证书载明内容，被申请人广东欧珀在生产销售的涉案 OPPOR830S 型号（合约机）的手机中内置有可以接入网易云音乐平台的移动手机客户端，并通过移动手机内置客户端方式，定向获取来源于网易云音乐平台提供的附件所列 623 首音乐作品。该行为涉嫌侵犯申请人腾讯公司享有的附件所列 623 首音乐作品的信息网络传播权。

5. 申请人腾讯公司提交的名称为网易科技的相关网页打印件

载明的内容如下：（1）被申请人广州网易、杭州网易法定代表人声称，BAT 大家的模式不同，阿里和百度还是流量模式，网易是内容供应商。三小虎（京东、小米和奇虎 360）利润加起来还没有网易多。（2）2014 年 8 月 18 日网易科技网页显示：网易云音乐用户四千万；网易云音乐内热门歌单《入耳便爱上的英文歌》短短一周的播放量就增加了 17 万次。

6. 担保人腾讯科技（深圳）有限公司广州分公司提供的担保资产经查证属实，法院依法对担保人提供的银行存款 300 万元（人民币）予以冻结。

综上，申请人腾讯公司对本裁定附件所列 623 首音乐作品依法享有信息网络传播权。五被申请人以互联网络、移动手机网易云音乐畅听流量包、内置网易云音乐移动手机客户端等方式，向公众大量提供涉案音乐作品。该行为涉嫌侵犯申请人腾讯公司对这些音乐作品依法享有的信息网络传播权，且被申请人向公众提供的音乐作品数量较大，造成了申请人腾讯公司巨大的经济损失。法院考虑到，在网络环境下，该行为如不及时予以禁止，将会使被申请人广州网易不当利用他人权利获得的市场份额进一步快速增长，损害申请人腾讯公司的利益，且这种损害将难以弥补。故对各被申请人通过网络传播本裁定附件所列 623 首音乐作品涉嫌侵权部分的行为理应禁止。担保人为申请人腾讯公司提出的行为保全申请进行担保，经查证属实，行为保全申请的担保程序合法。

湖北省武汉市中级人民法院经复议认为：

1. 法院经初步核查，腾讯公司提交了著作权授权书、音乐制品专辑、歌单等权利证据可以证明申请人是涉案音乐作品的独家信息网络传播权人。法院考虑到"网易云音乐"平台的网络传播属性，依据"网易云音乐"平台迅速发展的初步证据，认定不采取行为保全措施可能给申请人腾讯公司造成不可挽回的损失并无不妥。

2. 行为保全申请人腾讯公司针对被申请人湖北联通通过"网易云音乐畅听流量包"这一移动网络服务项目，向其移动用户提供涉案 623 首音乐作品的行为涉嫌侵害腾讯公司享有的信息网络传播权提出行为保全申请，该项申请与针对复议申请人的行为保全申请相互关联。

3. 三复议申请人除提交由网易雷火出具的关于该平台由网易雷火单独运营管理的书面陈词外，没有提交其他证据推翻行为保全对"网易云音乐"平台由三方复议申请人合作运营的认定。行为保全依据"网易云音乐"平台所使用的网络域名、网络经营许可证、"网易科技"宣称的杭州网易是涉案"网易云音乐"平台软件的开发者及"网易云音乐"网站题头、网站版权声明信息等证据，初步认定"网易云音乐"平台系由广州网易、杭州网易、网易雷火三方合作运营并无不当。

4. 听证中，经复议申请人和复议被申请人演示，在"网易云音乐"平台提供的页面尾部，直接点击链接代码可以播放涉案音乐作品，但通过复议申请人提供的域名地址进行网络连接并不能获得涉案音乐作品。同时，三复议申请人没有提交证据证明"网易云音乐"平台属于单纯提供网络链接技术及涉案音乐作品已获得合法授权。

5. 本案行为保全所附被禁歌曲清单第 216 号与第 217 号并非重复列明，而是两首不同表演的同名音乐作品。行为保全清单中的其他作品均经核查属实。根据"网易云音乐"平台传播的涉案作品信息，法院有理由确认这些音乐制品与腾讯公司主张行为保全的权利作品为同一作品，无需进行音源比对。

【本案裁判文书】

扫描二维码，可见裁判文书

Review and Judgment of Preliminary Injunction against "Cloud Music" Platform's Infringement of the Right to Network Dissemination of Information

——Shenzhen Tencent Computer Systems Co., Ltd. v. Guangzhou NetEase Computer Systems Co., Ltd., NetEase (Hangzhou) Network Co., Ltd., Hangzhou NetEase Leihuo Co., Ltd., China United Network Communications Limited Hubei Branch, Guangdong OPPO Mobile Telecommunications Corp., Ltd.

269

[Syllabus]

An injunction, as a temporary measure, is a provisional relief measure against the party that is suspected of infringement from pursuing a certain conduct or omission thereof. Five respondents disseminated the involved musical works to the public via different communications media through the "NetEase Cloud Music" platform, and such act shall be determined as an act of dissemination of information via the internet. The court upon examining the prima facie evidence held that it was much more likely that such an alleged act would constitute an infringement. Moreover, such an ongoing alleged infringing act may cause huge economic losses to the petitioner, and under such a circumstance, an injunction should be granted.

Online music is a newly developed cultural network communication medium that combines the network industry and the music industry, and involves issues related to copyright investment and copyright protection. It is more competitive in the industry, and the online music market is also an important juncture for the National Copyright Administration to clean the network environment this year. Allowing disorderly competition in online music go unchecked may damage the expansion of online productivity and cause online regulation to go out of control. At the same time, the injunction prescribed by the **Civil Procedure Law of the People's Republic of China** *has strong enforceability and has a certain deterrent effect on an infringer. The issuance and enforcement of the injunction in this case has been a kind of feasible copyright protection model for cracking down online music piracy, standardizing the online music market and regulating the network environment, providing an important reference for network administrative law enforcement, rapid check and crackdown over online music piracy, and protection of the legitimate rights of music right holders.*

[Case No.] (2014) YWHZZJZ No. 00005 and No. 00005-2 of Wuhan Intermediate People's Court of Hubei Province

[Cause of Action] Dispute over the infringement of the right to dissemination of musical works via the internet

[Collegial Panel Members] He Zhen　Xu Jixue　Chen Feng

[Keywords] Cloud music platform, right to network dissemination of information, preliminary injunction

[Relevant Legal Provisions]　Article 50 of the *Copyright Law of the People's Republic of China*, Article 100 of the *Civil Procedure Law of the People's Republic of China*.

[Basic Facts]

In a dispute over copyright arising between the petitioner Shenzhen Tencent Computer Systems Co., Ltd. ("**Tencent Company**") and the respondents Guangzhou NetEase Computer Systems Co., Ltd. ("**Guangzhou NetEase**"), NetEase (Hangzhou) Network Co., Ltd. ("**Hangzhou NetEase**"), Hangzhou NetEase Leihuo Co., Ltd. ("**NetEase Leihuo**"), China United Network Communications Limited Hubei Branch ("**Hubei Unicom**"), and Guangdong OPPO Mobile Telecommunications Co., Ltd. ("**Guangdong OPPO**"), Tencent Company filed an application for preliminary injunctions with the Wuhan Intermediate People's Court of Hubei Province on November 10th, 2014, requesting: 1. to order the respondents Guangzhou NetEase, Hangzhou NetEase and NetEase Leihuo stop the dissemination to the public of songs via the "NetEase Cloud Music" platform (music.163.com and its PC & mobile client), to which the petitioner enjoyed an exclusive copyright, wherein there were 623 songs including *Where Has the Time Gone, The Support of Love, Painted Heart*, etc.; 2. to order the respondent Hubei Unicom stop rendering the service of free data package for NetEase Cloud Music; 3. to order the respondent Guangdong OPPO stop its builit-in NetEase Cloud Music in its OPPO brand cellphones. In applying for the aforesaid injunctions, the petitioner Tencent Company submitted relevant evidence including notarial certificates of Wuhan Qintai Notary Public Office in Hubei [(2014) EQTNZZ Nos. 13911, 14057, 15782, 15783, 15784, 15785, 15786], music albums, printouts of related web pages as well as IP/ICP file information inquiry results from the Ministry of Industry and Information Technology, to support the fact that the copyright of musical works involved (music and lyrics, products, hereinafter collectively referred to as musical works) belonged to the petitioner. At the same time, the guarantor Tencent Technology

(Shenzhen) Co., Ltd. Guangzhou Branch provided a bank deposit of RMB3 million as security for the petitioner Tencent Company to apply for such injunctions.

 Holding

With regard to the application for preliminary injunctions filed and evidence submitted by the petitioner Tencent Company, the Wuhan Intermediate People's Court of Hubei Province formed a collegial panel pursuant to law to review the case. Upon review, the Court legally granted the following injunctions with respect to the application filed by the petitioner Tencent Company for the preliminary injunctions: 1. The respondents Guangzhou NetEase Computer Systems Co., Ltd., NetEase (Hangzhou) Network Co., Ltd. and Hangzhou NetEase Leihuo Co., Ltd. should stop provision to the public 623 musical works listed in the appendix attached hereto through the "NetEase Cloud Music" platform, as of the effective date of this ruling; 2. The respondent China United Network Communications Limited Hubei Branch should stop rendering the mobile network services to its mobile clients for the 623 musical works involved in the free data package of NetEase Cloud Music, as of the effective date of this ruling; 3. The respondent Guangdong OPPO Mobile Telecommunications Corp., Ltd. should stop its behavior of disseminating the 623 musical works involved, to its mobile clients via the NetEase Cloud Music client built in its mobile phones branded as OPPO R830S (contracted phones) within ten (10) days from the date immediately following the effective date of this ruling; 4. The bank deposit of RMB3 million in the account opened by Tencent Technology (Shenzhen) Co., Ltd. Guangzhou Branch at China Merchants Bank Guangzhou Branch Huanshi East Road Sub-branch (A/C No. 200583420610001) should be frozen; 5. Other injunction applications filed by the petitioner Guangzhou NetEase

Computer Systems Co., Ltd. should be dismissed; and 6. The petitioner Shenzhen Tencent Computer Systems Co., Ltd. should bring the case to the people's court within 30 days after this ruling comes into force, otherwise, injunctive measures specified herein shall be released.

After the court issued such injunctions, the respondents Hubei Unicom and Guangdong OPPO immediately stopped such alleged infringing acts and expressed that they would actively adhere to the injunction obligations of the court. Whereas, the respondents Guangzhou NetEase, Hangzhou NetEase and NetEase Leihuo appealed against such injunctions to the Wuhan Intermediate People's Court of Hubei Province for reconsideration. On December 3rd, 2014, the Wuhan Intermediate People's Court reviewed the application for reconsideration filed by the three respondents in a public hearing, and held that reasons for reconsideration proposed by the three respondents could not be established, and thus ruled to dismiss the application for reconsideration filed by the three respondents, i.e., Guangzhou NetEase Computer Systems Co., Ltd., NetEase (Hangzhou) Network Co., Ltd. and Hangzhou NetEase Leihuo Co., Ltd.

In the process of reconsideration, the petitioner Tencent Company discovered that the alleged infringing acts were continuing, and thus submitted a written application to the Wuhan Intermediate People's Court of Hubei Province, to penalize the respondents for the violation of the injunctions. The Court conducted a hearing over the application of violations lodged by the petitioner and imposed punitive measures accordingly. Upon the issuance of the decision over reconsideration, the alleged infringing acts were immediately ceased, pursuant to the requirements of the injunctions.

[Reasoning]

The Wuhan Intermediate People's Court of Hubei Province held upon review that:

I. Based on the music copyright licensing contracts, the involved music albums and other copyright documents submitted by the petitioner Tencent Company, the petitioner Tencent Company should be entitled to the rights to network dissemination of information of the 623 musical works including *Green Rose*, as listed in the appendix attached hereto.

II. According to the notarial certificate [(2014) EQTNZZ No. 14057] submitted by Wuhan Qintai Notary Public Office in Hubei to the petitioner Tencent Company, the respondents Guangzhou NetEase, Hangzhou NetEase and NetEase Leihuo jointly ran the NetEase Cloud Music platform (website: music.163.com) sponsored by Guangzhou NetEase and communicated to the public 623 musical works as listed in the appendix attached hereto via this platform. The three respondents were suspected of infringing the petitioner Tencent Company's right to network dissemination of information of the 623 musical works listed in the appendix attached hereto.

III. According to contents stated in the notarial certificate of Wuhan Qintai Notary Public Office in Hubei [(2014) EQTNZZ No. 13911] submitted by the petitioner Tencent Company, it could be confirmed that the respondent Hubei Unicom cooperated with the involved NetEase Cloud Music platform and disseminated the 623 music listed in the appendix as prepared by the petitioner Tencent Company to its mobile clients, through a free data package of NetEase Cloud Music. The above-mentioned acts committed by the respondent Hubei Unicom were suspected of infringing the petitioner's right to network dissemination of information of the musical works involved herein.

IV. According to contents stated in the notarial certificate of Wuhan Qintai Notary Public Office in Hubei [(2014) EQTNZZ No. 13911] submitted by the petitioner Tencent Company, the respondent Guangdong OPPO has a built-in mobile client to access NetEase Cloud Music platform on its mobile phones branded OPPO R830S (contracted phones) for production and sales, and by means of a build-in client on its mobile phones, acquired the 623 musical works provided by NetEase Cloud Music platform. Such acts were suspected of infringing the petitioner Tencent Company's right to network dissemination of information of 623 musical works listed in the appendix.

V. Contents specified in printouts of relevant webpages of NetEase Technology as submitted by the petitioner Tencent Company: (1) the legal representative of the respondents Guangzhou NetEase and Hangzhou NetEase claimed that they applied various BAT modes, Alibaba and Baidu adopted the traffic mode, while NetEase was a content supplier. The aggregate profits of the three large companies (JD, Xiaomi and Qihoo 360) were still less than that of NetEase. (2) According to the webpage of NetEase Technology on August 18th, 2014, NetEase Cloud Music had 40 million users; its hot songs list *English Songs that you Love to Hear* on its NetEase Cloud Music platform were played 170,000 times in just one week.

VI. The secured assets provided by the guarantor Tencent Technology (Shenzhen) Co., Ltd. Guangzhou Branch was verified to be genuine, and the court froze such bank deposits of RMB3 million provided by the guarantor.

Considering all of the above, the petitioner Tencent Company owned the right to network dissemination of information of the 623 musical works listed in the appendix attached hereto. The five respondents made available to the public the involved musical works by means of internet, free data package of NetEase Cloud Music in mobile phones, built-in mobile client of NetEase Cloud Music, etc. Such acts were suspected of infringing the petitioner Tencent Company's right to network dissemination of information of these musical works, moreover, the respondents offered such musical works to the public in a significant volume, causing huge economic losses to the petitioner Tencent Company. In the view of the Court, under the network environment, if such acts were not prohibited in a timely manner, the respondent Guangzhou NetEase may gain further growth in its market share acquired by taking improper advantage of others' rights, which would cause irreparable harm to the interests of the petitioner Tencent Company. Therefore, the suspected infringement of network dissemination of 623 musical works listed in the appendix attached hereto by all respondents should be prohibited. The security provided by the guarantor for injunctions lodged by the petitioner Tencent Company was verified, and the security procedure for the application of injunctions was legitimate.

The Wuhan Intermediate People's Court of Hubei province held upon reconsideration that:

I. Upon the preliminary verification by the Court, Tencent Company had submitted copyright licensing contract, music albums, song lists and other rights evidence, which were sufficient to support the fact that the petitioner was the exclusive owner of the right to network dissemination of the involved musical works. Considering the network dissemination feature of "NetEase Cloud Music" platform, and based on the prima facie evidence of the rapid development of "NetEase Cloud Music" platform, the Court determined that it was not improper to hold that failure to take injunctive measures might cause irreparable losses to the petitioner Tencent Company.

II. The petitioner Tencent Company lodged an application for injunctions against the respondent Hubei Unicom who provided the

623 musical works involved to its mobile users through the mobile service project of "free data package for NetEase Cloud Music", which was suspected of infringing the petitioner Tencent Company's right to network dissemination of information, and such an application for injunctions was related to the application for reconsideration filed by the respondents.

III. Except for the written statements issued by NetEase Leihuo that such a platform was operated and managed by NetEase Leihuo independently, the three respondents who applied for reconsideration of the injunction order failed to submit any other evidence which may have been sufficient to overthrow the injunction order that "NetEase Cloud Music" platform was jointly operated by the said three respondents. On the basis of evidence including the network domain applied by "NetEase Cloud Music" platform, internet business license, the fact declared by "NetEase Technology" that Hangzhou NetEase was the developer of the involved "NetEase Cloud Music" platform software, as well as the title and copyright disclaimer on "NetEase Cloud Music" website, it was not inappropriate to determine that "NetEase Cloud Music" platform was jointly operated by the three parties Guangzhou NetEase, Hangzhou NetEase and NetEase Leihuo.

IV. During the process of hearing and upon the demonstration of the petitioner and the respondents who applied for reconsideration, at the end of the page provided by the "NetEase Cloud Music" platform, the musical works involved could be directly played by clicking the link code, however, such musical works involved could not be obtained online through the domain provided by the three respondents. At the same time, the three respondents who applied for reconsideration failed to submit any evidence that may have supported the point that "NetEase Cloud Music" platform merely provided an internet link technology and that the involved musical works had been lawfully licensed.

V. No. 216 and No. 217 on the list of prohibited songs attached hereto in this case were not copies but were musical works of the same name but with different performance. Other works on the list had been verified to be true. On the basis of works involved that were disseminated via the "NetEase Cloud Music" platform, the Court had reason to confirm these music products are the same as the works for which Tencent Company claimed injunctions, and there was no need to compare the sound sources.

[Opinion of the Case (Chinese Version)]

Scan the QR code to see the Chinese version of the opinion

行为保全的实体审查要件、网游侵权案件中
难以弥补损害的认定、游戏整体下线
及玩家利益的保护

——暴雪娱乐有限公司等与成都七游科技有限公司等著作权侵权
及不正当竞争纠纷诉中行为保全案

【裁判要旨】

诉中行为保全应当审查原告胜诉可能性及原告是否受到难以弥补的损害。

被诉游戏的上线势必挤占原告新推游戏的市场份额。而且网络游戏具有生命周期短，传播速度快、范围广的特点，给原告造成的损害难以计算和量化。被诉游戏采用低俗营销方式也会给原告商誉带来损害。

被诉游戏重要组成部分均构成侵权，其余部分也存在较大侵权可能性，故应整体下线。但禁令期间不影响为被诉游戏玩家提供余额查询及退费等服务。

【案　　　号】广州知识产权法院（2015）粤知法著民初字第 2-1
　　　　　　　号、（2015）粤知法商民初字第 2-1 号
【案　　　由】著作权侵权及不正当竞争纠纷
【合议庭成员】龚麒天　庄　毅　彭　盎

【关 键 词】 网络游戏　诉中行为保全　难以弥补损害

【相关法条】 《中华人民共和国著作权法》第五十条，《中华人民
共和国民事诉讼法》第一百条

【基本案情】

在原告暴雪娱乐有限公司（以下简称暴雪娱乐）、原告上海网
之易网络科技发展有限公司（以下简称网之易公司）诉被告成都
七游科技有限公司（以下简称七游公司）、被告北京分播时代网络
科技有限公司（以下简称分播时代）、被告广州市动景计算机科技
有限公司（以下简称动景公司）著作权侵权及不正当竞争纠纷诉
中行为保全案中，原告暴雪娱乐是《魔兽世界》（2004 年 11 月 23
日美国首次发行）、《魔兽世界：燃烧的远征》（2007 年 1 月 16 日
美国首次发行）、《魔兽世界：巫妖王之怒》（2008 年 11 月 13 日
美国首次发表）、《魔兽世界：熊猫人之谜》（2012 年 9 月 25 日美
国首次发表）等计算机软件作品的著作权人。

《魔兽世界》系列游戏在国内获得诸多重要游戏奖项，如被中
国游戏产业年会评为 2006 年度、2007 年度十大最受欢迎的网络
游戏；在 2011 年首届中国游戏金浣熊奖评选中，被评为十大人气
网络游戏；在 2012 年度中国游戏英雄榜颁奖典礼上，被评为年度
最佳网络游戏。

2014 年 6 月起，原告暴雪娱乐通过中文官网为《魔兽世界：
德拉诺之王》游戏造势。11 月 20 日该游戏在中国正式上线运营，
由原告网之易公司独家运营。

《魔兽世界》系列游戏中的英雄有维纶、伊利丹·怒风、加
尔鲁什·地狱咆哮、萨尔等。怪兽有阿库麦尔、变异蹒跚者等。
这些英雄和怪兽形象在原告暴雪娱乐中文官网、英文出版物《魔

兽世界终极视觉宝典》、中文出版物《暴雪的艺术》及《魔兽世界·萨尔：巨龙的黄昏》中都可看到。上述网站及出版物均标明原告暴雪娱乐是著作权人。本两案中，原告主张其中 18 个英雄和 7 个怪兽形象美术作品的著作权。原告还主张"魔兽""德拉诺"构成知名商品的特有名称，"萨尔"构成知名角色名称，4 个游戏场景（包括标题界面、登陆界面和创建角色界面）构成知名商品的特有装潢。

被诉游戏原名《酋长萨尔：魔兽远征》，由被告七游公司开发。被告分播时代是被告七游公司股东，也是被诉游戏独家运营商。2014 年 8 月 25 日，被告分播时代在官网（www.rekoo.com）发布被诉游戏苹果版本公测，9 月 19 日发布安卓版本公测，12 月 19 日将该游戏更名为《全民魔兽：决战德拉诺》。被告动景公司经被告分播时代授权，在官网（www.9game.cn）向公众提供被诉游戏安卓版本下载。

将被诉游戏相关英雄和怪兽形象与原告主张的英雄和怪兽形象进行比较，两者构成实质相似。

关于被诉游戏的宣传和介绍，被告分播时代官网有以下表述："为了更完美的还原魔兽世界，《酋长萨尔》……无论是玩家操控的英雄还是副本中的小怪，不论是地图设计还是技能特效，都几乎 100% 还原了魔兽中的形象。……魔兽高玩林熊猫将在家中接受'美女上门服务'这一终极挑战。""《全民魔兽》是一款以魔兽世界为背景的 PRG 卡牌游戏……作为借顺风车的一款作品，完美呈现了《魔兽世界》的很多内容，其中剧情、英雄、场景都可以瞬间点燃粉丝们的激情。"

在该被告官方微博有玩家评论："最爱魔兽世界这么有挑战的游戏哦。……我们一起玩魔兽世界吧。"

原告认为，被诉游戏抄袭了原告游戏中的英雄和怪兽形象，使用了与原告游戏相似的名称、装潢。被告分播时代在宣传中反复声称被诉游戏是魔兽手游。三被告的行为共同侵犯了原告的著作权并构成不正当竞争。如果侵权行为持续，将会给原告造成难以弥补的损失。原告遂向广州知识产权法院起诉并同时申请行为保全，要求被诉游戏整体下线，其愿意提交 1000 万元现金担保。三被告则认为，被诉游戏软件登记在案外人名下，原告不能证明是涉案英雄和怪兽形象的著作权人，不能证明被告构成著作权侵权及不正当竞争，也不能证明受到难以弥补的损害，且采取行为保全措施将严重损害被告和游戏玩家利益，故请求驳回原告行为保全申请。

 裁判结果

　　广州知识产权法院于 2015 年 3 月 9 日作出行为保全裁定：1. 禁止被告七游公司复制、发行及通过信息网络传播《全民魔兽：决战德拉诺》（原名《酋长萨尔：魔兽远征》）游戏，效力维持至本两案判决生效日止；2. 禁止被告分播时代复制、发行、通过信息网络传播《全民魔兽：决战德拉诺》（原名《酋长萨尔：魔兽远征》）游戏和实施涉案不正当竞争行为，效力维持至本两案判决生效日止，行为保全期间不影响为该游戏玩家提供余额查询及退费等服务；3. 禁止被告动景公司通过其官网（www.9game.cn）传播《全民魔兽：决战德拉诺》（原名《酋长萨尔：魔兽远征》）游戏，效力维持至本两案判决生效日止，行为保全期间不影响为该游戏玩家提供余额查询及退费等服务；4. 驳回原告暴雪娱乐、原告网之易公司其他行为保全申请。

【裁判理由】

广州知识产权法院认为：

一、关于行为保全的实体审查要件

根据《中华人民共和国民事诉讼法》第一百条的规定，人民法院对于可能因当事人一方的行为，使判决难以执行或者造成当事人其他损害的案件，根据对方当事人的申请，可以裁定禁止其作出一定行为。据此，法院决定是否颁发禁令，应当首先审查原告胜诉可能性。根据《中华人民共和国民事诉讼法》第一百零一条的规定，如果情况紧急，不立即采取行为保全将会使权利人受到难以弥补损害的，权利人可以申请诉前行为保全。由于原告是在起诉同时申请行为保全，并主张情况紧急，故还需对被诉侵权行为是否使原告受到难以弥补损害进行审查。

二、关于原告胜诉可能性

我国及美国均为《保护文学和艺术作品伯尔尼公约》成员国，根据该公约及《中华人民共和国著作权法》第二条的规定，原告暴雪娱乐的作品受我国著作权法的保护。原告暴雪娱乐是《魔兽世界》系列游戏计算机软件作品的著作权人。据此，并结合原告暴雪娱乐官网及涉案合法出版物对《魔兽世界》英雄和怪兽介绍时的版权标记，足以证明其对所主张的18个英雄和7个怪兽形象美术作品享有著作权。被告未经原告许可，在被诉游戏中使用这些英雄和怪兽形象，侵犯了原告美术作品的复制、发行及信息网络传播等权利。同时，原告《魔兽世界》系列游戏在中国具有很高的市场知名度。故原告《魔兽世界：德拉诺之王》游戏构成知名游戏。又由于"魔兽"被相关公众视为《魔兽世界》的简称，"德拉诺"是《魔兽世界》虚构的地名，具有了区别商品来源的显著特征，故《魔兽世界：德拉诺之王》构成知名游戏特有名称。被告在原告《魔兽世界:德拉诺之王》游戏上线前后推出相似名称的游戏《全民魔兽：决战德拉诺》(原名《酋长萨尔：魔兽远征》)，主观上具有搭原告游戏知名度便车的故意，客观上容易导致相关公众的混淆,构成擅自使用他人知名商品特有名称的不正当竞争行为。另外，被告分播时代在宣传被诉游戏时多次提及魔兽世界，容易使相关公众误认该游戏是原告开发或与原告有授权许可等关系的手机游戏，构成虚假宣传。被告七游公司是被诉游戏的开发商，被告分播时代是独家运营商且是被告七游公司的股东，被告动景公司经被告分播时代授权向公众提供被诉游戏的下载服务，故原告主张三被告构成共同侵权，具有充分依据。在原告胜诉可能性高的情况下，被告关于如果原告败诉将会给其及玩家带来巨大损害的抗辩，明显缺乏说服力。另外，三被告共同实施了侵权行为，故被诉游戏软件是否登记在案外人名下，并不影响本案禁令是否颁发。

三、关于原告是否受到难以弥补的损害

被诉游戏是在原告《魔兽世界：德拉诺之王》游戏上线前后推出。虽然两者分属手机端和PC端的游戏,但两者都是网络游戏,且游戏名称相似，游戏中相关英雄和怪兽形象和名称相似，相关游戏界面相似，都采用玩家扮演英雄与怪兽作战的玩法。故两者是具有较强竞争关系的产品。被诉游戏的上线势必挤占原告新推游戏的市场份额。而且网络游戏具有生命周期短，传播速度快、范围广的特点，给原告造成的损害难以计算和量化。另外，被告分播时代在宣传被诉游戏时采用了低俗营销方式，在相关公众将被诉游戏与原告游戏混淆的情况下，会使相关公众对原告产生负面评价，从而给原告商誉带来损害。

四、关于被诉游戏应否整体下线及玩家利益的保护

被告虽提出相关英雄和怪物形象可以修改，但听证后提交的

修改方案仍然与原告主张的内容构成实质相似。另根据被诉游戏的名称、相关英雄和怪兽形象等重要组成部分均构成侵权，以及被诉游戏宣传 100% 还原魔兽形象等事实，该游戏其余英雄或怪兽形象也存在较大的侵权可能性。据此，原告要求被诉游戏整体下线，依据充分，应予支持。但行为保全期间不影响为被诉游戏玩家提供余额查询及退费等服务。

【本案裁判文书】

扫描二维码，可见裁判文书

Substantive Elements Reviewed for an Injunction, Affirmation of Irreparable Harm in Online Game Infringement Cases and Holistic Removal of a Game and Protection of Players' Interests

——Blizzard Entertainment Inc. et al.
v. Chengdu Qiyou Technology et al.

[Syllabus]

In the case of interim injunction, the possibility that the plaintiff wins the litigation and whether the plaintiff suffers from irreparable harm should be examined.

The launch of the disputed game would inevitably squeeze and occupy the market share of the new game launched by the plaintiff. At the same time, online games are characterized by short lifecycle, fast dissemination and broad circulation, due to which it is difficult to calculate and quantify the harm suffered by the plaintiff. Any vulgar marketing method of the disputed game would also harm the reputation of the plaintiff.

All important components of the disputed game constitute infringement, and the remaining components are also likely to be found infringing, hence the disputed game needs to be holistically removed. However, during the term of the injunction, the provision for balance inquiry, refund and other services for the players of the disputed game shall not be affected.

[Case No.] Guangzhou Intellectual Property Court (2015) YZFZMCZ No. 2 and (2015) YZFSMCZ No. 2

[Cause of Action] Dispute over copyright infringement and unfair competition

[Collegial Panel Members] Gong Qitian   Zhuang yi   Peng Ang

[Keywords] Online game, interim injunction, irreparable harm

[Relevant Legal Provisions] Article 50 of *Copyright Law of the People's Republic of China*, Article 100 of *Civil Procedure Law of the People's Republic of China*.

[Basic Facts]

The plaintiffs, Blizzard Entertainment Inc. (hereinafter referred to as "Blizzard Entertainment") and Shanghai EaseNet Network Technology Development Co., Ltd. (hereinafter referred to as "EaseNet") filed a suit for copyright infringement and unfair competition against the respondents, Chengdu Qiyou Technology Co., Ltd. (hereinafter referred to as "Qiyou"), Beijing Fenbo Times Internet Technology Co., Ltd. (hereinafter referred to as "Fenbo Times") and Guangzhou Dongjing Computer Technology Co., Ltd. (hereinafter referred to as "Dongjing"). The plaintiff Blizzard Entertainment is the copyright owner of computer software works such as World of Warcraft (first launched in the USA on November 23rd, 2004), World of Warcraft: The Burning Crusade (first launched in the USA on January 16th, 2007), World of Warcraft: Wrath of the Lich King (first launched in the USA on November 13th, 2008) and World of Warcraft: Mists of Pandaria (first launched in the USA on September 25th, 2012).

The World of Warcraft series of games have won many important game awards in China, such as the top 10 popular online games in 2006 and 2007 at the China Game Industry Annual Conference, the top 10 popular online games at the first Chinese Game Gold Raccoon Award in 2011, and the online game of the year at the award ceremony of List of Chinese Game Heroes in 2012.

From June 2014, the plaintiff Blizzard Entertainment started promoting its game World of Warcraft: Warlords of Draenor through its official Chinese website. On November 20th, the game was officially launched in China and was operated exclusively by the plaintiff EaseNet.

The heroes in the World of Warcraft series of games include Velen, Illidan Stormrage, Garrosh Hellscream and Thrall, etc. The monsters include Aku'mai, Deviate Shambler, etc. The designs of these heroes and monsters could be seen in Blizzard Entertainment's official Chinese website, English publication *Ultimate Visual Guide of World of Warcraft* and Chinese publications *Art of Blizzard and World of Warcraft Thrall: Twilight of Dragon*. The said websites and publications all indicated that the plaintiff Blizzard Entertainment was the copyright owner. In these two cases, the plaintiff claimed that it had copyright for fine-art works of 18 heroes and 7 monsters therein. The plaintiff also claimed that "Warcraft" and "Draenor" constituted the specific names of famous commodities, "Thrall" constituted a famous character name and that four game scenes (including title interface, login interface and role creation interface) constituted the specific decoration of famous commodities.

The disputed game, originally named as *Tribal Chief Thrall: Crusade of Warcraft*, was developed by the respondent Qiyou. The defendant Fenbo Times was a shareholder of respondent Qiyou and also the exclusive operator of the disputed game. On August 25th and September 19th 2014, respondent Fenbo Times launched the open beta iOS version and Android version respectively of the disputed game on its official website (www.rekoo.com), and on December 19th, it renamed the game as Everyone Warcraft: War of Draenor. Respondent Dongjing, with the authorization of respondent Fenbo Times, provided the Android version of the game to the public for download, in its official website (www.9game.cn).

The designs of relevant heroes and monsters of the disputed game were substantially similar with those claimed by the plaintiff, upon comparison.

With respect to the publicity and introduction of the disputed game, the official website of respondent Fenbo Times contained the following statements: "In order to recreate the World of Warcraft more perfectly, Tribal Chief Thrall...... whether it is the players controlling the heroes or the monsters in the game instance, and whether it is the map design or special skills, the designs of World of Warcraft are almost 100% recreated...... Panda Lin, top player of Warcraft, will accept the final challenge of 'beanty calls at your home' ."

"Everyone Warcraft is a card game with the background of World of Warcraft, which presents many contents of World of Warcraft perfectly, it ignites the passion of the fans with its plots, heros and scenes instantly."

In the official blog of the respondent Fenbo Times, some players commented: "I love the challenge of Warcraft so much ......Let's play World of Warcraft together."

The plaintiff believes that the disputed game copied the designs of heroes and monsters from the plaintiff's game and used the name and decoration similar to those used in the plaintiff's game. The respondent Fenbo Times repeatedly claimed in its publicity that the disputed game was the mobile version of Warcraft. The behavior of the three respondents jointly infringed the copyright of the plaintiff and constituted unfair competition. Further infringement would cause irreparable harm to the plaintiff. Therefore, the plaintiff instituted proceedings at the Guangzhou Intellectual Property Court and applied for an interim injunction, requesting that the disputed game be holistically removed. The plaintiff was willing to post a cash bond of RMB10 million. The three respondents contended that the disputed game software is registered under the name of a third party, the plaintiff could not prove that it was the copyright owner of the designs of the heroes and monsters involved in the case, the respondents constituted copyright infringement and unfair competition, or it suffered from irreparable harm, and that the issue of an injunction would seriously harm the interests of the respondents and game players. Therefore, the respondents requested that the plaintiff's application for injunction be rejected.

 Holding

The Guangzhou Intellectual Property Court issued an interim injunction on March 9th, 2015: 1. The respondent Qiyou was prohibited from reproducing, distributing and disseminating online the game *Everyone Warcraft: War of Draenor* (originally named as *Tribal Chief Thrall: Crusade of Warcraft*) for a term expiring upon the effective date of the judgments of the present two cases; 2. The respondent Fenbo Times was prohibited from reproducing, distributing and disseminating online the game *Everyone Warcraft: War of Draenor* (originally named as *Tribal Chief Thrall: Crusade of Warcraft*), and engaging in the alleged unfair competition for a term expiring upon the effective date of the judgments of the present two cases, provided that during the term of the injunction, the provision of balance inquiry, refund and other services for the game players would not be affected; 3. The respondent Dongjing was prohibited from disseminating the game *Everyone Warcraft: War of Draenor* (originally named as *Tribal Chief Thrall: Crusade of Warcraft*) through its official website (www.9game.cn) for a term expiring upon the effective date of the judgments of the present two case, provided during the injunction, the provision of balance inquiry, refund and other services for the game players shall not be affected; 4. The other injunction applications of the plaintiff Blizzard Entertainment and plaintiff EaseNet were dismissed.

[Reasoning]

Guangzhou Intellectual Property Court opined that:

With respect to the substantive review requirements for an injunction, according to Article 100 of the *Civil Procedure Law of the People's Republic of China*, whereas the conducts of one party may make the judgment hard to enforce or cause the parties other harms, the people's court may, at the request of the counterparty, prohibit it from conducting certain actions. Thus, while determining whether to issue an injunction, the court shall first review the plaintiff's possibility to win the case. According to Article 101 of *Civil Procedure Law of the People's Republic of China*, a rightholder may apply for an pre-litigation injunction in the case of urgency where the failure to immediately issue an injunction would cause such rightholder irreparable harm. As the plaintiff applied for injunction while instituting proceedings and claimed that the situation was urgent, it is also necessary to review whether the alleged infringement would cause the plaintiff irreparable harm.

With respect to the plaintiff's possibility to win the case, both China and the USA are member states of the Berne Convention for the Protection of Literary and Artistic Works, and according to the Convention and Article 2 of the *Copyright Law of the People's Republic of China*, the works of the plaintiff Blizzard Entertainment are protected by China's copyright law. Plaintiff Blizzard Entertainment is the copyright owner of computer software works of the World of Warcraft series games. In view of this and the copyright marks in the official website and legal publications of plaintiff Blizzard Entertainment involved in the case as introduction of heroes and monsters in the World of Warcrafts, there is sufficient proof that the plaintiff enjoys copyright for the artistic works of the designs of 18 heroes and 7 monsters claimed. The respondents' unauthorized use of the designs of these heroes and monsters in the game infringed the plaintiff's rights to reproduce, distribute and disseminate online its fine-art works. At the same time, the World of Warcraft series games of the plaintiff are very famous in the Chinese market. Therefore, the plaintiff's game World of Warcraft: Warlords of Draenor constituted a famous game. Since the relevant public view Warcraft as an abbreviation of the World of Warcraft, "Draenor" is a fictitious name in the World of Warcraft, and has distinctive features that distinguish the source of the commodities. Thus, World of Warcraft: Warlords of Draenor constitutes a specific name of a famous game. The respondents launched a similarly named game Everyone Warcraft: War of Draenor (originally named as Tribal Chief Thrall: Crusade of Warcraft) around the time the plaintiff's game World of Warcraft: Warlords of Draenor was launched. Subjectively, there was an intention to take a free ride on the popularity of the plaintiff's game. Objectively, it was likely to cause confusion among the relevant public. It thereby constituted unfair competition of unauthorized use of specific names of famous commodities of others. In addition, the respondent Fenbo Times repeatedly mentioned World of Warcraft when promoting the disputed game. This is false publicity that is likely to cause the relevant public to believe that the game is a mobile version developed or authorized by the plaintiff. The respondent Qiyou was the developer of the disputed game, respondent Fenbo Times was the exclusive operator and shareholder of respondent Qiyou and respondent Dongjing provided the download services for the disputed game to the public, with authorization by the respondent Fenbo Times; hence, there was sufficient evidence to establish the plaintiff's claim that the three respondents constituted joint infringement. With the plaintiff being likely to win, it was obviously unconvincing for the respondents to claim that the interim injunction would cause great harm to themselves and their players if the plaintiff loses the litigation. In addition, the three respondents jointly conducted infringement. Therefore, whether or not the disputed game software is registered under the name of a third party does not affect whether to issue the injunction in this case.

With respect to whether the plaintiff would be suffer from irreparable harm, the disputed game was launched around the time the plaintiff's game World of Warcraft: Warlords of Draenor was launched. Although the two are mobile and PC games, respectively, both are online games that have similar names, similarly designed and named heroes and monsters, similar game interfaces and similar model of heroes fighting monsters. Therefore, the two are products with a strong competitive relation. The launch of the disputed game will inevitably squeeze and occupy the market share of the newly launched game of the plaintiff. Furthermore, online games are characterized by short lifecycle, fast dissemination and broad circulation, making the plaintiff's harm hard to calculate and quantify. Moreover, the respondent Fenbo Times marketed the disputed game with vulgar approach. When confused about the disputed game and the plaintiff's game, the relevant public will make negative evaluation about the plaintiff, which will harm the plaintiff's reputation.

293

With respect to the holistic removal of the disputed game and the protection of players' interests, although the respondents proposed that the designs of relevant heroes and monsters could be modified, the modification proposal submitted after the hearing was still substantially similar to the content claimed by the plaintiff. In addition, according to the facts that the name, designs of relevant heroes and monsters and other important components of the disputed game are all infringing, and that the disputed game is promoted as 100% recreating the designs of World of Warcraft, the designs of the remaining heroes or monsters of that game are likely to be found infringing, too. Thus, the plaintiff's request to holistically remove the disputed game is sufficiently proven and shall be supported. However, the provision of services such as balance inquiry and refund to players of the disputed game shall not be affected during the term of the injunction.

[Opinion of the Case (Chinese Version)]

Scan the QR code to see the Chinese version of the opinion

思想与表达的划分、
涉文学作品侵害改编权的判定思路

——陈喆（笔名：琼瑶）与余征（笔名：于正）等
侵害著作权纠纷案

【裁判要旨】

著作权的客体是作品，但并非作品中的任何要素都受到著作权法的保护，思想与表达二分法是区分作品中受保护的要素和不受保护的要素的基本原则，其内涵是著作权法保护思想的表达而不保护思想本身。

文学作品的表达既不能仅仅局限为对白台词、修辞造句，也不能将文学作品中的主题、题材、普通人物关系认定为著作权法保护的表达。文学作品中，情节的前后衔接、逻辑顺序将全部情节紧密贯穿为完整的个性化表达，这种足够具体的人物设置、情节结构、内在逻辑关系的有机结合体可以成为著作权法保护的表达。

改编权即改变作品，创作出具有独创性的新作品的权利。改编权所直接控制的行为是改编行为，即改变作品，创作出具有独创性的新作品的行为，新作品应当保留原作品的基本表达，否则仅仅根据原作品的思想创作出来的新作品不受改编权的控制。

判断被诉行为是否侵犯权利人的改编权，通常需要满足接触和实质性相似两个要件。接触是指被诉侵权人有机会接触到、了解到或者感受到权利人享有著作权的作品。接触可以是一种推定。实质性相似的认定可以采用抽象分离法或整体观感法。判断文学作品是否构成实质性相似，根据案件具体情况，可以将两种方法结合使用，同时需要排除合理借鉴的情形。

【案　　　号】　北京市高级人民法院（2015）高民（知）终字第
　　　　　　　　1039号
【案　　　由】　侵害著作权纠纷
【合议庭成员】　谢甄珂　袁相军　钟　鸣
【法 官 助 理】　亓　雷
【关 键 词】　思想　接触　表达　实质性相似
【相 关 法 条】　《中华人民共和国著作权法》第十条第一款第（十四）项、
　　　　　　　　第十二条、第四十七条第（六）项

【基本案情】

原告琼瑶是台湾著名编剧。被告于正是大陆知名编剧。原告琼瑶主张的剧本《梅花烙》于1992年10月创作完成，未以纸质方式公开发表。小说《梅花烙》系根据剧本《梅花烙》改编而来，于1993年6月30日创作完成，1993年9月15日起在台湾地区公开发行，同年起在中国大陆公开发表，小说《梅花烙》作者是本案原告琼瑶。电视剧《梅花烙》于1993年10月13日起在我国台湾地区首次电视播出，并于1994年4月13日起在中国大陆地区首次电视播出，电视剧《梅花烙》内容与剧本《梅花烙》高度一致。电视剧《梅花烙》片头字幕显示署名编剧为林久愉，林久愉于2014年6月20日出具经公证认证的《声明书》，称其仅负责记录原告的创作讲述，执行剧本的文字统稿整理工作，剧本《梅花烙》系由原告琼瑶独立原创形成。被告于正系剧本《宫锁连城》载明的作者，系电视剧《宫锁连城》

的署名编剧。剧本《宫锁连城》创作完成时间为 2012 年 7 月 17 日，首次发表时间为 2014 年 4 月 8 日。电视剧《宫锁连城》根据剧本《宫锁连城》拍摄，剧情内容与剧本《宫锁连城》基本一致，于 2014 年 4 月 8 日在湖南卫视首播，片尾出品公司依次署名为：湖南经视公司、东阳欢娱公司、万达公司、东阳星瑞公司。剧本《宫锁连城》、电视剧《宫锁连城》在人物设置及人物关系、情节上与原告涉案作品均存在对应关系。剧本《宫锁连城》相对于原告涉案作品在整体上的情节排布及推演过程基本一致。原告琼瑶起诉至北京市第三中级人民法院，认为剧本《宫锁连城》侵害了其对《梅花烙》小说和剧本的改编权，电视剧《宫锁连城》的拍摄侵害了其摄制权，要求停止侵权、赔礼道歉和赔偿损失。

 裁判结果

　　北京市第三中级人民法院于 2014 年 12 月 25 日作出（2014）三中民初字第 07916 号民事判决，判决：1. 湖南经视公司、东阳欢娱公司、万达公司、东阳星瑞公司于判决生效之日起立即停止电视剧《宫锁连城》的复制、发行和传播行为；2. 余征于判决生效之日起十日内在新浪网、搜狐网、乐视网、凤凰网显著位置刊登致歉声明，向陈喆公开赔礼道歉，消除影响（致歉声明的内容须于判决生效后五日内送法院审核，逾期不履行，法院将在《法制日报》上刊登判决主要内容，所需费用由余征承担）；3. 余征、湖南经视公司、东阳欢娱公司、万达公司、东阳星瑞公司于判决生效之日起十日内连带赔偿陈喆经济损失及诉讼合理开支共计人民币 5,000,000 元；4. 驳回陈喆的其他诉讼请求。后余征等被告不服，向北京市高级人民法院提起上诉，北京市高级人民法院判决：驳回上诉，维持原判。

【裁判理由】

北京市高级人民法院认为：

一、《中华人民共和国著作权法》保护的文学作品的表达

思想与表达二分法是区分作品中受保护的要素和不受保护的要素的基本原则，其内涵是著作权法保护思想的表达而不保护思想本身。若被诉侵权作品与权利人的作品构成实质性相似，应当是表达构成实质性相似。表达不仅指文字、色彩、线条等符号的最终形式，当作品的内容被用于体现作者的思想、情感时，内容也属于受著作权法保护的表达，但创意、素材或公有领域的信息、创作形式、必要场景和唯一或有限表达则被排除在著作权法的保护范围之外。剧本和小说均属于文学作品，文学作品中思想与表达界限的划分较为复杂。文学作品的表达既不能仅仅局限为对白台词、修辞造句，也不能将文学作品中的主题、题材、普通人物关系认定为著作权法保护的表达。文学作品的表达，不仅表现为文字性的表达，也包括文字所表述的故事内容，但人物设置及其相互的关系，以及由具体事件的发生、发展和先后顺序等构成的情节，只有具体到一定程度，即文学作品的情节选择、结构安排、情节推进设计反映出作者独特的选择、判断、取舍，才能成为著作权法保护的表达。

文学作品中，情节的前后衔接、逻辑顺序将全部情节紧密贯穿为完整的个性化表达，这种足够具体的人物设置、情节结构、内在逻辑关系的有机结合体可以成为著作权法保护的表达。

二、侵害改编权的认定思路

《中华人民共和国著作权法》第十条第一款第（十四）项规定，改编权即改变作品，创作出具有独创性的新作品的权利。根据上述规定，改编权所直接控制的行为是改编行为，即改变作品，创作出具有独创性的新作品的行为，新作品应当保留原作品的基本表达，

否则仅仅根据原作品的思想创作出来的新作品不受改编权的控制。除法律另有规定外，未经许可利用他人的原作品实施改编行为，构成对原作品著作权人改编权的侵犯。判断被诉行为是否侵犯权利人的改编权，通常需要满足接触和实质性相似两个要件。

接触是指被诉侵权人有机会接触到、了解到或者感受到权利人享有著作权的作品。接触可以是一种推定。权利人的作品通过刊登、展览、广播、表演、放映等方式公开，也可以视为将作品公之于众进行了发表，被诉侵权人依据社会通常情况具有获知权利人作品的机会和可能，可以被推定为接触。电视剧《梅花烙》的公开播放可以视为剧本《梅花烙》的发表，并可据此推定余征、湖南经视公司、东阳欢娱公司、万达公司、东阳星瑞公司接触了剧本《梅花烙》。

著作权法保护思想的表达而不保护思想本身。若被诉侵权作品与权利人的作品构成实质性相似，应当是表达构成实质性相似。表达不仅指文字、色彩、线条等符号的最终形式，当作品的内容被用于体现作者的思想、情感时，内容也属于受著作权法保护的表达，但创意、素材或公有领域的信息、创作形式、必要场景和唯一或有限表达则被排除在著作权法的保护范围之外。判断是否构成实质性相似时，需首先判断权利人主张的作品要素是否属于著作权法保护的表达。

剧本和小说均属于文学作品，文学作品中思想与表达界限的划分较为复杂。文学作品的表达既不能仅仅局限为对白台词、修辞造句，也不能将文学作品中的主题、题材、普通人物关系认定为著作权法保护的表达。文学作品的表达，不仅表现为文字性的表达，也包括文字所表述的故事内容，但人物设置及其相互的关系，以及由具体事件的发生、发展和先后顺序等构成的情节，只有具体到一定程度，即文学作品的情节选择、结构安排、情节推进设计反映出作者独特的选择、判断、取舍，才能成为著作权法保护的表达。确定文学作品保护的表达是不断抽象过滤的过程。对于人物关系和人物设置，应对人物与情节的相互结合互动形成的表达进行比对。如果事件次序和人物互动均来源于在先权利作品，则构成实质性相似。文学作品中，情节的前后衔接、逻辑顺序将全部情节紧密贯穿为完整的个性化表达，这种足够具体的人物设置、情节结构、内在逻辑关系的有机结合体可以成为著作权法保护的表达。如果被诉侵权作品中包含足够具体的表达，且这种紧密贯穿的情节设置在被诉侵权作品中达到一定数量、比例，可以认定为构成实质性相似；或者被诉侵权作品中包含的紧密贯穿的情节设置已经占到了权利作品足够的比例，即使其在被诉侵权作品中所占比例不大，也足以使受众感知到来源于特定作品时，可以认定为构成实质性相似。

此外，需要明确的是，即使作品中的部分具体情节属于公共领域或者有限、唯一的表达，但是并不代表上述具体情节与其他情节的有机联合整体不具有独创性，不构成著作权法保护的表达。部分情节不构成实质性相似，并不代表整体不构成实质性相似。

本案中，原告琼瑶主张的 21 个情节中，其中 9 个情节构成著作权法保护的表达，剧本《宫锁连城》与上述 9 个情节构成实质性相似；原告琼瑶主张的人物设置及其相互关系，剧本《宫锁连城》与之构成实质性相似；剧本《宫锁连城》与涉案作品在整体上仍然构成实质性相似。

【本案裁判文书】

扫描二维码，可见裁判文书

Divide of Idea and Expression, and the Way to Judge Adaptation Right Infringement Concerning Literary Works

——Chen Zhe (pen name: Chiung Yao) v. Yu Zheng

(pen name: Yu Zheng) et al.

[Syllabus]

Works are the object of copyright. However, not all the elements in works are protected by the copyright law. Idea-expression dichotomy is the basic principle to distinguish the protected and unprotected elements in works. In essence, the copyright law protects expressions of ideas, instead of ideas per se. Neither can expressions in literary works be limited to dialogues, wording and phrasing, nor can the theme, subject matter and ordinary character relations in literary works be identified as the expressions protected by the copyright law. In literary works, plots are closely connected through successive scenes and logical sequence to form complete and individualized expressions. Such organic integration of sufficiently specific character setting, plot structure and inherent logical relations can become expressions protected by the copyright law.

The right of adaption refers to the right to change the work, and create a new work with originality. The acts under direct control of the right of adaption are those of adaptation, i.e. the acts to change the work and create a new work with originality. The new work shall retain the basic expressions in the original work. Otherwise, the right of adaption does not control the new work created only on basis of the ideas of the original work. For the accused acts to be found infringing the right of adaption of the right holder, the two requirements of access and substantial similarity usually need to be both met.

Access means that the accused infringer has the chance to access, know about or experience the copyrighted works of the right holder. Access can be presumed. Substantial similarity can be determined on basis of abstract separation or overall expression. To judgment whether or not the literary works are substantially similar, the two ways can be used together according to specific circumstances of the case, and reasonable reference shall be excluded.

[Case No.] Beijing High People's Court (2015) GM (Z) ZZ No. 1039

[Cause of Action] Copyright infringement dispute

[Collegial Panel Members] Xie Zhenke　Yuan Xiangjun Zhong Min

[Judge Assistant] Qi Lei

[Keywords] Ideas, access, expression, substantial similarity

[Relevant Legal Provisions] Subclause 1(14) of Article 10, Article 12 and Article 47(6) of the *Copyright Law of the People's Republic of China*

[Basic Facts]

The Plaintiff Chiung Yao is a famous script writer from Taiwan. The Defendant Yu Zheng is a famous script writer from the mainland of China. The script of "Meihualao" created by the Plaintiff Chiung Yao was completed in October 1992, and not published in paper form. The novel "Meihualao" was adapted from the script of "Meihualao", completed on June 30, 1993, and publicly distributed in Taiwan since September 15, 1993 and published in the Chinese mainland in the same year. The

Plaintiff Chiung Yao of this Case is the author of the novel "Meihualao". The TV series "Meihualao" was premiered in Taiwan on October 13, 1993, and in the Chinese mainland on April 13, 1994. The TV series "Meihualao" are highly similar to the script of "Meihualao". As shown in the opening credits of TV series "Meihualao", the script writer was Lin Jiuyu, who issued a notarized Statement on June 20, 2014 that she was only responsible for taking the dictation of the Plaintiff's creation and consolidating and editing of the script, and the script of "Meihualao" was independently created by the Plaintiff Chiung Yao. The Defendant Yu Zheng was the recorded author of the script of "Palace 3: the Lost Daughter", i.e. the named script writer of the TV series "Palace 3: the Lost Daughter". The script of " Palace 3: the Lost Daughter" was completed on July 17, 2012 and first published on April 8, 2014. The TV series "Palace 3: the Lost Daughter" was shot in accordance with the script of "Palace 3: the Lost Daughter", and its plot and content were basically the same as the script of "Palace 3: the Lost Daughter" in contents. The TV series "Palace 3: the Lost Daughter" was premiered in Hunan TV on April 8, 2014. It was stated in the ending credits of the TV series that production companies were Hunan eTV Culture Media Co., Ltd., Dongyang Huanyu Film and Television Culture Co., Ltd., Wanda Media Co., Ltd. and Dongyang Xingrui Film and Television Culture Media Co., Ltd. The script of "Palace 3: the Lost Daughter" and the TV series "Palace 3: the Lost Daughter" corresponded to the Plaintiff's work involved in character setting, character relations and plots. The script of "Palace 3: the Lost Daughter" was basically same as the Plaintiff's work involved in aspects of overall plot arrangement and process of progression. The Plaintiff Chiung Yao instituted a lawsuit to No.3 Intermediate People's Court of Beijing Municipality, alleging that the script of "Palace 3: the Lost Daughter" infringed her right of adaptation for the script and novel of "Meihualao", and the shooting of the TV series "Palace 3: the Lost Daughter" infringed her right of shooting, and requiring the termination of

303

the infringement, public apology and damages for loss.

 Holding

No.3 Intermediate People's Court of Beijing Municipality made the (2014) SZMCZ No. 07916 Civil Judgment on December 25, 2014, ruling that: I. Hunan eTV Culture Media Co., Ltd., Dongyang Huanyu Film and Television Culture Co., Ltd., Wanda Media Co., Ltd. and Dongyang Xingrui Film and Television Culture Media Co., Ltd. immediately cease the reproduction, distribution and dissemination of the TV series "Palace 3: the Lost Daughter" on the effective date of the Judgment; II. Yu Zheng make public apologetic statements at conspicuous positions of Sina.com, Sohu.com, LETV and ifeng. com to apologize to Chen Zhe and eliminate the influence (contents of the apologetic statement shall be submitted to the court within five days upon effectiveness of the Judgment for review, and in case of overdue performance, the court would publish the gist of this Judgment on the *Legal Daily*, with the necessary costs borne by Yu Zheng); III. Yu Zheng, Hunan eTV Culture Media Co., Ltd., Dongyang Huanyu Film and Television Culture Co., Ltd., Wanda Media Co., Ltd. and Dongyang Xingrui Film and Television Culture Media Co., Ltd. pay, jointly and severally, RMB 5,000,000 to compensate Chen Zhe for her economic losses and reasonable litigation costs within ten days upon effectiveness of the Judgment; IV. other claims by Chen Zhe be rejected. Yu Zheng et. al refused to accept the Judgment and appealed to Beijing High People's Court, which made the following judgment: the appeal be dismissed and the original judgment upheld.

[Reasoning]

Beijing High People's Court opined that:

I. The expressions in literary works protected by the copyright law

Idea-expression dichotomy is the basic principle to distinguish the protected and unprotected elements, whose essence is the copyright law protects expressions of ideas, instead of ideas per se. If the allegedly infringing work is substantially similar to the work of the right holder, it should be the expressions that are substantially similar. Expressions protectable under the copyright law refer to not only the finalized form of the text, colors, lines and other symbols, but also the content used to manifest the author's ideas and emotions. However, creative ideas, source material, or public domain information as well as forms of creation, necessary scenes and sole or limited expressions are excluded from the scope of protection of the copyright law. Both scripts and novels are literary works, in which the boundary between ideas and expressions is difficult to delineate. Neither can expressions in literary works be limited to dialogues, wording and phrasing, nor can the theme, subject matter and ordinary character relations in literary works be identified as the expressions protected by the copyright law. Expressions of a literary work are not only manifested by literal expressions, but also the story told through literal expressions. However, the setting of and relations among characters and the plots consisting of the occurrence, development and sequence of specific events cannot constitute expressions protected by the copyright law until they reach that certain extent that the author's unique choices, judgment and trade-off are reflected in the plot selection, structure arrangement and design of plot progression in a literary work.

In literary works, the tight and coherent connections and logistical sequence of plots from the beginning to the make the whole plot a complete and individual expression. The organic combination of such sufficiently specific character setting, plot structure and inherent logical relation may constitute expressions protected by the copyright law.

II. Way to judge infringement of the right of adaption

According to provisions of Item 14, Subclause 1 of Article 10 of *the Copyright Law of the People's Republic of China*, the right of adaption is the right to change the work, and create a new work with originality. Subject to provisions above, the acts under direct control of the right of adaption are those of adaptation, i.e. the acts to change the work and create a new work with originality. The new work shall retain basic expressions in the original work. Otherwise, the right of adaption does not control the new work created only on basis of the ideas of the original work. Unless otherwise specified by the law, unauthorized adaptation of the others' original works constitutes an infringement upon the adaptation right of the original copyright holder. For the accused acts to be found infringing the right of adaption of the right holder, the two requirements of access and substantial similarity usually need to be both met.

Access means that the accused infringer has the chance to access, know about or experience the copyrighted works of the right holder. Access can be presumed. When disclosed by such means as publication, exhibition, broadcasting, performance and screening, the works of the right holder may be deemed as published and made accessible to the alleged infringer in normal circumstances of the society. Thus, access can be presumed. The broadcast of the TV series "Meihualao" may be deemed as the publication of the script of "Meihualao". Therefore, it may be presumed that Yu Zheng, Hunan eTV Culture Media Co., Ltd., Dongyang Huanyu Film and Television Culture Co., Ltd., Wanda Media Co., Ltd. and Dongyang Xingrui Film and Television Culture Media Co., Ltd. accessed the script of "Meihualao".

The copyright law protects expressions of ideas, instead of ideas per se. If the allegedly infringing work is substantially similar to the work of the right holder, it should be the expressions that are substantially similar. Expressions do not merely refer to the text, colors, lines, and symbols of the final form of a work. When the content of a work is used to manifest the author's ideas and emotions, the content is also a type of expression protected by the copyright law. However, creative ideas, source material, or public domain information as well as forms of creation, necessary scenes, or sole or limited expressions are excluded from the scope of protection of the copyright law. To judgment whether or not substantial similarity is justified, one shall first judge whether or not the elements claimed by copyright holder belong to expressions protected by the copyright law.

Both scripts and novels are literary works, in which the boundary between ideas and expressions is difficult to delineate. Neither can expressions in literary works be limited to dialogues, wording and phrasing, nor can the theme, subject matter and ordinary character relations in literary works be identified as the expressions protected by the copyright law. Expressions of a literary work are not only manifested by literal expressions, but also the story told through literal expressions. However, the setting of and relations among characters and the plots consisting of the occurrence, development and sequence of specific events cannot constitute expressions protected by the copyright law until they reach that certain extent that the authors' unique choices, judgment and trade-off are reflected in the plot selection, structure arrangement and design of plot progression in a literary work. It is a process of abstracting and filtering to determine what are the protected expressions of a literary work. Comparison shall be made on expressions formed through combination and interaction of characters and plots when it comes to the character relations and setting. If both the sequence of events and interaction of characters originate from the prior copyrighted work, substantial similarity shall be justified. In literary works, plots are closely connected through successive scenes and logical sequence to form complete and individualized expressions. Such organic integration of sufficiently specific character setting, plot structure and inherent logical relations can become expressions protected by the copyright law. If the accused infringing work includes expressions which are specific enough, and such plot arrangements as running closely throughout the text reach a certain amount and portion in the alleged infringing work, substantial similarity shall be justified; or if such plot arrangements as running closely throughout the text of the accused infringing work account for a sufficient portion in the copyrighted work, substantial similarity shall be justified even if they only take a small portion in the accused infringing work, yet suffice to make the audiences feel like they originated from a certain work.

In addition, it needs to be clarified that, even though some specific plots in a work belong to the public domain or constitute limited or sole expressions, it does not mean that the organic combination of such plots and other plots are not original, or constitute expressions protected by the copyright law. Overall substantial similarity cannot be excluded by partial dissimilarity of plot.

In this Case, 9 out the 21 plots alleged by the Plaintiff Chiung Yao are expressions protected by the copyright law, are substantially similia to the script of "Palace 3: the Lost Daughter"; the script of "Palace 3: the Lost Daughter" is also substantially similar to the character setting and relations alleged by the Plaintiff Chiung Yao; and on the whole, script of "Palace 3: the Lost Daughter" is substantially similar to the work involved.

[Opinion of the Case (Chinese Version)]

Scan the QR code to see the Chinese version of the opinion

第四章　垄断、竞争案件

Chapter 4 Monopoly and Competition Cases

知名商品特有包装装潢权益归属的确定

——广药集团与加多宝公司等
擅自使用知名商品特有包装装潢纠纷案

【裁判要旨】

《中华人民共和国反不正当竞争法》第五条第（二）项规定的"知名商品"和"特有包装装潢"之间具有互为表里、不可割裂的关系，只有使用了特有包装装潢的商品，才能够成为反不正当竞争法调整的对象。抽象的商品名称或无确定内涵的商品概念，脱离于包装装潢所依附的具体商品，缺乏可供评价的实际使用行为，不具有依据《中华人民共和国反不正当竞争法》第五条第（二）项规定进行评价的意义。

在确定特有包装装潢的权益归属时，既要在遵循诚实信用原则的前提下鼓励诚实劳动，也应当尊重消费者基于包装装潢本身具有的显著特征而客观形成的对商品来源指向关系的认知。

【案 号】	最高人民法院（2015）民三终字第2号、（2015）民三终字第3号
【案 由】	擅自使用知名商品特有包装装潢纠纷
【合议庭成员】	宋晓明　夏君丽　周　翔　钱小红　佟　姝
【关 键 词】	不正当竞争　知名商品　特有包装装潢　权益归属

【相关法条】《中华人民共和国反不正当竞争法》第五条第（二）项

【基本案情】

2012 年 7 月 6 日，广州医药集团有限公司广药集团（以下简称广药集团）与广东加多宝饮料食品有限公司（以下简称加多宝公司）于同日分别向法院提起诉讼，均主张享有"红罐王老吉凉茶"知名商品特有包装装潢的权益，并据此诉指对方生产销售的红罐凉茶商品的包装装潢构成侵权。具体而言，作为"王老吉"注册商标的权利人，广药集团认为，因"王老吉"商标是包装装潢不可分割的组成部分，并发挥了指示商品来源的显著识别作用，消费者当然会认为红罐王老吉凉茶来源于"王老吉"商标的权利人，而配方、口味并不会影响消费者对商品的识别和判断。作为红罐王老吉凉茶曾经的实际经营者，加多宝公司认为，包装装潢权益与"王老吉"商标权的归属问题各自独立，互不影响。消费者喜爱的是由加多宝公司生产并选用特定配方的红罐王老吉凉茶，本案包装装潢由加多宝公司使用并与前述商品紧密结合，包装装潢的相关权益应归属于加多宝公司。

 裁判结果

广东省高级人民法院一审认为，"红罐王老吉凉茶"包装装潢的权益享有者应为广药集团，广州王老吉健康产业有限公司（以下简称大健康公司）经广药集团授权生产销售的红罐凉茶不构成侵权。由于加多宝公司不享有涉案包装装潢权益，故其生产销售的一面"王老吉"、一面"加多宝"和两面"加多宝"的红罐凉茶均构成侵权。一审法院遂判令加多宝公司停止侵权行为，刊登声明消除影响，并赔偿广药集团经济损失 1.5 亿元及合理维权费用 26 万余元。加多宝公司不服两案一审判决，向最高人民法院提起上诉。最高人民法院于 2017 年 7 月 7 日二审判决对广药集团及加多宝公司的诉讼请求均予以驳回。

【裁判理由】

　　法院生效裁判认为，包装装潢具有显著识别特征，并使用于具有一定知名度的商品之上，是与包装装潢有关的商业标识性权益获得反不正当竞争法保护的条件。在适用《中华人民共和国反不正当竞争法》第五条第（二）项的规定时，应对"特有包装装潢"与"知名商品"之间的关系作出正确理解，即二者具有互为表里、不可割裂的关系。只有使用了特有包装装潢的商品，才能够成为反不正当竞争法评述的对象。相反，抽象的商品名称，或无确定内涵的商品概念，脱离于包装装潢所依附的具体商品，缺乏可供评价的实际使用行为，不具有依据《中华人民共和国反不正当竞争法》第五条第（二）项规定进行评价的意义。"王老吉凉茶"作为一种商品名称，在双方纠纷发生之时，至少可以指代由广药集团生产的绿色纸盒或加多宝公司生产的红色罐装等不同包装装潢形式的凉茶商品。而本案界定"知名商品"的目的，是为了判断附着于其上的、特定的包装装潢形式，是否符合反不正当竞争法对商业标识性权益提供保护的条件。因此，该"知名商品"应当与涉案包装装潢形式具有明确的指向关系。一审法院脱离了商品与包装装潢所应具有的依附关系，将指代并不唯一的商品名称"王老吉凉茶"认定为本案的"知名商品"，缺乏事实与法律依据，对此予以纠正。

　　本案所涉知名商品特有包装装潢纠纷的产生，源于双方在签

315

订和履行商标许可使用合同的过程中，并未对可能产生于许可使用期间的衍生利益如何进行分割作出明确的约定。通常情况下，在商标许可使用关系终止后，被许可人应停止使用行为，被许可使用商标之上所积累的商誉，应同时归还于许可人。但本案纠纷发生的特殊之处在于，许可使用期间形成的特有包装装潢，既与被许可商标的使用存在密切联系，又因其具备反不正当竞争法下独立权益的属性，而产生了外溢于商标权之外的商誉特征。双方各自提出的权利主张，既涉及与商业标识性权益保护有关的一般性法律适用问题，也体现了本案所特有的包装装潢权益在形成过程中所包含的复杂历史和现实因素。注册商标制度与知名商品特有包装装潢权益保护制度虽然均属于对商业标识性权益提供保护的法律制度，但二者的权利来源和保护条件有所不同。注册商标与包装装潢可以各自发挥其独立的识别作用，并分属于不同的权利主体。红罐王老吉凉茶推出市场后，经过加多宝公司及其关联企业有效的营销活动，红罐王老吉凉茶使用的包装装潢因其知名度和独特性，已经形成了独立的商业标识性权益。但本案的特殊之处在于，作为涉案包装装潢实际经营者的加多宝公司，在设计、使用及宣传推广的过程中，始终将作为广药集团注册商标的"王老吉"文字在包装装潢中进行了突出使用，且从未着意阻断和清晰区分包装装潢与其中包含的注册商标之间的关系，客观上使包装装潢同时指向了加多宝公司与广药集团。消费者亦不会刻意区分法律意义上的商标权与知名商品特有包装装潢权益，而会自然地将红罐王老吉凉茶与广药集团、加多宝公司同时建立联系。实际上，涉案包装装潢中确实也同时蕴含了广药集团"王老吉"品牌的影响力，以及加多宝公司通过十余年的生产经营和宣传推广而形成、发展而来的商品知名度和包装装潢的显著识别效果。综合考虑上述因素，结合红罐王老吉凉茶的历史发展过程、双方的合作背景、消费者的认知及公平原则的考量，因广药集团及其前身、加多宝公司及其关联企业，均对涉案包装装潢权益的形成、发展和商誉建树，各自发挥了积极的作用，将涉案包装装潢权益完全判归一方所有，均会导致显失公平的结果，并可能损及社会公众利益。因此，涉案知名商品特有包装装潢权益，在遵循诚实信用原则和尊重消费者认知并不损害他人合法权益的前提下，可由广药集团与加多宝公司共同享有。

【本案裁判文书】

扫描二维码，可见裁判文书

Determination on the Ownership of Packaging and Decoration Specific to Famous Commodities

——GPHL v. JDB Company et al.

[Syllabus]

*The "famous commodities" and "specific packaging and decoration" stipulated in Item 2, Article 5 of **the Anti-unfair Competition Law** are mutually interdependent and inseparable; only the commodities that use specific packaging or decoration can be the object regulated by **the Anti-unfair Competition Law**. Abstract commodity names or commodity concepts without definitive connotations are detached from the concrete commodities on which packaging and decoration depend, short of evaluable conducts of actual usage, and thus unevaluable under Item 2, Article 5 of **the Anti-unfair Competition Law**.*

The determination of the ownership of the rights and interests of specific packaging and decoration shall both encourage honest work on the premise of following the principle of good faith, and respect consumers' cognition on the source of commodities objectively formed based on the distinctive features of packaging and decoration per se.

[Case No.] Supreme People's Court (2015) MSZZ No.2 and (2015) MSZZ No.3

[Cause of Action] Disputes over unauthorized use of the packaging and decoration specific to a famous commodity

[Collegial Panel Members] Song Xiaoming   Xia Junli
Zhou Xiang   Qian Xiaohong   Tong Shu

[Keywords] Unfair competition, famous commodity, specific packaging and decoration, ownership

[Relevant Legal Provisions] Item 2, Article 5 of *Anti-unfair Competition Law of the People's Republic of China*

[Basic Facts]

On July 6, 2012, Guangzhou Pharmaceutical Holdings Limited (hereinafter referred to as "GPHL") and Guangdong Jiaduobao Beverage and Food Co., Ltd. (hereinafter referred to as "JDB Company") respectively instituted legal proceedings in a court on the same day, each asserting its rights and interests of the packaging and decoration specific to a famous commodity, "Red-Canned Wanglaoji Herbal Tea", and alleging on this basis that the packaging and decoration of the red-canned herbal tea produced and sold by the other party constituted infringement. Specifically speaking, GPHL, as the holder of registered trademark "Wanglaoji" believes that since "Wanglaoji" is an inseparable part of the packaging and decoration and distinctively indicates the source of commodity, consumers would take it for granted that the Red-Canned Wanglaoji Herbal Tea originates from the holder of trademark "Wanglaoji", and the recipe and taste would not affect the consumers' identification and judgment of the commodity. JDB Company, as the former actual operator of Red-Canned Wanglaoji Herbal Tea, believes that the rights and interests of the packaging and decoration and the ownership of trademark right of "Wanglaoji" are independent from, and do not affect, each other. What consumers love is the Red-Canned Wanglaoji Herbal Tea produced by JDB Company with specifically selected recipe, and the packaging and decoration in this Case is used by JDB Company and closely integrated with the said commodity; thus the rights and interests relating to the packaging and decoration shall belong to JDB Company.

Holding

In the first instance, Guangdong High People's Court held that the rights and interests of the packaging and decoration of "Red-Canned Wanglaoji Herbal Tea" shall belong to GPHL and that the production and sale of red-canned herbal tea by Guangzhou Wanglaoji Health Industry Co., Ltd. (hereinafter referred to as "Health Company") with the authorization by GPHL did not constitute infringement. Since JDB Company did not own the rights and interests of the packaging and decoration concerned, its production and sale of both red-canned herbal tea with "王老吉 (Wanglaoji)" and "加多宝 (JDB)"on either side and that with "加多宝 (JDB)" on both sides constituted infringement. Hence, the Court in the first instance ordered JDB Company to cease the infringement, publish a statement to eliminate the effect, and compensate GPHL 150 million yuan for economic losses and more than 260,000 yuan for reasonable enforcement costs. JDB Company appealed both judgments of the first instance to the Supreme People's Court. The Supreme People's Court made the second-instance judgment on July 7, 2017, dismissing all the claims of both GPHL and JDB Company.

[Reasoning]

The Court held in the effective judgment that distinctive features of packaging and decoration for recognition and their application to fairly famous commodities are the conditions for the rights and interests of the commercial indications connected with packaging and decoration to be protected by *the Anti-unfair Competition Law*. The application of Item 2,

Article 5 of *the Anti-unfair Competition Law* shall correctly understand the relationship between "specific packaging and decoration" and "famous commodity", as being mutually interdependent and inseparable. Only the commodity that uses the specific packaging and decoration is evaluable by *the Anti-unfair Competition Law*. On the contrary, abstract commodity names or commodity concepts without definitive connotations are detached from the concrete commodities on which packaging and decoration depend, short of evaluable conducts of actual usage, and thus unevaluable under Item 2, Article 5 of *the Anti-unfair Competition Law*. When dispute occurred between the two parties, "Wanglaoji Herbal Tea", as a kind of commodity name, could at least refer to variously packaged and decorated herbal tea products such as the green-boxed one produced by GPHL and red-canned one produced by JDB Company. The purpose of defining "famous commodity" is to judge whether the specific packaging and decoration attached thereto meet the conditions for the rights and interests of commercial indications to be protectable by *the Anti-unfair Competition Law*. Hence, such "famous commodity" shall be clearly directed to the packaging and decoration concerned. The court of first instance disregarded the dependence of the packaging and decoration on the commodity, and found the commodity name "Wanglaoji Herbal Tea", which has non-specific references, as the "famous commodity" in this Case. This decision lacks factual and legal basis and is hereby corrected.

This dispute over the packaging and decoration specific to the famous commodity arose from the failure of both parties to clearly contract, while entering into and performing the trademark license contract, how to allocate the derivative benefits accruable during the term of license. Usually, once the trademark license terminates, the licensee shall immediately stop its use, and the goodwill accumulated on the licensed trademark shall be simultaneously returned to the licensor. The dispute in this Case occurred in an unusual way in the sense that the specific packaging and decoration introduced during the licensed use not only closely related to the licensed trademark, but also created features of goodwill beyond trademark rights due to their attribute as independent rights and interests under *the Anti-unfair Competition Law*. The claims proposed by the parties both entail the general application of law on the protection of rights and interests of commercial indications, and reflect the complex historical and realistic factors involved in the formation process of the rights and interests of the specific packaging and decoration in this Case. The registered trademark system and the protection system of the rights and interests of the packaging and decoration specific to famous commodities have different sources of rights and conditions for protection though they both belong to the legal system to protect the rights and interests of commercial indications. Registered trademarks and packaging and decoration can each play an independent role of recognition, and respectively belong to different rightholders. After the Red-canned Wanlaoji Herbal Tea was launched to the market and effectively marketed by JDB Company and its affiliates, the packaging and decoration used on the Red-canned Wanlaoji Herbal Tea has generated independent rights and interests of commercial indications due to its popularity and specificity. This Case is exceptional because in the course of design, use and promotion, JDB Company, as the actual operator of the packaging and decoration concerned, always highlighted the word "Wanglaoji", a registered trademark of GPHL, on its packaging and decoration, and never intended to break and clearly distinguish the relation between the packaging and decoration and the registered trademark contained therein, which objectively caused the packaging and decoration to simultaneously refer to JDB Company and GPHL. Consumers would not deliberately differentiate, in the legal sense, the trademark rights and the rights and interests of the packaging and decoration specific to famous commodities, but would naturally relate the Red-canned Wanglaoji Herbal Tea to GPHL and JDB Company at the same time. Actually, the packaging and decoration concerned did contain the influence of GPHL's brand "Wanglaoji" and the commodity popularity formed and developed by JDB Company through production, operation and promotion for more than ten years as well as the remarkable recognitive effects of the packaging and decoration. In an overall consideration of the abovementioned factors, as well as the development history of Red-canned Wanglaoji Herbal Tea, cooperation background between the parties, consumers' cognition and the principle of equity, on account of the positive role of GPHL and its predecessor and that of JDB Company and its affiliates in the forming and developing the rights and interests of the packaging and decoration concerned and establishing the goodwill, it would result in obvious unfairness and might harm public interests if the rights and interests of the packaging and decoration are all awarded to either party. Therefore, on the premise of compliance with the principle of good faith and respect for consumers' cognition, without prejudicing the lawful rights and interests of others, the rights and interests of the packaging and decoration specific to the famous commodity concerned may be jointly owned by GPHL and JDB Company.

[Opinion of the Case (Chinese Version)]

Scan the QR code to see the Chinese version of the opinion

互联网领域相关市场界定及滥用市场支配地位行为的分析方法

——奇虎公司与腾讯公司滥用市场支配地位纠纷案

【裁判要旨】

在反垄断案件的审理中，界定相关市场通常是重要的分析步骤。但是，能否明确界定相关市场取决于案件具体情况。在滥用市场支配地位的案件中，界定相关市场是评估经营者的市场力量及被诉垄断行为对竞争影响的工具，其本身并非目的。如果通过排除或者妨碍竞争的直接证据，能够对经营者的市场地位及被诉垄断行为的市场影响进行评估，则不需要在每一个滥用市场支配地位的案件中，都明确而清楚地界定相关市场。

假定垄断者测试（HMT）是普遍适用的界定相关市场的分析思路。在实际运用时，假定垄断者测试可以通过价格上涨（SSNIP）或质量下降（SSNDQ）等方法进行。互联网即时通信服务的免费特征使用户具有较高的价格敏感度，采用价格上涨的测试方法将导致相关市场界定过宽，应当采用质量下降的假定垄断者测试进行定性分析。

基于互联网即时通信服务低成本、高覆盖的特点，在界定其相关地域市场时，应当根据多数需求者选择商品的实际区域、法律法规的规定、境外竞争者的现状及进入相关地域市场的及时性等因素，进行综合评估。

在互联网领域中，市场份额只是判断市场支配地位的一项比较粗糙且可能具有误导性的指标，其在认定市场支配力方面的地位和作用必须根据案件具体情况确定。

【案　　　号】最高人民法院（2013）民三终字第 4 号
【案　　　由】滥用市场支配地位纠纷
【合议庭成员】王　闯　王艳芳　朱　理
【关　键　词】垄断　滥用市场支配地位　相关市场　市场份额
【相关法条】《中华人民共和国反垄断法》第十七条、第十八条、
　　　　　　　第十九条

【基本案情】

此案由奇虎公司诉至广东省高级人民法院，指控腾讯公司滥用其在即时通信软件及服务相关市场的市场支配地位。2010 年 11 月 3 日，腾讯公司发布《致广大 QQ 用户的一封信》，在装有 360 软件的电脑上停止运行 QQ 软件。11 月 4 日，360 安全中心宣布，在国家有关部门的强力干预下，目前 QQ 和 360 软件已经实现了完全兼容。2010 年 9 月，腾讯 QQ 即时通信软件与 QQ 软件管理一起打包安装，安装过程中并未提示用户将同时安装 QQ 软件管理。2010 年 9 月 21 日，腾讯公司发出公告称，正在使用的 QQ 软件管理和 QQ 医生将自动升级为 QQ 电脑管家。奇虎公司主张，腾讯公司拒绝向安装有 360 软件的用户提供相关的软件服务，强制用户在腾讯 QQ 和奇虎 360 之间"二选一"，构成反垄断法所禁止的限制交易；腾讯公司将 QQ 软件管家与即时通信软件相捆绑，以升级 QQ 软件管家的名义安装 QQ 医生，构成反垄断法所禁止的捆绑销售。

广东省高级人民法院一审认为：1.关于相关市场界定。奇虎公司关于综合性即时通信服务构成一个独立的相关商品市场以及本案相关地域市场应为中国大陆市场的主张不能成立。本案相关商品市场远远超出综合性即时通信服务市场，相关地域市场应为全球市场。但是，该院并未明确界定本案相关商品市场的范围。2.关于市场支配地位认定。由于奇虎公司对本案相关商品市场界定错误，其所提供的证据不足以证明腾讯公司在相关商品市场上具有垄断地位。奇虎公司的诉讼请求缺乏事实和法律依据，不能成立。遂判决驳回奇虎公司的全部诉讼请求。

奇虎公司不服，提出上诉。其主要上诉理由为：1.一审判决对本案相关商品市场未作认定，属于案件基本事实认定不清。2.一审判决在分析相关商品市场时基本方法错误，对于本案的免费产品不应直接适用假定垄断者测试（即"SSNIP测试"）界定相关市场，且其运用SSNIP价格增长测试也是错误的。本案相关商品市场应界定为综合了文字、语音、视频的个人电脑端即时通信软件和服务。3.一审判决对相关地域市场的认定明显错误，本案中相关地域市场应为中国大陆地区。4.一审判决认定腾讯公司在相关市场不具有支配地位是错误的。腾讯公司在相关市场的市场份额均超过二分之一，应当推定其具有市场支配地位。5.腾讯公司实施了滥用市场支配地位的行为，依法应当承担法律责任。

裁判结果

最高人民法院于2014年10月8日作出（2013）民三终字第4号民事判决：驳回上诉、维持原判。

【裁判理由】

最高人民法院针对该上诉理由，将争议焦点归纳为五个方面共计 22 个具体争议问题，并对每一争议问题逐一进行了分析。特别是，对于相关市场界定的作用、目的、方法等，最高人民法院在判决中根据互联网领域的独特特点，对于传统反垄断法的分析方法进行了创新和发展，在全球领域内首次对互联网领域相关市场的界定方法给出了创造性的答案。例如，在相关市场界定是否是滥用市场支配地位垄断纠纷的必经步骤这一问题上，业界普遍认为，准确界定相关市场是认定市场支配地位的前提。此谓传统的"相关市场（relative market——市场支配力（market power）——竞争效应（competition effects）（R -M-C）"分析范式。最高人民法院的判决在回溯相关市场的目的与作用的基础上，结合互联网领域的特点，雄辩地说明了相关市场界定的工具性，并提出了不以相关市场界定为前提的"市场支配力——竞争效应（M-C）"分析范式和"行为——竞争效应（C-C）"分析范式。

最高人民法院审理认为：本案中涉及的争议焦点主要包括，一是如何界定本案中的相关市场，二是被上诉人是否具有市场支配地位，三是被上诉人是否构成反垄断法所禁止的滥用市场支配地位行为等几个方面。

一、如何界定本案中的相关市场

该争议焦点可以进一步细化为一些具体问题，择要概括如下：

首先，并非在任何滥用市场支配地位的案件中均必须明确而清楚地界定相关市场。竞争行为都是在一定的市场范围内发生和展开的，界定相关市场可以明确经营者之间竞争的市场范围及其面对的竞争约束。在滥用市场支配地位的案件中，合理地界定相关市场，对于正确认定经营者的市场地位、分析经营者的行为对市场竞争的影响、判断经营者行为是否违法，以及在违法情况下需承担的法律责任等关键问题，具有重要意义。因此，在反垄断案件的审理中，界定相关市场通常是重要的分析步骤。尽管如此，是否能够明确界定相关市场取决于案件具体情况，尤其是案件证据、相关数据的可获得性、相关领域竞争的复杂性等。在滥用市场支配地位案件的审理中，界定相关市场是评估经营者的市场力量及被诉垄断行为对竞争的影响的工具，其本身并非目的。即使不明确界定相关市场，也可以通过排除或者妨碍竞争的直接证据对被诉经营者的市场地位及被诉垄断行为可能的市场影响进行评估。因此，并非在每一个滥用市场支配地位的案件中均必须明确而清楚地界定相关市场。一审法院实际上已经对本案相关市场进行了界定，只是由于本案相关市场的边界具有模糊性，一审法院仅对其边界的可能性进行了分析而没有对相关市场的边界给出明确结论。有鉴于此，奇虎公司关于一审法院未对本案相关商品市场作出明确界定，属于本案基本事实认定不清的理由不能成立。

其次，关于"假定垄断者测试"方法可否适用于免费商品领域问题。法院生效裁判认为：第一，作为界定相关市场的一种分析思路，假定垄断者测试（HMT）具有普遍的适用性。实践中，假定垄断者测试的分析方法有多种，既可以通过数量不大但有意义且并非短暂的价格上涨（SSNIP）的方法进行，又可以通过数量不大但有意义且并非短暂的质量下降（SSNDQ）的方法进行。同时，作为一种分析思路或者思考方法，假定垄断者测试在实际运用时既可以通过定性分析的方法进行，又可以在条件允许的情况下通过定量分析的方法进行。第二，在实践中，选择何种方法进行假定垄断者测试取决于案件所涉市场竞争领域以及可获得的相关数据的具体情况。如果特定市场领域的商品同质化特征比较明显，价格竞争是较为重要的竞争形式，则采用数量不大但有意义且并非短暂的价格上涨（SSNIP）的方法较为可行。但是如果在产品差异化非常明显且质量、服务、创新、消费者体验等非价格竞争成为重要竞争形式的领域，采用数量不大但有意义且并非短暂的价格上涨（SSNIP）的方法则存在较大困难。特别是，当特定领域商品的市场均衡价格为零时，运用 SSNIP 方法尤为困难。在运用 SSNIP 方法时，通常需要确定适当的基准价格，进行 5% ~ 10% 幅度的价格上涨，然后确定需求者的反应。在基准价格为零的情况下，如果进行 5% ~ 10% 幅度的价格增长，增长后其价格仍为零；如果将价格从零提升到一个较小的正价格，则相当于价格增长幅度的无限增大，意味着商品特性或者经营模式发生较大变化，因而难以进行 SSNIP 测试。第三，关于假定垄断者测试在本案中的可适用性问题。互联网服务提供商在互联网领域的竞争中更加注重质量、服务、创新等方面的竞争而不是价格竞争。在免费的互联网基础即时通信服务已经长期存在并成为通行商业模式的情况下，用户具有极高的价格敏感度，改变免费策略转而收取哪怕是较小数额的费用都可能导致用户的大量流失。同时，将价格由免费转变为收费也意味着商品特性和经营模式的重大变化，即由免费商品转变为收费商品，由间接盈利模式转变为直接盈利模式。在这种情况下，如果采取基于相对价格上涨的假定垄断者测试，很可能将不具有替代关系的商品纳入相关市场中，导致相关市场界定过宽。因此，基于相对价格上涨的假定垄断者测试并不完全适宜在本案中适用。尽管基于相对价格上涨的假定垄断者测试难以在本案中完全适用，但仍可以采取该方法的变通形式，例如基于质量下降的假定垄断者测试。由于质量下降程度较难评估以及相关数据难以获得，因此可以采用质量下降的假定垄断者测试进行定性分析而不是定量分析。

　　再次，关于本案相关市场是否应确定为互联网应用平台问题。

上诉人认为，互联网应用平台与本案的相关市场界定无关；被上诉人则认为，互联网竞争实际上是平台的竞争，本案的相关市场范围远远超出了即时通信服务市场。法院生效裁判针对互联网领域平台竞争的特点，阐述了相关市场界定时应如何考虑平台竞争的特点及处理方式，认为：第一，互联网竞争一定程度地呈现出平台竞争的特征。被诉垄断行为发生时，互联网的平台竞争特征已经比较明显。互联网经营者通过特定的切入点进入互联网领域，在不同类型和需求的消费者之间发挥中介作用，以此创造价值。第二，判断本案相关商品市场是否应确定为互联网应用平台，其关键问题在于，网络平台之间为争夺用户注意力和广告主的相互竞争是否完全跨越了由产品或者服务特点所决定的界限，并给经营者施加了足够强大的竞争约束。这一问题的答案最终取决于实证检验。在缺乏确切的实证数据的情况下，至少注意如下方面：首先，互联网应用平台之间争夺用户注意力和广告主的竞争以其提供的关键核心产品或者服务为基础。其次，互联网应用平台的关键核心产品或者服务在属性、特征、功能、用途等方面上存在较大的不同。虽然广告主可能不关心这些产品或者服务的差异，只关心广告的价格和效果，因而可能将不同的互联网应用平台视为彼此可以替代，但是对于免费端的广大用户而言，其很难将不同平台提供的功能和用途完全不同的产品或者服务视为可以有效地相互替代。一个试图查找某个历史人物生平的用户通常会选择使用搜索引擎而不是即时通信，其几乎不会认为两者可以相互替代。再次，互联网应用平台关键核心产品或者服务的特性、功能、用途等差异决定了其所争夺的主要用户群体和广告主可能存在差异，因而在获取经济利益的模式、目标用户群、所提供的后续市场产品等方面存在较大区别。最后，本案中应该关注的是被上诉人是否利用了其在即时通信领域中可能的市场支配力量排除、限制互联网安全软件领域的竞争，将其在即时通信领域中可能存在的市场支配力量延伸到安全软件领域，这一竞争过程更多地发生在免费的用户端。鉴于上述理由，在本案相关市场界定阶段互联网平台竞争的特性不是主要考虑因素。第三，本案中对互联网企业平台竞争特征的考虑方式。相关市场界定的目的是为了明确经营者所面对的竞争约束，合理认定经营者的市场地位，并正确判断其行为对市场竞争的影响。即使不在相关市场界定阶段主要考虑互联网平台竞争的特性，但为了正确认定经营者的市场地位，仍然可以在识别经营者的市场地位和市场控制力时予以适当考虑。因此，对于本案，不在相关市场界定阶段主要考虑互联网平台竞争的特性并不意味着忽视这一特性，而是为了以更恰当的方式考虑这一特性。

最后，关于即时通信服务相关地域市场界定需要注意的问题。法院生效裁判认为：本案相关地域市场的界定，应从中国大陆地区的即时通信服务市场这一目标地域开始，对本案相关地域市场进行考察。因为基于互联网的即时通信服务可以低成本、低代价到达或者覆盖全球，并无额外的、值得关注的运输成本、价格成本或者技术障碍，所以在界定相关地域市场时，将主要考虑多数需求者选择商品的实际区域、法律法规的规定、境外竞争者的现状及其进入相关地域市场的及时性等因素。由于每一个因素均不是决定性的，因此需要根据上述因素进行综合评估。首先，中国大陆地区境内绝大多数用户均选择使用中国大陆地区范围内的经营者提供的即时通信服务。中国大陆地区境内用户对于国际即时通信产品并无较高的关注度。其次，我国有关互联网的行政法规规章等对经营即时通信服务规定了明确的要求和条件。我国对即时通信等增值电信业务实行行政许可制度，外国经营者通常不能直接进入我国大陆境内经营，需要以中外合资经营企业的方式进入并取得相应的行政许可。再次，位于境外的即时通信服务经营者的实际情况。在本案被诉垄断行为发生前，多数主要国际即时通信经营者例如 MSN、雅虎、Skype、谷歌等均已经通过合资的方式进入中国大陆地区市场。因此，在被诉垄断行为发生时，尚未进入我国大陆境内的主要国际即时通信服务经营者已经很少。如果我国大陆境内的即时通信服务质量小幅下降，已没有多少境外即时通信服务经营者可供境内用户选择。最后，境外即时通信服务经营者在较短的时间内（例如一年）及时进入中国大陆地区并发展到足以制约境内经营者的规模存在较大困难。境外即时通信服务经营者首先需要通过合资方式建立企业、满足一系列许可条件并取得相应的行政许可，这在相当程度上延缓了境外经营者的进入时间。综上，本案相关地域市场应为中国大陆地区市场。

综合本案其他证据和实际情况，本案相关市场应界定为中国大陆地区即时通信服务市场，既包括个人电脑端即时通信服务，又包括移动端即时通信服务；既包括综合性即时通信服务，又包括文字、音频以及视频等非综合性即时通信服务。

二、被上诉人是否具有市场支配地位

对于经营者在相关市场中的市场份额在认定其市场支配力方面的地位和作用，法院生效裁判认为：市场份额在认定市场支配力方面的地位和作用必须根据案件具体情况确定。一般而言，市场份额越高，持续的时间越长，就越可能预示着市场支配地位的存在。尽管如此，市场份额只是判断市场支配地位的一项比较粗糙且可能具有误导性的指标。在市场进入比较容易，或者高市场份额源于经营者更高的市场效率或者提供了更优异的产品，或者市场外产品对经营者形成较强的竞争约束等情况下，高的市场份额并不能直接推断出市场支配地位的存在。特别是，互联网环境下的竞争存在高度动态的特征，相关市场的边界远不如传统领域那样清晰，在此情况下，更不能高估市场份额的指示作用，而应更多地关注市场进入、经营者的市场行为、对竞争的影响等有助于判断市场支配地位的具体事实和证据。

结合上述思路，法院生效裁判从市场份额、相关市场的竞争状况、被诉经营者控制商品价格、数量或者其他交易条件的能力、该经营者的财力和技术条件、其他经营者对该经营者在交易上的依赖程度、其他经营者进入相关市场的难易程度等方面，对被上诉人是否具有市场支配地位进行考量和分析，并特别考虑了腾讯公司实施"二选一"行为仅仅持续一天即导致其竞争对手 MSN 当月覆盖人数增长 2300 多万，多个竞争对手争抢即时通信服务市场的事实。最终认定本案现有证据并不足以支持被上诉人具有市场支配地位的结论。

三、被上诉人是否构成《中华人民共和国反垄断法》所禁止的滥用市场支配地位行为

法院生效裁判打破了传统的分析滥用市场支配地位行为的"三步法"，采用了更为灵活的分析步骤和方法，认为：原则上，如果被诉经营者不具有市场支配地位，则无需对其是否滥用市场支配地位进行分析，可以直接认定其不构成反垄断法所禁止的滥用市场支配地位行为。不过，在相关市场边界较为模糊、被诉经营者是否具有市场支配地位不甚明确时，可以进一步分析被诉垄断行为对竞争的影响效果，以检验关于其是否具有市场支配地位的结论正确与否。此外，即使被诉经营者具有市场支配地位，判断其是否构成滥用市场支配地位，也需要综合评估该行为对消费者和竞争造成的消极效果和可能具有的积极效果，进而对该行为的合法性与否作出判断。本案主要涉及两个方面的问题：

一是关于被上诉人实施的"产品不兼容"行为（用户二选一）是否构成反垄断法禁止的限制交易行为。根据《中华人民共和国反垄断法》第十七条的规定，具有市场支配地位的经营者，没有正当理由，

限定交易相对人只能与其进行交易或者只能与其指定的经营者进行交易的，构成滥用市场支配地位。上诉人主张，被上诉人没有正当理由，强制用户停止使用并卸载上诉人的软件，构成反垄断法所禁止的滥用市场支配地位限制交易行为。对此，法院生效裁判认为，虽然被上诉人实施的"产品不兼容"行为对用户造成了不便，但是并未导致排除或者限制竞争的明显效果。这一方面说明被上诉人实施的"产品不兼容"行为不构成反垄断法所禁止的滥用市场支配地位行为，也从另一方面佐证了被上诉人不具有市场支配地位的结论。

二是被上诉人是否构成反垄断法所禁止的搭售行为。根据《中华人民共和国反垄断法》第十七条的规定，具有市场支配地位的经营者，没有正当理由搭售商品，或者在交易时附加其他不合理的交易条件的，构成滥用市场支配地位。上诉人主张，被上诉人将QQ软件管家与即时通信软件捆绑搭售，并且以升级QQ软件管家的名义安装QQ医生，不符合交易惯例、消费习惯或者商品的功能，消费者选择权受到了限制，不具有正当理由；一审判决关于被诉搭售行为产生排除、限制竞争效果的举证责任分配错误。对此，法院生效裁判认为，上诉人关于被上诉人实施了滥用市场支配地位行为的上诉理由不能成立。

【本案裁判文书】

扫描二维码，可见裁判文书

Analysis Methods of Internet-Related Market Definition and Abuse of Dominant Market Position

——Qihoo v. Tencent on Abuse of Dominant Market Position

[Syllabus]

In handling anti-monopoly cases, defining the relevant market is an important analytical step. However, clearly defining the relevant market depends on the case's specific circumstances. In a case of abuse of dominant market position, the definition of relevant market itself is not the purpose, but a tool to assess the business operator's dominant market position and impact of the alleged monopolistic practice on competition. If the business operator's market position and market impact of the alleged monopolistic practice can be assessed through direct evidence of elimination or hindrance to competition, it will be unnecessary to clearly and conclusively define the relevant market in every case involving abuse of dominant market position.

Hypothetical Monopolist Testing (HMT) is a generally applicable analytical method that defines the relevant market. In practice, it is assumed that HMT can be conducted through methods such as Small but Significant and Non-transitory Increase in Price (SSNIP) or Small but Significant and Non-transitory Decrease in Quality (SSNDQ). The free-of-charge features of Internet-based instant messaging (IM) services, makes users highly sensitive to price. As the SSNIP test method will lead to an excessively broad definition of the relevant market, SSNDQ should be adopted for qualitative analysis.

Keeping in mind IM service's low cost and high coverage in defining the relevant geographical market, a comprehensive assessment can be made based on the actual region where majority of users select the goods, provisions of laws and regulations, status quo of overseas competitors and timely access to relevant geographical markets and other factors.

In the Internet sector, market share is a relatively crude and potentially misleading indicator for evaluating dominant market position. Its position and role in determining dominant market position must be determined based on the circumstances of specific cases.

[Case No.] Supreme People's Court (2013) MSZZ No.4

[Cause of Action] Dispute over misuse of dominant market position

[Collegial Panel Members] Wang Chuang   Wang Yanfang   Zhu li

[Keywords] Monopoly, abuse of dominant market position, relevant market, market share

[Relevant Legal Provisions] Article 17, Article 18 and Article 19 of *Anti-Monopoly Law of the People's Republic of China*

[Basic Facts]

This case was filed by Beijing Qihoo Technology Co., Ltd. (Qihoo) in the High People's Court of Guangdong Province, alleging that Tencent misused its dominant market position with respect to relevant IM software and service market. On November 3rd, 2010, Tencent released *A letter to QQ users* requesting them to stop running QQ on computers that had Qihoo 360 software. On November 4th, after strong intervention of relevant departments of the State, 360 Security Center announced that the current QQ version and 360 software were fully compatible. In September 2010,

Tencent QQ Instant Messaging software and QQ Software Management were provided to users for installation as a package. However, users were not prompted that QQ Software Management would be installed when QQ Instant Messaging software was installed. On September 21st, 2010, Tencent issued a notice that current QQ Software Management and QQ Doctor will be automatically upgraded to QQ Computer Housekeeper. Qihoo claimed that Tencent refused to provide related software services to users who had installed Qihoo 360 software and forced users to choose between Tencent QQ and Qihoo 360, thus constituting a restrictive trade practice, which is prohibited under the *Anti-Monopoly Law*. Tencent's act of bundling QQ Computer Housekeeper with its Instant Messaging software and installing QQ Doctor under the guise of upgrading QQ Housekeeper constituted a bundled sale, which is prohibited under the *Anti-Monopoly Law*.

The case was filed in the court of first instance, the High People's Court of Guangdong Province, which held that: 1. On the definition of relevant market, Qihoo's claim that integrated IM service constitutes an independent relevant commodity market and relevant geographical market, which in this case was the Mainland China market, could not be established. The relevant commodity market in this case goes far beyond integrated IM service market and the relevant geographical market should be the global market. However, the court did not clearly define the scope of relevant commodity market in this case. 2. On the dominant market position, as Qihoo misjudged the relevant commodity market in this case, the evidence it provided did not prove that Tencent had a monopolistic position in the relevant commodity market. Qihoo's litigation claims lacked factual and legal basis, and thus could not be established. Therefore, Qihoo's entire claim was rejected in the judgment.

Not accepting the judgment, Qihoo filed an appeal. The main points of contention in the appeal are: (1) The first-instance judgment did not determine the relevant commodity market in this case, and the basic facts of the case were not clearly established. (2) Basic method used in the first-instance judgment for the analysis of the relevant commodity market is incorrect. Hypothetical Monopolist Test (i.e. SSNIP Test) should not be directly applicable to free-of-charge products, to define relevant market in this case, and it is incorrect to use the SSNIP Test. Relevant commodity market in this case should be defined as a personal computer-side instant messaging software and service that integrates text, voice and video. (3) Determination of relevant geographical market in the first-instance judgment is obviously incorrect. Relevant geographical market in this case should be Mainland China. (4) The verdict of the first-instance judgment that Tencent did not possess dominant position in the relevant market is incorrect. Tencent's share in the relevant market is more than half, and thus it should be presumed to possess a dominant market position. (5) Tencent has abused its dominant position in the market and should bear legal liability according to law.

 Holding

On October 8th, 2014, the Supreme People's Court rendered the Civil Judgment (2013) MSZZ No.4, and rejected the appeal and upheld the original judgment.

[Reasoning]

Based on these grounds of appeal, the Supreme People's Court summarized 22 specific controversial issues in terms of five aspects, and analyzed each of the issues individually. In particular, with respect to the role, purpose and method of defining the relevant market, the Supreme People's Court made innovations and developments in the analysis of traditional *Anti-Monopoly Law* in the judgment, based on the Internet sector's unique features and gave a creative answer on the method of defining the relevant market in the global field. For example, on the issue of whether defining relevant market is a unavoidable step in resolution of a monopoly dispute related to abuse of dominant market position, the industry widely recognizes that accurate definition of the relevant market is a prerequisite for determining dominant market position. This refers to the traditional analysis paradigm of "Relevant market - Market power - Competition effects (R-M-C)". The Supreme People's Court's judgment reconsidered the purpose and role of the relevant market based on the Internet's characteristics, illustrated the tool of defining relevant market and proposed an analysis paradigm of "Market power - Competition effect (MC)" and "Conduct - Competition effect (CC)", both not based on determination of relevant market.

The Supreme People's Court held that: The focus of dispute involved in this case mainly include: first, how to define relevant market in this case; second, whether or not the appellee possesses dominant market position; and third, whether or not the act of the appellee constitutes abuse of dominant market position and other aspects that are prohibited by *Anti-Monopoly Law*.

I. How to define the relevant market in this case.

The focal point of the dispute can be further divided into numerous specific issues, which can be summarized as follows:

First of all, it is not necessary to define relevant market clearly, in a specific case involving abuse of dominant market position. Competition takes place and is carried out within a certain market scope. Defining relevant market can define the market scope and the competition constraints faced by business operators. In a case of abuse of dominant market position, a reasonable definition of relevant market is of great importance in correctly identifying the business operator's market position, analyzing the influence of the business operator's behavior on market competition, judging whether the business operator's acts are illegal or not, and determining legal liabilities and other key issues. Therefore, in handling anti-monopoly cases, definition of relevant market is usually an important analytical step. Nevertheless, a clear definition of the relevant market depends on specific case circumstances, particularly on the evidence in the case, availability of relevant data and complexity of competition in the relevant field. In handling cases of abuse of dominant market position, definition of the relevant market is a tool for assessing the business operator's dominant market position and influence of alleged monopolistic act on the competition, and is not the purpose in itself. Even if the relevant market is not clearly defined, possible market impact of the alleged business operator's market position and alleged monopolistic act may be assessed through direct evidence of elimination or hindrance to competition. Therefore, it is not necessary to clearly define relevant market in every case of abuse of dominant market position. The court of first instance has actually defined relevant market in this case. As the boundary of relevant market in this case is ambiguous, the court of first instance merely analyzed the possibility of its boundary without arriving at any definite conclusion on the relevant market's boundary. In view of this, Qihoo's grounds for appeal that the failure of the court of first instance to clearly define relevant commodity market in this case, is a failure to find basic facts of the case, cannot be established.

Second, on the issue of whether the method of Hypothetical Monopolist Test is applicable to free commodities, the judgment held that: (1) As an analytical way of defining the relevant market, it is assumed that the Hypothetical Monopolistic Test (HMT) is universally applicable. In practice, there are serveral methods of hypothetical monopolist test that can be conducted, either by using the SSNIP method or the SSNDQ method. At the same time, as an analysis or thinking method, it is assumed that HMT can be conducted using both qualitative and quantitative analysis when conditions permit, in practice. (2) In practice, choosing the HMT method depends on the specific field of market competition involved in the case and relevant data available. If the homogeneity of commodities in a particular market field is pronounced and price competition is a relatively important form of competition, it is more feasible to adopt the SSNIP method. However, in a field where product differentiation is obvious and where non-price competition factors such as quality, service, innovation, consumer experience etc. become important competitive forms, it will be difficult to adopt the SSNIP method. In particular, using the SSNIP method is difficult when the market equilibrium price of commodities in a particular field is zero. When using the SSNIP method, it is usually necessary to determine the appropriate benchmark price, and make a price increase of between 5% and 10% to determine the consumer's reaction. Where the benchmark price is zero, price increased by 5% and 10% will still be zero. If the price is increased from zero to a smaller positive price, it will be equivalent to an indefinite price increase, which means that the characteristics of commodities or business models have undergone major changes, making it difficult to conduct the SSNIP test. (3) On applicability of HMT in this case, Internet service providers are placing greater emphasis on quality, service and innovation rather than price competition in Internet competition. In circumstances where free internet-based IM service has existed for a long time and has become a pervasive business model, users are highly sensitive to price. Therefore, changing toll-free tactics to charging even a small amount of fees can result in a massive effect on users. Likewise, changing from free-of-charge to charging fees also means a major change in commodity characteristics and business model, i.e. changing from free goods to paid goods, from indirect profitability model to direct profitability model. Under such circumstances, if HMT based on relative increase in price is adopted, it is likely to include commodities without substitutability into the relevant market, resulting in an overly broad definition of the relevant market. Therefore, HMT based on relative increase in price is not entirely suitable for this case. Although it is difficult for HMT based on relative increase in price to be fully applicable in this case, many alternatives to this method are still available, such as HMT based on decrease in quality. As it is difficult to assess quality degradation and obtain relevant data, HMT based on decrease in quality can be used for qualitative analysis rather than quantitative analysis.

Thirdly, whether relevant market in this case should be identified as an Internet application platform, the appellant believes that Internet application platform has nothing to do with definition of relevant market in this case. The appellee held that Internet competition is actually a platform competition and scope of relevant market in this case is far beyond the IM service market. In light of the competition feature of the Internet platform, the judgment expounds how to consider the feature and approach of platform competition in defining the relevant market, and held that: (1) Internet competition shows features of platform competition to some extent. When the sued monopolistic act occurred, the Internet platform competition feature becomes obvious. Internet operators enter the Internet field through a specific entry point to play an intermediary role for different types of consumers with different demands, to create value. (2) Judging whether the relevant commodity market in this case should be identified as an Internet application platform. The key issue lies in whether the competition between network platforms for the users and advertisers completely crosses the boundary determined by the characteristics of products or services, and imposes enough competitive constraints on the business operators. The answer to this question ultimately depends on empirical testing. In the absence of definitive empirical data, attention shall be paid to the following aspects at least: Firstly, competition between Internet application platforms for user attention and advertiser competition is based on key core products or services they provide. Secondly, key core products or Internet application platform services differ in terms of attributes, features, functions and usages. Although advertisers may not care about differences in these products or services but only care about prices and effectiveness of advertisements, and from their perspectives, different Internet application platforms may be considered to be alternatives to each other, it is very difficult for majority of free users to consider products or services of different platforms that have completely different functions and usages to be effective alternatives to each other. A user trying to find out the life of a historical figure typically uses a search engine instead of instant messaging, and hardly ever thinks the two can replace each other. Thirdly, differences in characteristics, functions and usages of key core products or services of Internet application platforms determine that there may be differences between major user groups and advertisers for whom they compete. Therefore, there are obvious differences in the mode of obtaining economic benefits, target user groups, and follow-up market products provided. Finally, the case should focus on whether the appellee has taken advantage of their potential dominant market position in the field of instant messaging to eliminate and hinder competition in Internet security software, and extended its dominant market position in the field of instant messaging to the field of security software, and if this competitive process occurs more often for free users. In view of the above grounds, the nature of competition in the Internet platform in the defining the relevant market in this case, is not considered a major factor. (3) The way of considering the competitive feature of the Internet enterprise platform, in this case. The purpose of defining the relevant market is to clarify competition constraints faced by business operators, reasonably determine their market position and correctly judge the impact of their actions on market competition. Even if the Internet platform's competition feature is not considered at the stage of defining the relevant market, due consideration can still be given to such a feature in recognizing the market position and dominant market position of the business operator. Therefore, in this case, failure to mainly consider the Internet platform's competition feature while defining the relevant market does not mean ignoring this feature, but rather considering this feature in a more appropriate way.

Finally, issues that need to be clarified when defining the relevant geographical market for IM service. The judgment held that definition of the relevant geographical market in this case should begin with the target area of the IM service market in Mainland China. As Internet-based IM services can be delivered at low cost, and can be available to or cover the entire world without additional or noteworthy shipping costs, price costs, or technical hurdles, the actual area where majority of users select the goods, provisions of laws and regulations, status quo of overseas competitors and timeliness of entering the relevant geographical market will be considered in defining the relevant geographical market. As each factor is not decisive, a comprehensive assessment based on the above factors is required. (1) Vast majority of users in Mainland China choose to use IM services provided by business operators in Mainland China. Users in Mainland China do not pay much attention to international IM products. (2) China's Internet-related administrative regulations and rules clearly lay out the requirements and conditions for operating IM services. China implements a system of administrative license for value-added telecommunications services such as instant messaging. Foreign business operators usually cannot directly enter Mainland China, and need to enter by establishing Sino-foreign joint ventures and obtain corresponding administrative licenses. (3) The actual situation of IM service operators located overseas. Prior to filing of this case of alleged monopoly, most international instant messaging operators such as MSN, Yahoo, Skype, Google, etc., entered the Mainland China market through joint ventures. Therefore, when the alleged monopolistic act took place, there were very few major international instant messaging service operators that had not yet entered Mainland China. If the quality of instant messaging service in Mainland China had decreased, there would not have been many overseas IM service operators available for domestic users to choose from. (4) It is quite difficult for overseas instant messaging service operators to enter Mainland China in a relatively short period of time (for example, one year) and to develop enough to restrict scale of domestic operators. Overseas instant messaging service operator need to first establish a joint venture, satisfy a series of licensing conditions and obtain appropriate administrative licenses, which to a certain extent, delays entry of the foreign business operator. In summary, the relevant geographical market in this case should be the Mainland China market.

Based on other evidence and actual situation of this case, the relevant market in this case should be defined as the IM market in Mainland China, including both PC-based and mobile-based IM services; both integrated IM services and non-integrated IM services such as text, audio and video.

II. Whether the appellee has dominant market position.

With respect to the position and role of business operator's market share in the relevant market in determining its dominant market position, the judgment held that the position and role of market share in determining the dominant market position must be determined according to specific case circumstances. In general, higher the market share and longer its duration, the more likely it is to indicate the existence of dominant market position. However, market share is only a relatively crude and potentially misleading indicator of dominant market position. Under circumstances where the market is relatively easy to enter, or high market share stems from the business operator's higher market efficiency or provision of better products, or products outside the market impose a strong competitive constraint on business operators, then high market share does not directly infer existence of dominant market position. In particular, competition in the Internet environment is highly dynamic. The boundary of the relevant market is far less clear than those in traditional fields. In this case, the role of market share as an indicator of dominant market position cannot be overestimated. Instead, more attention should be paid to market entry, business operator's market behavior, impact of competition and other specific facts and evidences that can help determine dominant market position.

Combining the above ideas, the judgment considered and analyzed whether the appellee possesses dominant position in the market based on aspects such as market share, competition condition in relevant market, capacity of the accused business operator controlling price, quantity or other trading conditions of goods or business operator's financial and technical conditions, degree of dependency of other business operators on the business operator with respect to transactions, and degree of difficulty with which other business operators enter the relevant market, especially the fact that when Tencent forced its users to choose between Tencent QQ and Qihoo 360 on Nov. 3, 2010, the monthly users of MSN, one of Tencent's competititors, increased 23 million in that month and many competitors entered, competing for Instant Messaging market. It was finally determined that existing evidence in this case was not sufficient to support the conclusion that the appellee possessed dominant market position.

III. Whether the appellee's act constitutes abuse of the dominant market position as prohibited by the *Anti-Monopoly Law*.

The judgment broke from the traditional "three-step" approach of analyzing the abuse of dominant market position and adopted a more flexible analytical procedure and approach. It considered that: In principle, if the accused business operator does not have a dominant market position, it is not necessary to analyze whether it has abused its dominant market position, and it can be directly determined that its act does not constitute abuse of dominant market position as prohibited by the *Anti-Monopoly Law*. However, when the relevant market boundary is vague and it is not clear whether or not the accused business operator possessed the dominant market position, the effect of the alleged monopolistic act on competition may be further analyzed to test whether the conclusion of its dominant market position is correct or not. In addition, even if the accused business operator possessed the dominant market position, to judge whether the act constitutes abuse of dominant market position, it is necessary to comprehensively evaluate the possible negative and positive effect that such an act has on consumers and competition, and further judge the legitimacy of the act. This case mainly involves two aspects:

First, whether the act of "product incompatibility" (the user has to choose one of two products) conducted by the appellee constitutes a restrictive trade practice as prohibited by the *Anti-Monopoly Law*. According to provisions of Article 17 of the *Anti-Monopoly Law*, an act of a business operator with market dominance that requires counterparties to do business only with it or operators designated by it without justified ground, shall constitute abuse of the dominant market position. In this respect, the judgment held that although the act of "product incompatibility" conducted by the appellee caused inconvenience to the user, it did not result in the obvious effect of eliminating or restricting competition. It shows that the act of "product incompatibility" conducted by the appellee does not constitute abuse of market dominant position as prohibited by the *Anti-Monopoly Law*. Thus, it supported the conclusion that the appellee did not possess the dominant market position.

Second, whether the act of the appellee constituted a bundling as prohibited by the *Anti-Monopoly Law*. According to the provisions of Article 17 of the *Anti-Monopoly Law*, the act of a business operator with market dominance conducting a bundling or attaching unreasonable trade conditions without justified grounds shall constitute abuse of dominant market position. In this respect, the judgment held that the appellant's appeal against the appellee's abuse of dominant market position was not well grounded.

[Opinion of the Case (Chinese Version)]

Scan the QR code to see the Chinese version of the opinion

经营者占有市场支配地位的认定

——吴小秦与陕西广电网络传媒（集团）股份有限公司捆绑交易纠纷案

【裁判要旨】

作为特定区域内唯一合法经营有线电视传输业务的经营者及电视节目集中播控者，在市场准入、市场份额、经营地位、经营规模等各要素上均具有优势，可以认定该经营者占有市场支配地位。

经营者利用市场支配地位，将数字电视基本收视维护费和数字电视付费节目费捆绑在一起向消费者收取，侵害了消费者的消费选择权，不利于其他服务提供者进入数字电视服务市场。经营者即使存在两项服务分别收费的例外情形，也不足以否认其构成反垄断法所禁止的搭售。

349

【案　　　号】最高人民法院（2016）最高法民再98号
【案　　　由】捆绑交易纠纷
【合议庭成员】王艳芳　钱小红　杜微科
【关　键　词】垄断　搭售　经营者　市场支配地位
【相关法条】《中华人民共和国反垄断法》第十七条第一款第（五）项

【基本案情】

原告吴小秦诉称：2012 年 5 月 10 日，其前往陕西广电网络传媒（集团）股份有限公司（以下简称广电公司）缴纳数字电视基本收视维护费得知，该项费用由每月 25 元调至 30 元，吴小秦遂缴纳了 3 个月费用 90 元，其中数字电视基本收视维护费 75 元、数字电视节目费 15 元。之后，吴小秦获悉数字电视节目应由用户自由选择，自愿订购。吴小秦认为，广电公司属于公用企业，在数字电视市场内具有支配地位，其收取数字电视节目费的行为剥夺了自己的自主选择权，构成搭售，故诉至法院，请求判令：确认被告 2012 年 5 月 10 日收取其数字电视节目费 15 元的行为无效，被告返还原告 15 元。

广电公司辩称：广电公司作为陕西省内唯一电视节目集中播控者，向选择收看基本收视节目之外的消费者收取费用，符合反垄断法的规定；广电公司具备陕西省有线电视市场支配地位，鼓励用户选择有线电视套餐，但并未滥用市场支配地位，强行规定用户在基本收视业务之外必须消费的服务项目，用户有自主选择权；垄断行为的认定属于行政权力，而不是司法权力，原告没有请求认定垄断行为无效的权利；广电公司虽然推出了一系列满足用户进行个性化选择的电视套餐，但从没有进行强制搭售的行为，保证了绝大多数群众收看更多电视节目的选择权利；故请求驳回原告要求确认广电公司增加节目并收取费用无效的请求；愿意积极解决吴小秦的第二项诉讼请求。

法院经审理查明：2012 年 5 月 10 日，吴小秦前往广电公司缴纳数字电视基本收视维护费时获悉，数字电视基本收视维护费每月最低标准由 25 元上调至 30 元。吴小秦缴纳了 2012 年 5 月 10 日至 8 月 9 日的数字电视基本收视维护费 90 元。广电公司向吴小秦出具的收费专用发票载明：数字电视基本收视维护费75元及数字电视节目费15元。之后，吴小秦通过广电公司客户服务中心（服务电话96766）咨询，广电公司节目升级增加了不同的收费节目，有不同的套餐，其中最低套餐基本收视费每年360元，用户每次最少应缴纳3个月费用。广电公司是经陕西省政府批准，陕西境内唯一合法经营有线电视传输业务的经营者和唯一电视节目集中播控者。广电公司承认其在有线电视传输业务中在陕西省占有支配地位。

另查，2004年12月2日国家发展改革委、国家广电总局印发的《有线电视基本收视维护费管理暂行办法》规定：有线电视基本收视维护费实行政府定价，收费标准由价格主管部门制定。2005年7月11日国家广电总局关于印发《推进试点单位有线电视数字化整体转换的若干意见（试行）》的通知规定，各试点单位在推进整体转换过程中，要重视付费频道等新业务的推广，供用户自由选择，自愿订购。陕西省物价局于2006年5月29日出台的《关于全省数字电视基本收视维护费标准的通知》规定：数字电视基本收视维护费收费标准为：以居民用户收看一台电视机使用一个接收终端为计费单位。全省县城以上城市居民用户每主终端每月25元；有线数字电视用户可根据实际情况自愿选择按月、按季或按年度缴纳基本收视维护费。国家发展改革委、国家广电总局于2009年8月25日出台的《关于加强有线电视收费管理等有关问题的通知》指出：有线电视基本收视维护费实行政府定价；有线电视增值业务服务和数字电视付费节目收费，由有线电视运营机构自行确定。

二审中，广电公司提供了四份收费专用发票复印件，证明在5月10日前后，广电公司的营业厅收取过25元的月服务费，因无原件，吴小秦不予质证。庭后广电公司提供了其中三张的原件，双方进行了核对与质证。该票据上均显示一年交费金额为300元，即每月25元。广电公司提供了五张票据的原件，包括一审提供过原件的三张，交易地点均为咸阳市。由此证明广电公司在5月10日前后，提供过每月25元的收费服务。

再审中，广电公司提交了其2016年网站收费套餐截图、关于印发《2016年大众业务实施办法（试行）的通知》、2016年部分客户收费发票。

 裁判结果

陕西省西安市中级人民法院于2013年1月5日作出（2012）西民四初字第438号民事判决：1.确认陕西广电网络传媒（集团）股份有限公司2012年5月10日收取原告吴小秦数字电视节目费15元的行为无效；2.陕西广电网络传媒（集团）股份有限公司于本判决生效之日起十日内返还吴小秦15元。陕西广电网络传媒（集团）股份有限公司提起上诉，陕西省高级人民法院于2013年9月12日作出（2013）陕民三终字第38号民事判决：1.撤销一审判决；2.驳回吴小秦的诉讼请求。吴小秦不服二审判决，向最高人民法院提出再审申请。最高人民法院于2016年5月31日作出（2016）最高法民再98号民事判决：1.撤销陕西省高级人民法院（2013）陕民三终字第38号民事判决；2.维持陕西省西安市中级人民法院（2012）西民四初字第438号民事判决。

【裁判理由】

法院生效裁判认为：本案争议焦点包括：一是本案诉争行为是否违反了《中华人民共和国反垄断法》第十七条第一款第（五）

项之规定。二是一审法院适用《中华人民共和国反垄断法》是否适当。

一、关于本案诉争行为是否违反了《中华人民共和国反垄断法》第十七条第（五）项之规定

依据《中华人民共和国反垄断法》第十七条第一款第（五）项规定，禁止具有市场支配地位的经营者没有正当理由搭售商品或者在交易时附加其他不合理的交易条件。本案中，广电公司在一审答辩中明确认可其"是经陕西省政府批准，陕西境内唯一合法经营有线电视传输业务的经营者。作为陕西省内唯一电视节目集中播控者，广电公司具备陕西省有线电视市场支配地位，鼓励用户选择更丰富的有线电视套餐，但并未滥用市场支配地位，也未强行规定用户在基本收视业务之外必须消费的服务项目。"二审中，广电公司虽对此不予认可，但并未举出其不具有市场支配地位的相应证据。再审审查过程中，广电公司对一、二审法院认定其具有市场支配地位的事实并未提出异议。鉴于广电公司作为陕西境内唯一合法经营有线电视传输业务的经营者，陕西省内唯一电视节目集中播控者，一、二审法院在查明事实的基础上认定在有线电视传输市场中，广电公司在市场准入、市场份额、经营地位、经营规模等各要素上均具有优势，占有支配地位，并无不当。

关于广电公司在向吴小秦提供服务时是否构成搭售的问题。《中华人民共和国反垄断法》第十七条第一款第（五）项规定禁止具有市场支配地位的经营者没有正当理由搭售商品。本案中，根据原审法院查明的事实，广电公司在提供服务时其工作人员告知吴小秦每月最低收费标准已从 2012 年 3 月起由 25 元上调为 30 元，每次最少缴纳一个季度，并未告知吴小秦可以单独缴纳数字电视基本收视维护费或者数字电视付费节目费。吴小秦通过广电公司

客户服务中心（服务电话号码 96766）咨询获悉，广电公司节目升级，增加了不同的收费节目，有不同的套餐，其中最低套餐基本收视费为每年 360 元，每月 30 元，用户每次最少应缴纳 3 个月费用。根据前述事实并结合广电公司给吴小秦开具的收费专用发票记载的收费项目——数字电视基本收视维护费 75 元及数字电视节目费 15 元的事实，可以认定广电公司实际上是将数字电视基本收视节目和数字电视付费节目捆绑在一起向吴小秦销售，并没有告知吴小秦是否可以单独选购数字电视基本收视服务的服务项目。此外，从广电公司客户服务中心（服务电话号码 96766）的答复中亦可佐证广电公司在提供此服务时，是将数字电视基本收视维护费和数字电视付费节目费一起收取并提供。虽然广电公司在二审中提交了其向其他用户单独收取数字电视基本收视维护费的相关票据，但该证据仅能证明广电公司在收取该费用时存在客户服务中心说明的套餐之外的例外情形。再审中，广电公司并未对客户服务中心说明的套餐之外的例外情形作出合理解释，其提交的单独收取相关费用的票据亦发生在本案诉讼之后，不足以证明诉讼时的情形，对此不予采信。因此，存在客户服务中心说明的套餐之外的例外情形并不足以否认广电公司将数字电视基本收视维护费和数字电视付费节目费一起收取的普遍做法。二审法院认定广电公司不仅提供了组合服务，也提供了基本服务，证据不足，应予纠正。因此，现有证据不能证明普通消费者可以仅缴纳电视基本收视维护费或者数字电视付费节目费，即不能证明消费者选择权的存在。二审法院在不能证明是否有选择权的情况下直接认为本案属于未告知消费者有选择权而涉及侵犯消费者知情权的问题，进而在此基础上，认定为广电公司的销售行为未构成反垄断法所规制的没有正当理由的搭售，事实和法律依据不足，应予纠正。

根据本院查明的事实，数字电视基本收视维护费和数字电视付费节目费属于两项单独的服务。在原审诉讼及本院诉讼中，广电公司未证明将两项服务一起提供符合提供数字电视服务的交易习惯；同时，如将数字电视基本收视维护费和数字电视付费节目费分别收取，现亦无证据证明会损害该两种服务的性能和使用价值；广电公司更未对前述行为说明其正当理由，在此情形下，广电公司利用其市场支配地位，将数字电视基本收视维护费和数字电视付费节目费一起收取，客观上影响消费者选择其他服务提供者提供相关数字付费节目，同时也不利于其他服务提供者进入电视服务市场，对市场竞争具有不利的效果。因此一审法院认定其违反了《中华人民共和国反垄断法》第十七条第一款第（五）项之规定，并无不当。吴小秦部分再审申请理由成立，予以支持。

二、关于一审法院适用《中华人民共和国反垄断法》是否适当

本案诉讼中，广电公司在答辩中认为本案的发生实质上是一个有关吴小秦基于《消费者权益保护法》所应当享受的权利是否被侵犯的纠纷，而与垄断行为无关，认为一审法院不应当依照《中华人民共和国反垄断法》及相关规定，认为其处于市场支配地位，从而确认其收费行为无效。根据《最高人民法院关于适用〈中华人民共和国民事诉讼法〉的解释》第二百二十六条及第二百二十八条的规定，人民法院应当根据当事人的诉讼请求、答辩意见以及证据交换的情况，归纳争议焦点，并就归纳的争议焦点征求当事人的意见。在法庭审理时，应当围绕当事人争议的事实、证据和法律适用等焦点问题进行。根据查明的事实，吴小秦在其诉状中明确主张"被告收取原告数字电视节目费，实际上是为原告在提供上述服务范围外增加提供服务内容，对此原告应当具有自主选择权。被告属于公用企业或者其他依法具有独占地位

的经营者，在数字电视市场内具有支配地位。被告的上述行为违反了《中华人民共和国反垄断法》第十七条第一款第（五）项关于'禁止具有市场支配地位的经营者从事没有正当理由搭售商品，或者在交易时附加其他不合理的交易条件的滥用市场支配地位行为'，侵害了原告的合法权益。原告依照《最高人民法院关于审理因垄断行为引发的民事纠纷案件应用法律若干问题的规定》，提起民事诉讼，请求人民法院依法确认被告的捆绑交易行为无效，判令其返还原告15元。"在该诉状中，吴小秦并未主张其消费者权益受到损害，因此一审法院根据吴小秦的诉讼请求适用《反垄断法》进行审理，并无不当。

综上，广电公司在陕西省境内有线电视传输服务市场上具有市场支配地位，其将数字电视基本收视服务和数字电视付费节目服务捆绑在一起向吴小秦销售，违反了《中华人民共和国反垄断法》第十七条第一款第（五）项之规定。吴小秦关于确认广电公司收取其数字电视节目费15元的行为无效和请求判令返还15元的再审请求成立。一审判决认定事实清楚，适用法律正确，应予维持，二审判决认定事实依据不足，适用法律有误，应予纠正。

【本案裁判文书】

扫描二维码，可见裁判文书

Recognition of Operator's Dominant Market Position
——Wu Xiaoqin v. Shaanxi Broadcast & TV Network Intermediary (Group) Co., Ltd.

[Syllabus]

A sole operator engaged in legitimate cable TV transmission business and an entity engaged in the centralized broadcast control of TV programs in a specific area has advantages in market access, market share, operating status, operation scale, and other elements, and may be recognized as having a dominant market position.

357

*By taking advantage of its dominant market position, the operator bundles basic maintenance fee for receiving digital TV programs with the fee for paid digital TV programs, and collects them together from a consumer, which infringes the consumer's right of choice, and disadvantages other service providers for accessing the digital TV service market. Even though there exist exceptions where the operator separately charges these two fees , it is insufficient to deny its constitution of tie-in sale prohibited by the **Anti-Monopoly Law**.*

[Case No.] Supreme People's Court (2016) ZGFMZ No. 98
[Cause of Action] Dispute over Bundled Transaction
[Collegial Panel Members] Wang Yanfang　Qian Xiaohong Du Weike

[Keywords] Monopoly, bundled transaction, operator, dominant market position

[Relevant Legal Provisions] Item (5), Paragraph 1, Article 17 of *the Anti-Monopoly Law of the People's Republic of China*

[Basic Facts]

Plaintiff Wu Xiaoqin alleged that: When he paid the basic maintenance fee for receiving digital TV programs to Shaanxi Broadcast & TV Network Intermediary (Group) Co., Ltd. (hereinafter referred to as "BC & TV Company") on May 10th, 2012, he learned that this fee had been adjusted from RMB25 per month to RMB30 per month. Wu Xiaoqin paid RMB90 for three months, including RMB75 as the basic maintenance fee for receiving digital TV programs and RMB15 as the fee for digital TV programs. Afterwards, Wu Xiaoqin learned that digital programs should be freely chosen and voluntarily subscribed by subscribers. Wu Xiaoqin believed that as a utilities enterprise, BC & TV Company had a dominant position in the digital TV market, and its charging of the digital TV program fee deprived him of the right of choice and constituted a tie-in sale. Therefore, he instituted a lawsuit to the court and requested the court to invalidate the defendant BC & TV Company's charging of the digital TV program fee of RMB15 on May 10th, 2012 and order the defendant to refund him RMB15.

BC & TV Company contended that: It was consistent with *the Anti-Monopoly Law* for it, the only the centralized broadcaster of TV programs in Shaanxi Province, to charge fees from consumers who chose to receive programs beyond the basic ones; BC & TV Company had a dominant position in the provincial cable TV market, and encouraged subscribers to choose cable TV packages, but did not abuse its dominant market position or force its subscribers to buy service items beyond basic TV program services. The subscribers had the right of free choice; the finding monopolistic conduct was an administrative power rather than a judicial one. The plaintiff had no right to request for the invalidation of monopolistic conducts; although BC & TV Company launched a series of TV program packages for subscribers to choose, it had never made any compulsory tie-in sale, which guaranteed most people's right to choose more TV programs. Therefore, BC & TV Company requested the court to dismiss the plaintiff's claim to invalidate BC & TV Company's increased number of TV programs and charge of fees; and BC & TV Company was willing to actively resolve the plaintiff's second claim.

The court found through trial that: When Wu Xiaoqin paid the basic maintenance fee for receiving digital TV programs to BC & TV Company on May 10th, 2012, he learned that the minimum monthly basic maintenance fee for receiving digital TV programs increased from RMB25 to RMB30. Wu Xiaoqin paid RMB90 as the basic maintenance fee for receiving digital TV programs for the period from May 10th to August 9th, 2012. The special invoice issued by BC & TV Company to Wu Xiaoqin recorded RMB75 of the basic maintenance fee for receiving digital TV programs and RMB15 of the fee for paid digital TV programs. Afterwards, Wu Xiaoqin consulted BC & TV Company's the customer service center (service telephone: 96766) and learned that BC & TV Company's program update added various paid programs in different packages, the cheapest of which cost RMB360 per year, with each installment payable by subscribers for at least three months. With the approval of the People's Government of Shaanxi Province, BC & TV Company was the only operator engaged in legitimate operation of cable TV transmission business and the only entity engaged in the centralized broadcast control of TV programs within Shaanxi Province. BC & TV Company admitted its dominant position in the cable TV transmission business within Shaanxi Province.

It was also found that: As prescribed in *the Interim Measures for the*

Administration of Basic Maintenance Fees for Receiving Cable TV Programs issued by the National Development and Reform Commission and the State Administration of Radio, Film and Television on December 2nd, 2004, the basic maintenance fee for receiving cable TV programs shall be priced by the government and the fee rates shall be set by the price authorities. As prescribed in *the Several Opinions on Promoting the Integral Transition of Cable TV Digitalization by Pilot Entities (for Trial Implementation)* issued by the State Administration of Radio, Film and Television on July 11th, 2005, in the process of promoting the overall transition, all pilot entities shall pay attention to the promotion of paid channels and other new business for subscribers to freely choose and voluntarily subscribe. As provided in *the Notice on the Standards of Basic Maintenance Fees for Receiving Digital TV Programs across the Province* issued by the Pricing Bureau of Shaanxi Province on May 29th, 2006, the standard for basic maintenance fee for receiving digital TV programs was that on the basis of one terminal per residential TV set, the maintenance fee for each terminal for urban residential subscribers at or above the county level across the Province was RMB25 per month; and subscribers of digital cable TV programs may, according to their actual circumstances, voluntarily choose to pay the basic maintenance fees for receiving TV programs on a monthly, quarterly or annual basis. As noted in *the Notice on Issues concerning Strengthening the Administration of Fee Charging of Cable TV Programs* issued by the National Development and Reform Commission and the State Administration of Radio, Film and Television on August 25th, 2009, the basic maintenance fees for receiving cable TV programs shall be priced by the government, and the fee rates of value-added cable TV business services and paid digital TV programs shall be set by the cable TV operators themselves.

During the second instance, BC & TV Company submitted the photocopies of four special invoices for charges, proving that around May 10th, the outlet of BC & TV Company collected a monthly service fee at RMB25.

Given the absence of originals, Wu Xiaoqin refused cross-examination. After the hearing, BC & TV Company submitted the originals for three of them, which both parties verified and cross-examined. All these invoices showed that the annual payment was RMB300, i.e. RMB25 per month. BC & TV Company submitted the originals of five invoices, including the originals of the three invoices submitted during the first instance, all transacted in Xianyang City. They proved that around May 10th, BC & TV Company provided paid services for RMB25 per month.

In the retrial, BC & TV Company submitted the screenshots of fee packages on its website as of 2016, *the Notice on Issuing the Measures for the Implementation of Public Business in 2016 (for Trial Implementation)*, and the 2016 invoices of some subscribers.

 Holding

On January 5th, 2013, the Intermediate People's Court of Xi'an City, Shaanxi Province rendered a civil judgment (No. 438 [2012], First, Civil Division IV, IPC, Xi'an): 1) it is invalid for BC & TV Company to charge the plaintiff Wu Xiaoqin RMB15 on May 10th, 2012 for digital TV fee; and 2) BC & TV Company shall, within ten (10) days after the judgment's effective date, refund Wu Xiaoqin RMB15. BC & TV Company appealed on September 12th, 2013, and the High People's Court of Shaanxi Province rendered a civil judgment (No. 38 [2013], Final, Civil Division III, HPC, Shaanxi) that: 1) the judgment of the first instance shall be set aside; and 2) the claims of Wu Xiaoqin shall be dismissed. Unsatisfied with the second-instance judgment, Wu Xiaoqin requested the Supreme People's Court for a retrial. On May 31st, 2016, the Supreme People's Court rendered a civil judgment (No. 98 [2016], Civil Retrial, Supreme People's Court) that: 1) the civil judgment (No. 38 [2013], Final, Civil Division III, HPC,

Shaanxi) rendered by the High People's Court of Shaanxi Province shall be set aside; and 2) the civil judgment (No. 438 [2012], First, Civil Division IV, IPC, Xi'an) rendered by the Intermediate People's Court of Xi'an City, Shaanxi Province shall be affirmed.

[Reasoning]

In the effective judgment, the Supreme People's Court focused the disputes on 1) whether the disputed conduct violated Item (5), Paragraph 1, Article 17 of *the Anti-Monopoly Law* and 2) whether the court of first instance appropriately applied *the Anti-Monopoly Law*.

1. Whether the disputed conduct violated Item (5), Paragraph 1, Article 17 of *the Anti-Monopoly Law*

Item (5), Article 17 of *the Anti-Monopoly Law* prohibits a business operator with a dominant market position from implementing tie-in sale or attaching other unreasonable trading conditions at the time of trading without just cause. In its defense during the first instance of this case, BC & TV Company explicitly conceded that it "was the only business operator that was legally engaged in the cable TV transmission business within Shaanxi Province with the approval of the People's Government of Shaanxi Province. As the only the centralized broadcaster of TV programs in Shaanxi Province, BC & TV Company had a dominant position in the provincial cable TV market, and encouraged subscribers to choose cable TV packages, but did not abuse its dominant market position or force its subscribers to buy service items beyond basic TV program services." While denying this during the second instance, BC & TV Company failed to produce the corresponding evidence proving that it did not have a dominant market position. In the process of retrial examination, BC & TV Company raised no objection to the fact found by the courts of first and second instance that it had a dominant market position. Given that

BC & TV Company was the only legal operator engaged in cable TV transmission business and the entity engaging in the centralized broadcast control of TV programs within Shaanxi Province, and on the basis of the facts found, the courts of first and second instance did not error in recognizing that in the cable TV transmission business market, BC & TV Company had advantages in market access, market share, operating status, scale of operation, and other elements and had the dominant market position.

Did BC & TV Company made a tie-in sale while serving Wu Xiaoqin? Item (5), Paragraph 1 of Article 17 of *the Anti-Monopoly Law* prohibits a business operator with a dominant market position from engaging in tie-in sale without just cause. In this case, according to facts found by the original courts, when providing services, the personnel of BC & TV Company notified Wu Xiaoqin that from March 2012, the minimum monthly fee rate had increased from RMB25 to RMB30, with each installment payable for at least a quarter; however, they failed to notify Wu Xiaoqin that he may separately pay the basic maintenance fee for receiving digital TV programs or the fee for paid digital TV programs. Afterwards, Wu Xiaoqin consulted BC & TV Company's customer service center (service telephone: 96766) and learned that BC & TV Company's program update increased the number of paid programs with various packages, the cheapest of which cost RMB360 per year (RMB30 per month), with each installment payable by subscribers for at least three months. According to the aforesaid facts and in light of the fact that among the charge items recorded on the special invoices issued by BC & TV Company to Wu Xiaoqin, i.e. RMB75 for the basic maintenance fee for receiving digital TV programs and RMB15 for paid digital TV programs, it was recognizable that BC & TV Company actually bundled the basic digital TV programs with the paid digital TV programs and sold them together to Wu Xiaoqin without notifying Wu Xiaoqin whether or not he could separately choose the service item of receiving the basic digital

363

TV programs. In addition, the reply of BC & TV Company's customer service center (service telephone: 96766) also corroborated that BC & TV Company charged together the basic maintenance fee for receiving digital TV programs and the fee for paid digital TV programs and provided the services together. Although BC & TV Company submitted, during the second instance, relevant documents for its separate charge of the basic maintenance fee for receiving digital TV programs from other subscribers, such evidence could only prove that when BC & TV Company collected such charge, there were exceptions to the package detailed by the customer service center. In the retrial, BC & TV Company failed to make reasonable explanations on exceptions to the package detailed by the customer service center. Furthermore, BC & TV Company's submission of receipts in which the relevant fees were separately charged occurred after this lawsuit was instituted, which was insufficient to prove the circumstances of this lawsuit and is not admitted. Therefore, exceptions to the package explained by the customer service center was insufficient to deny BC & TV Company's common practice of charging together the basic maintenance fee for receiving digital TV programs and the fee for paid digital TV programs. The recognition of the court of second instance that BC & TV Company not only provided portfolio services, but basic services is insufficiently evidenced and shall be corrected. Therefore, the existing evidence could not prove that an ordinary consumer could only pay the basic maintenance fee for receiving digital TV programs or the fee for paid digital TV programs, or that there existed the consumers' right of choice. Without the right of choice proven, the court of second instance directly concluded that this case was about the failure to inform the consumer of his right of choice and henceforth the infringement of his right to know. On this basis, the second-instance court held that BC & TV Company's sale did not constitute a tie-in sale without just cause as provided in *the Anti-Monopoly Law*, which judgment lacked factual and legal basis and shall be corrected.

In accordance with the facts found by this court, the basic maintenance fee for receiving digital TV programs and the fee for paid digital TV programs were for two separate services. In the trials of first and second instance and that of this court, BC & TV Company failed to prove that the combined provision of both services conformed to the trading practices of digital TV services. Moreover, there was no evidence proving that the separate charges of the basic maintenance fee for receiving digital TV program and the fee for paid digital TV programs would impair the performance and usage value of these two services; and BC & TV Company did not state the just cause for the aforesaid conduct. Under these circumstances, by taking advantage of its dominant market position, BC & TV Company's combined charging of the basic maintenance fee for receiving digital TV programs and the fee for paid digital TV programs objectively affected the consumer's choice of relevant paid digital TV programs provided by other service providers, and disadvantaged other service providers for accessing the TV service market, and had adverse impact on market competition. Therefore, the court of first instance did not error in holding that the defendant's conduct violated the provisions of Item (5), Paragraph 1, Article 17 of *the Anti-Monopoly Law*. Some grounds of Wu Xiaoqin's application for retrial were tenable and upheld.

II. Whether the court of first instance appropriately applied *the Anti-Monopoly Law*

In its defense in this case, BC & TV Company contended that the occurrence of this case was in essence a dispute over whether the right enjoyable by Wu Xiaoqin under *the Law on the Protection of Consumer Rights and Interests* was infringed, which was irrelevant to monopolistic conduct. BC & TV Company argued that the court of first instance should not have recognized its dominant market position and invalidated its charges in accordance with *the Anti-Monopoly Law* and relevant provisions. Pursuant to Articles 226 and 228 of *the Interpretation of the Supreme People's Court on the Application of the Civil Procedure Law of the People's Republic of China*, a people's court shall, as per the claims and answers of the parties as well as the circumstances on evidence exchange, summarize the focus of disputes and consult the parties on the summarized focus. The court shall focus the trial on focal issues such as the facts disputed by the parties, evidence, and application of law. According to the facts found, Wu Xiaoqin clearly claimed in his complaint that, "The digital TV program fee charged by the defendant was actually an additional service provided to the plaintiff beyond the scope of the aforesaid services, which the plaintiff should have the right to autonomously choose. The defendant was a utilities enterprise or other operator enjoying a lawful monopoly and had a dominant position in the digital TV market. The aforesaid conduct of the defendant violated Item (5), Paragraph 1, Article 17 of *the Anti-Monopoly Law* that "business operators with a dominant market position are prohibited from implementing tie-in sale or abusing their dominant market position by imposing other unreasonable trading conditions at the time of trade without just cause," and thus impaired the lawful rights and interests of the plaintiff. The Plaintiff instituted a civil lawsuit in accordance with *the Provisions of the Supreme People's Court on Several Issues concerning the Application of Law in the Trial of Civil Dispute Cases Arising from Monopolistic Conduct* and requested the people's court to invalidate the defendant's bundled transaction according to the law and order it to refund the plaintiff RMB15." In that complaint, Wu Xiaoqin did not claim that his consumer rights and interests were impaired. Therefore, the court of first instance did not error in applying *the Anti-Monopoly Law* to Wu Xiao Qin's claims.

In conclusion, BC & TV Company had a dominant market position in the cable TV transmission service market within Shaanxi Province, bundled service for receiving digital TV programs with the paid digital TV programs and sold them together to Wu Xiaoqin, which violated Item

(5), Paragraph 1, Article 17 of *the Anti-Monopoly Law*. Wu Xiaoqin's retrial claims to invalidate BC & TV Company's charge of RMB15 for digital TV programs and have the RMB15 refunded were tenable. The first-instance judgment was clear in its finding of facts and correct in its application of law, and shall be affirmed. The second-instance judgment was insufficient in its factual basis and wrong in its application of law, and shall be corrected.

[Opinion of the Case (Chinese Version)]

Scan the QR code to see the Chinese version of the opinion

互联网市场背景下对反不正当竞争法
第二条规定的适用及技术创新、
自由竞争和不正当竞争的界限

——北京奇虎科技有限公司、奇智软件（北京）有限公司

与腾讯科技（深圳）有限公司、

深圳市腾讯计算机系统有限公司不正当竞争纠纷案

【裁判要旨】

经营者在市场交易中，应当遵循自愿、平等、公平、诚实信用的原则，遵守公认的商业道德，互联网市场领域同样如此。

认定竞争行为是否构成不正当竞争，关键在于该行为是否违反了诚实信用原则和互联网行业公认的商业道德，是否损害了他人的合法权益。

技术创新可以刺激竞争，竞争又可以促进技术创新。技术本身虽然是中立的，但技术也可以成为进行不正当竞争的工具。技术革新应当成为公平自由竞争的工具，而非干涉他人正当商业模式的借口。

【案　　　号】　最高人民法院（2013）民三终字第 5 号

【案　　　由】　不正当竞争纠纷

【合议庭成员】　王　闯　王艳芳　朱　理　等

【关　键　词】　不正当竞争　互联网市场　诚实信用　公平竞争
　　　　　　　　技术创新

【相关法条】 《中华人民共和国反不正当竞争法》第二条、第十四条、第二十条

【基本案情】

在上诉人北京奇虎科技有限公司（以下简称奇虎公司）、奇智软件（北京）有限公司（以下简称奇智公司）与被上诉人腾讯科技（深圳）有限公司（以下简称腾讯公司）、深圳市腾讯计算机系统有限公司（以下简称腾讯计算机公司）不正当竞争纠纷案（以下简称"腾讯QQ"不正当竞争案）中，奇虎公司、奇智公司针对QQ软件专门开发了扣扣保镖，在相关网站上宣传扣扣保镖全面保护QQ用户安全，并提供下载。本案中，在安装了扣扣保镖软件后，该软件会自动对QQ软件进行体检，然后显示"体检得分4分，QQ存在严重的健康问题"；"共检查了40项，其中31项有问题，建议立即修复！重新体检"；"在QQ的运行过程中，会扫描您电脑里的文件（腾讯称之为安全扫描），为避免您的隐私泄露，您可禁止QQ扫描您的文件"等用语。同时，以红色字体警示用户QQ存在严重的健康问题，以绿色字体提供一键修复帮助，同时将"没有安装360安全卫士，电脑处于危险之中；升级QQ安全中心；阻止QQ扫描我的文件"列为危险项目；查杀QQ木马时，显示"如果您不安装360安全卫士，将无法使用木马查杀功能"，并以绿色功能键提供360安全卫士的安装及下载服务；经过一键修复，扣扣保镖将QQ软件的安全沟通界面替换成扣扣保镖界面。2011年6月10日，腾讯公司、腾讯计算机公司以奇虎公司、奇智公司的上述行为构成不正当竞争为由，提起诉讼。广东省高级人民法院一审认为，奇虎公司、奇智公司针对QQ软件专门开发的扣扣保镖破坏了合法运行的QQ软件及其服务的安

全性、完整性，使腾讯公司、腾讯计算机公司丧失合法增值业务的交易机会及广告、游戏等收入，扣扣保镖通过篡改 QQ 的功能界面从而取代 QQ 软件的部分功能以推销自己的产品，上述行为违反了诚实信用和公平竞争的原则，构成不正当竞争行为。奇虎公司、奇智公司针对腾讯公司、腾讯计算机公司的经营，故意捏造、散布虚伪事实，损害了腾讯公司、腾讯计算机公司的商业信誉和商品声誉，构成商业诋毁。遂判决奇虎公司、奇智公司公开赔礼道歉、消除影响，并连带赔偿腾讯公司、腾讯计算机公司经济损失及合理维权费用共计 500 万元。奇虎公司、奇智公司不服，提起上诉。

 裁判结果

最高人民法院于 2014 年 2 月 18 日作出（2013）民三终字第 5 号民事判决：驳回上诉、维持原判。

【裁判理由】

最高人民法院二审认为：在市场竞争中，经营者通常可以根据市场需要和消费者需求自由选择商业模式，这是市场经济的必然要求。腾讯公司、腾讯计算机公司为谋取市场利益，通过开发 QQ 软件，以该软件为核心搭建一个综合性互联网业务平台，并提供免费的即时通讯服务，吸引相关消费者体验、使用其增值业务，同时亦以该平台为媒介吸引相关广告商投放广告，以此创造商业机会并取得相关广告收入。这种免费平台与广告或增值服务相结合的商业模式是本案争议发生时，互联网行业惯常的经营方式，也符合我国互联网市场发展的阶段性特征。事实上，本案奇虎公司、奇智公司也采用这种商业模式。这种商业模式并不违反反不正当竞争法的原则精神和禁止性规定，腾讯公司、腾讯计算机公司以此谋求商业利益的行为应受保护，他人不得以不正当干扰方式损害其正当权益。奇虎公司、奇智公司专门针对 QQ 软件开发、经营扣扣保镖，以帮助、诱导等方式破坏 QQ 软件及其服务的安全性、完整性，减少了腾讯公司、腾讯计算机公司的经济收益和增值服务交易机会，干扰了其正当经营活动，损害了其合法权益。正当的市场竞争是竞争者通过必要的付出而进行的诚实竞争。不付出劳动或者不正当地利用他人已经取得的市场成果，为自己谋取商业机会，从而获取竞争优势的行为，属于不正当竞争行为。奇虎公司、奇智公司在经营扣扣保镖时，将自己的产品和服务嵌入 QQ 软件界面，取代了腾讯公司、腾讯计算机公司 QQ 软件的部分功能，其根本目的在于依附 QQ 软件强大用户群，通过对 QQ 软件及其服务进行贬损的手段来推销、推广 360 安全卫士，从而增加奇虎公司、奇智公司的市场交易机会并获取市场竞争优势，此行为本质上属于不正当地利用他人市场成果，为自己谋取商业机会从而获取竞争优势的行为。据此，奇虎公司、奇智公司的上述行为均违反了诚实信用和公平竞争原则，构成不正当竞争。

关于技术创新、自由竞争和不正当竞争的界限的问题。奇虎公司认为其行为是互联网自由和创新精神的体现，认为一审法院违反行业发展规律，苛刻适用反不正当竞争法的一般原则，会限制竞争和打击创新。最高人民法院认为，互联网的发展有赖于自由竞争和科技创新，互联网行业鼓励自由竞争和创新，但这并不等于互联网领域是一个为所欲为的法外空间，竞争自由和创新自由必须以不侵犯他人合法权益为边界，互联网的健康发展需要有序的市场环境和明确的市场竞争规则作为保障。是否属于互联网精神鼓励的自由竞争和创新，仍然需要基于是否有利于建立平等公平的竞争秩序、是否符合消费者的一般利益和社会公共利益为标准来进行判断，而不是仅有某些技术上的进步即认为属于自由竞争和创新。否则，任何人均可以技术进步为借口，对他人的技术产品或者服务进行任意干涉，就导致借技术进步、创新之名，而行"丛林法则"之实。技术创新可以刺激竞争，竞争又可以促进技术创新。技术本身虽然是中立的，但技术也可以成为进行不正当竞争的工具。技术革新应当成为公平自由竞争的工具，而非干涉他人正当商业模式的借口。本案中，奇虎公司以技术创新为名，专门开发扣扣保镖对腾讯公司 QQ 软件进行深度干预，难以认定其符合互联网自由和创新之精神，最高人民法院对其上诉理由不予支持。

【本案裁判文书】

扫描二维码，可见裁判文书

Applicability of Article 2 of Law Against Unfair Competition and the Boundary Among Technological Innovation, Free Competition and Unfair Competition in the Context of Internet Market

——Qihoo and QGOA v. Tencent Company
and Tencent Computer Company

[Syllabus]

Operators shall comply with the principles of voluntariness, equality, fairness, honesty and credibility in market transactions and observe the generally recognized business ethics. It also applys to the internet market. The key to determining whether a behavior constitutes unfair competition is whether it violates the principle of honesty and credibility and generally recognized business ethics in the internet industry and harms the legitimate rights and interests of others.

Technological innovation can stimulate competition, which in turn can further promote technological innovation. Neutral as it is, technology also can be used as a tool for unfair competition. Technological innovation should become a tool for fair and free competition, rather than an excuse to interfere with the legitimate business model of others.

[Case No.] Supreme People's Court (2013) MSZZ No. 5

[Cause of Action] Dispute over unfair competition

[Collegial Panel Members] Wang Chuang   Wang Yanfang

Zhu li etc.

[Keywords] Unfair competition, internet market, honesty and credibility, fair competition, technological innovation

[Relevant Legal Provisions] Article 2, 14 and 20 of *Law of the People's Republic of China Against Unfair Competition*

[Basic Facts]

In this dispute on unfair competition (hereinafter referred to as "Tencent QQ" unfair competition case) between the Appellants Beijing Qihoo Technology Co., Ltd. (hereinafter referred to as "Qihoo") and QGOA Software (Beijing) Co., Ltd. (hereinafter referred to as "QGOA") and the Appellees Tencent Technology (Shenzhen) Co., Ltd. (hereinafter referred to as "Tencent Company") and Shenzhen Tencent Computer System Co., Ltd. (hereinafter referred to as "Tencent Computer Company"), Qihoo and QGOA developed QQ Safeguard to work specifically against QQ software and publicized on relevant websites that QQ Safeguard could comprehensively protect the security of QQ users, and offered the software for download. In this case, once installed, the QQ Safeguard software would automatically test QQ software, and then display messages such as "The test score is 4, and QQ has a serious health problem", "Totally 40 items have been tested. 31 of them have problems. It is suggested to repair immediately! and test again"; "While running, QQ will scan the files on your computer (Tencent calls it a security scan); you can prohibit QQ from scanning your files and avoid breach of your privacy." Meanwhile, it reminded users of serious problems in QQ in red fonts, provided one-click repair help in green font, and listed as dangerous items "Your computer is in danger as 360 Safeguard has not been installed; upgrade QQ

Security Center; and prevent QQ from scanning my files". While searching for and killing Trojans in QQ, it would display a message "If you do not install 360 Safeguard, you will be unable to use Trojan search and kill function", and provide the installation and download services for 360 Safeguard with a green button. After performing the one-click repair, QQ Safeguard would replace QQ software's secure communication interface with the QQ Safeguard interface. On June 10th, 2011, Tencent Company and Tencent Computer Company instituted a lawsuit, claiming that such conducts of Qihoo and QGOA constituted unfair competition. In the first instance, High People's Court of Guangdong Province held that QQ Safeguard developed by Qihoo and QGOA specifically against QQ software destroyed the security and integrity of the legitimately running QQ software and services, deprived Tencent Company and Tencent Computer Company of transaction opportunities of legitimate value-added services and income from advertisements, games and others, and that QQ Safeguard replaced some functions of QQ software to promote its own products by altering the functional interface of QQ, which conduct violated the principle of honesty and credibility and that of fair competition, and constituted unfair competition. Qihoo and QGOA willfully fabricated and distributed false information against the operation of Tencent Company and Tencent Computer Company, which damaged the commercial reputation and commodity goodwill of Tencent Company and Tencent Computer Company and constituted commercial disparagement. Therefore, the court ruled that Qihoo and QGOA make public apology, eliminate the influence and jointly and severally indemnify Tencent Company and Tencent Computer Company RMB5 million in total for economic losses and reasonable enforcement expenses. Unsatisfied with this judgment, Qihoo and QGOA appealed.

Holding

The Supreme People's Court made a civil judgment (2013) MSZZ No. 5 on February 18ᵗʰ, 2014, dismissing the appeal and upholding the original judgment.

[Reasoning]

In the second instance, the Supreme People's Court opined that in market competition, operators can usually select the commercial model freely according to the demands of the market and consumers, which is a necessary requirement of market economy. In order to seek market benefit, Tencent Company and Tencent Computer Company developed QQ software, built around it a comprehensive internet business platform, and provided instant messaging services free of charge to attract both relevant consumers to experience and use their value added services and relevant advertisers to advertise on their platform, so as to create business opportunities and obtain relevant advertising income. Such a business model of combining a free platform with advertisement or value added services was a common operational model in the internet industry when the dispute in this case occurred, and also conformed to the stage characteristics of development of the internet market in China. In fact, Qihoo and QGOA in this case also used this business model. This business model did not violate the principled spirit and prohibitive provisions of *the Law against Unfair Competition*; the behavior of Tencent Company and Tencent Computer Company to seek commercial benefit shall be protected, and others shall not damage their legitimate rights and interests in an improper manner. Qihoo and QGOA developed and operated QQ Safeguard specifically against QQ software, destroyed the security and integrity of QQ software and its services through aiding and abetting, reduced Tencent Company and Tencent Computer Company's economic income and value-added service transaction opportunities, disturbed their proper operational activities and harmed their legitimate rights and interests. Fair competition is honest competition among competitors by making necessary efforts. Seeking competitive advantage without making the efforts or by unfairly using others' market achievements for one's own business opportunities and competitive advantages is unfair competition. While operating QQ Safeguard, Qihoo and QGOA embedded their own products and services into QQ software's interface, and replaced some functions of Tencent Company and Tencent Computer Company's QQ software. Their fundamental purpose was to sell and promote 360 Safeguard by relying on the strong user group of QQ software and by disparaging QQ software and its services, so as to increase the market transaction opportunities of Qihoo and QGOA and obtain competitive advantage in the market. In essence, this behavior is an improper use of others' market achievements for one's own business opportunities, so as to obtain competitive advantage. Thus, the said behavior of Qihoo and QGOA violated the principles of honesty and credibility and that of fair competition, and constituted unfair competition.

Issues regarding the boundary among technological innovation, free competition and unfair competition.

Qihoo contended that its behavior manifested the free and innovative spirit of internet, and that the court of first instance violated the laws of industrial development and oppressively applied the general principles of the *Law Against Unfair Competition*, which would limit competition and discourage innovation. The Supreme People's Court held that internet's development relies on free competition and scientific and technological innovation. The encouragement of free competition and innovation in the internet industry does not mean that internet is an arbitrary space beyond the law, and freedom of competition and innovation must be bounded by the principle of not infringing others' legitimate rights and interests.

Furthermore, the sound development of internet shall be guaranteed by an orderly market environment and clear rules for market competition. Whether a behavior is free competition and innovation encouraged by the spirit of the internet needs to be determined based on whether it helps to establish an equal and fair competition order and whether it conforms to the general interest of consumers and the public interest of the society. Free competition and innovation cannot be found as long as there is some progress in technology. Otherwise, anyone may arbitrarily interfere with others' technological products or services with the excuse of technological progress, which will create a "law of the jungle" under the disguise of technological progress and innovation. Technological innovation may stimulate competition, which in turn can further promote technological innovation. Neutral as it is, technology can also become a tool of unfair competition. Technological innovation should become a tool of fair and free competition, rather than an excuse to interfere with the legitimate business model of others. In this case, Qihoo specifically developed QQ Safeguard to deeply interfere with Tencent's QQ software in the name of technological innovation, which can hardly be found to comply with internet's spirit of freedom and innovation. Hence, the Supreme People's Court did not support the grounds of the appeal.

[Opinion of the Case (Chinese Version)]

Scan the QR code to see the Chinese version of the opinion

商业秘密侵权诉讼中行为保全措施的
审查与适用

—— 美国礼来公司、礼来（中国）研发公司诉黄孟炜
侵害技术秘密纠纷案

【裁判要旨】

2013年1月1日施行的《中华人民共和国民事诉讼法》规定了行为保全措施，有利于商业秘密权利人及时有效地寻求救济措施。法院要综合考虑：原告胜诉的实质可能性、如不采取行为保全措施将遭受无可挽回损失的实质性威胁、原告可能受到的损害大于对被告的任何潜在损害、采取行为保全措施不违反公共利益等因素作出裁定。

【案　　　号】　上海市第一中级人民法院（2013）沪一中民五（知）
　　　　　　　　初字第119号
【案　　　由】　侵害技术秘密纠纷
【合议庭成员】　唐　震　陈瑶瑶　陈荣祥
【关　键　词】　侵害商业秘密　行为保全
【相关法条】　《中华人民共和国民事诉讼法》第一百条

【基本案情】

申请人（原告）美国礼来公司（Eli Lilly and Company）。

申请人（原告）礼来（中国）研发有限公司（以下简称礼来中国公司）。

被申请人（被告）黄孟炜。

2013年7月2日，美国礼来公司、礼来中国公司向上海市第一中级人民法院（以下简称上海一中院）起诉状告黄孟炜侵害技术秘密，同时向该院提出行为保全的申请，要求法院责令被告不得披露、使用或者允许他人使用从申请人处盗取的21个商业秘密文件。

申请人称：被申请人于2012年5月入职礼来中国公司，担任化学主任研究员工作。礼来中国公司与被申请人签订了《保密协议》，并进行了相应的培训。2013年1月，被申请人从礼来中国公司的服务器上下载了48个申请人所拥有的文件（其中21个为原告核心机密商业文件），并将上述文件私自存储至被申请人所拥有的设备中。经交涉，2013年2月，被申请人签署同意函，向申请人承认："我从公司的服务器上下载了三十三（33）个属于公司的保密文件……"，并承诺："我允许公司或公司指定的人员检查第一手非公司装置和第二手非公司装置，以确定我没有进一步转发、修改、使用或打印任何公司文件。如果公司或其指定人员在非公司装置中发现任何公司文件或内容，我授权公司或其指定人员删除这些公司文件及相关内容……"。此后，申请人曾数次派员联系被申请人，要求其配合删除机密商业文件，并由申请人派员检查并确认上述机密商业文件已被删除。但是，被申请人无视申请人的交涉和努力，拒绝履行同意函约定的事项。鉴于被申请人严重违反公司制度，申请人于2013年2月27日致信被申请人宣布解除双方劳动关系。申请人认为，被申请人私自下载的21个核心机密商业文件，系申请人的商业秘密，被申请人对此明知且已在承诺书中予以认可。由于被申请人未履行承诺，致使申请人的商业秘密处于随时可能因被申请人披露、使用或者许可他人使用而被外泄的危险境地，对申请人造成无法弥补的损害。据此，申请人依法请求法院责令被申请人不得披露、使用或者允许他人使用从申请人处盗取的 21 个商业秘密文件。为支持其申请，申请人还向法院提供了涉案 21 个商业秘密文件的名称及内容、被申请人的承诺书、公证书、员工信息设备配备表格、劳动关系终止通知函、直接及间接成本统计表等证据材料。申请人就上述申请还提供了担保金人民币 10 万元。

 裁判结果

上海一中院裁定禁止被申请人黄孟炜披露、使用或允许他人使用申请人美国礼来公司、礼来（中国）研发有限公司主张作为商业秘密保护的 21 个文件。被申请人黄孟炜在裁定指定的期限内未申请复议，该裁定发生法律效力。

【裁判理由】

本案系国内首例依据《中华人民共和国民事诉讼法》（2013 年 1 月 1 日起施行）在商业秘密侵权诉讼中适用行为保全措施的案件，凸显了新时期下人民法院顺应社会需求，依法加强知识产权司法保护的实践努力。在案件的审理过程中，法院主要从以下方面加以认识和把握：

一、商业秘密侵权诉讼中行为保全措施的裁量因素

商业秘密侵权诉讼中，行为保全能够及时有效保护权利人的利益，作用十分重要。但是，行为保全是一种特殊的救济措施，不仅能够保障未来生效判决的顺利执行，而且在一定程度上会使得申请人提前获得终局救济全部或部分的利益。因此，在司法实践中，仅

仅是存在未经授权的披露或者使用的一般可能性，法院不能采取行为保全。通常而言，行为保全的适用要综合考虑原告胜诉的实质可能性；如不采取行为保全将遭受无可挽回损失的实质性威胁；原告可能受到的损害大于对被告的任何潜在损害；采取行为保全不违反公共利益等因素作出裁定。本案特殊性还在于：1. 被申请人黄孟炜已经确认其违反公司规定下载了33个属于公司的保密文件（其中包括了21个权利人主张作为商业秘密保护的文件），并承诺授权公司指定人员删除上述文件。据此，被申请人通过非法手段获取权利人作为商业秘密保护的保密文件的事实是显而易见的。2. 商业秘密存在着"一旦丧失就永远丧失"的特性。涉案商业文件已经处于被申请人的掌控之下，一旦被申请人外泄，上述电子文件的内容很可能就会被竞争对手获悉或者进入公知领域，从而丧失秘密性，使得权利人的利益遭受无可挽回的损失。3. 从案件事实来看，被申请人作为自然人主体，相对于权利人而言，禁止被申请人披露、使用或允许他人使用涉案商业文件并不会对其造成损害。更何况，权利人也向法院提交了担保金，以防止万一可能出现的损害。综合上述因素，合议庭对被申请人采取行为保全措施，同时告知其申复议的时限，以利于被申请人行使自己的抗辩权利。

二、商业秘密侵权诉讼中行为保全措施的裁判要点

本案系首例商业秘密侵权诉讼中适用行为保全措施的案件，如何适用法律无先例可循。在审理过程中，合议庭还着重把握了以下裁判要点：一是诉讼请求与行为保全申请统一的问题。权利人起诉时，请求法院判令被告停止侵犯原告商业秘密，并明确具体内容为要求被告删除及不得披露、使用或允许他人使用涉案21个商业文件。合议庭认为，法院审查权利人行为保全申请时只能局限于其诉讼请求的范围之内，而不允许另行增加，且应当符合《中

华人民共和国反不正当竞争法》第十条（该法于 2017 年 11 月 4 日第十二届全国人民代表大会常务委员会第三十次会议修订，新法条为第九条）规定的商业秘密侵权手段，故最终裁定被申请人"不得披露、使用或允许他人使用涉案 21 个文件"。二是行为保全与终局裁判的关系问题。本案处于审理阶段，商业秘密能否成立，是否属于我国《反不正当竞争法》所保护的法律利益尚未定论。行为保全作为阶段性诉讼措施，禁令裁定不能埋下与最终裁判相互矛盾的隐患。因此，裁定主文采取的表述为"禁止被申请人黄孟炜披露、使用或允许他人使用申请人美国礼来公司、礼来（中国）研发有限公司主张作为商业秘密保护的 21 个文件"，这就意味着，涉案的 21 件文件目前仅系申请人主张作为商业秘密保护的文件，而非经由法院依法审查，最终作为商业秘密保护的信息。三是裁判与执行兼顾问题。仅从裁定主文而言，21 个文件内容尚不清晰，执行部门执行时将不具有针对性和可行性。因此，我们在裁定主文后附上涉案 21 个文件的具体名称。这说明尽管被申请人违反公司规定下载了 33 件文件，但只有违反裁定要求，披露、使用或允许他人使用裁定所附的 21 件文件，才要承担相应的法律责任。

三、商业秘密侵权诉讼中行为保全措施的执行方式

行为保全的内容是法院裁决当事人作出一定行为或者禁止作出一定行为，行为保全不同于财产保全，执行的对象是人的行为，而非物本身。正是由于行为保全的特殊性，行为保全的执行需要当事人的配合。而且，禁止当事人实施一定行为比要求当事人作出一定行为执行难度更大。因为要求当事人作出一定行为可以被外在感知，某些时候也能即时履行完毕；而禁止当事人实施一定行为则有赖于当事人的自觉性。而这种自觉性并不能为法院执行人员所能客观感知，从而增加了裁定执行的不确定性。合议庭认为，这种不作为行

为的裁定，主要依赖生效法律文书的威慑力。只有增强生效法律文书的威慑力，才能保证当事人自觉履行法院裁定。因此，在本案裁定作出之后，法院并未简单地送达法律文书，而是传唤被申请人到法院谈话，当庭告知其裁定的内容及违反裁定的后果。事实上，对于拒不履行法院已经发生法律效力判决、裁定的，法院可以依据《中华人民共和国民事诉讼法》第一百一十条的规定，根据情节轻重对行为人处以罚款、拘留；构成犯罪的，依法追究刑事责任。应当说，这种告诫取得了较好的法律效果。被申请人当庭书面承诺表示愿意遵守法院裁定，并在事后提交法院的答辩材料中，陈述其已经损毁了存储下载文件的硬盘装置，并附上照片佐证。

【本案裁判文书】

扫描二维码，可见裁判文书

Review and Application of Behavioral Preservation in Trade Secret Infringement Litigations

——Eli Lilly and Company and Lilly (China) Research and Development Co., Ltd. v. Huang Mengwei

[Syllabus]

*The revised **Civil Procedure Law** entering into force on January 1, 2013 stipulates the preliminary injunction, which helps the obligee of trade secret seek remedies in a timely and effective manner. Before entering an injunction, the court shall consider such factors as the substantial possibility of the plaintiff wining the case, the substantial danger of irreparable harm caused by denial of injunction, the possible harm to the plaintiff outweighing any potential harm to the defendant, and injunction's non-infringement on public interests.*

385

[Case No.] Shanghai No. 1 Intermediate People's Court (2013) HYZMW(Z) CZ No. 119

[Cause of Action] Dispute over infringement upon technological secrets

[Collegial Panel Members] Tang Zhen　Chen Yaoyao Chen Rongxiang

[Keywords] Infringement upon trade secrets, preliminary injunction

[Relevant Legal Provisions] Article 100 of *the Civil Procedure Law of the People's Republic of China*

[Basic Facts]

Claimant (Plaintiff): Eli Lilly and Company

Claimant (Plaintiff): Lilly (China) Research and Development Co., Ltd. (hereinafter referred to as "Lilly China").

Respondent (Defendant): Huang Mengwei

On July 2, 2013, Eli Lilly and Company and Lilly China filed a lawsuit with Shanghai No. 1 Intermediate People's Court (hereinafter referred to as "Shanghai No. 1 Intermediate Court") against Huang Mengwei for infringing technological secret and applied to the court for behavioral preservation, requesting the court to order the Defendant not to disclose, use or allow others to use the 21 confidential documents stolen from the Claimants.

The Claimants alleged that the Respondent joined Lilly China in May 2012 as a chief chemistry researcher. Lilly China signed a Confidentiality Agreement with the Respondent and provided corresponding trainings. In January 2013, the Respondent downloaded 48 documents owned by the Claimants from the server of Lilly China (including 21 core confidential documents of the Plaintiffs) and stored such documents in the device owned by the Respondent without authorization. Upon negotiation, the Respondent signed a letter of consent in February 2013, admitting to the Claimants, "I downloaded thirty-three (33) confidential documents belonging to the company from the company's server…", and undertaking, "I allow the company or persons designated by the company to check the first-hand device not belonging to the company and the second-hand device not belonging to the company to determine that I did not forward, modify, use or print any company document. If the company or persons designated by the company find any document or information of the company in device not belonging to the company, I authorize the company or persons designated by the company to delete such document or information. ..." After that, the Claimants repeatedly designated persons to contact the Respondent and required him to delete confidential commercial documents. The Claimants also designated persons to check and confirm whether the confidential commercial documents were deleted. However, the Respondent ignored the negotiations and efforts of the Claimants and refused to perform the obligations agreed in the letter of consent. As the Respondent seriously violated the rules and regulations of the company, the Claimants sent a letter to the Respondent on February 27, 2013, announcing the termination of their labor relation. The Claimants believed that the 21 core confidential commercial documents downloaded by the Respondent without authorization were trade secrets of the Claimants and the Respondent knew and admitted it in the letter of undertaking. The Respondent's failure to fulfill his undertaking had exposed the Claimants' trade secrets to the danger of leakage due to disclosure or use by the Respondent or use by others permitted by him, which would cause irreparable harm to the Claimants. Therefore, in accordance with law, the Claimants requested the court to order the Respondent not to disclose, use or allow others to use the 21 trade secret documents stolen from the Claimants. To support their application, the Claimants also provided the court with the names and content of the 21 trade secret documents involved, the Respondent's letter of undertaking, the certificate of notarization, table of information devices allocated to employees, the termination notice of labor relation, the statistical statement of direct and indirect costs and other evidentiary materials. The Claimants also deposited RMB 100,000 with the court as security bond for the above application.

Holding

Shanghai No. 1 Intermediate Court ordered that the Respondent Huang Mengwei be prohibited from disclosing, using or allowing others to use the 21 documents claimed by Eli Lilly and Company and Lilly China Research and Development Co., Ltd. as protected trade secrets. As the Respondent Huang Mengwei did not apply for reconsideration within the time limit specified by the order, that order came into force.

[Reasoning]

As the first case where behavioral preservation was applied to a trade secret dispute under the new *Civil Procedure Law* (effective as of January 1, 2013), this case highlighted the practical efforts made by the people' court in the new era to comply with societal needs, and strengthen the judicial protection of intellectual property according to law. During the trial, the court mainly considered the following factors:

I. Factors to be considered for behavioral preservation in trade secret infringement litigations

In trade secret infringement litigations, a preliminary injunction plays an important role in protecting the interests of the obligee in a timely and effective manner. However, as a special relief, preliminary injunctions can not only ensure the smooth enforcement of the upcoming effective judgment, but also enable its claimant to obtain, in advance, all or part of the interests of the final relief. Therefore, in judicial practice, the court shall not enter an injunction simply when there exist general possibilities of unauthorized disclosure or use. Before entering an injunction, the court shall usually consider such factors as the substantial possibility of the plaintiff wining the case, the substantial danger of irreparable harm caused by denial of injunction, the possible harm to the plaintiff outweighing any potential harm to the defendant, and injunction's non-infringement on public interests. What makes this case special is that: 1) the Respondent Huang Mengwei had confirmed that he downloaded 33 confidential documents belonging to the company (including 21 documents claimed by the obligees for trade secret protection) in violation of rules and regulations of the company, and undertaken to authorize persons designated by the company to delete such documents. Therefore, it is obvious that the Respondent obtained by illegal means the confidential documents claimed by the obligees for trade secret protection. 2) A trade secret, once lost, is lost forever. The commercial documents involved were already under the control of the Respondent. Once disclosed by the Respondent, the content of such electronic documents may be known to competitors or enter the public domain and then lose its confidentiality, leaving the interest of the obligees irreparably harmed. 3) Based on the facts of this case, the Respondent, as a natural person in contrast with the obligees, would not be harmed if he was prohibited from disclosing, using or allowing others to use the commercial documents. In addition, the obligees deposited security bond to the court for any damage that might occur. Based on the above facts, the collegial panel granted a behavioral injunction against the Respondent and informed him of the time limit for applying for reconsideration to facilitate the exercise of his right of defense.

II. Key points to be considered for behavioral preservation in trade secret infringement litigations

As the first case for the application of behavioral preservation to trade secrete infringement litigation, this case had no precedent to follow with respect to the application of law. During the trial, the collegial panel mainly considered the following key points: 1) the consistency between the claims of the Plaintiffs and the application for injunction. When filing the lawsuit, the obligees requested the court to order the Respondent to stop infringing the trade secrets of the Plaintiffs, and specifically, to order the Respondent to delete and not disclose, use or allow others to use the 21 commercial documents involved. The collegial panel held that its review of the obligees' injunction application shall be limited to their litigious claims without allowing additions, and shall conform to the means of trade secret infringement as set forth in Article 10 of *the Anti-unfair Competition Law* (Article 9 in the law as amended at the 30th Session of the Standing Committee of the 12th National People's Congress held on November 4, 2017). Therefore, the Respondent was ordered "not to disclose, use or allow others to use the 21 documents involved". 2) The relation between the preliminary injunction and the final judgment. When the trial was underway, it was pending whether the documents involved constituted trade secrets and belonged to the legal interests protected by *the Anti-unfair Competition Law*. As a temporary litigious measure, the injunction order shall be free from the danger of conflicting with the final judgment. Therefore, the order was worded as "the Respondent Huang Mengwei be prohibited from disclosing, using or allowing others to use the 21 documents claimed by Eli Lilly and Company and Lilly China Research and Development Co., Ltd. as protected trade secrets", which means that the 21 documents involved were just documents claimed by the applicant to be protected as trade secrets, instead of information finally confirmed by the court to be protected as trade secrets upon review under law. 3) Balance between trial and enforcement. As the content of the 21 documents involved was not clear in the text of the order, the enforcement departments would lack specificity and feasibility during enforcement. Therefore, we appendixed a list of the names of the 21 documents involved to the text of the order. This suggested that although the Respondent downloaded 33 documents in violation of the rules and regulations of the company, he shall only be legally liable for disclosing, using or allowing others to use the 21 appendixed documents in violation of the order.

III. Enforcement models of behavioral preservation in trade secret infringement litigations

A behavioral injunction is about the court ordering a party to do or not to do a certain activity. Different from property preservation, a behavioral injunction is enforced against a person's behavior, instead of a property per se. Due to a behavioral injunction's special characteristics, its enforcement requires the party's cooperation. Moreover, enforcement is more difficult when the injunction orders the party not to do something than doing something because a positive action by a party is perceivable from outside, and sometimes completable instantaneously while the prohibition of a party's behavior depends on his conscientiousness, which is not objectively perceivable by the enforcement staff of the court, and makes the enforcement of court orders less certain. The collegial panel held that such negative injunctions mainly depend on deterrent force of effective legal instruments. Only by strengthening the deterrent force of effective legal instruments can the parties' conscientious compliance with court orders be ensured. Therefore, after entering the judgment, the court not only serviced the legal instrument, but also summoned the Respondent to the court and informed him of the content of the order and the consequence of violating it. In fact, in case a party refuses to comply with effective court judgments or orders, the court may, in accordance with Article 111 of *the Civil Procedure Law*, fine or detain the party based on the severity of circumstances, and hold him criminally liable if crime is committed. It is fair to say that such warning has generated good legal effect. In the court, the Respondent undertook in writing that it was willing to comply with the court order and then represented in later submission to the court that it had destroyed the hard disks that stored the downloaded documents, and attached photos to corroborate such representations.

[Opinion of the Case (Chinese Version)]

Scan the QR code to see the Chinese version of the opinion

解决权利冲突的原则：
保护在先权利与权利共存并重

——北京趣拿信息技术有限公司与广州市去哪信息技术有限公司
不正当竞争纠纷案

【裁判要旨】

权利冲突的实质是利益冲突，重新确定和明晰权利边界的过程是一个对冲突的利益进行衡量和取舍的过程，体现了司法裁判的价值取向。

【案　　　号】	广东省高级人民法院（2013）粤高法民三终字第565号
【案　　　由】	不正当竞争纠纷案
【合议庭成员】	岳利浩　喻　洁　石静涵
【关　键　词】	不正当竞争　知名服务特有名称　域名
【相关法条】	《最高人民法院关于审理涉及计算机网络域名民事纠纷案件使用法律若干问题的解释》

【基本案情】

2005年5月9日，庄辰超注册了"qunar.com"域名并创建了"去哪儿"网。北京趣拿信息技术有限公司（以下简称北京趣拿公司）于2006年3月17日经工商登记成立后，"qunar.com"域名由庄辰超（北京趣拿公司法定代表人）转让给公司。经过多年使用，"去哪儿""去哪儿网""qunar.com"等服务标识成为知名服务的特有名称。

广州市去哪信息技术有限公司（以下简称广州去哪公司）前身为广州市龙游仙踪旅行社有限公司，成立于 2003 年 12 月 10 日，经营范围与北京趣拿公司相近。2003 年 6 月 6 日，"quna.com"域名登记注册。经过多次转让，苑景恩（广州去哪公司法定代表人）于 2009 年 5 月 9 日受让取得该域名。2009 年 5 月 26 日，广州去哪公司经核准变更为现名，"quna.com"域名也随即转让给公司。公司随后注册了"123quna.com""mquna.com"域名，并使用"去哪""去哪儿""去哪网""quna.com"名义对外宣传和经营。

2011 年 4 月 25 日，北京趣拿公司以广州去哪公司使用"去哪""去哪儿""去哪网""quna.com"名义对外宣传和经营构成不正当竞争为由，向一审法院提起诉讼，请求判令广州去哪公司停止不正当竞争行为并赔偿经济损失人民币 300 万元，等。

 裁判结果

广州市中级人民法院于 2013 年 6 月 9 日作出（2011）穗中法民三初字第 217 号民事判决。认为：北京趣拿公司、广州去哪公司均提供旅游网络服务，构成竞争关系。北京趣拿公司使用的商业标记"去哪儿""去哪儿网""qunar.com"属于知名服务特有的名称。广州去哪公司使用"去哪""去哪儿""去哪网""quna.com"商业标记的行为构成对北京趣拿公司知名服务特有的名称的侵害。广州去哪公司在其企业字号中使用"去哪"字样的行为构成不正当竞争。广州去哪公司使用"quna.com""123quna.com""mquna.com"域名的行为构成对北京趣拿公司域名权益的侵害。一审法院据此判决：1.广州去哪公司停止使用"去哪"作为其企业字号；2.广州去哪公司公司停止使用"去哪""去哪儿""去哪网""quna.com"作为其服务标记；3.广州去哪公司停止使用"quna.com""123quna.com""mquna.com"域名，并限期将上述域名移转给北京趣拿公司；4.广州去哪公司赔偿北京趣拿公司经济损失人民币35万元；5.驳回北京趣拿公司的其他诉讼请求。

广州去哪公司不服一审判决上诉至广东省高级人民法院。理由是该公司享有的域名"quna.com"是于2003年6月6日合法登记注册的，是在先权利。该公司受让并使用"quna.com"域名，以及随后注册"123quna.com""mquna.com"域名没有恶意。

二审法院于2014年3月19日作出二审判决。认为：北京趣拿公司使用的"去哪儿""去哪儿网""qunar.com"构成知名服务的特有名称；广州去哪公司使用"去哪"作为企业字号构成不正当竞争行为。但是，广州去哪公司使用域名"quna.com""123quna.com""mquna.com"属于对在先权利的使用，有合法依据。二审法院据此维持了一审判决关于广州去哪公司停止使用"去哪"企业字号及"去哪"等标识的判项；撤销了"广州去哪公司停止使用'quna.com''123quna.com''mquna.com'域名，并限期将上述域名移转给北京趣拿公司"的判项；并把赔偿数额相应减少为人民币25万元。

【裁判理由】

二审的主要争议焦点是广州去哪公司使用域名"quna.com""123quna.com""mquna.com"是否有合法依据。

《最高人民法院关于审理涉及计算机网络域名民事纠纷案件使用法律若干问题的解释》第四条规定："人民法院审理域名纠纷案件，对符合以下各项条件的，应当认定被告注册、使用域名等行为构成侵权或者不正当竞争：（一）原告请求保护的民事权益合法有效；（二）被告域名或其主要部分构成对原告驰名商标的复制、模仿、翻译或音译；或者与原告的注册商标、域名等相同或近似，足以造成相关公众的误认；（三）被告对该域名或其主要部分不享有权益，也无注册、使用该域名的正当理由；（四）被告对该域名的注册、使用具有恶意。"因此，判断广州去哪公司是否构成不正当竞争行为的关键，是看该公司使用域名的行为是否符合上述全部四个要件。

首先，关于使用"quna.com"域名的问题。二审法院认为，广州去哪公司对域名"quna.com"享有合法权益，使用该域名有正当理由，因此不符合上述第三个要件，广州去哪公司不构成不正当竞争行为。理由是：（一）2003 年 6 月 6 日，"quna.com"域名初次登记注册。而"qunar.com"域名被注册并创建网站的时间是 2005 年 5 月 9 日，较"quna.com"域名初次登记注册的时间要晚将近两年。因此，"quna.com"域名的注册是正当的。"quna.com"域名后经多次转让，于 2009 年 5 月 9 日由苑景恩（广州去哪公司的法定代表人）受让取得，2009 年 7 月 3 日由广州去哪公司受让取得，这种转让行为亦不违反法律规定。广州去哪公司使用合法受让的"quna.com"域名，法律不应干涉。（二）2010 年 8 月 27 日，北京趣拿公司曾就广州去哪公司的"quna.com"域名向亚洲域名争议解决中心北京秘书处提交投诉书，请求移转广州去哪公司名下的上述域名给北京趣拿公司。专家组认为，投诉人不能同时满足相关《统一域名争议解决政策》规定的三个条件；从而缺乏理由支持"裁决被投诉人将争议域名转移给投诉人"的请求。进一步证明广州去哪公司使用"quna.com"域名有正当理由；（三）由于域名有长度和总量限制，故允许近似域名注册，因此北京趣拿公司的"qunar.com"域名与广州去哪公司的"quna.com"域名因仅相差一个字母"r"，虽然构成相近似，但是对于在使用过程中可能产生混淆的情况，双方均有容忍的义务。如果以两个域名在使用过程中产生混淆的结果，反推广州去哪公司使用"quna.com"域名存在恶意，进而推定广州去哪公司取得"quna.com"域名没有正当理由，因此构成不正当竞争行为，不符合推理逻辑。

其次，关于使用"123quna.com""mquna.com"域名的问题。相较北京趣拿公司的"qunar.com"域名而言，"123quna.com""mquna.com"域名与广州去哪公司使用的"quna.com"域名更为近似。由于广州去哪公司使用"quna.com"域名有正当理由，随后注册的"123quna.com""mquna.com"域名也应当允许注册和使用。综上，广州去哪公司上诉认为该公司使用域名"quna.com""123quna.com""mquna.com"有合法依据的理由成立，二审法院依法予以支持。

二审法院同时指出，本案双方当事人均享有来源合法的域名权益，双方需要彼此容忍，互相尊重，长期共存。一方不能因为在经营过程中知名度提升，就剥夺另一方的生存空间；另一方也不能恶意攀附知名度较高一方的商誉，以谋取不正当的商业利益。据此，广州去哪公司虽然有权继续使用"quna.com""123quna.com""mquna.com"域名，但是也有义务在与域名相关的搜索链接及网站上加注区别性标识，以使消费者将上述域名与北京趣拿公司"去哪儿""去哪儿网""qunar.com"等知名服务特有名称相区分。

【本案裁判文书】

扫描二维码，可见裁判文书

The Principle for Resolving Conflict of Rights: Attach Equal Importance to Protection of Prior Rights and Coexistence of Rights

——Beijing Quna Information Technology Co., Ltd. v. Guangzhou Quna Information Technology Co., Ltd.

[Syllabus]

A conflict of rights is substantially that of interests. The process to redefine and clarify the boundary of rights represents that to measure and trade-off conflicting interests, and reflects the value orientation of judgment.

399

[Case No.] Guangdong High People's Court (2013) YGFMSZZ No.565

[Cause of Action] A dispute over unfair competition

[Collegial Panel Members] Yue Lihao   Yu Jie   Shi Jinghan

[Keywords] Unfair competition, specific name of famous service, domain name

[Relevant Legal Provisions] Article 4 of the *Interpretation of the Supreme People's Court on Several Issues concerning the Application of Law in the Trial of Civil Dispute Cases Regarding Computer Network Domain Names*

[Basic Facts]

On May 9th, 2005, Zhuang Chenchao registered the domain name "qunar.com" and established the "qunar" website. After Beijing Quna Information Technology Co., Ltd. (hereinafter referred to as "Beijing Quna Company") was incorporated and registered on March 17th, 2006, the domain name "qunar.com" was transferred by Zhuang Chenchao (legal representative of Beijing Quna Company) to Beijing Quna Company. After years of use, the service logos such as "去哪儿", "去哪儿网" and "qunar.com" became specific names of famous service.

Guangzhou Quna Information Technology Co., Ltd. (hereinafter referred to as "Guangzhou Quna Company") was formerly known as Guangzhou Longyou Xianzong Travel Agency Co., Ltd., founded on December 10th, 2003, and covering a scope of business similar to that of Beijing Quna Company. On June 6th, 2003, the domain name "quna.com" was registered. After several transfers, it was acquired by Yuan Jingen (the legal representative of Guangzhou Quna Company) on May 9th, 2009. On May 26th, 2009, Guangzhou Quna Company got its present name after approved renaming, and the domain name "quna.com" was transferred to this company soon afterwards. Guangzhou Quna Company subsequently registered domain names "123quna.com" and "mquna.com", and used "去哪", "去哪儿", "去哪网" and "quna.com" in its external publicity materials and operations.

On April 25, 2011, Beijing Quna Company filed a lawsuit in the court of first instance against Guangzhou Quna Company, alleging that its use of "去哪", "去哪儿", "去哪网" and "quna.com" in its external publicity materials and operations constituted unfair competition, and requested the court to rule that Guangzhou Quna Company immediately cease the unfair competition and pay a damage of RMB 3 million for the economic losses.

Holding

Guangzhou Intermediate People's Court rendered a civil judgment (2011) SZFMSCZ No.217 on June 9th, 2013, holding that: Both Beijing Quna Company and Guangzhou Quna Company provided online travel service, and there existed competition between them. The commercial marks "去哪儿", "去哪儿网" and "qunar.com" used by Beijing Quna Company were specific names of famous service. Guangzhou Quna Company's use of the commercial marks "去哪", "去哪儿", "去哪网" and "quna.com" constituted an infringement of the specific names of the famous service of Beijing Quna Company, and Guangzhou Quna Company's use of the word "quna" in its company name constituted unfair competition. Guangzhou Quna Company's use of the domain names "quna.com", "123quna.com" and "mquna.com" constituted an infringement of the interests in the domain name of Beijing Quna Company. Thus, the court of first instance ruled: 1) Guangzhou Quna Company stop using "quna" as its company name; 2) Guangzhou Quna Company stop using "去哪", "去哪儿", "去哪网" and "quna.com" as its service marks; 3) Guangzhou Quna Company stop using the domain names "quna.com", "123quna.com" and "mquna.com", and transfer these domain names to Beijing Quna Company within the stipulated time limit; 4) Guangzhou Quna Company pay RMB350,000 to Beijing Quna Company to compensate its economic losses; and 5) All other claims of Beijing Quna Company be rejected.

Unsatisfied with the judgment of first instance, Guangzhou Quna Company appealed to High People's Court of Guangdong Province, arguing that its domain name "quna.com" was legitimately registered on June 6th, 2003, and was thus a prior right. Furthermore, it had no malicious intent in acquiring the domain name "quna.com" and subsequently registering the domain names "123quna.com" and "mquna.com".

The court of second instance delivered a judgment on March 19th, 2014, holding that: "去哪儿", "去哪儿网" and "qunar.com" used by Beijing Quna Company constituted specific names of famous service; Guangzhou Quna Company's use of the word "quna" as its company name constituted unfair competition. However, the use of domain names "quna.com", "123quna.com" and "mquna.com" by Guangzhou Quna Company was the exercise of prior rights, which had a legal basis. Therefore, the court of second instance upheld the decision of the court of first instance that Guangzhou Quna Company stop using "quna|" in its company name and using marks like "去哪"; set aside the first-instance decision that Guangzhou Quna Company stop using the domain names "quna.com", "123quna.com" and "mquna.com" and transfer these domain names to Beijing Quna Company within the stipulated time limit; and reduced the amount of compensation to RMB250,000 accordingly.

[Reasoning]

The court of second instance believed it correct for the court of first instance to find as unfair competition Guangzhou Quna Company's use of the word "quna" in its company name and use of marks such as "去 哪". The dispute of second instance focused on whether the use of domain names "quna.com", "123quna.com" and "mquna. com" by Guangzhou Quna Company had legal basis. According to Article 4 of *the Interpretation of the Supreme People's Court on Several Issues concerning the Application of Law in the Trial of Civil Dispute Cases Regarding Computer Network Domain Names*, "in the trial of domain name dispute cases, the people's court shall find the respondent's registration and use of a domain name to be an infringement or unfair competition when the following conditions are satisfied: 1) the civil rights and interests claimed by the plaintiff for protection are legitimate and valid; 2) the defendant's domain name or its main part constitutes the reproduction, imitation, translation or transliteration of the plaintiff's well-known trademark, or is same as or similar to the plaintiff's registered trademark and domain name, etc., enough to cause confusion among the relevant public; 3) the defendant has neither rights and interests in the domain name or its main part, nor just cause to register or use such domain name; 4) the defendant registers or uses the domain name with a malicious intent." Therefore, the key to determining whether Guangzhou Quna Company conducted unfair competition was whether its use of the domain names satisfied all of the four elements above.

Firstly, on the use of the domain name "quna.com", the court of second instance opined that Guangzhou Quna Company enjoyed legitimate rights and interests in the domain name "quna.com", and had just cause to use it; failing this third requirement, Guangzhou Quna Company's action did not constitute unfair competition. The reason is as follows: 1) On June 6th, 2003, the domain name "quna.com" was registered for the first time, but it was not until May 9th, 2005, about 2 years after such initial registration of "quna.com", that the domain name "qunar.com" was registered and website created. Therefore, the registration of "quna.com" was legitimate. After several transfers, the domain name "quna.com" was acquired by Yuan Jingen (legal representative of Guangzhou Quna Company) on May 9th, 2009, and later by Guangzhou Quna Company on July 3rd, 2009. Such transfers did not break the law, either. The law shall not interfere with Guangzhou Quna Company's use of its legally acquired domain name "quna.com". 2) On August 27th, 2010, Beijing Quna Company submitted a complaint letter against the domain name "quna.com" of Guangzhou Quna Company to the Beijing Secretariat of the Asian Domain Name Dispute Resolution Center, requesting that this domain name be transferred to Beijing Quna Company. According to the expert group, the complainant could not satisfy the three conditions stipulated in *Uniform Domain Name Dispute Resolution Policy*, hence, there was no reason to grant its request to "order the respondent to transfer the disputed domain name to the complainant". This further proved that Guangzhou Quna Company had just cause to use the domain name "quna.com"; 3) As domain names were limited in length and quantity, similar domain names are registerable. The only difference between Beijing Quna Company's domain name "qunar.com" and Guangzhou Quna Company's domain name "quna.com" was the dropped letter "r". Although the two domain names are similar, the two parties are obliged to tolerate the possible confusion between these two domain names in their use. It is illogical to deduce Guangzhou Quna Company's malice in using the domain name "quna.com" from the confusion resulting from the use of these two domain names, and proceed to presume that Guangzhou Quna Company had no just cause to acquire the domain name "quna.com", and therefore conducted unfair competition.

Secondly, on the use of the domain names "123quna.com" and "mquna.com". The domain names "123quna.com" and "mquna.com" are more similar to the domain name "quna.com" used by Guangzhou Quna Company than Beijing Quna Company's domain name "qunar.com". As Guangzhou Quna Company had just cause to use the domain name "quna.com", the domain names "123quna.com" and "mquna.com" registered afterwards shall also be allowed to be registered and used. In conclusion, there was valid reasons for Guangzhou Quna Company to argue that it had a legal basis to use the domain names "quna.com", "123quna.com" and "mquna.com". The court of second instance supported its appeal according to law.

As also noted by the court of second instance, both parties in this case enjoyed the rights and interests in domain names with legitimate sources, therefore shall tolerate, respect and co-exist in long term with each other. Neither may one party deprive the other of its living space because the former's popularity increased in operation; nor may the other party maliciously exploit the higher goodwill of the more famous party for improper business benefits. Therefore, Guangzhou Quna Company shall have the right to continuously use the domain names "quna.com", "123quna.com" and "mquna.com", but be obligated to add corresponding distinguishing marks on the domain name-related search links and websites so that consumers could distinguish the abovementioned domain names from "去哪儿", "去哪儿网" and "qunar.com", which are specific names of Beijing Quna Company's famous service.

[Opinion of the Case (Chinese Version)]

Scan the QR code to see the Chinese version of the opinion

商业秘密中客户名单的认定，
以及侵权人承担停止侵权民事责任的适用

——鹤壁市反光材料有限公司与宋俊超、
鹤壁睿明特科技有限公司、李建发侵害商业秘密纠纷案

【裁判要旨】

商业秘密中的客户名单不是简单的客户名称，还应包含名单以外影响交易的深度信息。权利人与客户之间的增值税发票、发货清单、汇款凭证、要货通知单、包裹票据等，包含了客户的交易习惯、交易需求、价格承受能力等区别于公知信息的特殊客户信息，具有现实或者潜在的商业价值，构成了经营信息的秘密点，经权利人采取合理保密措施后，构成商业秘密。

【案　　　号】	河南省高级人民法院（2016）豫民终 347 号
【案　　　由】	侵害商业秘密纠纷
【合议庭成员】	赵　筝　赵艳斌　焦新慧
【关　键　词】	侵害商业秘密　客户名单　适用停止侵权
【相关法条】	《中华人民共和国反不正当竞争法》（1993年）第十条 ①，《最高人民法院关于审理不正当竞争民事案件应用法律若干问题的解释》第十六条

---

① 该法于 2017 年 11 月 4 日修订，新法法条为第九条。

【基本案情】

上诉人宋俊超、鹤壁睿明特科技有限公司（以下简称睿明特公司）与被上诉人鹤壁市反光材料有限公司（以下简称反光材料公司）、原审被告李建发侵害商业秘密纠纷一案。反光材料公司成立于 1996 年 4 月 4 日，经营范围为反光材料及应用反光材料制品、镀膜制品、加工销售等。反光材料公司提交了该公司 2010 年（5 页）、2011 年（4 页）、2012 年（4 页）、2013 年（3 页）、2014 年（2 页）共计 18 页与东北地区客户的交易记录明细表。包含有"日期""客户名称""品种""规格""数量""单价""收入""地址""联系人""联系电话""备注"等信息。宋俊超自 2006 年起在反光材料公司任业务员，主要负责黑龙江省、吉林省、辽宁省及内蒙古自治区的销售及客户拓展工作。反光材料公司与宋俊超先后签订两份劳动合同，并约定有保密条款、竞业限制条款。反光材料公司对其经营信息制定有保密制度，对客户及潜在客户信息采取了必要的保密措施，同时向宋俊超及其他业务员支付了保密费用。之后，反光材料公司发现宋俊超自行购买反光布，向法院申请诉前保全及诉讼，请求查封宋俊超存放的收货人为宋翔的 14 件反光布，判令宋俊超、睿明特公司、李建发停止侵权，赔偿合理费用及损失 50 万元。

鹤壁市山城区睿欣反光材料经营部（以下简称睿欣经营部）成立于 2006 年 4 月 3 日，经营者姓名为李建发，联系电话为 130xxxxxxx9。鹤壁市睿欣商贸有限公司（以下简称睿欣公司）成立于 2011 年 6 月 22 日，经营范围为钢材、建材、五金交电、涂板、反光护栏。法定代表人两次变更的联系电话均为 130xxxxxxx9。2011 年 11 月 12 日，宋翔办理了该公司经营项目变更，增加的经营项目为：反光材料制品、服装、纺织品、卫生用品、橡胶制品等。2013 年 8 月 27 日，宋翔办理了睿欣公司法定代表人的变更手续。另外，在睿欣公司经营期间，宋翔还参与了办理营业执照、公司事项变更、提交年检报告等公司工商登记手续的相关工作。睿欣公司于 2015 年 1 月 19 日名称变更为睿明特公司。宋俊超的身份证号码为 4106xxxxxxxxx1537，宋翔的身份证号码为 4106xxxxxxxxx7510，两个名字系同一人。号码为 130xxxxxxx9 的 SIM 卡由宋俊超使用。宋俊超以宋翔名义先后 10 次通过郑州德邦物流有限公司鹤壁分公司向东北地区发送货物，货品有"反光布、3 纤"等，"反光条、2 纤""布、5 纤"等。宋俊超于 2014 年 2 月 8 日通过中铁股份有限公司鹤壁市营业部向东北地区发送货物。宋俊超先后 7 次通过上海佳吉快运有限公司鹤壁分公司向东北地区发送货物，货品有"布、3""布、4""布、9"等。部分客户名单与反光材料公司客户名单相同。睿欣公司的银行往来账目显示，自 2011 年 8 月 1 日至 2015 年 7 月 31 日期间，睿欣公司与东北地区客户中，与反光材料公司交易客户相重复的客户 10 户，供货交易 38 笔，交易金额 830,512.50 元。宋俊超以个人名义从睿欣公司账户取款 27 笔，金额为 1,270,603.42 元。

 裁判结果

河南省鹤壁市中级人民法院于 2015 年 12 月 25 日作出（2015）鹤民初字第 96 号民事判决：判令宋俊超、睿明特公司停止对反光材料公司商业秘密的侵权行为，并在两年内不准使用反光材料公司所拥有的商业秘密，赔偿 35 万元。一审宣判后，宋俊超、睿明特公司不服，向河南省高级人民法院提起上诉，请求撤销一审判决，驳回反光材料公司的诉讼请求。河南省高级人民法院于 2017 年 8 月 2 日作出（2016）豫民终 347 号民事判决：驳回上诉，维持原判。

【裁判理由】

河南省高级人民法院终审认为：

一、关于反光材料公司主张的客户名单是否构成商业秘密

《中华人民共和国反不正当竞争法》第十条规定："本条所称的商业秘密，是指不为公众所知悉、能为权利人带来经济利益、具有实用性并经权利人采取保密措施的技术信息和经营信息"。本案中，反光材料公司将向东北地区客户出具的增值税发票、发货清单、与客户资金往来汇款凭证、要货通知单、包裹票、出差工作日程表及出差计划上载明的客户信息汇总、整理，形成了包含详细经营信息的客户名单，并为此耗费了大量的时间、金钱和劳动。其中，"成交日期"能够反映客户的要货规律，"品种""规格""数量"能够说明客户的独特需求，"单价"能够说明客户对价格的承受能力、价格成交的底线，"备注"反映了客户的特殊信息，这些内容构成了反光材料公司经营信息的秘密点，体现了反光材料公司特有的客户信息，不能从公开的信息中获取。以上证据符合"不为公众所知悉"的认定条件。反光材料公司提供的交易记录及客户来往票据，涵盖时间长，包含客户众多，这些经营信息具有现实的或者潜在的商业价值，有的已成为有长期业务往来的客户，有的虽未建立业务关系但亦是反光材料公司获得交易机会的重要资源，经营信息的客户已与反光材料公司形成了稳定的供货渠道，保持着良好的交易关系，在生产经营中具有实用性，能够为反光

材料公司带来经济利益、竞争优势。以上证据符合"能为权利人带来经济利益、具有实用性"的认定条件。反光材料公司为上述经营信息制定了具体的保密制度，对客户及潜在客户信息采取了必要的保密措施，与宋俊超签订的劳动合同书中明确约定了保密条款、竞业限制条款，反光材料公司也向宋俊超及其他业务员支付了相应的保密费用。以上证据证明了反光材料公司为上述经营信息采取了合理的"保密措施"。综上，反光材料公司制作的客户名单构成商业秘密。

二、关于宋俊超、睿明特公司是否侵犯了反光材料公司的商业秘密

宋俊超自 2006 年起在反光材料公司任业务员，主要负责黑龙江省、吉林省、辽宁省及内蒙古自治区的销售及客户拓展，对在工作中接触到的关于反光材料公司商业秘密的客户资料等经营信息十分熟知。宋俊超以宋翔名义先后 18 次向东北地区发送货物，部分货物品名与反光材料类似，部分客户名单也与反光材料公司客户名单相同。因此，可以认定宋俊超擅自与反光材料公司的客户进行交易。宋俊超多次参与睿明特公司营业执照办理、公司事项变更、提交年检报告等工商登记的相关工作，睿明特公司法定代表人经两次变更的联系电话均为宋俊超使用的 130xxxxxxx9 号码，宋俊超也以个人名义从睿明特公司账户上支取 27 笔，共计1,270,603.42 元款项，综上可以认定宋俊超与睿欣公司存在紧密联系。宋俊超在反光材料公司工作期间，签署了保密协议，反光材料公司也向其支付了保密费用，宋俊超应负有对反光材料公司的忠实义务，包括对工作中接触到的经营信息进行保密的义务。宋俊超应对公司的相关管理规定及客户名单的非公开性、商业价值清楚明了，但仍私自与反光材料公司的客户进行交易，主观上

具有侵权故意。宋俊超违反保密约定，披露、使用、允许他人使用反光材料公司经营信息的行为，侵害了反光材料公司的商业秘密。睿明特公司经宋俊超 2011 年 11 月 12 日办理变更经营项目后与反光材料公司的主要经营项目部分重合，在宋俊超与睿明特公司的紧密联系下，睿明特公司与反光材料公司长期联系的客户在较短时间内即发生了业务交易。据睿明特公司的银行往来账目显示，自 2011 年 8 月 1 日至 2015 年 7 月 31 日期间，睿明特公司与东北地区交易客户中，与反光材料公司交易客户部分相同，且交易数额较大，可以认定睿明特公司使用的客户信息与反光材料公司的经营信息存在相同或实质性相同。进而可以认定睿明特公司通过宋俊超实际接触到了反光材料公司的经营信息。结合睿明特公司未举证证明其业务往来系客户自行要求与其交易的事实，可以推定睿明特公司不正当地获取、使用了宋俊超所掌握的反光材料公司所拥有的客户名单与反光材料公司的特定客户进行交易，侵害了反光材料公司对客户名单享有商业秘密的权利，主观上具有共同故意。综上，宋俊超、睿明特公司对反光材料公司的商业秘密构成共同侵权。

三、关于侵权责任如何承担

由于反光材料公司的损失及宋俊超、睿明特公司的获利均无法计算，根据宋俊超、睿明特公司侵权行为的性质、主观过错、交易时间、交易的数量，反光材料公司以往的同类产品交易价格以及为获取客户经营信息付出的努力等因素，酌情确定宋俊超、睿明特公司赔偿反光材料公司 35 万元。为了避免反光材料公司遭受侵权损害，防止宋俊超、睿明特公司因侵权而继续获利，依照《最高人民法院关于审理不正当竞争民事案件应用法律若干问题的解释》第十六条："人民法院对于侵犯商业秘密行为判决停止侵害的民事责任时，停止侵害的时间一般持续到该项商业秘密已为公众知悉时为止。依据前款规定判决停止侵害的时间如果明显不合理的，可以在依法保护权利人该项商业秘密竞争优势的情况下，判决侵权人在一定期限或者范围内停止使用该项商业秘密"之规定，判决宋俊超、睿明特公司立即停止对反光材料公司商业秘密的侵权行为并在两年内不准使用反光材料公司所拥有的商业秘密。

【本案裁判文书】

扫描二维码，可见裁判文书

Ascertainment of the Client List in Trade Secret and Application of Injunctive Order against Infringer

——Hebi Reflective Material Co., Ltd. v. Song Junchao, Hebi Ruimingte Technology Co., Ltd., and Li Jianfa

[Syllabus]

The Client List infringed accounts for a large proportion of disputes over trade secret. The Client List in the trade secret is not an ordinary list of client name, but should also contain in-depth information affecting the transaction. Important information, such as VAT invoice, delivery list, remittance voucher, notice of goods requisition, parcel bill, etc. between the Obligee and the client, includes the special client information that is different from the publicly-known information, such as, trading habits, trading needs, and price tolerance of the client. Such information has real or potential commercial value and constitutes the secrets of business information., and It would be a trade secret after the Obligee takes reasonable confidentiality measures.

After the court recognized determined the occurrence of the infringement and ordered the iInfringer to stop the infringement and compensate the loss, the infringer continued to use the trade secret already in control, causing greater injuries to the Obligee. To this end, in accordance with the provisions of Article 16 of the [Inserted: injuri]Interpretation of the

Supreme People's Court on Some Issues Concerning the Application of Law in the Trial of Civil Cases Involving Unfair Competition, the infringer was ordered to stop misappropriating using the trade secret within a specified period, thereby preventing the infringer from continuing to infringe.

[Case No.] Henan High People's Court (2016) YuMingZhong No. 347

[Cause of Action] Disputes over Missappropriation of trade secret

[Collegial Panel Members] Zhao Zheng Zhao Yanbin Jiao Xinhui

[Keywords] Missappropriation of trade secret, client list, application of injunction

[Relevant Legal Provisions] Article 10 of the *Anti-Unfair Competition Law of the People's Republic of China* (this law was amended on November 4, 2017, and Article 9 of the Amendment)

Article 16 of *Interpretation of the Supreme People's Court on Some Issues Concerning the Application of Law in the Trial of Civil Cases Involving Unfair Competition*

[Basic Facts]

In the case of disputes over missaproriationof trade secret among the Appellant Song Junchao, Hebi Ruimingte Technology Co., Ltd. (hereinafter referred to as Ruimingte Company), the Appellee Hebi Reflective Material Co., Ltd. (hereinafter referred to as Reflective Material Company), and Li Jianfa (Defendant in first instance), the Obligee, Reflective Material Company, was established on April 4, 1996, and its business scope covers the processing and sales of reflective materials and applications of reflective materials and coated products. Song Junchao was a sale person at Reflective Material Company since 2006, responsible for sales and customer development in Heilongjiang, Jilin, Liaoning, and Inner Mongolia Autonomous Region. Reflective Material Company has entered into two labor contracts with Song

Junchao, which included confidentiality clauses and non-competition clauses. Reflective Material Company has established a confidentiality system for its business information, taken necessary confidentiality measures for information of clients and potential clients, and paid confidential fees to Song Junchao and other salespeople. After noticing Song Junchao purchased the reflective cloth on his behalf, Reflective Material Company filed a law suit and asked for preliminary injujnction, and demanded to seize 14 pieces of reflective fabric stored by Song Junchao, of which the consignee is Song Junchao, and to enjoin Song Junchao, Ruimingte, and Li Jianfa from the misappropriation, and to compensate for reasonable expenses and losses of RMB500,000.

[Inserted: fabri][Inserted: ople][Inserted: p][Inserted: ,][Inserted: the] [Deleted:m][Deleted:n][Deleted:loth]

Hebi Shancheng Ruixin Reflective Material Business Department (hereinafter referred to as Ruixin Business Department) was established on April 3, 2006. The name of its operator is Li Jianfa, and the contact number is 13033895409. Hebi Ruixin Trading Co., Ltd. (hereinafter referred to as Ruixin Company) was established on June 22, 2011. Its business scope covers steel, building materials, hardware, electricity, coated panels, and reflective fences. The contact number of the legal representative, upon two changes, is 13033895409. On November 12, 2011, Song Xiang applied for the change of the company's business scope. The expanded scope encompassed reflective material products, clothing, textiles, sanitary products, rubber products, etc. On August 27, 2013, Song Xiang handled the procedures for changing legal representative of Ruixin Company. In addition, during the operation of Ruixin Company, Song Xiang also participated in the work related to the business registration procedures of the company, such as applying for a business license, changing company's business scope, and submitting annual inspection reports. Ruixin Company changed its name to Ruimingte Company on January 19, 2015. The ID number of Song

Junchao is 410621197603181537. The ID number of Song Xiang is 410611198102187510. These two names referred to the same person. Song Junchao uses SIM card with the number of 13033895409. Song Jun has sent goods to Northeast China in the name of Song Xiang through Zhengzhou Debon Logistics Limited Hebi Branch over ten times. The goods sent include "reflective cloth, 3 fibers" and "reflective strips, 2 fibers", "cloth, 5 fibers", etc. On February 8, 2014, Song Junchao delivered goods to Northeast China through Hebi Business Department of China Railway Corporation. Song Junchao has sent goods to Northeast China through Shanghai Jiaji Express Co., Ltd. Hebi Branch for 7 times. The goods include "cloth, 3", "cloth, 4" "cloth, 9" and so on. Some of the client lists are the same as the client list of Reflective Material Company. The current account of Ruixin Company shows that from August 1, 2011 to July 31, 2015, among the client of Ruixin Company in Northeast China, there were 10 clients who were the trading clients of Reflective Material Company and there were 38 supply transactions, amounting to RMB830, 512.50. Song Junchao, at his own capacity, withdrew the money from the accounts of Ruixin Company for 27 times, totaling to RMB1, 270, 603.42.

Holding

Henan Hebi Intermediate People's Court rendered (2015) HeMingChuZi No. 96 Civil Judgment on December 25, 2015, which demanded Song Junchao and Ruimingte Company to cease misappropriating the trade secret in two years to come and to pay the damage of RMB 350,000. After the judgment was granted in the first instance, Song Junchao and Ruimingte Company were dissatisfied with it and appealed to Henan Higher People's Court, seeking the reverse of the first-instance decision and dismissing the claims of Reflective Material Company. On August 2, 2017, Henan Higher People's Court issued the (2016) YM No. 347 Civil Judgment to dismiss the appeal and affirm the original judgment.

[Reasoning]

As the court of the appeal, Henan Higher People's Court held that:

I. Whether the Client List claimed by Reflective Material Company constitutes a trade secret

Article 10 of the Anti-Unfair Competition Law of the People's Republic of China stipulates that "trade secret", for the purpose of this Article, means the utilized technical information and business information, which is unknown by the public, may create business interests or profit for its Obligee, and also is maintained confidentially by its Obligee. In this case, Reflective Material Company collected and recorded the client information stated in VAT invoice issued to clients in Northeast China, the delivery list, remittance voucher for fund transfer with clients, notice of goods requisition, the parcel bill, the travel schedule and travel plan, to form a Client List with detailed business information, and thus spent a lot of time and money and contributed amount of labor. Among them, "variety", "specification" and "quantity" can explain the unique needs of clients; "transaction date" can reflect the regular pattern when the client demands for goods; "unit price" can explain the price affordability of clients and the bottom line of price transactions; "Remarks" reflect the special information of clients. All of these items constitute the secret in the business information of Reflective Material Company, reflects the unique client information of Reflective Material Company, and cannot be obtained from the public information. The above evidence matches the requirement of "not known to the public." Transaction records and client transaction bills provided by Reflective Material Company cover a long time and a large number of clients. Such business information has real or potential business value. Some clients have established long-term business dealings with Reflective Material Company. Some clients have not established business relationships with Reflective Material Company, but they are also important resources for Reflective Material

417

Company to obtain trading opportunities. The clients designated in the business information have formed stable supply channels and maintained good trading relationships with Reflective Material Company. Therefore, such information has practical utility in the operation of the business and can bring economic benefits and competitive advantages to Reflective Material Company. The above evidence meets the requirement of "causing economic benefits to the Obligee and having practicality." Reflective Material Company has established a specific confidentiality system for the above business information, and taken necessary confidentiality measures for the information of clients and potential clients. The labor contract entered into with Song Junchao clearly stipulates the confidentiality clause and competition restriction clause. Reflective Material Company also paid the corresponding confidentiality fees to Song Junchao and other salespeople. The above evidence proves that Reflective Material Company has taken reasonable "confidential measures" for the above business information. In summary, the Client List produced by Reflective Material Company constitutes a trade secret.

II. Do Song Junchao and Ruimingte Company misappropriate the trade secret of Reflective Material Company?

Song Junchao was a salesman of Reflective Material Company since 2006. He was responsible for sales and customer development in Heilongjiang Province, Jilin Province, Liaoning Province, and Inner Mongolia Autonomous Region, and knew very well the client information related to the trade secret of Reflective Material Company. Song Junchao delivered goods to Northeast China 18 times under the name of Song Xiang. Some of the products were named similar to reflective materials. Some of the client lists were also the same as the client list of Reflective Material Company. It can be ascertained that Song Junchao traded with clients of Reflective Material Company without permission. Song Junchao has participated in the work relevant to the business registration of Ruimingte

Company, such as application of corporate business license, change of corporate business scope, and submission of annual inspection reports. The contact number of the legal representative of Ruimingte Company, upon two changes, is 13033895409 used by Song Junchao. Song Junchao also withdrew money at his personal capacity from the account of Ruimingte Company for 27 times, with a total of RMB 27, 127,060.42. Thus, it can be ascertained that Song Junchao had a close relationship with Ruixin Company. Song Junchao entered into a non-disclosure agreement with Reflective Material Company. Reflective Material Company also paid confidentiality fees to Song Junchao. Song Junchao was obligated to keep confidential the business information obtained at work. Song Junchao should be aware of the company's relevant management regulations, the non-publicity, and commercial value of client list, but he still conducted transactions at his personal capacity with clients of Reflective Material Company. Thus, he knowingly committed the misappropriation. The act of Song Junchao in breaching confidentiality agreement, disclosing, using, and allowing others to use the business information of Reflective Material Company misappropriate trade secrets of Reflective Material Company. The business scope of Ruimingte Company changed by Song Junchao on November 12, 2011 partially overlapped with the business scope of Reflective Material Company. Under the close ties by Song Junchao and Ruimingte Company, Ruimingte Company conducted the business transaction in a short period with the clients, with whom Reflective Material Company had contacted in a long term. According to current accounts of Ruimingte Company, some of the clients in Northeast China, who traded with Ruimingte Company from August 1, 2011, to July 31, 2015, were the same clients of Reflective Material Company, and the transaction amount was significant. It can be ascertained that client information used by Ruimingte Company is the same or substantially the same with business information of Reflective Material Company. It can be further ascertained that Ruimingte Company actually accesses to the business information of Reflective Material Company through Song Junchao. Due to the fact that Ruimingte Company did not provide evidence to prove that the transaction was initiated by the clients, it can be presumed that Ruimingte Company improperly obtained and used the client list of Reflective Material Company, which was acquired by Song Junchao, to conduct transactions with the particular clients of Reflective Material Company. Such acts infringe on the rights of Reflective Material Company over trade secret of client list, constituting a common subjective intention. Song Junchao and Ruimingte Company jointly infringed on the trade secret of Reflective Material Company.

III. Whether the defendants were liable

According to Article 16 of Interpretation of the Supreme People's Court on Some Issues Concerning the Application of Law in the Trial of Civil Cases Involving Unfair Competition, when the People's Court imposes civil liability for misappropriation of trade secrets, the time frame for stopping the infringement generally endures until the trade secret has been known to the public. If the period of time during which the misappropriation would have been enjoined would apparently unreasonable, a judgment may be rendered to order the infringer to cease misappropriating the trade secret for a certain period of time or within a particular scope, provided that the competitive advantage bestowed on the Obligee by such trade secret is protected in accordance with the law. As it is impossible to calculate the loss of Reflective Material Company and the profits of Song Junchao and Ruimingte Company, the court determines, as appropriate, that Song Junchao and Ruiming Special Company should compensate RM 350,000 to Reflective Material Company, based on the nature of misappropriation of Song Junchao and Ruimingte Company, knowingness, the trading time and number of transactions, previous transaction price of similar products of Reflective Material Company, and efforts made by Reflective Material Company to collect client business information. In order to preclude the potential damages to be suffered by by Reflective Material Company, and to eliminate the continued profits obtained by Song Junchao and Ruimingte Company as a result of misappropriation, Song Junchao and Ruimingte Company must immediately stop misappropriating the trade secret of Reflective Material Company in two years to come.

[Opinion of the Case (Chinese Version)]

Scan the QR code to see the Chinese version of the opinion

第五章　植物新品种案件

Chapter 5 New Plant Varieties Cases

为确保新品种继续生产，
判令持父本母本双方当事人相互授权许可

——天津天隆种业科技有限公司与江苏徐农种业科技有限公司
侵害植物新品种权纠纷案

【裁判要旨】

　　分别持有植物新品种父本与母本的双方当事人，因不能达成相互授权许可协议，导致植物新品种不能继续生产，损害双方各自利益，也不符合合作育种的目的。为维护社会公共利益，保障国家粮食安全，促进植物新品种转化实施，确保已广为种植的新品种继续生产，在衡量父本与母本对植物新品种生产具有基本相同价值基础上，人民法院可以直接判令双方当事人相互授权许可并相互免除相应的许可费。

【案　　　号】	江苏省高级人民法院（2011）苏知民终字第 0194 号、（2012）苏知民终字第 0055 号
【案　　　由】	植物新品种权纠纷
【合议庭成员】	宋　健　顾　韬　袁　滔
【关　键　词】	民事　侵害植物新品种权　相互授权许可
【相 关 法 条】	《中华人民共和国合同法》第五条,《中华人民共和国植物新品种保护条例》第二条、第六条、第三十九条

【基本案情】

天津天隆种业科技有限公司（以下简称天隆公司）与江苏徐农种业科技有限公司（以下简称徐农公司）相互以对方为被告，分别向法院提起两起植物新品种侵权诉讼。

北方杂交粳稻工程技术中心（与辽宁省稻作研究所为一套机构两块牌子）、徐州农科所共同培育成功的三系杂交粳稻9优418水稻品种，于2000年11月10日通过国家农作物品种审定。9优418水稻品种来源于母本9201A、父本C418。2003年12月30日，辽宁省稻作研究所向国家农业部提出C418水稻品种植物新品种权申请，于2007年5月1日获得授权，并许可天隆公司独占实施C418植物新品种权。2003年9月25日，徐州农科所就其选育的徐9201A水稻品种向国家农业部申请植物新品种权保护，于2007年1月1日获得授权。2008年1月3日，徐州农科所许可徐农公司独占实施徐9201A植物新品种权。经审理查明，徐农公司和天隆公司生产9优418使用的配组完全相同，都使用父本C418和母本徐9201A。

2010年11月14日，一审法院根据天隆公司申请，委托农业部合肥测试中心对天隆公司公证保全的被控侵权品种与授权品种C418是否存在亲子关系进行DNA鉴定。检验结论：利用国家标准GB/T20396－2006中的48个水稻SSR标记，对9优418和C418的DNA进行标记分析，结果显示，在测试的所有标记中，9优418完全继承了C418的带型，可以认定9优418与C418存在亲子关系。

2010年8月5日，一审法院根据徐农公司申请，委托农业部合肥测试中心对徐农公司公证保全的被控侵权品种与C418和徐9201A是否存在亲子关系进行鉴定。检验结论：利用国家标准

GB/T20396 — 2006 中的 48 个水稻 SSR 标记，对被控侵权品种与 C418 和徐 9201A 的 DNA 进行标记分析，结果显示：在测试的所有标记中，被控侵权品种完全继承了 C418 和徐 9201A 的带型，可以认定被控侵权品种与 C418 和徐 9201A 存在亲子关系。

根据天隆公司提交的 C418 品种权申请请求书，其说明书内容包括：C418 是北方杂粳中心国际首创"籼粳架桥"制恢技术，和利用籼粳中间材料构建籼粳有利基因集团培育出形态倾籼且有特异亲和力的粳型恢复系。C418 具有较好的特异亲和性，这是通过"籼粳架桥"方法培育出来的恢复系所具有的一种性能，体现在杂种一代更好地协调籼粳两大基因组生态差异和遗传差异，因而较好地解决了通常籼粳杂种存在的结实率偏低，籽粒充实度差，对温度敏感、早衰等障碍。C418 具有籼粳综合优良性状，所配制的杂交组合一般都表现较高的结实率和一定的耐寒性。

根据徐农公司和徐州农科所共同致函天津市种子管理站，称其自主选育的中粳不育系徐 9201A 于 1996 年通过，在审定之前命名为"9201A"，简称"9A"，审定时命名为"徐 9201A"。以徐 9201A 为母本先后选配出 9 优 138、9 优 418、9 优 24 等三系杂交粳稻组合。在 2000 年填报全国农作物品种审定申请书时关于亲本的内容仍延用 1995 年配组时的品种来源 9201A × C418。徐 9201A 于 2003 年 7 月申请农业部新品种权保护，在品种权申请请求书的品种说明中已注明徐 9201A 配组育成了 9 优 138、9 优 418、9 优 24、9 优 686、9 优 88 等杂交组合。徐 9201A 与 9201A 是同一个中粳稻不育系。天隆公司侵权使用 9201A 就是侵权使用徐 9201A。

裁判结果

　　就天隆公司诉徐农公司一案，南京市中级人民法院于 2011 年 8 月 31 日作出（2009）宁民三初字第 63 号民事判决：1. 徐农公司立即停止销售 9 优 418 杂交粳稻种子，未经权利人许可不得将植物新品种 C418 种子重复使用于生产 9 优 418 杂交粳稻种子；2. 徐农公司于判决生效之日起十五日内赔偿天隆公司经济损失 50 万元；3. 驳回天隆公司的其他诉讼请求。一审案件受理费 15,294 元，由徐农公司负担。

　　就徐农公司诉天隆公司一案，南京市中级人民法院于 2011 年 9 月 8 日作出（2010）宁知民初字第 069 号民事判决：1. 天隆公司于判决生效之日起立即停止对徐农公司涉案徐 9201A 植物新品种权之独占实施权的侵害；2. 天隆公司于判决生效之日起 10 日内赔偿徐农公司经济损失 200 万元；3. 驳回徐农公司的其他诉讼请求。

　　徐农公司、天隆公司不服一审判决，就上述两案分别提起上诉。江苏省高级人民法院于 2013 年 12 月 29 日合并作出（2011）苏知民终字第 0194 号、（2012）苏知民终字第 0055 号民事判决：1. 撤销江苏省南京市中级人民法院（2009）宁民三初字第 63 号、（2010）宁知民初字第 069 号民事判决。2. 天津天隆种业科技有限公司于本判决生效之日起十五日内补偿江苏徐农种业科技有限公司 50 万元整。3. 驳回天津天隆种业科技有限公司、江苏徐农种业科技有限公司的其他诉讼请求。

【裁判理由】

　　法院生效裁判认为植物新品种权作为一种重要的知识产权应当受到尊重和保护。《中华人民共和国植物新品种保护条例》第六条明确规定："完成育种的单位或者个人对其授权品种，享有排他的独占权。任何单位或者个人未经品种权所有人许可，不得为商业目的生产或者销售该授权品种的繁殖材料，不得为商业目的将该授权品种的繁殖材料重复使用于生产另一品种的繁殖材料"，但需要指出的是，该规定并不适用于本案情形。首先，9优418的合作培育源于上世纪九十年代国内杂交水稻科研大合作，本身系无偿配组。9优418品种性状优良，在江苏、安徽、河南等地广泛种植，受到广大种植农户的普遍欢迎，已成为中粳杂交水稻的当家品种，而双方当事人相互指控对方侵权，本身也足以表明9优418品种具有较高的经济价值和市场前景，涉及辽宁稻作所与徐州农科所合作双方以及本案双方当事人的重大经济利益。在二审期间，法院做了大量调解工作，希望双方当事人能够相互授权许可，使9优418这一优良品种能够继续获得生产，双方当事人也均同意就涉案品种权相互授权许可，但仅因一审判令天隆公司赔偿徐农公司200万元，徐农公司赔偿天隆公司50万元，就其中的150万元赔偿差额双方当事人不能达成妥协，故调解不成。天隆公司与徐农公司不能达成妥协，致使9优418品种不能继续生产，不能认为仅关涉双方的利益，实际上已经损害了国家粮食安全战略的实施，有损公共利益，且不符合当初辽宁稻作所与徐州农科所合作育种的根本目的，也不符合促进植物新品种转化实施的根本要求。从表面上看，双方当事人的行为系维护各自的知识产权，但实际结果是损害知识产权的运用和科技成果的转化。鉴于该两案已关涉国家粮食生产安全等公共利益，影响9优418这一优良品种的推广，双方当事人在行使涉案植物新品种独占实施许可权时均应当受到限制，即在生产9优418水稻品种时，均应当允许对方使用已方的亲本繁殖材料，这一结果显然有利于辽宁稻作所与徐州农科所合作双方及本案双方当事人的共同利益，也有利于广大种植农户的利益,故一审判令该两案双方当事人相互停止侵权并赔偿对方损失不当,应予纠正。其次,9优418是三系杂交组合,综合双亲优良性状,杂种优势显著,其中母本不育系作用重要,而父本C418的选育也成功解决了三系杂交粳稻配套的重大问题,在9优418配组中父本与母本具有相同的地位及作用。法院判决,9优418水稻品种的合作双方徐州农科所和辽宁省稻作研究所及其本案当事人徐农公司和天隆公司均有权使用对方获得授权的亲本繁殖材料,且应当相互免除许可使用费,但仅限于生产和销售9优418这一水稻品种,不得用于其他商业目的。因徐农公司为推广9优418品种付出了许多商业努力并进行种植技术攻关,而天隆公司是在9优418品种已获得市场广泛认可的情况下进入该生产领域,其明显减少了推广该品种的市场成本,为体现公平合理,法院同时判令天隆公司给予徐农公司50万元的经济补偿。最后,鉴于双方当事人各自生产9优418,事实上存在着一定的市场竞争和利益冲突,法院告诫双方当事人应当遵守我国反不正当竞争法的相关规定,诚实经营,有序竞争,确保质量,尤其应当清晰标注各自的商业标识,防止发生新的争议和纠纷,共同维护好9优418品种的良好声誉。

【本案裁判文书】

扫描二维码,可见裁判文书

Order the Parties Separately Holding the Male plant and the Female plant of a New Plant Variety to Cross License to Each Other to Ensure Continuous Production of the New Plant Variety

——Tianjin Tianlong Seed Technology Co., Ltd. v. Jiangsu Xunong Seed Technology Co., Ltd.

[Syllabus]

As the parties who separately hold the male plant and the female plant of a new plant variety have failed to reach an agreement on cross liscensing to each other, continuous production of the new plant variety has become impossible, which will impair the interests of both parties and does not meet the purpose of cooperative breeding. In order to safeguard public interests, guarantee the national grain security, and promote the commercialization and implementation of widely-planted new plant varieties, on the basis of the judgement that the same value exists with both the male plant and the female plant in the production of a new plant variety, the people's court may directly order that both parties should grant authorization and license to each other and mutually exempt the corresponding royalties.

431

[Case No.] Jiangsu High People's Court (2011) SZMZZ No. 0194 and (2012) SZMZZ No. 0055

[Cause of Action] New plant variety right dispute

[Collegial Panel Members] Song Jian   Gu Tao   Yuan Tao

[Keywords] Civil, infringement upon rights to new plant varieties, cross authorization and licensing

[Relevant Legal Provisions] Article 5 of the *Contract Law of the People's Republic of China* and Articles 2, 6 and 39 of the *Regulation of the People's Republic of China on the Protection of New Varieties of Plants*

[Basic Facts]

Tianjin Tianlong Seed Technology Co., Ltd. (hereinafter referred to as "Tianlong Company") and Jiangsu Xunong Seed Technology Co., Ltd. (hereinafter referred to as "Xunong Company") respectively filed lawsuits with the court regarding infringement upon rights to a new plant variety , each with the other party as defendant.

The 9A/418 rice variety, a three-line japonica hybrid rice variety, jointly cultivated by the Northern Japonica Hybrid Rice Engineering Technology Center (same institute as the Liaoning Rice Research Institute, despite of the different names) and the Xuzhou Institute of Agricultural Sciences, passed the National Crop Variety Validation on November 10, 2000. The 9A/418 rice variety is generated from female plant 9201A and male plant C418. On December 30, 2003, the Liaoning Rice Research Institute applied to the Ministry of Agriculture for rights to new plant variety with respect to the C418 rice variety, obtained the approval on May 1, 2007, and were granted the exclusive license to Tianlong Company for exercising new plant variety rights with regard to C418. On September 25, 2003, the Xuzhou Institute of Agricultural Sciences applied to the Ministry of Agriculture for protection of new plant variety rights with regard to the Xu 9201A rice variety it bred, and obtained the approval on January 1, 2007. On January 3, 2008, the Xuzhou Institute of Agricultural Sciences licensed the exclusive right to Xunong Company to exercise the new plant variety rights with respect to Xu 9201A . After the court investigation, it was found that Xunong Company and Tianlong Company used the same combination to produce 9A/418, namely, C418 as the male plant and Xu 9201A as the female plant.

On November 14, 2010, upon request by Tianlong Company, the court of first instance commissioned Hefei Test Center of Ministry of Agriculture to conduct parenthood DNA identification on whether there was parenthood between the alleged infringing variety under notarized preservation of Tianlong Company and the authorized variety C418. The following findings were obtained from the test. Having applied the 48 rice SSR markers in the national standard GB/T20396-2006, a marker analysis was made on the DNA of 9A/418 and C418. The results showed that in all markers tested, 9A/418 fully inherits the DNA band pattern of C418 and it may be concluded that there exists parenthood between 9A/418 and C418.

On August 5, 2010, upon request by Xunong Company, the court of first instance authorized the Hefei Test Center of Ministry of Agriculture to identify whether there was parenthood between the alleged infringing variety under notarized preservation by Xunong Company, and C418 and Xu 9201A. The following findings were obtained. Having applied 48 rice SSR markers in the national standard GB/T20396-2006, a marker analysis was made on DNA of the alleged infringing variety and C418 and Xu 9201A. The results showed that in all markers tested, the alleged infringing variety fully inherited the DNA band pattern of C418 and Xu 9201A, it may be concluded that there is parenthood between the alleged infringing variety and C418 and Xu 9201A.

In the written request of the application for the C418 variety rights submitted by Tianlong Company, the contents of the specification document included: C418, a japonica-type restorer line with a form close to indica and specific affinity, was cultivated by using the "indica-japonica bridge" restorer production technique first invented by North China Japonica Hybrid Rice Center and by using intermediate materials between indica and japonica varieties to construct favorable genetic groups from indica and japonica varieties. C418 has higher specific affinity, which is a property possessed by restorer lines cultivated by the "indica-japonica bridge" method, as manifested in the first offspring generation's better coordination of the ecological and genetic differences between the genomes of indica and japonica varieties, thus providing a better solution to the weaknesses generally manifested by indica and japonica hybrids, such as low seed setting rate, poor grain plumpness, temperature sensitivity, and premature aging. C418 combines the excellent traits of indica and japonica varieties, and the hybrid combinations that it produces generally show a higher seed setting rate and some cold tolerance.

In their letter to Tianjin Seed Management Station, Xunong Company and Xuzhou Agricultural Science Institute claimed that Xu 9201A, a middle-season japonica sterile line that they independently bred, passed the national validation for crop varieties in 1996. Prior to the validation, it had been named "9201A", abbreviated as "9A"; and after the validation, it was renamed as "Xu 9201A". Adopting Xu 9201A as the female parent, they had successively bred various three-line japonica hybrid rice combinations, including 9 A/138, 9A/418, and 9A/24. In the application for national validation of the crop variety filed in 2000, the variety origins were indicated still as 9201A×C418", the same as when the two genetic groups were combined in 1995. In the application to the Ministry of Agriculture for the protection of the new variety rights to Xu 9201A filed in July 2003, it was indicated in the variety specification as a part of the written application the variety rights, that Xu 9201A has been combined with other genetic groups to breed various hybrid combinations, including 9A/138, 9A/418, 9A/24, 9A/686, and 9A/88. Xu 9201A and 9201A are the same middle-season japonica sterile line. Tianlong Company's infringement upon the rights to use 9201A was an infringement upon the rights to use Xu 9201A.

 Holding

With respect to the case of Tianlong Company v.s. Xunong Company, on August 31, 2011, the Intermediate People's Court of Nanjing Municipality, rendered the (2009) NMSCZ No. 63 Civil Judgment: I. the court orders Xunong Company to immediately cease selling the seeds of the japonica hybrid rice 9A/418 and orders that without permission from the right-holder, Xunongcompany is not allowed use the seeds of the new plant variety C418 repeatedly in the production of the seeds of the japonica hybrid rice 9A/418; II. the court orders Xunong Company to pay, within 15 days since the judgment has come into effect, RMB 500,000 to Tianlong Company as compensation for its economic loss; III. the court rejects Tianlong Company's other litigation requests. The legal fees RMB 15,294of the first-instance trial is to be borne by Xunong Company.

With respect to the case of Xunong Company v.s. Tianlong Company, on September 8, 2011, the Intermediate People's Court of Nanjing Municipality rendered the (2010) NZMCZ No. 069 Civil Judgment: I. The court orders Tianlong Company, immediately on the day the judgment comes into effect, to cease infringing Xunong Company's exclusive right to the new plant variety Xu 9201A involved in the case; II. the court orders Tianlong Company to pay, within 10 days of the judgment's coming into effect, RMB 2,000,000 toXunong Company as compensation for its economic loss; III. the court rejects Xunong Company's other litigation requests.

Unconvinced by the first-instance judgments, Xunong Company and Tianlong Company both appealed for the above-mentioned cases respectively. On December 29, 2013, the High People's Court of Jiangsu Province combined the two cases and rendered the (2011) SZMZZ No. 0194 and (2012) SZMZZ No. 0055 Civil Judgments: I. the court revokes the (2009) NMSCZ No. 63 and (2010) NZMCZ No. 069 Civil Judgments rendered by the Intermediate People's Court of Nanjing Municipality, Jiangsu Province; II. the court orders Tianjin Tianlong Seeds Science and Technology Co., Ltd. to pay, within 15 days since the judgment has come into effect, RMB 500,000 to Jiangsu Xunong Seeds Science and Technology Co., Ltd. as compensation; III. the court rejects the other litigation requests of Tianjin Tianlong Seeds Science and Technology Co., Ltd. and Jiangsu Xunong Seeds Science and Technology Co., Ltd.

[Reasoning]

In the effective judgments, the court believes: the right to a new plant variety, as a type of important intellectual property right, should be respected and protected. Article 6 of the *Regulation on the Protection of New Plant Varieties* clearly provides: an entity or individual enjoys an exclusive right to a variety which they have bred and for which rights have been granted to the entity or individual. No entity or individual, without permission from the holder of the variety rights, shall produce or sell for commercial purposes the propagation material of the variety for which rights have been granted, or to repeatedly use the propagation material of the variety for which rights have been granted, in the production of the propagation material of another variety for commercial purposes. However, it is necessary to point out that this provision does not apply to the situation in this case. First, the cooperative cultivation of 9A/418, combining rice groups free of charge, traces its origin back to the large-scale cooperation in hybrid rice research that took place in the 1990s in China. The variety 9A/418 has excellent traits and has been widely planted in Jiangsu, Anhui, Henan, and other places. It has been generally welcomed by many farmers and has become the leading variety of middle-season japonica hybrid rice. The infringement of rights complained by both parties in itself shows that the variety 9A/418 has a high economic value and better market prospects compared with other varieties. The alleged mutual infringement has an important bearing upon enormous economic interests on the part of the collaborating parties, Liaoning Rice Institute and Xuzhou Agricultural Science Institute, as well as both parties to this case. During the second instance of this case, the court carried out significant mediation work in the hope that the parties to the case could engage in cross licensing to allow the continued production of the excellent variety 9A/418. The parties agreed to cross license the variety rights involved in the case, but the mediation was not successful, for the only reason that the first-instance court had ordered Tianlong Company to pay Xunong Company compensation in the amount of RMB 2,000,000 and had ordered Xunong Company to pay Tianlong Company compensation in the amount of RMB 500,000, and the parties could not reach a settlement on the RMB 1,500,000 net balance of compensation. As Tianlong Company and Xunong Company could not reach a settlement, production of the variety 9 You 418 could not continue. This could not be considered to affect only the interests of the two parties in this case. In fact, this outcome impaired the implementation of national food security strategy and was detrimental to public interests. In addition, this was not consistent with the fundamental purposes of the breeding cooperation initially carried out by Liaoning Rice Research Institute and Xuzhou Agricultural Science Institute, nor did it comply with the fundamental requirements for promoting commercialization and application of new plant varieties. At the surface of the issue, the actions of the parties to this case were undertaken to protect their own intellectual property rights, but the actual results were that the use of intellectual property rights and the commercialization and application of scientific and technological progress. Considering that public interests were involved in the two cases, such as national food production security, and the promotion of the excellent variety 9A/418 was affected, the parties should both be subject to some constraints when they exercise their exclusive licensing rights to the new plant variety involved in the case. In the production of the rice variety 9A/418, each party should permit the other party to use the propagation material of its own parent variety. This result was clearly beneficial to the common interests of Liaoning Rice Research Institute and Xuzhou Agricultural Science Institute—the two cooperating parties, and the parties to this case. This result would take care of many farmers' interests. Therefore, it was inappropriate for the first-instance court to order the parties of the two cases to respectively cease infringing each other's rights and to pay each other compensation for economic losses. The court's mistakes should be corrected. Second, 9A/418 is a three-line hybrid combination that combines the excellent traits of the two parents and has notable heterosis. The role of the female parent sterile line is important, and the selective breeding of male parent C418 also successfully solved significant problems related to three-line japonica hybrid rice. In the 9A/418 combined groups, the male parent has the same status and function as the female parent. The court gave the decision that Xuzhou Agricultural Science Institute and Liaoning Rice Research Institute, the two parties cooperating for the development of the rice variety 9A/418, as well as Xunong Company and Tianlong Company, the parties to this case, all had the rights to use the propagation material of the parent variety for which rights have been granted, and that they should mutually exempt each other from the relevant licensing fees. However, the rights and exemption only applied to the production and sale of the rice variety 9A/418 and could not be used for other commercial purposes. Xunong Company expended significant business efforts and carried out research on planting technology in promoting the variety 9A/418, whereas Tianlong Company only entered into production of the variety 9A/418 after it had been widely recognized by the market; therefore, the latter's market costs for promoting the variety were significantly reduced. For the sake of fairness and reasonableness, the court also ordered Tianlong Company to pay Xunong Company RMB 500,000 as economic compensation. Finally, given that each party produced 9A/418 on its own, as a matter of fact, there existed some market competition and conflict of interest between them, and the court warned that the parties shall abide by the relevant provisions of the Anti-Unfair Competition Law of China, operate their businesses honestly, compete in an orderly manner, and ensure the quality of their products. In particular, they shall clearly display their respective business logos in order to prevent new controversies and disputes from arising, and both parties shall jointly preserve the good reputation of the variety 9A/418.

[Opinion of the Case (Chinese Version)]

Scan the QR code to see the Chinese version of the opinion

第六章　集成电路布图设计案件

Chapter 6 Integrated Circuit Layout Design Cases

集成电路布图设计专有权的侵权判定

——钜泉光电科技（上海）股份有限公司与深圳市锐能微科技
有限公司、上海雅创电子零件有限公司侵害集成电路布图
设计专有权纠纷案

【裁判要旨】

由于集成电路布图设计的创新空间有限，因此在布图设计侵权判定中，对于两个布图设计构成相同或者实质性相似的认定应当采用较为严格的标准。

原告应当对其主张保护的集成电路布图设计具有独创性承担举证责任，原告提供的证据以及所作的说明可以证明其主张保护的布图设计不属于常规设计的，则应当认为原告已经完成初步的举证责任。被告主张相关布图设计是常规设计的，应当提供反证加以证明。

受保护的布图设计中任何具有独创性的部分均受法律保护，而不论其在整个布图设计中的大小或者所起的作用。复制受保护的布图设计的全部或者其中任何具有独创性的部分的行为均构成侵权。

法律并不禁止对他人芯片的布图设计进行摄片进而分析其电路原理的反向工程行为，但是，法律并不允许在反向工程的基础上直接复制他人的布图设计。

【案　　　号】　上海市高级人民法院（2014）沪高民三（知）终字第

12 号

【案   由】 侵害集成电路布图设计专有权纠纷

【合议庭成员】 丁文联 马剑峰 徐卓斌

【关 键 词】 集成电路布图设计专有权 复制 实质性相似
               独创性 反向工程

【相关法条】 《集成电路布图设计保护条例》第二条、第三条第一
               款、第四条、第七条、第二十三条、第三十条、第
               三十三条第一款

【基本案情】

在上诉人（原审原告）钜泉光电科技（上海）股份有限公司（以下简称钜泉公司）与上诉人（原审被告）深圳市锐能微科技有限公司（以下简称锐能微公司）、原审被告上海雅创电子零件有限公司（以下简称雅创公司）侵害集成电路布图设计专有权纠纷案中，钜泉公司于 2008 年 3 月 1 日完成名称为"ATT7021AU"的布图设计创作，同年进行布图设计登记。该集成电路布图设计登记的图样共有 16 层，登记文件中的"ATT7021AU 集成电路布图设计结构、技术、功能简要说明"记载：1. 达成业界相同芯片（单相电能计量）功能 / 性能最优化面积的版图设计诉求；2. 数模混合高抗干扰 / 高静电保护芯片版图设计；3. 采用电路设计技术和金属层、扩散层、信号流合理布局等版图技术实现灵敏信号噪声屏蔽，大小信号干扰隔离。

国家知识产权局专利复审委员会经审查，未发现钜泉公司涉案布图设计专有权存在不符合《集成电路布图设计保护条例》（以下简称《条例》）规定可以被撤销的缺陷，故终止了锐能微公司提出的撤销程序。

　　2010 年 1 月 20 日，钜泉公司经公证在雅创公司经营场所购买集成电路芯片 100 片，该芯片显示的型号为 RN8209G。雅创公司确认该芯片系其销售，锐能微公司确认 RN8209、RN8209G 芯片系其制造、销售。锐能微公司网站中显示：2010 年 9 月 RN8209 销售量突破 1000 万片。从锐能微公司查封的部分增值税专用发票显示销售 RN8209G 芯片共计 1120 片，单价大多在 5.50 元至 4.80 元之间，有 1 张发票显示单价约为 2 元；销售 RN8209 芯片共计 6610 片，单价在 4.80 元至 4.20 元之间。

　　北京紫图知识产权司法鉴定中心（以下简称紫图鉴定中心）接受上海市第一中级人民法院委托进行司法鉴定，鉴定结论为：1.RN8209、RN8209G 与原告主张的独创点 5（数字地轨与模拟地轨衔接的布图）相同；2.RN8209、RN8209G 与原告主张的独创点 7（模拟数字转换电路的布图）中第二区段独立升压器电路的布图相同；3. 依据现有证据应认定上述 1、2 点具有独创性，不是常规设计。

　　2006 年，钜泉公司分别与陈强、赵琮签订劳动合同和保密合同，钜泉公司聘用陈强为销售经理，聘用赵琮在研发部门从事 IC 设计工作。后陈强至锐能微公司担任总经理，赵琮亦至锐能微公司任职。庭审中，赵琮陈述称：在钜泉公司看到过钜泉公司的 ATT7021AU 集成电路布图设计；锐能微公司没有对钜泉公司 ATT7021AU 芯片进行反向工程。

　　原告认为，两被告的行为侵犯其集成电路布图设计专有权，遂诉至法院，请求判令两被告停止侵权、公开赔礼道歉、赔偿经济损失人民币 1500 万元。

裁判结果

　　上海市第一中级人民法院于 2013 年 12 月 24 日一审判决：锐能微公司立即停止侵害钜泉公司享有的 ATT7021AU（登记号为 BS.08500145.7）集成电路布图设计专有权；锐能微公司赔偿钜泉公司经济损失以及为制止侵权行为所支付的合理开支共计人民币 320 万元；驳回钜泉公司的其余诉讼请求。钜泉公司、锐能微公司均不服一审判决，向上海市高级人民法院提起上诉。上海市高级人民法院于 2014 年 9 月 23 日二审判决驳回上诉，维持原判。

【裁判理由】

　　上海市高级人民法院认为：

　　一、涉案 RN8209、RN8209G 芯片的相应布图设计与钜泉公司 ATT7021AU 集成电路布图设计中的"数字地轨与模拟地轨衔接的布图"和"独立升压器电路布图"是否相同

　　由于集成电路布图设计的创新空间有限，因此在布图设计侵权判定中对于两个布图设计构成相同或者实质性相似的认定应当采用较为严格的标准。涉案 RN8209、RN8209G 芯片的"数字地轨与模拟地轨衔接的布图""独立升压器电路布图"的主要特征与钜泉公司"数字地轨与模拟地轨衔接的布图""独立升压器电路布图"的主要特征均一一对应相同。虽然在考虑 M2 层后，双方布图设计中一条布线的走向会有区别，但是布线与互连的元件之间组合的三维配置并未实质性改变。至于锐能微公司主张的衔接处位置、轨的宽度、具体布图的布局、尺寸、形状的差异以及 M1、M2、M3 层以及 PL 层的 MOS 管尺寸等不同，均属于细微的、次要的差异，也未实质性改变布线与互连的元件之间组合的三维配

置，而 ST 层的不同是双方使用不同工艺造成的，上述不同点均不足以改变两者布图设计实质性相似的判断。因此，本案中，即使按照较为严格的判定标准，锐能微公司涉案 RN8209、RN8209G 芯片的相应布图设计也与钜泉公司 ATT7021AU 集成电路布图设计中的"数字地轨与模拟地轨衔接的布图"和"独立升压器电路布图"构成实质性相似。

二、钜泉公司 ATT7021AU 集成电路布图设计中的"数字地轨与模拟地轨衔接的布图"和"独立升压器电路布图"是否具有独创性

根据《条例》第四条的规定，布图设计具有独创性，是指该布图设计是创作者自己的智力劳动成果，并且在其创作时该布图设计在布图设计创作者和集成电路制造者中不是公认的常规设计。并且，钜泉公司应当对其主张保护的集成电路布图设计具有独创性承担举证责任，但是钜泉公司并无必要也不可能穷尽所有的相关常规布图设计来证明其主张保护的布图设计属于非常规设计。只要钜泉公司提供的证据以及所作的说明可以证明其主张保护的布图设计不属于常规设计的，则应当认为钜泉公司已经完成了初步的举证责任。在此情况下，锐能微公司主张相关布图设计是常规设计的，则锐能微公司只要能够提供一份相同或者实质性相似的常规布图设计，即足以推翻钜泉公司关于非常规设计的主张。本案中，钜泉公司对于 ATT7021AU 集成电路布图设计中的"数字地轨与模拟地轨衔接的布图""独立升压器电路布图"具有独创性的主张，已经提供《集成电路布图设计登记证书》、专利复审委员会认为不存在被撤销缺陷的决定以及鉴定结论等证据完成了初步的举证责任。在此情况下，锐能微公司提供的证据，或者是电路原理图，或者是特征点与钜泉公司布图设计并不相同的布图设

计，尚不足以证明钜泉公司 ATT7021AU 集成电路布图设计中的"数字地轨与模拟地轨衔接的布图""独立升压器电路布图"是常规设计。因此，可以认定钜泉公司的"数字地轨与模拟地轨衔接的布图"和"独立升压器电路布图"具有独创性。

三、锐能微公司生产、销售涉案 RN8209、RN8209G 芯片的行为是否侵犯钜泉公司享有的 ATT7021AU 集成电路布图设计专有权

根据《条例》第三十条的规定，复制受保护的布图设计的全部或者其中任何具有独创性的部分的行为均构成侵权。由此可见，受保护的布图设计中任何具有独创性的部分均受法律保护，而不论其在整个布图设计中的大小或者所起的作用。本案所涉"数字地轨与模拟地轨衔接的布图""独立升压器电路布图"存在常规的布图设计，锐能微公司完全可以使用该些常规设计；或者，可以通过自行研发创作出具有独创性的不同的布图设计。但是，锐能微公司没有采取上述做法，而是直接复制钜泉公司 ATT7021AU 集成电路布图设计中具有独创性的"数字地轨与模拟地轨衔接的布图""独立升压器电路布图"用于制造涉案 RN8209、RN8209G 芯片并进行销售，其行为已经构成侵权。

实现相同或相似功能的芯片必然在电路原理上存在相似性，而电路原理不属于《条例》规定可赋予专有权的部分，因此法律并不禁止对他人芯片的布图设计进行摄片进而分析其电路原理的反向工程行为。但是，法律并不允许在反向工程的基础上直接复制他人的布图设计，因为这将大幅度减少竞争对手在时间和成本上的投入，从而极大地削弱被模仿企业的竞争优势，最终将降低整个集成电路行业创新的积极性。本案中，锐能微公司之所以对钜泉公司 ATT7021AU 集成电路布图设计进行部分复制，既不是

为个人目的，亦不是单纯为评价、分析、研究、教学等目的，而是为了研制新的集成电路以进行商业利用；锐能微公司认可其并非通过反向工程获得钜泉公司 ATT7021AU 集成电路布图设计；锐能微公司未经许可直接复制了钜泉公司 ATT7021AU 集成电路布图设计中具有独创性的"数字地轨与模拟地轨衔接的布图"和"独立升压器电路布图"用于制造涉案 RN8209、RN8209G 芯片并进行销售。因此，无论锐能微公司涉案 RN8209、RN8209G 芯片的布图设计是否具有独创性，其行为均不适用《条例》第二十三条的规定。

综上，锐能微公司认可其接触了钜泉公司的 ATT7021AU 集成电路布图设计。现锐能微公司未经钜泉公司许可，在其生产、销售的涉案 RN8209、RN8209G 芯片中包含了钜泉公司 ATT7021AU 集成电路布图设计中具有独创性的"数字地轨与模拟地轨衔接的布图"和"独立升压器电路布图"，其行为已经侵犯了钜泉公司 ATT7021AU 集成电路布图设计专有权，应当承担相应的民事责任。

四、一审法院确定的赔偿数额是否合理

由于锐能微公司拒绝提供其财务资料，可以将钜泉公司主张的锐能微公司在其网站页面显示的 1000 万片的销售数量作为本案赔偿数额的计算依据；本案中，双方均未提交证据证明被控侵权产品的销售利润；鉴定报告明确钜泉公司主张的其余独创性部分双方并不相同或实质性相似，故钜泉公司以其余模块双方亦存在相同部分为由要求锐能微公司以全部获利进行赔偿的主张，缺乏依据；"数字地轨与模拟地轨衔接的布图"和"独立升压器电路布图"在被控侵权芯片中所起的作用确非核心和主要作用且所占的布图面积确实较小；通过直接复制钜泉公司的"数字地轨与模拟地轨衔接的布图"和"独立升压器电路布图",锐能微公司节约了自行研发的投入,缩短了芯片研发时间,并据此获得了市场竞争优势,因此也不能完全按照该两项布图在芯片中所占的比例来确定赔偿数额。综上,上海市第一中级人民法院根据本案实际情况判决锐能微公司赔偿钜泉公司包括合理支出在内的经济损失人民币 320 万元,并无不当。

【本案裁判文书】

扫描二维码,可见裁判文书

Judgment on Infringement on Exclusive Right of Integrated Circuit Layout Design

——HiTrend Technology (Shanghai) Co., Ltd. v. Renergy Micro-Technologies (Shenzhen) Co., Ltd. and Shanghai Yachuang Texin Electronics Co., Ltd.

[Syllabus]

Due to limited space for innovation in layout design of integrated circuits, in the judgment on layout design infringement, stricter standards should be adopted to ascertain identicalness or substantial similarity between two layout designs.

The plaintiff shall bear the burden of proof for the layout design of the integrated circuit for which it claims protection. If the evidence provided and the explanations made by the plaintiff can prove that the layout design for which it claims protection is not a conventional design, it will be deemed that the plaintiff has satisfied the preliminary burden of proof. If the defendant claims that the relevant layout design is a conventional design, it should provide evidence to prove otherwise.

Any original part of the protected layout design shall be protected by law, regardless of its size or role in the overall layout design. The act of reproducing all or any original parts of the protected layout design constitutes infringement.

The law does not prohibit the act of conducting reverse engineering by photographing the layout design of other people's chips and analyzing the principle behind the circuit design. However, the law does not allow direct copying of other people's layout designs through reverse engineering.

[Case No.] Shanghai Higher People's Court (2014) HGMS (Z) ZZ No. 12

[Cause of Action] Dispute over infringement of integrated circuit layout design

[Collegial Panel Members] Ding Wenlian   Ma Jianfeng
Xu Zhuobin

[Keywords] Exclusive right of integrated circuits (IC) layout design, reproduction, substantial similarity, originality, reverse engineering

[Relevant Legal Provisions] Article 2, Clause 1 of Article 3, Article 4, Article 7, Article 23, Article 30 and Clause 1 of Article 33 of *Regulations on Protection of Integrated Circuit Layout Design*

[Basic Facts]

In the case of dispute over infringement of exclusive right of integrated circuit layout design among the appellant (plaintiff in the court of first instance, HiTrend Technology (Shanghai) Co., Ltd., referred to as HiTrend Company), the respondent (the defendant in the court of first instance, Renergy Micro-Technologies(Shenzhen) Co., Ltd., referred to as Renergy Company) and the defendant in the court of first instance (Shanghai Yachuang Texin Electronics Co., Ltd., referred to as Yachuang Company), HiTrend Company completed its IC layout design titled "ATT7021AU" on March 1st, 2008 and registered the layout design in the same year. The registered IC layout design drawing indicates 16 layers. It is noted in the "Brief Description on Structure, Technology and Functions of ATT7021AU IC Layout Design" included the registration documents that: 1. Satisfying the best of breed layout design requirements of function/performance-optimized area (single-phase energy measurement); 2. A chip layout design with Digital-analog hybrid high anti-interference/ high-electrostatic protection; 3. Applying circuit design technology and layout technology, such as rational layout of metal layer, diffusion layer and signal flow, to achieve sensitive signal noise shielding and isolation of big and small signal interference.

The review by the Patent Reexamination Board of the State Intellectual Property Office did not find any defect warranting revocation in the exclusive right of the layout design of HiTrend Company according to *Regulations on the Protection of Layout Design of Integrated Circuits* (the *Regulations*); hence, the revocation proposed by Renergy Company was terminated.

On January 20th, 2010, HiTrend Company purchased 100 pieces of integrated circuit chips at Yachuang Company's business site, with notarization and the model number being RN8209G. Yachuang Company confirmed that it sold those chips and Renergy Company confirmed that RN8209 and RN8209G chips were manufactured and sold by them. The website of Renergy Company shows: As of September 2010, the sales volume of RN8209 exceeded 10 million pieces. Some VAT special invoices seized from Renergy Company indicated that a total of 1,120 RN8209G chips were sold, at a unit price ranging mostly between RMB4.80 and RMB5.50, with one invoice bearing the unit price as about RMB2; a total of 6,610 pieces of RN8209 chips were sold, with the unit price ranging between RMB4.20 and RMB4.80.

Beijing Zitu Intellectual Property Judicial Appraisal Center (referred to as Zitu Appraisal Center) was commissioned by Shanghai No. 1 Intermediate People's Court for carrying out the judicial appraisal. The appraisal conclusions are shown as follows: 1. RN8209 and RN8209G are the same as the Original Feature No. 5 claimed by the plaintiff (layout for connection of digital ground rack and analog ground rack); 2. RN8209 and RN8209G are the same with the layout of independent booster circuit in the second section of the Original Feature No. 7 claimed by the plaintiff (layout of the analog-to-digital conversion circuit) ; 3. Based on existing evidences, Item 1 and Item 2 afore-mentioned are ascertained to be original and exclusive, and not conventional.

In 2006, HiTrend Company signed labor contracts and confidentiality agreements with Chen Qiang and Zhao Cong. HiTrend Company hired Chen Qiang as the sales manager and Zhao Wei to engage in IC design work in the R&D department. Later on, Chen Qiang worked at Renergy Company as its General Manager and Zhao Wei also worked at Renergy Company. During the trial, Zhao Wei stated that he had seen the layout design of ATT7021AU IC chip of HiTrend Company while he was working at HiTrend Company; Renergy Company did not reverse engineer HiTrend Company's ATT7021AU IC chip.

The plaintiff held that the acts of the two defendants infringed on the exclusive right of IC layout design, and thus filed a lawsuit with the court, requiring the two defendants to cease the infringement, make public apology, and compensate RMB15 million for its economic losses.

⚖ Holding

On December 24ᵗʰ, 2013, the court of first instance, Shanghai No. 1 Intermediate People's Court ruled that Renergy Company should immediately cease the infringement on the exclusive right of ATT7021AU (registration no. of BS.08500145.7) IC layout design held by HiTrend Company; Renergy Company should compensate RMB3.2 million to HiTrend Company for its economic losses and reasonable expenses for stopping the infringement; the remaining litigation requests of HiTrend Company were rejected. HiTrend Company did not accept the compensation award of the court of first instance, and Renergy Company refused to accept the decision of the court of first instance, and they both appealed to Shanghai Higher People's Court. Shanghai Higher People's Court rejected the appeals on September 23ʳᵈ, 2014 and upheld the original judgment.

455

[Reasoning]

Shanghai Higher Intermediate People's Court held that:

I. Whether the corresponding layout designs of RN8209 and RN8209G chips involved in the case are the same as the "layout for connection of digital ground rack and analog ground rack" and the "independent booster circuit layout" in ATT7021AU IC layout design of HiTrend Company

Due to limited space for innovation in layout design of integrated circuits, stricter standards should be adopted for the ascertainment of identicalness or substantial similarity of two layout designs in the judgment of layout design infringement. The main features of "layout for connection of digital ground rack and analog ground rack" and "independent booster circuit layout" of RN8209 and RN8209G chips are corresponding and identical to the main features of "layout for connection of digital ground rack and analog ground rack" and "independent booster circuit layout" of HiTrend Company. Although the wiring in the layout designs of the parties differed considering the M2 layer, the three-dimensional configuration of the combination between wiring and the interconnected components had not changed substantially. As for the difference claimed by Renergy Company with respect to connection position, rack width, arrangement of specific layout, size and shape, and the difference in size of MOS tube in M1, M2, M3 and PL layers, all of these are minor and insignificant, and do not substantially change the three-dimensional configuration of the combination between the wiring and the interconnected components. The difference in ST layer is caused by the parties using different processes. The above differences are not sufficient to change the judgment that the two layout designs is substantially similar to each other. Therefore, in this case, even in accordance with the more stringent judgement criteria, the corresponding layout designs of RN8209 and RN8209G chips of Renergy Company constitute a substantial similarity with the "layout for connection of digital ground rack and analog ground rack" and "independent booster circuit layout" in the ATT7021AU IC layout design of HiTrend Company.

II. Is there originality in the "layout for connection of digital ground rack and analog ground rack" and "independent booster circuit layout" in ATT7021AU IC layout design of HiTrend Company?

According to the provisions of Article 4 of the *Regulations*, originality of layout design means that the layout design is the result of the inventor's own intellectual work, and at the time of its creation, the layout design is not a standard design generally accepted by layout design inventors and integrated circuit manufacturers. Moreover, HiTrend Company should bear the burden of proof for the originality of the integrated circuit layout design for which it claims protection, but it is neither necessary nor possible for HiTrend Company to exhaust all relevant conventional layout designs to prove that its layout design is an unconventional design. As long as the evidence provided and the explanations made by HiTrend Company can prove that the layout design it claimed protection for is not a conventional design, it should be deemed that HiTrend Company has satisfied the preliminary burden of proof. Under this circumstance, Renergy Company claimed that the relevant layout design is a conventional design, and it will be able to overturn the non-conventional design claim of HiTrend Company, by providing an identical or substantially similar conventional layout design. In this case, to substantiate its claim that "layout for connection of digital ground rack and analog ground rack" and "independent booster circuit layout" in ATT7021AU IC layout design are original, HiTrend Company has already provided the *Registration Certificate for IC Layout Design*, and the conclusion of the Review Board that there is no defect that warrants a revocation of the registration, as well as the appraisal conclusion and other evidences. These actions are sufficient to meet the requirements of preliminary burden of proof. Under this circumstance, the evidence provided by Renergy Company, or the circuit schematic diagram, or the layout design where the feature points differ from layout design of HiTrend Company, are insufficient to prove that "layout for connection of digital ground rack and analog ground rack" and "independent booster circuit layout" in ATT7021AU IC layout design are conventional. Therefore, it can be ascertained that the "layout for connection of digital ground rack and analog ground rack" and "independent booster circuit layout" of HiTrend Company have originality.

III. Whether the conducts of Renergy company in producing and selling RN8209 and RN8209G chips violate the Plaintiff's exclusive rights to ATT7021AU IC layout design

According to Article 30 of the *Regulations*, reproduction of all or any of the original parts of the protected layout design constitutes an infringement. It can be seen that any original part of the protected layout design is protected by law, regardless of its size or role in the overall layout design. In this case, there are conventional designs readily available for "layout for connection of digital ground rack and analog ground rack" and "independent booster circuit layout". Renergy Company have the choices either to adopt these conventional designs, or to develop different layout designs with originality by themselves. However, Renergy Company did not take either of the above approaches, but instead directly copied the "layout for connection of digital ground rack and analog ground rack" and "independent booster circuit layout" in ATT7021AU IC layout design of HiTrend Company, to manufacture and sell RN8209 and RN8209G chips. Such practice has already constituted infringement.

Chips that achieve the same or similar functions must have similarities in circuit work mechanisms, which do not meet the criteria of being protected with exclusive rights as stipulated in the *Regulations*. Therefore, the law does not prohibit the act of conducting reverse engineering by photographing the layout design of other people's chips and analyzing the circuit work mechanisms. However, the law does not allow the direct copying of other people's layout designs through reverse engineering, as it will massively reduce the time and costs invested by the imitators, thus severely weakening the competitive advantage of the businesses that created the original design, and ultimately lower the incentives for innovation in the entire integrated circuit industry. In this case, the motivation of Renergy Company partially copying the HiTrend Company's ATT7021AU IC layout design was neither for personal purpose, nor for the purpose of evaluation, analysis, research, teaching, etc., but for developing a new IC for commercial exploitation. Renergy Company admitted that it did not obtain HiTrend Company's ATT7021AU IC layout design through reverse engineering; instead it directly copied the original "layout for connection of digital ground rack and analog ground rack" and "independent booster circuit layout" in HiTrend Company's ATT7021AU IC layout design, to manufacture and sell RN8209 and RN8209G chips. Therefore, regardless of whether or not Renergy Company's RN8209 and RN8209G chip layout design are original, Article 23 of the Regulations shall not apply to any of its practices.

In summary, Renergy Company admitted the fact that it accessed HighTrend Company's ATT7021AU IC layout design. Without the permission of HiTrend Company, Renergy Company incorporated the original "layout for connection of digital ground rack and analog ground rack" and "independent booster circuit layout" of ATT7021AU IC layout design into its RN8209 and RN8209G chips that it produced and sold. Such practices violated the exclusive right of HiTrend Company to ATT7021AU IC layout design and thus should bear the relevant civil liabilities.

IV. Whether the amount of compensation decided by the court of first instance is reasonable?

As Renergy Company refused to provide its financial information, and therefore the information on sale of 10 million pieces as displayed on its website could be used as the basis for calculating the amount of compensation in this case. In this case, neither party submitted evidence to prove the profit from the sales of the alleged infringing products; the appraisal report clarifies that the other original parts claimed by HiTrend Company are not identical or substantially similar with that of Renergy Company, so there is absence of evidence on the part of HiTrend Company to claim compensation on the full profits of Renergy Company on the ground that there is similarity in other modules. The "layout for connection of digital ground rack and analog ground rack" and "independent booster circuit layout" don't play a core and important role in the alleged infringing chip, and the layout occupies a really small area. By directly copying HiTrend Company's "layout for connection of digital ground rack and analog ground rack" and "independent booster circuit layout", Renergy Company saved on investment in research and development, shortened chip development time, and accordingly, obtained a competitive advantage in the market. Therefore, the amount of compensation cannot be determined completely in line with the proportion of the two layouts of the whole chip. In summary, there is no inappropriateness in Shanghai No. 1 Intermediate People's Court's ruling to rule according to the actual situation of the case that Renergy Company shall compensate RMB3.2 million to HiTrend Company for its economic losses and reasonable expenses.

[Opinion of the Case (Chinese Version)]

Scan the QR code to see the Chinese version of the opinion

第七章　知识产权刑事案件

Chapter 7 Criminal Cases of Intellectual Property Right

销售记录刷信誉行为的辩解无以证实，
不予采信

——郭明升、郭明锋、孙淑标假冒注册商标案

【裁判要旨】

　　假冒注册商标犯罪的非法经营数额、违法所得数额，可以综合考虑被告人供述、证人证言、被害人陈述、网络销售电子数据、被告人银行账户往来记录、送货单、快递公司电脑系统记录、被告人等所作记账等证据认定。被告人辩解称网络销售记录存在刷信誉的不真实交易，但无证据证实的，对其辩解不予采纳。

【案　　　　号】 江苏省宿迁市中级人民法院（2015）宿中知刑初字第
　　　　　　　　　　0004号

【案　　　　由】 假冒注册商标

【合议庭成员】 程黎明　朱　庚　白　金

【关　键　词】 刑事　假冒注册商标罪　非法经营数额　网络销售

【相关法条】 《中华人民共和国刑法》第二百一十三条

【基本案情】

　　公诉机关指控：2013年11月底至2014年6月期间，被告人郭明升为谋取非法利益，伙同被告人孙淑标、郭明锋在未经三星（中

国）投资有限公司授权许可的情况下，从他人处批发假冒三星手机裸机及配件进行组装，利用其在淘宝网上开设的"三星数码专柜"网店进行"正品行货"宣传，并以明显低于市场价格公开对外销售，共计销售假冒的三星手机 20,000 余部，销售金额 2000 余万元，非法获利 200 余万元，应当以假冒注册商标罪追究其刑事责任。被告人郭明升在共同犯罪中起主要作用，系主犯。被告人郭明锋、孙淑标在共同犯罪中起辅助作用，系从犯，应当从轻处罚。

被告人郭明升、孙淑标、郭明锋及其辩护人对其未经"SΛMSUNG"商标注册人授权许可，组装假冒的三星手机，并通过淘宝网店进行销售的犯罪事实无异议，但对非法经营额、非法获利提出异议，辩解称其淘宝网店存在请人刷信誉的行为，真实交易量只有 10,000 多部。

法院经审理查明："SΛMSUNG"是三星电子株式会社在中国注册的商标，该商标有效期至 2021 年 7 月 27 日；三星（中国）投资有限公司是三星电子株式会社在中国投资设立，并经三星电子株式会社特别授权负责三星电子株式会社名下商标、专利、著作权等知识产权管理和法律事务的公司。2013 年 11 月，被告人郭明升通过网络中介购买店主为"汪亮"、账号为 play2011-1985 的淘宝店铺，并改名为"三星数码专柜"，在未经三星（中国）投资公司授权许可的情况下，从深圳市华强北远望数码城、深圳福田区通天地手机市场批发假冒的三星 I8552 手机裸机及配件进行组装，并通过"三星数码专柜"在淘宝网上以"正品行货"进行宣传、销售。被告人郭明锋负责该网店的客服工作及客服人员的管理，被告人孙淑标负责假冒的三星 I8552 手机裸机及配件的进货、包装及联系快递公司发货。至 2014 年 6 月，该网店共计组装、销售假冒三星 I8552 手机 20,000 余部，非法经营额 2000 余万元，非法获利 200 余万元。

裁判结果

江苏省宿迁市中级人民法院于 2015 年 9 月 8 日作出（2015）宿中知刑初字第 0004 号刑事判决，以被告人郭明升犯假冒注册商标罪，判处有期徒刑五年，并处罚金人民币 160 万元；被告人孙淑标犯假冒注册商标罪，判处有期徒刑三年，缓刑五年，并处罚金人民币20 万元。被告人郭明锋犯假冒注册商标罪，判处有期徒刑三年，缓刑四年，并处罚金人民币 20 万元。宣判后，三被告人均没有提出上诉，该判决已经生效。

【裁判理由】

法院生效裁判认为，被告人郭明升、郭明锋、孙淑标在未经"SAMSUNG"商标注册人授权许可的情况下，购进假冒"SAMSUNG"注册商标的手机机头及配件，组装假冒"SAMSUNG"注册商标的手机，并通过网店对外以"正品行货"销售，属于未经注册商标所有人许可在同一种商品上使用与其相同的商标的行为，非法经营数额达 2000 余万元，非法获利 200 余万元，属情节特别严重，其行为构成假冒注册商标罪。

被告人郭明升、郭明锋、孙淑标虽然辩解称其网店售销记录存在刷信誉的情况，对公诉机关指控的非法经营数额、非法获利提出异议，但三被告人在公安机关的多次供述，以及公安机关查获的送货单、支付宝向被告人郭明锋银行账户付款记录、郭明锋银行账户对外付款记录、"三星数码专柜"淘宝记录、快递公司电脑系统记录、公安机关现场扣押的笔记等证据之间能够互相印证，综合公诉机关提供的证据，可以认定公诉机关关于三被告人共计销售假冒的三星 I8552 手机 20,000 余部，销售金额 2000 余万元，非法获利 200 余万元的指控能够成立，三被告人关于销售记录存在刷信誉行为的辩解无证据予以证实，不予采信。被告人郭明升、郭明锋、孙淑标，系共同犯罪，被告人郭明升起主要作用，是主犯；被告人郭明锋、孙淑标在共同犯罪中起辅助作用，是从犯，依法可以从轻处罚。

【本案裁判文书】

扫描二维码，可见裁判文书

Defending Statement of Faking Credibility through Unreal Sales Records Is Groundless and Unacceptable

——Guo Mingsheng, Guo Mingfeng and Sun Shubiao

[Syllabus]

For the criminal activities of counterfeiting a registered trademark, the amounts of illegal business revenue and illegal gains can be ascertained by taking into full account of such evidences as confessions of defendants, testimony of witnesses, statements of victims, electronic data of online sale, records and bank accounts of defendants, delivery bills, data records of delivery companies, and accounting ledgers kept by defendants. Where a defendant contends that there exist fake records of online retail dealings in order to fake credibility, but provides no evidence to substantiate the contention, such a contention may not be adopted.

[Case No.] Suqian Intermediate People's Court of Jiangsu (2015) SZZXCZ No. 0004
[Cause of Action] Counterfeiting a registered trademark
[Collegial Panel Members] Cheng Liming   Zhu Geng   Bai Jin
[Keywords] Criminal, crime of counterfeiting a registered trademark, amount of illegal business revenue, online sale

[Relevant Legal Provisions] Article 213 of the *Criminal Law of the People's Republic of China*

[Basic Facts]

The public prosecutor accused that: from the end of November 2013 to June 2014, without the licensing of Samsung (China) Investment Co., Ltd., for the purpose of seeking illegal profits, and in collusion with defendants Sun Shubiao and Guo Mingfeng, the defendant Guo Mingsheng purchased counterfeit bare SAMSUNG mobile phones and accessories through wholesale from other persons, assembled them, publicized them as "genuine and authentic" in his online store "SAMSUNG Digital Shoppe" on Taobao, and sold them at a price significantly lower than the market price. They sold a total of over 20,000 counterfeit SAMSUNG mobile phones, with the sales revenue of over RMB 20 million and the illegal profits of over RMB 2 million. This constitutes their criminal liabilities for the crime of counterfeiting a registered trademark. In the joint criminal activities, Guo Mingsheng played a leading role and was the principal offender; and Guo Mingfeng and Sun Shubiao played an assistant role and were accessory offenders, entailinglighter punishments.

The defendants Guo Mingsheng, Sun Shubiao and Guo Mingfeng confirmed without dissents the criminal facts that they assembled counterfeit SAMSUNG mobile phones, and publicized and sold them through their online store on Taobao, but filed an objection to the amount of illegal business revenue and illegal profits. They contended that the real volume of business was over 10000 sets because they hired some pretended shoppers to fake the credibility of their online store.

Based on court investigation, it was ascertained by the court that

"SΛMSUNG" is a trademark that has been registered in China by Samsung Electronics Co. Ltd. with validity until July 27, 2021; and Samsung (China) Investment Co., Ltd. is a company established by Samsung Electronics Co. Ltd. in China and is specially authorized by Samsung Electronics Co. Ltd. to deal with the management and legal affairs concerning trademarks, patents, copyrights and other IPs owned by Samsung Electronics Co. Ltd. In November 2013, the defendant Guo Mingsheng purchased a Taobao online store (account no. play2011-1985) of which the storekeeper was "Wang Liang", changed its name to "SΛMSUNG Digital Counter". Without the licensing from Samsung (China) Investment Co., Ltd., he purchased counterfeit bare SΛMSUNG I8552 mobile phones and accessories through wholesale from Yuanwang Digital Mall at Huaqiangbei, Shenzhen and from Tongtiandi Telecommunication Market in Futian District, Shenzhen, assembled them together, and publicized and sold them as "genuine and authentic ones" through his online store "SΛMSUNG Digital Counter" on Taobao. The defendant Guo Mingfeng was responsible for customer service and managing customer service staff at the online store, and the defendant Sun Shubiao was responsible for sourcing, packaging and contacting with delivery companies for shipment of counterfeit SΛMSUNG I8552 mobile phones. Up until June 2014, the online store assembled and sold a total of over 20,000 counterfeit SΛMSUNG I8552 mobile phones, on an aggregated basis, with the total sales revnue of over RMB 20 million and the illegal profit of over RMB 2 million.

 Holding

Suqian Intermediate People's Court of Jiangsu issued (2015) SZZXCZ No. 0004 Criminal Judgment on September 8, 2015, stating that the defendant Guo Mingsheng committed the crime of counterfeiting a registered trademark and were sentenced to a five-year term of imprisonment and a fine of RMB 1.6 million; the defendant Sun Shubiao committed the crime of counterfeiting a registered trademark and were sentenced to a three-year term of imprisonment with a five-year probation and a fine of RMB 200,000; and the defendant Guo Mingfeng committed the crime of counterfeiting a registered trademark and were sentenced to a three-year term of imprisonment with a four-year probation and a fine of RMB 200,000. Since the judgment was announced, none of the three defendants had filed an appeal, and the judgment has taken into effect.

[Reasoning]

It is held by the court in the effective judgment that the defendants Guo Mingsheng, Guo Mingfeng and Sun Shubiao, without the licensing of Samsung (China) Investment Co., Ltd., purchased counterfeit bare SAMSUNG mobile phones and accessories, assembled into mobile phones under the registered trademark "SAMSUNG", and sold them as "genuine and authentic ones" through their online store. Their activities constituted the illegal behavior of using the same trademark on the same product without the licensing of a registered trademark owner. With sales amount of over RMB 20 million and the illegal profits of over RMB 2 million, it constitutes a very severe violation of the crime of counterfeiting a registered trademark. The defendants Guo Mingsheng, Guo Mingfeng and Sun Shubiao filed an objection to the amount of illegal business revenue and illegal profit by defending that they hired some pretended shoppers to fake the credibility of the online store. However, the three defendants' confessions and the delivery bills, records of fund transfers from Alipay to Guo Mingfeng's bank account, records of payments from Guo Mingfeng's bank account, records of the Taobao online store "SΛMSUNG Digital Counter", data records of delivery companies, records seized on sitepublic security department and other evidences collected by public security department reconcile and validate each other to establish the public prosecution department's charge that they sold a total of over 20,000 counterfeit SΛMSUNG I8552 mobile phones, with the sales revenue of over RMB 20 million and the illegal profit of over RMB 2 million, and the three defendants' defending statement of faking credibility though unreal sales records is not supported by evidences and is found unacceptable. The defendants Guo Mingsheng, Guo Mingfeng and Sun Shubiao were joint offenders, of which the defendant Guo Mingsheng played a leading role and was the principal offender; and Guo Mingfeng and Sun Shubiao played an assistant role and were accessory offenders and therefore should be given lighter punishments.

[Opinion of the Case (Chinese Version)]

Scan the QR code to see the Chinese version of the opinion